Investing in Children
Families, and Comm

Investing in Children, Youth, Families, and Communities

Strengths-Based Research and Policy

edited by
Kenneth I. Maton
Cynthia J. Schellenbach
Bonnie J. Leadbeater
Andrea L. Solarz

American Psychological Association
Washington, DC

Published by
American Psychological Association
750 First Street, NE
Washington, DC 20002
www.apa.org

First Printing September 2003
Second Printing April 2005

To order
APA Order Department
P.O. Box 92984
Washington, DC 20090-2984
Tel: (800) 374-2721; Direct: (202) 336-5510
Fax: (202) 336-5502; TDD/TTY: (202) 336-6123
Online: www.apa.org/books/
E-mail: order@apa.org

In the U.K., Europe, Africa, and the Middle East, copies may be ordered from
American Psychological Association
3 Henrietta Street
Covent Garden, London
WC2E 8LU England

Typeset in Goudy by Stephen McDougal, Mechanicsville, MD

Printer: United Book Press, Inc., Baltimore, MD
Cover Designer: Watermark Design Office, Alexandria, VA
Technical/Production Editor: Rosemary Moulton

Library of Congress Cataloging-in-Publication Data

Investing in children, youth, families, and communities : strengths-based research and policy / edited by Kenneth I. Maton . . . [et al.].
   p. cm.
  Includes bibliographical references and index.
  ISBN 1-59147-062-5
  1. Social policy—Research. 2. Social psychology—Research. 3. Reinforcement (Psychology) 4. Affirmations. I. Maton, Kenneth I.

HN17.I7 2003
361.6'1'072—dc22   2003015829

British Library Cataloguing-in-Publication Data
A CIP record is available from the British Library.

Printed in the United States of America
First Edition

CONTENTS

Contributors   ix

Acknowledgments   xiii

I. Setting the Stage   1

    Chapter 1.   Strengths-Based Research and Policy:
                 An Introduction   3
                 Kenneth I. Maton, Daniel W. Dodgen,
                 Bonnie J. Leadbeater, Irwin N. Sandler,
                 Cynthia J. Schellenbach, and Andrea L. Solarz

    Chapter 2.   Research and Policy for Building Strengths:
                 Processes and Contexts of Individual, Family,
                 and Community Development   13
                 Bonnie J. Leadbeater, Cynthia J. Schellenbach,
                 Kenneth I. Maton, and Daniel W. Dodgen

    Chapter 3.   Adversities, Strengths, and Public Policy   31
                 Irwin N. Sandler, Tim S. Ayers, Jesse C. Suter,
                 Amy Schultz, and Joan Twohey-Jacobs

II. Overcoming Adverse Circumstances Affecting the
    Individual and the Family   51

    Chapter 4.   Strengths-Building Public Policy for Children
                 of Divorce   53
                 Sanford L. Braver, Kathleen N. Hipke,
                 Ira M. Ellman, and Irwin N. Sandler

Chapter 5.   Resilient Outcomes in Abused and Neglected
             Children: Bases for Strengths-Based Intervention
             and Prevention Policies   73
             Penelope K. Trickett, Dawn A. Kurtz, and
             Karabelle Pizzigati

Chapter 6.   The Strengths, Competence, and Resilience of
             Women Facing Domestic Violence: How Can
             Research and Policy Support Them?   97
             Sarah L. Cook, Jennifer L. Woolard, and
             Harriet C. McCollum

Chapter 7.   Enhancing the Developmental Outcomes of
             Adolescent Parents and Their Children   117
             Cynthia J. Schellenbach, Bonnie J. Leadbeater,
             and Kristin Anderson Moore

Chapter 8.   Fostering Resilience in Children of Alcoholic
             Parents   137
             Laurie Chassin, Adam C. Carle,
             Denis Nissim-Sabat, and Karol L. Kumpfer

Chapter 9.   Mental Health Services: A Family Systems
             Approach   157
             William Beardslee and Jane Knitzer

Chapter 10. Children and Families Coping With Pediatric
             Chronic Illnesses   173
             Cynthia A. Gerhardt, Natalie Walders,
             Susan L. Rosenthal, and Dennis D. Drotar

III. **Overcoming Adverse Circumstances in the Community
      and Society**   191

Chapter 11. Building Protection, Support, and Opportunity
             for Inner-City Children and Youth and
             Their Families   193
             Patrick H. Tolan, Lonnie R. Sherrod,
             Deborah Gorman-Smith, and David B. Henry

Chapter 12. Opportunities for Schools to Promote
             Resilience in Children and Youth   213
             Emilie Phillips Smith, Gloria Swindler Boutte,
             Edward Zigler, and Matia Finn-Stevenson

Chapter 13. The Organization of Schooling and
Adolescent Development 233
*Edward Seidman, J. Lawrence Aber, and
Sabine E. French*

Chapter 14. Resilience in Children Exposed to Negative
Peer Influences......................... 251
*Janis B. Kupersmidt, John D. Coie, and
James C. Howell*

Chapter 15. Racial and Ethnic Status: Risk and Protective
Processes Among African American
Families 269
*Algea O. Harrison-Hale, Vonnie C. McLoyd,
and Brian Smedley*

Chapter 16. Acculturation and Enculturation Among
Latino Youth 285
*Nancy A. Gonzales, George P. Knight,
Dina Birman, and Amalia A. Sirolli*

Chapter 17. Community Violence and Children:
Preventing Exposure and Reducing Harm 303
*James Garbarino, W. Rodney Hammond,
James Mercy, and Betty R. Yung*

Chapter 18. Community Development as a Response to
Community-Level Adversity: Ecological
Theory and Research and Strengths-Based
Policy 321
*Douglas D. Perkins, Bill Crim, Pamela Silberman,
and Barbara B. Brown*

IV. Conclusions and Future Directions **341**

Chapter 19. A Blueprint for the Future................. 343
*Andrea L. Solarz, Bonnie J. Leadbeater,
Irwin N. Sandler, Kenneth I. Maton,
Cynthia J. Schellenbach, and Daniel W. Dodgen*

Index.. 355

About the Editors............................. 379

CONTRIBUTORS

J. Lawrence Aber, National Center for Children in Poverty, New York

Tim S. Ayers, Program for Prevention Research, Department of Psychology, Arizona State University, Tempe

William Beardslee, Department of Psychiatry, Children's Hospital, Boston, MA

Dina Birman, Department of Psychology, University of Illinois at Chicago

Gloria Swindler Boutte, Department of Education, Benedict College, Columbia, SC

Sanford L. Braver, Program for Prevention Research, Department of Psychology, Arizona State University, Tempe

Barbara B. Brown, Department of Family and Consumer Studies, University of Utah, Salt Lake City

Adam C. Carle, Department of Psychology, Arizona State University, Tempe

Laurie Chassin, Department of Psychology, Arizona State University, Tempe

John D. Coie, Department of Psychology, Duke University, Durham, NC

Sarah L. Cook, Department of Psychology, Georgia State University, Atlanta

Bill Crim, Center for Poverty Research and Action—Utah Issues, Salt Lake City

Daniel W. Dodgen, Public Policy Office, American Psychological Association, Washington, DC

Dennis D. Drotar, Department of Pediatrics, Rainbow Babies and Children's Hospital, Case Western Reserve School of Medicine, Cleveland, OH

Ira M. Ellman, Arizona State University College of Law, Tempe

Matia Finn-Stevenson, Child Study Center and Bush Center in Child Development and Social Policy, Yale University, New Haven, CT

Sabine E. French, Department of Psychology, University of California, Riverside

James Garbarino, Department of Human Development and Family Sciences, Family Life Development Center, Cornell University, Ithaca, NY

Cynthia A. Gerhardt, Division of Hematology/Oncology, Columbus Children's Research Institute, Columbus, OH

Nancy A. Gonzales, Department of Psychology, Program for Prevention Research, Arizona State University, Tempe

Deborah Gorman-Smith, Institute for Juvenile Research, Department of Psychiatry, University of Illinois at Chicago

W. Rodney Hammond, Division of Violence Prevention, National Center for Injury Prevention and Control, Centers for Disease Control and Prevention, Atlanta, GA

Algea O. Harrison-Hale, Department of Psychology, Oakland University, Rochester, MI

David B. Henry, Institute for Juvenile Research, Department of Psychiatry, University of Illinois at Chicago

Kathleen N. Hipke, Medical School, Wisconsin Psychiatric Institute and Clinics, University of Wisconsin—Madison

James C. Howell, National Youth Gang Center, Pinehurst, NC

George P. Knight, Department of Psychology, Program for Prevention Research, Arizona State University, Tempe

Jane Knitzer, National Center for Children in Poverty, School of Public Health, Columbia University, New York

Karol L. Kumpfer, Department of Health Promotion and Education, College of Health, University of Utah, Salt Lake City

Janis B. Kupersmidt, Department of Psychology, University of North Carolina at Chapel Hill

Dawn A. Kurtz, Young Adolescent Project, School of Social Work, University of Southern California, Los Angeles

Bonnie J. Leadbeater, Department of Psychology, University of Victoria, Victoria, British Columbia, Canada

Kenneth I. Maton, Department of Psychology, University of Maryland Baltimore County, Baltimore

Harriet C. McCollum (née Russell), Private Consultant and Mediator, Pinehurst, NC

Vonnie C. McLoyd, Department of Psychology, University of North Carolina at Chapel Hill

James Mercy, Division of Violence Prevention, National Center for Injury Prevention and Control, Centers for Disease Control and Prevention, Atlanta, GA

Kristin Anderson Moore, Child Trends, Washington, DC

Denis Nissim-Sabat, Senior Policy Analyst, Public Policy Office, American Psychological Association, Washington, DC

Douglas D. Perkins, Program in Community Research and Action, Department of Human and Organizational Development, Peabody College, Vanderbilt University, Nashville, TN

Karabelle Pizzigati, Independent Policy Specialist, Kensington, MD

Susan L. Rosenthal, Children's Hospital, University of Texas Medical Branch at Galveston

Irwin N. Sandler, Department of Psychology, Program for Prevention Research, Arizona State University, Tempe

Cynthia J. Schellenbach, Department of Sociology and Anthropology, Oakland University, Rochester, MI

Amy Schultz, Department of Psychology, Arizona State University, Tempe

Edward Seidman, Department of Psychology, New York University, New York

Lonnie R. Sherrod, Department of Psychology, Fordham University, Bronx, NY

Pamela Silberman, Center for Poverty Research and Action—Utah Issues, Salt Lake City

Amalia A. Sirolli, Department of Psychology, Arizona State University, Tempe

Brian Smedley, Institute of Medicine, Washington, DC

Emilie Phillips Smith, Prevention Development and Evaluation Branch, Division of Violence Prevention, Centers for Disease Control and Prevention, Atlanta, GA

Andrea L. Solarz, Independent Consultant, Arlington, VA

Jesse C. Suter, Department of Psychology, University of Vermont, Burlington

Patrick H. Tolan, Institute for Juvenile Research, Department of Psychiatry, Families and Community Research Group, University of Illinois at Chicago

Penelope K. Trickett, School of Social Work, University of Southern California, Los Angeles

Joan Twohey-Jacobs, Department of Psychology, Arizona State University, Tempe

Natalie Walders, Case Western Reserve University, Cleveland, OH

Jennifer L. Woolard, Department of Psychology, Georgetown University, Washington, DC

Betty R. Yung, School of Professional Psychology, Ellis Institute, Wright State University, Dayton, OH

Edward Zigler, Bush Center in Child Development and Social Policy, Yale University, New Haven, CT

ACKNOWLEDGMENTS

This book reflects the contributions of many individuals who gave their time, expertise, and support. The coeditors are especially grateful to the chapter coauthors for contributing to this effort. Participating in this project required the investment of a significant amount of their time, as well as a great deal of flexibility and good humor. Irwin N. Sandler and Daniel N. Dodgen, in addition to coauthoring chapters, worked closely with the coeditors throughout the life of the project as members of the Division 27/37 Task Force on Strengths-Based Research and Policy. We very much value both their substantial intellectual contributions and their good comradeship.

Many coauthors participated in one or both of two workshop meetings convened to refine the "strengths-based" concept and clarify the focus of the volume. These workshop meetings were made possible through support from the Substance Abuse and Mental Health Services Administration Center for Mental Health Services and the American Psychological Association (APA). We are grateful for this support and for guidance from Nancy Davis, project officer at the Center for Mental Health Services.

The input of the numerous academic and policy experts who reviewed drafts of the individual chapters—as well as that of the individuals who reviewed the full manuscript on behalf of APA—was very helpful for finalizing the manuscript. Also appreciated is feedback from the University of Maryland Baltimore County graduate students who reviewed and made comments on draft chapters as part of a community psychology course with Ken Maton.

Leni Santo Domingo provided invaluable administrative support for the project and was always willing to respond quickly to our requests. Susan Reynolds in APA Books was very supportive in the initial stages of the project; Linda McCarter and Rosemary Moulton provided helpful feedback and guidance as the manuscript went through the review and production process.

Finally, we wish to thank the Society for Community Research and Action: Division of Community Psychology (APA Division 27) and the Division of Child, Youth, and Family Services (APA Division 37). We are indebted to them for their financial and ongoing organizational support for this initiative.

I

SETTING THE STAGE

1

STRENGTHS-BASED RESEARCH AND POLICY: AN INTRODUCTION

KENNETH I. MATON, DANIEL W. DODGEN, BONNIE J. LEADBEATER,
IRWIN N. SANDLER, CYNTHIA J. SCHELLENBACH,
AND ANDREA L. SOLARZ

A growing movement has emerged that promotes a strengths-based approach to research and social policy and seeks to counter the limitations of traditional deficits-based orientations. We refer to this as a "movement" in the sense that it is an unorganized collection of groups that share a common worldview and are generally moving in the same direction. This movement encompasses researchers, advocates, and policymakers who have organized themselves around different issues such as resilience, health promotion, school reform, and community development and have developed different formal or informal organizational structures. Table 1.1 briefly contrasts the focuses of deficits-based approaches with those of strengths-based alternatives in 10 content areas.

The specific rationale, terminology, and strengths-based approaches emerging in these areas vary, reflecting in part the different types of deficits models that have traditionally influenced each (see column 1 of Table 1.1). The common element across content areas is that they transform deficits-based approaches to ones based on strengths, as shown in column 2 of Table

TABLE 1.1
Deficits-Based Approaches and Strengths-Based Alternatives
in 10 Selected Content Areas

Deficits-based approach	Strengths-based alternative	Area or field embodying the strengths-based alternative
Understand how problems and disorders develop	Understand how healthy development occurs, especially competencies and resilience	Developmental psychology Resilience
Provide clinical treatment for children and adults with identified problems	Build competencies and capacities to prevent later development of problems	Competence-based prevention
Prevent discrete problems in youths and adults	Promote youth development Promote health and psychological wellness	Youth development field Health and mental health promotion
Blame the victim Ignore social environment's role in causing problems	Empower groups lacking power Strengthen and transform environments	Community psychology
Focus on negative emotions, cognitions, behaviors, traits, outcomes	Focus on positive emotions, cognitions, behaviors, traits, outcomes	Positive psychology
Provide minimalist case management of difficult populations	Promote client development, quality of life, advocacy	Strengths perspective in social work and allied fields
Isolate, punish, and pathologize families that are different	Support all families Build on family strengths and value family resilience	Family support and family diversity movements
Engage in tracking and remediation of less capable students	Expect all children to succeed Capitalize on child, teacher, and community strengths	Whole-school educational reform
Follow expert- or government-defined prescriptions for remedying problems in communities	Identify and build on existing assets in communities Facilitate community capacity building	Assets-based community development
Devalue cultural differences and view them as a problem for society	Value cultural differences and view them as an asset to society	Multicultural psychology

1.1. This transformation is based on the guiding belief that society will benefit greatly if a strengths-based approach is emphasized instead of the prevailing deficiency-based focus that guides most social research and policy. A brief overview of this emerging strengths-based approach is presented in the first part of this introductory chapter. In the second part, we describe the particular strengths-based research and policy focus of the current volume.

THE EMERGING STRENGTHS-BASED APPROACH

A central feature of many of the deficits-based approaches (see column 1 of Table 1.1) is that individuals, families, and communities who are the subjects of policies are too often viewed as deficient and different, and so in need of "fixing." Furthermore, social scientists, professional help givers, and lawmakers may unintentionally contribute to the belief that those in need are the source of problems that can only be fixed by experts, rather than a source of solutions to these problems. They frame the problems from the perspective of their discipline or their institutions and empower the experts in the helping or service professions to diagnose the problem and administer the solutions. For example, Cook, Woolard, and Russell (see chap. 6, this volume) note that policies in the area of domestic violence are designed with the view that affected women are passive, resigned victims rather than active problem solvers seeking to positively influence their futures. Deficits-based social polices often disempower individuals, families, or communities facing truly difficult situations and seek solutions by diagnosing, fixing, punishing, or simply ignoring those affected. Entire population groups—especially those lacking economic resources and political voice in our society—may thus be stigmatized and stereotyped as lacking competence, motivation, or even redeeming social value. Beyond that, they are framed as the objects of policies, rather than the active participants in the creation of solutions.

In direct contrast to a deficits approach, strengths-based alternatives (see column 2 of Table 1.1) begin with a focus on the positive potential of individuals, families, and communities. Strengths, not weaknesses, command primary attention. These strengths are defined broadly and at multiple levels of analysis: individual, family, and community. For individuals, strengths encompass varied cognitive, affective, psychological, moral, and behavioral capacities such as self-efficacy, positive coping, practical knowledge, special talents, and persistence, to name but a few. For families and communities, strengths encompass varied instrumental, relational, structural, and cultural characteristics such as providing useful roles, facilitating meaningful relationships, setting valuable goals, using adaptive decision-making processes, providing culturally prescribed norms that regulate behavior in healthy and purposeful ways, and facilitating a positive sense of belonging to a valued community, again to name but a few.

The strengths-based approaches described in Table 1.1 differ on a number of important dimensions. Some approaches focus on increasing understanding and research knowledge, whereas others focus on social action and application (i.e., research vs. action). Strengths-based approaches also vary in whether they focus on identifying and capitalizing on existing strengths or building new strengths (i.e., tapping vs. building strengths). The development of strengths is sometimes viewed as a means to a future goal, such as to prevent future problems, whereas in other cases the development of strengths is viewed as a positive, sufficient outcome in its own right (i.e., strengths as means vs. ends). The focus of attention (i.e., level of analysis) ranges from the individual, child, and family to the community and society. Finally, some approaches target strengths as the *content* focus of the intervention (e.g., building strengths among those receiving interventions), and others target strengths as central to the *process* of intervention (e.g., engaging the strengths of local staff or citizens in designing, implementing, and evaluating interventions).

STRATEGIC GOALS

In our view, strengths-based research and policy are most likely to be effective when they encompass all of the above approaches. Taking into account these various approaches, we have found that four strategic goals can be discerned that are fundamental to strengths-based research and social policy:

1. Recognize and build on existing strengths in individuals, families, and communities.
2. Build new strengths in individuals, families, and communities.
3. Strengthen the larger social environments in which individuals, families, and communities are embedded.
4. Engage individuals, families, and communities in a strengths-based process of designing, implementing, and evaluating interventions.

Recognizing and Building on Existing Strengths

Recognizing and building on existing strengths in individuals, families, and communities represents a core element of many strengths-based approaches. For example, in whole-school reform, all students in inner-city communities, rather than only a select few, are seen as capable of success and expected to succeed (Comer, Haynes, Joyner, & Ben-Avie, 1996; Finnan & Levin, 2000). Accordingly, in Levin's accelerated schools intervention, inner-city students were viewed as particularly able to benefit from the "gifted and talented" curricular approaches used in specialized elementary school programs (Finnan & Levin, 2000). In the case of strengths-based social work practice, individuals with severe mental illness are viewed as having the potential to develop meaningful relationships and to lead meaning-rich lives, rather than being viewed as society's "casualties" (Saleebey, 1992). Family diversity adherents emphasize the importance of understanding and using the distinct strengths of ethnic minority families as an integral part of the helping process (e.g., Boyd-Franklin, 1989). In the cultural strengths perspective, the salient, traditional features of diverse cultural subgroups are viewed as assets both for the group that has them and for the larger society, rather than as a subgroup handicap or societal problem (e.g., Trickett, Watts, & Birman, 1994). Finally, central to community development work is the view that each neighborhood or community has unique strengths that need to be identified and tapped.

It should be emphasized that a positive view of the strengths of "at-risk" individuals, families, and communities does not ignore their problems or difficulties or the critical need to ameliorate or prevent the harm caused by these difficulties. The key assumption of this strengths-based approach is that individuals, families, and communities are defined not by their difficulty, but rather by their multiple strengths, and that the amelioration of current difficulties or the prevention of future difficulties begins with the identification and marshaling of these strengths.

Building New Strengths

Building new strengths in individuals, families, and communities is a second major facet of many strengths-based approaches. A central finding of developmental psychology and resiliency research is that acquiring key competencies and capacities is an integral part of the healthy development of children and youth and at the same time serves a protective function for those facing adverse life circumstances (e.g., Masten & Coatsworth, 1998; Rutter, 1987). Thus, competence-based prevention programs focus on fostering resilience in high-risk children and youth by contributing to the development of specific competencies and capacities shown through research to serve such a protective function (e.g., Durlak, 1997; Sandler, Wolchik, MacKinnon, Ayers, & Roosa, 1997; Weissberg & Greenberg, 1998). These programs prevent negative outcomes by building positive strengths in individuals, families, and communities.

Furthermore, the development of critical cognitive, affective, moral, and behavioral competencies and capacities represents, in and of itself, a socially valuable outcome of programs and policy. This view is emphasized by several approaches to building strengths, including positive youth development initiatives (e.g., Catalano, Berglund, Ryan, Lonczak, & Hawkins, 1998; Moore, Evans, Brooks-Gunn, & Roth, 2001; Pittman, 1996), health and mental health promotion (e.g., Cicchetti, Rappaport, Sandler, & Weissberg, 2000; Cowen, 1994; Millstein, Petersen, & Nightingale, 1993), and positive psychology (e.g., Aspinwall & Staudinger, 2003; Seligman & Csikszentmihalyi, 2000).

Strengthening the Larger Social Environments

It has been increasingly recognized that the larger social environments in which individuals, families, and communities are embedded substantially influence—and limit—intervention efforts to bring about positive change. Thus, our very best social policies and programs have relatively limited potential to make a substantial, sustainable, positive difference if they do not influence these larger environments (see also Maton, 2000). For example, the larger social environments that influence outcomes for children and youth include families, schools, faith-based organizations, neighborhoods, and cultural and economic structures. Consistent with this realization, the family support movement emphasizes the centrality of enhanced programs and policies that strengthen families by providing a range of social, psychological, cultural, and economic supports (e.g., Lerner, Sparks, & McCubbin, 1999; Weick & Saleebey, 1995). Community psychology and assets-based community development each focus on empowering community groups and enhancing the capacities of community institutions in efforts to prevent social problems and enhance the general quality and viability of community life (e.g., Benson, 1997; Kretzmann & McKnight, 1993; Maton, 2000; Rappaport, 1981; Saegert, Thompson, & Warren, 2001).

Engaging Individuals, Families, and Communities in the Design, Implementation, and Evaluation of Interventions

A number of strengths-based approaches emphasize the importance of engaging the unique perspectives, competencies, and capacities of both those who implement programs (e.g., teachers, community workers, agency staff) and those affected by programs (i.e., citizens) in social program design, implementation, and evaluation. For example, community psychology, whole-school reform, and assets-based community development all stress that change efforts are more likely to be successfully implemented, and to be sustained over time, if they emerge from a process that is empowering, capacity building, participatory, and collaborative for all those involved. The idea that individuals, families, and communities—the traditional focus of social policy—should become part of generating solutions to social problems is directly contrary to the expert-driven, top-down, prescriptive approach that is intrinsic to the deficits model.

Taken together, these four goals represent the foundation of a strengths-based movement that seeks to counter existing deficits-based approaches. To the extent they become an integral part of research and policy, we believe the capacity of the country to positively influence the well-being of its children, youth, citizens, families, and communities will be greatly enhanced.

THE CURRENT VOLUME

This volume seeks to examine the implications of a strengths-based approach for research and social policy across a broad array of issues. This effort emerged as part of an ongoing collaboration between two divisions of the American Psychological Association: the Society for Community Research and Action: Division of Community Psychology (Division 27) and Child, Youth, and Family Services (Division 37).[1] The primary purpose of the collaboration is to influence social and behavioral science researchers and social policymakers to adopt a more strengths-based perspective and reduce their reliance on deficits-based approaches. It assumes that sound policy development should be based on and integrally related to scientific research knowledge and that research questions and funding in turn are importantly influenced by social policy. Based on this view, one of the unique aspects of the volume is that each chapter is coauthored by scholars with complementary strengths: expertise in the psychosocial aspects of an issue and expertise in social policy. This approach enhances the linkages between extant research knowledge and the resulting policy implications, and as a result these chapters speak meaningfully both to academicians and to policymakers and experts.

The focus of this volume is on children, youth, families, and communities facing adverse circumstances. This organizational structure around adversities reflects the transformative theme of the volume—from deficits to strengths. Thus, we begin where we believe society currently is focused—"do something" about deficits—and illustrate through each of the chapters how this can be transformed to a focus on strengths. For each chapter, academic researchers were asked to review the current research evidence on a specific adversity (e.g., divorce, parental mental illness, school transition, ethnic minority status), focusing on what is known about strengths such as protective processes or enabling conditions that help those facing the adversity to adapt successfully. Each chapter is also transformative in moving from social science research evidence to public policy. Policy expert coauthors were asked to develop strengths-based policy implications consistent with the literature reviewed. In some cases, they were able to establish strong connections between research evidence and policy implications; in other cases, where research evidence was weaker, the policy implications represent the authors' informed opinion about the most promising directions.

[1]The two divisions developed the Division 27/37 Task Force on Strengths-Based Research and Policy. Members include Dan Dodgen, Bonnie Leadbeater, Ken Maton (co-chair), Cynthia Schellenbach (co-chair), Irwin Sandler, and Andrea Solarz.

The chapters purposely focus on several levels of analysis, reflecting our commitment to a view of children, families, and communities as constituents of an integrated ecology in which each reciprocally influences the others over time. This stands in contrast to many deficits-based approaches in which people are separated from the contexts that influence their lives. It is our view that the combination of strengths-based and multilevel or ecological perspectives holds great promise for developing meaningful social research and effective social policy. The multilevel emphasis on strengths and resilience is not a cry to dismantle successful person-centered programs that help combat specific adversities, but rather to transform and broaden the focus of such efforts, and to provide a complementary strategy to help promote a healthier, more resilient society.

This volume is divided into four parts. The first part sets the framework for the remainder of the volume. This introductory chapter provides a brief overview of the strengths-based perspective. Chapter 2 presents a process-based, contextual model for understanding the development of strengths at the individual, family, and community levels of analysis. The final chapter in Part 1 outlines the nature of adversities and their commonalities and provides empirical evidence from two national databases that demonstrate the adaptive importance of strengths for those facing adversities.

The second part of this volume includes seven chapters that focus on adversities at the individual and family levels of analysis. These chapters review research and develop strengths-based policy implications for children facing parental divorce (chap. 4), child abuse and neglect (chap. 5), alcoholic parents (chap. 8), parental mental illness (chap. 9), or pediatric chronic illness (chap. 10), as well as for families in which the mother is experiencing domestic violence (chap. 6), or is an adolescent parent (chap. 7). The strengths-based approaches of resilience research, competence-based primary prevention, and family support are strongly represented in this section of the volume.

Part III of this book focuses on strengths-based approaches to adverse circumstances at the community and societal levels, including growing up in the inner city (chap. 11), social–environmental contributors to school failure (chap. 12), the transition to secondary school (chap. 13), exposure to negative peer influence (chap. 14), community violence (chapter 17), and community-level adversity (chap. 18). Also considered in this section are strengths-based aspects of racial and ethnic minority status (chap. 15) and the ways in which strengths-based approaches can promote positive outcomes for immigrants adapting to a new culture (chap. 16). The strengths-based traditions of positive youth development, community psychology, whole-school reform, assets-based community development, and multicultural psychology are strongly represented in this section of the volume.

The fourth part contains the final chapter, an overarching blueprint to move U.S. society toward a strengths-based social policy (chap. 19). Based on the key research and policy implications from the preceding chapters, the authors propose a general set of recommendations to frame future research and policy development from a strengths-based perspective.

The current volume represents the fruits of the first stage of our collaboration. The next stage of our work will focus on advocating for strengths-based policies. We plan to develop summary materials based on this volume that can be used to promote strengths-based policies to policymakers, to hold congressional briefings on the issues presented in this volume, and to collaborate with allied organizations to advance strengths-based social policies. It is our view that the current volume, as one part of the larger movement away from a deficits-based and toward a strengths-based approach, will serve as a strong foundation for policy advocacy work for students, researchers, and policymakers.

REFERENCES

Aspinwall, L. G., & Staudinger, U. M. (Eds.). (2003). *A psychology of human strengths: Fundamental questions and future directions for a positive psychology*. Washington, DC: American Psychological Association.

Benson, P. L. (1997). *All kids are our kids: What communities must do to raise caring and responsible children and adolescents*. San Francisco: Jossey-Bass.

Boyd-Franklin, N. (1989). *Black families in therapy: A multisystems approach*. New York: Guilford Press.

Catalano, R. F., Berglund, M. L., Ryan, J. A. M., Lonczak, H. S., & Hawkins, J. D. (1998). *Positive youth development in the United States: Research findings of positive youth development programs*. Retrieved February 1, 2002, from http://www.aspe.hhs.gov/hsp/positiveyouthdev99/

Cicchetti, D., Rappaport, J., Sandler, I., & Weissberg, R. P. (Eds.). (2000). *The promotion of wellness in children and adolescents*. Washington, DC: Child Welfare League of America Press.

Comer, J. P., Haynes, N. M., Joyner, E. T., & Ben-Avie, M. (Eds.). (1996). *Rallying the whole village: The Comer process for reforming education*. New York: Teachers College Press.

Cowen, E. L. (1994). The enhancement of psychological wellness: Challenges and opportunities. *American Journal of Community Psychology, 22*, 149–179.

Durlak, J. A. (1997). *Successful prevention programs for children and adolescents*. New York: Plenum Press.

Finnan, C., & Levin, H. M. (2000). Changing school cultures. In H. Altrichter & J. Elliot (Eds.), *Images of educational change* (pp. 87–98). Buckingham, England: Open University Press.

Kretzmann, J. P., & McKnight, J. L. (1993). *Building communities from the inside out: A path toward finding and mobilizing a community's assets*. Chicago: Assisting Christians to Act.

Lerner, R. M., Sparks, E. E., & McCubbin, L. D. (1999). *Family diversity and family policy: Strengthening families for America's children*. Boston: Kluwer Academic.

Masten, A. S., & Coatsworth, J. D. (1998). The development of competence in favorable and unfavorable environments: Lessons from research on successful children. *American Psychologist, 53*, 205–220.

Maton, K. I. (2000). Making a difference: The social ecology of social transformation. *American Journal of Community Psychology, 28*, 25–57.

Millstein, S. G., Petersen, A. C., & Nightingale, E. O. (1993). *Promoting the health of adolescents: New directions for the twenty-first century*. New York: Oxford University Press.

Moore, K. A., Evans, J., Brooks-Gunn, J., & Roth, J. (2001). What are good child outcomes? In A. Thornton (Ed.), *The well-being of children and families: Research and data needs* (pp. 59–84). Ann Arbor: University of Michigan Press.

Pittman, K. J. (1996, September). *Prevention problems or promoting development: Competing priorities or inseparable goals?* Retrieved June 12, 2003 from www.iyfnet.org/programs/dyo.html

Rappaport, J. (1981). In praise of paradox: A social policy of empowerment over prevention. *American Journal of Community Psychology, 9*, 1–21.

Rutter, M. (1987). Psychosocial resilience and protective mechanisms. *American Journal of Orthopsychiatry, 57*, 316–331.

Saegert, S., Thompson, J. P., & Warren, M. R. (Eds.). (2001). *Social capital and poor communities*. New York: Russell Sage Foundation.

Saleebey, D. (Ed.). (1992). *The strengths perspective in social work practice*. New York: Longman.

Sandler, I. N., Wolchik, S. A., MacKinnon, D., Ayers, T. S., & Roosa, M. W. (1997). Developing linkages between theory and intervention in stress and coping processes. In S. A. Wolchik & I. N. Sandler (Eds.), *Handbook of children's coping* (pp. 3–41). New York: Plenum Press.

Seligman, M. E. P., & Csikszentmihalyi, M. (2000). Positive psychology: An introduction. *American Psychologist, 55*, 5–14.

Trickett, E. J., Watts, R. J., & Birman, D. (Eds.). (1994). *Human diversity: Perspectives on people in context*. San Francisco: Jossey-Bass.

Weick, A., & Saleebey, D. (1995, March). Supporting family strengths: Orienting policy and practice toward the 21st century. *Families in Society, 76*, 141–149.

Weissberg, R. P., & Greenberg, M. T. (1998). School and community competence-enhancement and prevention programs. In I. E. Sigel & A. Renninger (Eds.), *Handbook of child psychology: Vol. 4. Child psychology in practice* (5th ed., pp. 955–998). New York: Wiley.

2

RESEARCH AND POLICY FOR BUILDING STRENGTHS: PROCESSES AND CONTEXTS OF INDIVIDUAL, FAMILY, AND COMMUNITY DEVELOPMENT

BONNIE J. LEADBEATER, CYNTHIA J. SCHELLENBACH, KENNETH I. MATON, AND DANIEL W. DODGEN

Research evidence that has accumulated over the past 2 decades from several academic disciplines has catalyzed a strengths-based approach to understanding individual, family, and community development. In the past, research and policy development typically emphasized the individual vulnerabilities, deficits, pathology, deviance, or risk factors associated with negative outcomes for children or families. In contrast, a strengths-based approach seeks to illuminate and understand the individual and environmental characteristics and protective processes that create and support positive developmental outcomes. The need for broader, more integrated theories of individual, family, and community development has also pushed researchers to collaborate across disciplines and to consider the linkages among viable communities, well-functioning families, and individual well-being.

* * *

A strengths-based approach to research and policy is based on the recognition that there is substantial variation in the adjustment of individuals, families, and communities experiencing adverse circumstances. Research seeking to explain why some (even the majority of) individuals show adaptive functioning in adverse circumstances has begun to identify the interactive, protective processes that build, maintain, or engage strengths at individual, family, and community levels to enable adaptive functioning.

In this chapter, we show how the key constructs of strengths building, protective processes, competence, and adaptive functioning can be considered at several levels as characteristics of individuals, families, and communities. We also demonstrate the interdependence of adaptive functioning at each of these levels. Strengths at one level have direct and indirect effects on strengths at each of the other levels. Policies and programs also can address adversities that encompass individual (e.g., chronic health risks), family (e.g., poverty), or social–cultural (e.g., discrimination) circumstances. However, the interdependence of effects across these levels also creates multiple, interrelated targets for effectively integrating policy and programming. These integrated efforts are critical for promoting child, youth, family, institutional, and community strengths.

In this chapter we outline the brief history of strengths-based research approaches. We argue that both risk and protective processes influence the development and well-being of children, families, and communities. Moreover, because the well-being of individuals, families, and communities is interwoven, policies and programs that target individuals, families, or communities have effects that reverberate on the other levels. We end by suggesting priorities for strengths-based research and directions for policy and programming that are derived from this perspective.

STRENGTHS-BASED RESEARCH, PAST AND PRESENT

Since the late 1960s, researchers have been investigating the competencies, resilience, resources, and protective processes that lead some individuals to thrive despite adverse life circumstances. Werner's (1993) formative research with the resilient children of Kauai, Hawaii, focused on children and youth "who pulled themselves up by their own bootstraps, with informal support from kith and kin" (p. 513). She added that "no children were recipients of intervention services," emphasizing the focus of this research on illuminating the preexisting strengths of individuals that afforded them protection against risks. Haggerty, Sherrod, Garmezy, and Rutter (1996) studied the characteristics of stress-resistant children who "retained competence despite the presence of adverse circumstances in which adversity takes the form of biological, psychological, or societal shortcomings" (p. 11). This early research revealed individual capacities (e.g., high intelligence, easy disposition), personality characteristics (e.g., internal locus of control, sociable or optimistic attitudes), and achievements (e.g., being at grade level, having positive peer relationships) that compensate for inadequate resources, protect against risks, or help children to resist maladaptive behaviors in adverse circumstances.

The early emphasis in resilience research on personal bootstrapping and invulnerability despite risk initially preempted more detailed investigations of the family, cultural, and societal contexts that support resilience. Indeed, the almost exclusive attention to individual stress resistance has given rise to outcries against resilience models. Researchers, policy analysts, and service providers have feared that emphasis on individuals' or even families' capacities to rise above adversity will perpetuate blaming victims of adverse circumstances for their own deficits or failure to pull themselves up. Even well-meaning efforts to provide services to fix or correct deficits can negatively stigmatize individuals who experience adversity in their families or communities. A singular focus on individuals also can detract research attention, intervention efforts, and funding from community- and institutional-level interventions that could correct the adverse circumstances that impede or overwhelm individual effort. With the movement of resilience parlance into the public domain, some of these fears have borne fruit in self-help books directing survivors to rise above adversity and research and treatments that promote the development of personal traits or assets but do not work to affect family- or community-level adversities or resources.

The early research, however, did draw attention to the environmental risk and protective factors that predict differences in groups of individuals' capacities for resilience or stress resistance (Masten, Best, & Garmezy, 1990; Werner & Smith, 1992). As Gore and Eckenrode (1994) noted, "within a traditional model of risk and resiliency it is assumed that high levels of existing protective resources significantly offset the mental health and behavioral impact of risk" (p. 55). Studies of network supports for individual capacities have focused particular attention on the advantages of close parent–child or extended family relationships (see reviews by McLoyd, 1998; Masten & Coatsworth, 1998). Similarly, theories seeking to explain how positive outcomes come about for individuals facing adverse circumstances emphasize the need to understand the complex transactions of antecedent conditions, initial levels of adjustment or vulnerability, and the interactions among environmental risk and protective factors.

Researchers have begun only recently to make the roles of contextual factors explicit and to extend concepts of resilience or strengths building to family, institutional, neighborhood, and community levels of analysis. In the following section we consider models developed by researchers in developmental, family, and community psychology to illuminate essential principles of a strengths-based research and policy focus. Individuals, families, and communities are viewed as interdependent systems that experience multidimensional changes over time in response to evolving risk and protective processes. They act as self-determining collaborators in strengths-building policy development (rather than as the recipients of services that seek to correct deficits, treat pathology, or punish deviance). Individuals, families, and communities facing adverse circumstances can collaborate with professionals and academics to define relevant problems and to generate, disseminate, and apply solutions. Attention is focused on the ways in which protective processes (intrapsychic, situational, and environmental) support adaptive outcomes for individuals, families, and communities facing adverse circumstances. Strengths-building policies and practices can contribute to adaptive outcomes at many points in time by creating and enhancing protective processes and resources.

NEW DIRECTIONS IN STRENGTHS-BASED RESEARCH

Perhaps because of its relative longevity compared to research on family and community development, research on the resilience of individuals has helped to characterize many of the essential features of strength-building processes. However, going beyond the development of characteristics in individuals that support adaptive functioning, researchers have begun to draw attention to the necessity of understanding development as context based, multidimensional, nonstatic, and process oriented. This research builds on but also goes beyond early efforts to identify the correlates of competent children and youth. It also investigates the ways that competence is engendered, maintained, promoted, or even diminished across the life span.

Individual competence is context based. In their review of research on the development of individual competence, Masten and Coatsworth (1998) defined *resilience* as "manifested competence [in a person] in the context of significant challenges to adaptation or development" (p. 205). They defined *competence* as a

> pattern of effective adaptation in the environment either broadly defined in terms of reasonable success with major developmental tasks expected for a given age and gender *in the context of his or her culture, society and time* or more narrowly defined in terms of specific domains of achievement such as academics, peer acceptance, or athletics. (emphasis added, p. 206)

In other words, understanding the effects of social–cultural and historical contexts on the development of individuals, families, and communities (for example, changes in the face of racism, rates of divorce, roles for women, markets, and job opportunities) is essential for promoting individual competence.

Individual competence is multidimensional (Cicchetti & Garmezy, 1993; Luthar, Cicchetti, & Becker, 2000; Luthar, Doernberger, & Zigler,

1993; Masten & Coatsworth, 1998). The development of competence in one domain may or may not be accompanied by competence in others. For example, poor, ethnic minority children's academic success may be accompanied by internal struggles with psychological distress rather than good emotional health (Luthar et al., 2000).

Individual competence is dynamic. Continuities and discontinuities in the capacity for competence in adverse circumstances also need to be understood. Changes in children's competence are often preceded by critical changes in their environmental supports (Egeland, Carlson, & Sroufe, 1993). In addition, continued harmful exposure to adverse circumstances such as poverty, unstable housing, or domestic violence can overwhelm resources that support competence, as exemplified in a study of inner-city adolescent mothers' transitions to early adulthood (Leadbeater, 1998; Leadbeater & Way, 2001). In the course of their life cycles, children, families, and communities develop new vulnerabilities and strengths over time, and these risk and protective processes, in turn, interact with children's competencies in dealing with subsequent challenges, opportunities, or threats to their well-being.

How children and youth develop, maintain, and express competence in contexts of adversity can also vary depending on their developmental stage, family resources and expectations, and environmental circumstances (Cicchetti & Garmezy, 1993; Masten & Coatsworth, 1998; Werner, 1993). An adolescent, for example, can be aware of the importance of planning for the future in a way that a young child is not. This developing cognition can enhance an adolescent's ability to resist negative behaviors or maintain adaptive ones when he or she is exposed to delinquent peers (see chap. 14, this volume; Gest, Neemann, Hubbard, Masten, & Tellegen, 1993). On the other hand, future-oriented youths from communities with high unemployment that offer few prospects for earning a living wage may be more likely to engage in illegal behaviors when exposed to delinquent peers if they see this as a means for gaining status or resources that are otherwise inaccessible (Fagan & Wilkinson, 1998). The adolescent's cognitive gains interact with environmental risks and protective processes to determine adaptive functioning.

The development of individual competence is a process rather than a static outcome. Changes in risk and protective factors continue to challenge and support individual competencies across an individual's life span. Competencies are not acquired once and for all and forever. They are reworked in evolving life circumstances that offer new resources and new challenges. According to Pianta and Walsh (1998), "Resilience is best perceived in terms of a process that involves multiple factors interacting over time, from which occasionally precipitates success in a particular developmental domain or function" (p. 411). Research has begun to specify the ways that protective processes operate to support the development and maintenance of individual competencies. *Protective processes* include experiences, events, and relationships that operate to:

1. interrupt or reverse downward developmental trajectories;
2. diminish the causes or impact of stressful situations;
3. reduce the negative chain reactions that characterize pathogenic family or school situations;
4. promote the development and maintenance of self-efficacy;
5. create beliefs or loyalties that are incompatible with deviant behaviors; and
6. provide opportunities for positive education, vocational, and personal growth (Connell, Spencer, & Aber, 1994; Cowen, Wyman, Work, & Iker, 1995; Jessor, Van Den Bos, Vanderryn, Costa, & Turbin, 1995).

These processes vary in their emphasis on individual characteristics or contextual factors and also differ in focusing on general protective processes (those that act independent of adverse circumstances) or on risk-specific processes (those that affect strengths development only in adverse circumstances), again suggesting multiple interrelated targets for policy and programming efforts.

PROCESSES OF STRENGTHS BUILDING

The continuities and discontinuities in the development of individual competence in several domains and of the contextual factors and protective process that are critical to fostering and sustaining these competencies must be recognized in a working definition of strengths building. A process-oriented definition not only emphasizes people's capacities to rise above or resist adversity at a given point in time, but also brings attention to the interrelations among individuals, families, and communities across time. At the individual level, strengths-building research and policy should make this interdependence explicit and should emphasize long-term goals that promote specific protective processes such as those listed above.

Intraindividual continuities and discontinuities in adaptive behaviors occur over the life span. The building and maintenance of competence is a function of protective processes that inevitably fluctuate across an individual's life span, as illustrated in Figure 2.1. In the course of their daily lives, people all encounter stresses in the form of, for example, relationship changes or losses, illnesses, or economic difficulties. Their capacity to deal with these challenges is also dependant on their storehouse of protective processes in the form of social supports, access to medical care, or financial savings or earning potential. Interrelations among individual vulnerabilities and competencies, as well as risk and protective factors, may serve to diminish adversity and increase protective processes over time for a person in adverse circumstances (as is exemplified in the positive trajectory depicted in Figure 2.1 after age 25); however, other patterns are also possible as risks and protective processes change.

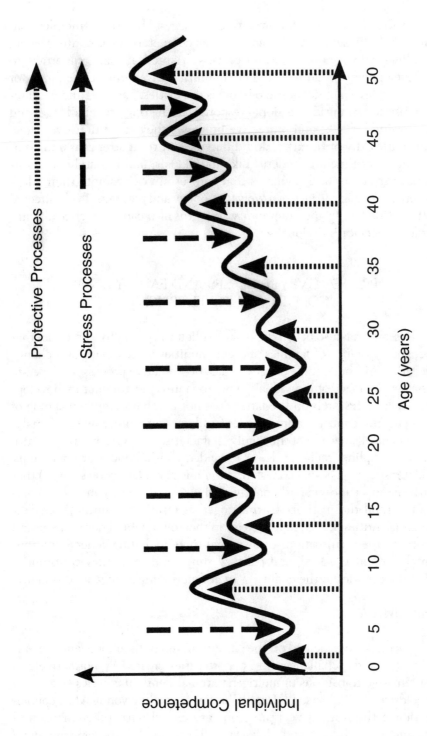

Figure 2.1. Interplay of protective and stress processes and their influence on individual competence across the life span.

In the section that follows, we also suggest that the principles that characterize the development of individual competencies as context based, multidimensional, nonstatic, and process oriented also are important to the development of families and communities. Strengths at the family or community level are not static outcomes or entities. Families and communities also show multidimensional responses to the ongoing challenges and opportunities or risks and protective processes they encounter over time. Continuities, discontinuities, and differences in their strengths and competencies over time are evident. Like individuals, families and communities have strengths and resources that can sustain or promote their adaptive functioning in the face of adversities. Policy and program efforts directed at supporting family and community strengths also can have critically important effects for individuals.

PROTECTIVE PROCESSES AND FAMILY AND COMMUNITY DEVELOPMENT

Research has also begun the make explicit the protective processes that affect the capacities of families and communities to deal with and change adversities. Although some of the features of protective process that operate in the development of individuals apply to family and community development analysis, research on the latter does not involve a simple mapping of developmental concepts onto broader family or community levels of analyses or a mere elaboration of the family characteristics (e.g., parental warmth, positive discipline, racial pride, or extended family bonds) or community characteristics (e.g., social cohesion, economic resources, good schools) that positively affect individuals' adaptive behaviors. Rather, families or communities (and the institutions that together form communities) are self-regulating entities or organized systems in their own right. They undergo and respond to the perturbations of historical time, including general environmental, economic, social, and political shifts, and they show continuities and discontinuities in the quality of their functioning as organized systems.

Family Systems

Theories have focused on the patterns of relations among family members that undergo challenges and opportunities created by normative and nonnormative transitions of multigenerational family life cycles (Carter & McGoldrick, 1988; Gerson, 1995). Families formed by young adult couples experience the normative transitions associated with pregnancies and parenting young children and adolescents who, themselves, become the young adults who form new families and leave their parents, who regroup as a couple and as grandparents. Today's families are frequently structured differently than the once-typical nuclear family of mother, father, and child; however, the life cycle of families with children continues to be subject to these normative transitions as well as to stressful life events that threaten family functioning, such as illnesses, divorce, unemployment episodes, and poverty. Family functioning in the face of family-level adversities reflects resources and protective processes inherent in individual family members, in the family system, and in the family's specific cultural, ethnic, and community contexts.

Resiliency research with families has focused particularly on minority-group families dealing with adversities related to discrimination (McCubbin, Thompson, Thompson, & Fromer, 1998). This research emphasizes, for example, "the family's relational process of adaptation and the family's appraisal processes involving ethnicity and culture which facilitate the family's functioning and achieve harmony while promoting the well-being and development of its members" (McCubbin, Futrell, Thompson, & Thompson, 1998, p. 332). Protective "relational processes" operate to maintain families' integrity. Research with divorced and remarried families has also begun to illuminate the processes that support effective family functioning in the face of dramatic, often adverse, changes in relationships between parents, and between children and parents, that are frequently accompanied by economic stress (see chap. 4, this volume).

As shown in Figure 2.2, analogous to individual development, family functioning can be portrayed as an organized system that creates and follows a trajectory in responding to stress and protective processes over time. Aspects of adaptive family functioning (including, for example, family cohesion, parental warmth, and effective disciplinary practices) fluctuate as families cope with stressful life events, mobilize their resources, and interact with changing community adversities and resources (McLoyd, 1998). Moreover, the life cycle stage or baseline resources of a family may importantly influence their capacity to respond. For example, families with very young parents who are undergoing transitions to early adulthood have very different challenges and resources than families with older parents who have acquired life skills, network supports, and work experiences that may aid family functioning during normative transitions and in times of adversity (Leadbeater & Way, 2001).

Community Organizations

Similar to family systems theorists, investigators of community strengths-building processes focus attention on relational constructs, in this case those that represent the interdependence of individuals, families, and the larger community (including community settings, institutions, political representation, values, economies, and so forth; see chap. 18, this volume; Baldwin et al., 1993; Bronfenbrenner, 1979; Maton, 2000; Seidman, 1990). The term

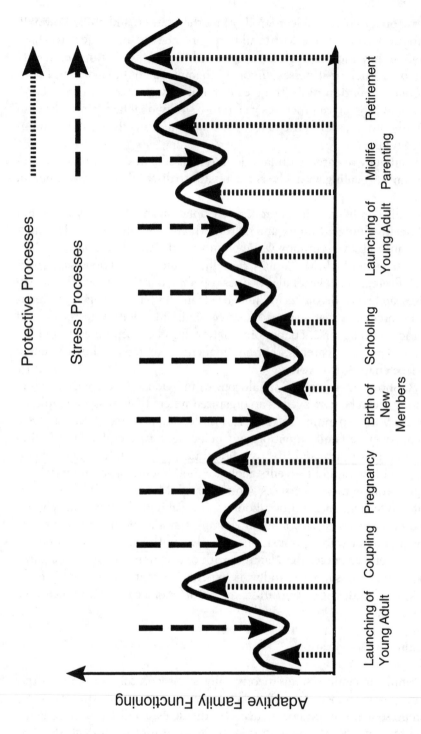

Figure 2.2. Interplay of protective and stress processes and their influence on adaptive family functioning across multigenerational life cycle transitions.

community is used to convey simultaneously a local geographical area as well as the networks of personal and institutional relations it encompasses. Community-level adaptive functioning, adverse circumstances, stressors, and protective resources touch directly on and transact with individual and family life cycles and well-being, but again no simple mapping of individual-level protective processes onto community-level functioning is possible.

Moreover, the widespread nature of community-level adversities calls for a different focus for strengths building. Community-level adversities include overlapping problems that are centered in economic, social, and environmental adversities. These include such concerns as neighborhood decline, inadequate housing, and high levels of crime and disorder, which can be compounded by a lack of a political voice for the citizens who are most affected by these disorders (see chap. 18, this volume). Resolving community-level adversities may have large payoffs given that the development and resilience of individuals or families depends on the viability and adequate functioning of their communities. On the other hand, individual and family resources can be overwhelmed in the face of high levels of community violence, disorganization, or poverty (see chaps. 11 and 17, this volume).

Research on the patterns of reciprocal relations, transactions, and interdependencies among people and social systems has been the focus of community psychology researchers. For example, Seidman (1990, p. 92) referred to the temporal patterns of these reciprocal relations as "social regularities," underscoring their constancy or self-sustaining tendencies over time. Figure 2.3 portrays a developmental trajectory of a community that is building on its strengths over time. Biases in beliefs, stereotyping, resource and power inequalities, or institutional dysfunctions can serve to create negative social regularities that undermine the psychosocial functioning of community members. On the other hand, responsive community-level, institutional, and societal-level interventions and policies that address peremptory social regularities (e.g., by removing race-related barriers or reducing neighborhood disorder and enhancing community capacity or political empowerment of marginalized groups) can increase the likelihood of growth-promoting interactions for children, youth, and families (Maton, 2000; see chap. 18, this volume).

As with individuals and families, communities fluctuate in their ability to support the well-being of their constituents across time in response to the challenges and opportunities or risk and protective processes. For example, poor communities with active, organized , stable residents may be better able to respond to community-level adversities than communities with isolated citizens or fragmented interest groups. Highly supportive community settings such as churches or mutual help groups can augment community cohesion and buffer stressful events (Maton, 1989). Institutions are also organized community-based systems that affect children's adjustment. For example, the timing of the transition from elementary to middle schools has also been shown to affect children's school performance (see chap. 13, this volume).

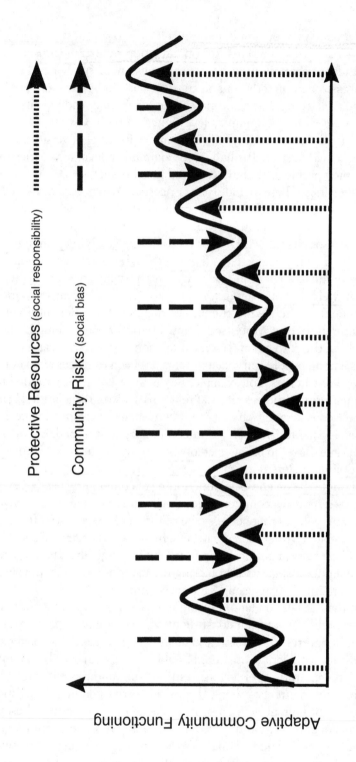

Figure 2.3. Interplay of protective resources and community risks (social regularities) on adaptive community functioning over historical time.

TABLE 2.1

Emphasis of Problem-Focused Versus Strengths-Based Research and Policy Approaches

Problem-focused approaches	Strengths-based approaches
Correct deficits or maladaptative behaviors	Build strengths and resources
Have a short-term impact	Have a long-term impact
Provide crisis intervention	Provide primary prevention
Involve reactive planning	Involve proactive planning
Create good endpoints	Build and sustain strengths
Target risks in populations	Target variations in risks and strengths of populations

GUIDING PRINCIPLES FOR STRENGTHS-BASED RESEARCH AND POLICY

A strengths-based approach to research and policy development requires significant changes in focus. The directions of these changes are outlined in Table 2.1. To build a stronger empirical foundation for strengths-based policy, researchers need to be aware of (a) the diversity of individual, family, and community responses to adverse circumstances rather than generalized population responses; (b) the strengths, competencies, and resources needed for preventing or dealing with adversities rather than the deficits, pathologies, and deviance that can result from them; (c) the long-term pathways or life-span trajectories that are affected by variations in strengths available to respond to adversities, rather than short-term responses that are elicited by recurring crises; and (d) the interrelations among individual, family, and community levels of development rather than the characteristics of adapted individuals or community assets. This knowledge can be used to create targeted policy responses that can identify, enhance, and sustain strengths; follow long-term goals; and prioritize integrated strategies that have effects that cut across individual, family, and community levels of functioning and across several specific adversities.

Targeted programs and policies are needed to build new strengths and enhance the existing strengths of high-risk groups in ways that reflect the diversity of their responses to adversities. Findings of diversity of responses to adversities within high-risk populations challenge the generalizability and often the validity of risk-based statistics. Adversities can have very different effects on individuals, families, or communities who do or do not have the resources to deal with them. Too often, comparisons of groups experiencing challenging circumstances (e.g., poor teenage mothers) are compared to apparently normative groups (e.g., poor women who delayed childbearing). Not surprisingly, the "at-risk" group is found to be, on average, deficient or deviant in some way (such as having lower levels of education or income or poorer parenting skills). This is problematic and can misguide public opinion and policy when, despite higher risk, <u>the majority in the "defective" group are</u> <u>very similar to the normative one.</u>

For example, although 1987 statistics (Allan Guttmacher Institute, 1994) showed that teen mothers were at risk for not finishing high school (29% did not finish) when compared to women who gave birth at age 20 or over (9% did not finish), the large majority of teenage mothers (71%) did in fact earn a high school diploma. Because of this emphasis on risk, researchers know very little about the experiences of the majority of young mothers who graduate, or the approximately one in five teenage mothers who go on to college. Instead of focusing on low-level income support that maintains disadvantage over the short term, a strengths-based perspective emphasizes that concentrated supports (e.g., income assistance, career planning, accessible and affordable day care) are needed to make these normal transitions to adulthood possible for young mothers.

Focusing on within-group differences also forces researchers to ask which individuals, families, or communities who are coping with what adverse circumstances will experience negative or positive outcomes and to prioritize programs that identify, sustain, or build strengths while reducing adversities. For example, the treatment of people with mental illnesses, like depression or psychotic disorders, traditionally has focused on case management of the ill persons in one-to-one relationships with health care providers. Their status as parents and the effects of the illness on their children are dealt with by attempts to improve the individual's functioning and has only rarely focused on resources in their families or communities that could sustain good parenting despite episodes of illness (see chap. 9, this volume). In addition, accessible school or community-based recreation facilities that offer affordable sports and talent activities and programs for youths and families could serve multiple functions for families dealing with a parent's mental illness, including overcoming social isolation, providing respite after-school care, enhancing parenting skills and health education, and providing financial planning assistance. Similarly, policies that create safe, stable housing for low-income families in economically diverse neighborhoods would also help stabilize the neighborhood resources or support networks that these families need to assist them in times of crisis. Stable housing for poor families also means that their children are not moving from school to school, decreases their isolation from conventional peers, and increases the likelihood that they will find supportive adults and opportunities for engagement in their school environment, reducing the long-term negative effects of poverty on these children.

Policy and programming need to give support that is adequate enough and long enough to help families establish the foundations they need to sustain positive trajectories over time (rather than minimal support that maintains minimal standards of living and downward trajectories across generations). Welfare policies that universally prescribe time limits for high-risk groups, like teenage mothers, can abort these women's efforts toward educational or financial advancement just as they qualify for college entry or job promotion. Financial stresses that accompany postsecondary education or work, such as tuition and books, child care or transportation costs, health insurance, and living expenses, can force single mothers to choose low-wage jobs over education. A more tapered approach to reducing income assistance that allows financial and health benefits to continue to support advanced education or work apprenticeships would be a more forward-looking strategy for sustaining the resources of single mothers and their children in the long term. Similarly, support of school, family, and community cooperative programs that improve educational and career opportunities for girls (and boys) from poor families and increase their motivation for postsecondary education is a preventive rather than deficits-based welfare reform strategy that could have long-term benefits for these families and communities.

BUILDING STRENGTHS IN RESEARCH-POLICY COLLABORATIONS

Research and policy efforts have long been pushed by different goals, priorities, orientations, methods, and time schedules. Policymakers are oriented toward making decisions that have immediate effects on social actions that are intended to advance public welfare or serve a particular constituency. Individual plights, bottom lines, popular opinion, and economic concerns weigh heavily throughout this decision-making process. Policy dialogue takes the form of verbal debates often among strongly held views and competing interests.

On the other hand, research is oriented toward the generation and, frequently, regeneration of knowledge in changing social circumstances. Paradigmatic research methods create specific mechanisms for verifying knowledge claims. Research dialogue moves slowly. It is fueled by data collection and analysis as well as procedures for evaluation and interpretation of written findings through critical peer review.

The major players in research and policy are often segregated into separate spheres of practice (universities versus government agencies), where they use different sources of information and develop divergent sets of terminology. These factors further institutionalize the gaps between the two worlds. This volume addresses how policy can pose questions for research and how research can respond more effectively to policy questions. In each chapter, collaborations between academics and policy advocates illuminate the implications of research on strengths building for policy development, as well as the critical influence of social policy on research questions and funding. The chapters also explore how to disseminate better research knowledge to policymakers and how to make researchers more aware of the worldviews and needs of policymakers.

Investing in children, youths, families, and communities requires a prevention, wellness, competency, and future-oriented approach to building strengths. It requires giving up quick-fix, short-term investment strategies. Research and policy must be ready to weather intermittent continuities and discontinuities in risk statistics and eschew crisis-driven actions for longer-term benefits. Like the stock market, these short-term investments are subject to extremes and fluctuations, but long-term strategies can generate higher yields. Investment risks can also be reduced by increasing decision makers' access to research evidence. Strengths-building policy decisions rest on the foundation of several decades of careful scientific research that augments investment certainty. Children, youths, families, and communities are interdependent entities that undergo and respond to the perturbations of daily life. Strengths-based policy, informed by the available research, can help build the foundations that enable individuals, families, and communities to respond competently to life's ongoing challenges and opportunities.

REFERENCES

Allan Guttmacher Institute. (1994). *Sex and America's teenagers*. New York: Author.

Baldwin, A. L., Baldwin, C. P., Kasser, T., Zax, M., Sameroff, A., & Seifer, R. (1993). Contextual risk and resiliency during late adolescence. *Development and Psychopathology, 5*, 741–761.

Bronfenbrenner, U. (1979). *The ecology of human development*. Cambridge, MA: Harvard University.

Carter, E. A., & McGoldrick, M. (1988). *The changing family life-cycle: A framework for family therapy* (2nd ed.). New York: Gardner Press.

Cicchetti, D., & Garmezy, N. (1993). Prospects and promise in the study of resilience. *Development and Psychopathology, 5*, 497–502.

Connell, J. P., Spencer, M. B., & Aber, J. L. (1994). Educational risk and resilience in African-American youth: Context, self, action, and outcomes in school. *Child Development, 65*, 493–506.

Cowen, E. L., Wyman, P. A., Work, W. C., & Iker, M. R. (1995). A preventive intervention for enhancing resilience among highly stressed urban children. *Journal of Primary Prevention, 15*, 247–260.

Egeland, B. R., Carlson, E., & Sroufe, L. A. (1993). Resilience as process. *Development and Psychopathology, 5*, 517–528.

Fagan, J., & Wilkinson, D. K. (1998). Social context and functions of adolescent violence. In D. S. Elliott, B. A. Hamburg, & K. R. Williams, (Eds.), *Violence in American schools* (pp. 55–94). New York: Cambridge University Press.

Gerson, R. (1995). The family life cycle: Phases, stages, and crises. In R. H. Mikesell, D. D. Lusterman, & S. H. McDaniel (Eds.), *Integrating family therapy: Handbook of family psychology and systems theory* (pp. 91–111). Washington, DC: American Psychological Association.

Gest, S. D., Neemann, J., Hubbard, J. J., Masten, A. S., & Tellegen, A. (1993). Parenting quality, adversity, and conduct problems in adolescence: Testing process-oriented models of resilience. *Development and Psychopathology, 5,* 663–682.

Gore, S., & Eckenrode, J. (1994). Context and process in research on risk and resilience. In R. J. Haggerty, L. R. Sherrod, N. Garmezy, & M. Rutter (Eds.), *Stress, risk, and resilience in children and adolescents: Processes, mechanisms, and interventions* (pp. 19–63). New York: Cambridge University Press.

Haggerty, R. J., Sherrod, L. R., Garmezy, N., & Rutter, M. (Eds.). (1996). *Stress, risk, and resilience in children and adolescents: Processes, mechanisms, and interventions.* New York: Cambridge University Press.

Jessor, R., Van Den Bos, J., Vanderryn, J., Costa, F., & Turbin, M. S. (1995). Protective factors in adolescent problem behavior: Moderator effects and developmental change. *Developmental Psychology, 31,* 923–933.

Leadbeater, B. J. (1998). The goals of welfare reform reconsidered: Supporting the transition to work for inner-city adolescent mothers. *Children's Services: Social Policy, Research and Practice, 2,* 23–44.

Leadbeater, B. J., & Way, N. (2001). *Growing up fast: Early adult transitions of inner-city adolescent mothers.* New York: Erlbaum.

Luthar, S. S., Cicchetti, D., & Becker, B. (2000). The construct of resilience: A critical evaluation and guidelines for future work. *Child Development, 71,* 543–562.

Luthar, S. S., Doernberger, C. H., & Zigler, E. (1993). Resilience is not a unidimensional construct: Insights from a prospective study of inner-city adolescents. *Development and Psychopathology, 5,* 703–717.

Masten, A. S., Best, K. M., & Garmezy, N. (1990). Resilience and development: Contributions from the study of children who overcome adversity. *Development and Psychopathology, 2,* 425–444.

Masten, A. S., & Coatsworth, J. D. (1998). The development of competence in favorable and unfavorable environments: Lessons from research on successful children. *American Psychologist, 53,* 205–220.

Maton, K. (1989). Community settings as buffers of life stress? Highly supportive churches, mutual help groups and senior centers. *American Journal of Community Psychology, 17,* 203–232.

Maton, K. (2000). Making a difference: The social ecology of social transformation. *American Journal of Community Psychology, 28,* 25–57.

McCubbin, H. I., Futrell, J. A., Thompson, E. A., & Thompson, A. I. (1998). Resilient families in an ethnic and cultural context. In H. I. McCubbin, E. A. Thompson, A. I. Thompson, & J. A. Futrell (Eds.), *Resiliency in African-American families* (pp. 329–351). Thousand Oaks, CA: Sage.

McCubbin, H. I., Thompson, E. A., Thompson, A. I., & Fromer, J. E. (1998). *Resiliency in native and immigrant families.* Thousand Oaks, NJ: Sage.

McLoyd, V. (1998). Socioeconomic disadvantage and child development. *American Psychologist, 53,* 185–202.

Pianta, R. C., & Walsh, D. J. (1998). Applying the construct of resilience in schools: Cautions from a developmental systems perspective. *School Psychology Review*, *27*, 407–417.

Seidman, E. (1990). Pursuing the meaning and utility of social regularities for community psychology. In P. Tolan & C. Keys (Eds.), *Researching community psychology: Issues of theory and methods* (pp. 91–100). Washington, DC: American Psychological Association.

Werner, E. E. (1993). Risk, resilience and recovery: Perspectives from the Kauai Longitudinal Study. *Developmental Psychopathology*, *5*, 503–515.

Werner, E. E., & Smith, R. S. (1992). *Overcoming the odds: High risk children from birth to adulthood*. Ithaca, NY: Cornell University Press.

3

ADVERSITIES, STRENGTHS, AND PUBLIC POLICY

IRWIN N. SANDLER, TIM S. AYERS, JESSE C. SUTER, AMY SCHULTZ, AND JOAN TWOHEY-JACOBS

The promotion of strengths can reduce risk for problem outcomes. Although policies to promote strengths can be justified because they produce positive, culturally valued developmental outcomes (see chap. 2, this volume), public policy is often driven by the goal to reduce problem outcomes, such as mental health problems, delinquency, and drug abuse. We argue that the goals of building strengths and preventing problems are synergistic: A policy that promotes strengths may also provide the most sustainable and effective approach to reducing problem outcomes. For example, there is now considerable evidence that early intervention programs promoting healthy social, cognitive, and physical development in at-risk, disadvantaged infants reduces their likelihood of involvement in antisocial behavior in adolescence and early adulthood (Yoshikawa, 1994).

* * *

In support of the argument that promoting strengths reduces problem outcomes, we first present empirical evidence from two national samples to show that the presence of strengths reduces the effects of cumulative adversities on problem outcomes. We then present a framework of the theoretical mechanisms by which strengths reduce the effects of adversities on problem outcomes. Finally, we discuss how public policies may synergistically build strengths and reduce problem outcomes.

RESEARCH ON ADVERSITIES, STRENGTHS, AND SERIOUS PROBLEMS OF CHILDREN AND YOUTH

There is considerable evidence that exposure to multiple adversities has a cumulative effect, increasing the probability of problems in the domains of mental health, substance use, and social adaptation (Rutter, 1979; Sameroff & Fiese, 2000). In these studies, researchers have traditionally treated each adversity as equivalent and have found that a simple count of the number of adversities was associated with a dramatic increase in the risk for problem outcomes. For example, Furstenberg, Cook, Eccles, Elder, and Sameroff (1999) created an additive index of the number of adversities to which children were exposed at different ecological levels (e.g., individual, family, peer, community). They found that the odds for poor mental health outcomes was 5.7 times greater for children exposed to 8 or more risk factors compared with those exposed to 0 to 3 risk factors. This chapter provides further evidence to support the relation between exposure to cumulative adversity and risk for poor mental health. However, because public policies are often developed for specific adversities (e.g., poverty, divorce, parental mental illness), our analyses differ from previous studies on cumulative risk by assessing the effects of specific individual adversities and combinations of adversities, rather than a simple count of the number of adversities.

The major focus of our analyses is on addressing whether the presence of strengths reduces the likelihood of problem outcomes under conditions of adversity. The accomplishment of positive adaptation under conditions of adversity is referred to as *resilience*, and an exciting literature has developed over the past two decades to describe factors that contribute to resilience and the processes that explain these effects (Luthar, Cicchetti, & Becker, 2000; Masten & Coatsworth, 1998). Within this literature, protective factors have been proposed to have either a main effect of reducing problem outcomes across levels of adversity or an interactive effect of reducing problem outcomes, *particularly* under conditions of high adversity (Luthar et al., 2000). Werner (2000), in a review of the longitudinal studies on resilience, identified protective factors at the level of individuals (e.g., internal locus of control, positive temperament, achievement motivation), families (e.g., close bond with primary caregiver, mother's education), and communities (e.g., mentors, supportive teachers, successful school experiences). Luthar et al. noted that protective factors have been characterized either as enduring personal traits of individuals or as a process. For purposes of our data analyses, we define *strengths*[1] as indicators of positive person–environment transactions in two domains, school and after-school or community activities. Theoreti-

---

[1]We use the term *strengths* rather than *protective factors* for purposes of consistency with the volume and because we save the term *protective* to refer to a particular model of how strengths reduce the negative effects of adversity.

cally, although positive involvements in school and community activities may result from the presence of enduring characteristics of individuals, families, or communities, they also reflect the existence of processes of positive person–environment transactions. Similar to Sameroff and Fiese (2000), we were interested in distinguishing strengths from the absence of failures. Therefore, we designated strengths as the high end of the distribution on school and activity engagement. We addressed two questions about the effects of these strengths: Do strengths reduce the probability of serious behavior problems across each of the levels of cumulative adversity? And are the effects of strengths cumulative, so that the presence of two strengths affords greater reduction in risk than the presence of a single strength?

For our analyses we used data from two nationally representative samples, the National Longitudinal Study of Youth (NLSY; Center for Human Resource Research, 1999) and the National Study of America's Families (NSAF; Urban Institute, 1999). The data sets have comparable information but are also different in important ways. The NSAF data set is cross-sectional and retrospective, whereas the NLSY is prospective. Somewhat different measures were used in the two data sets to assess adversities, strengths, and behavior problems. In each case we created categories that represented extreme groups so as to study the relations between adversities, strengths, and serious levels of child behavior problems. With the NSAF data set we assessed the issue of how adversities cumulate within a single level of the social ecology— the family—and with the NLSY data set we assessed how adversities cumulate across levels of the social ecology—individual, family, and community. The use of two data sets allowed us to assess whether the findings on the cumulative effects of adversities and the effects of strengths were robust across methodologies and the unique characteristics of each study.

FINDINGS FROM NATIONAL DATA SETS

National Survey of America's Families

The NSAF is a study of the economic, health, and social well-being of a nationally representative sample of 44,461 American families in 1997 (Urban Institute, 1999). Because the sample overrepresented low-income families, all analyses were weighted (using the provided public-use weights) to reflect results for a nationally representative sample. Data were collected through telephone interviews with the most knowledgeable adult in the household. Four variables were identified as adversities: poor parent mental health,[2]

[2]Poor parent mental health was defined as a score of less than 67 on a 100-point scale of items reflecting symptoms of anxiety, depression, and loss of behavioral and emotional control (Stewart, Hays, & Ware, 1988). Using the full NSAF data set, we found that 17% scored below the cutoff point.

poor parent physical health,[3] family poverty (family income at or below the national poverty level), and single parent (one parent in the household). We used two measures of strengths: high levels of participation in activities or clubs and volunteering,[4] and positive school engagement.[5] The outcome measure was having a high level of behavior problems as measured by items derived from the Child Behavior Checklist.[6]

We analyzed data separately for the younger (6- to 11-year-old) and older (12- to 17-year-old) samples using logistic regression. An additive model entering all adversities and all strengths simultaneously was used to predict the dichotomous outcome of high behavior problems. For both the younger and the older samples, each of the adversities and strengths contributed significantly to the prediction of behavior problems. The predicted probability of behavior problems at each combination of adversities and strengths is shown in Table 3.1. The effect of cumulative adversities can be seen by looking down the columns. Illustratively, in the absence of strengths, for 12- to 17-year-olds, the probability of behavior problems is .07 for zero adversities, ranges from .11 to .20 for different single adversities, ranges from .18 to .40 for different combinations of two adversities, ranges from .38 to .55 for different combinations of three adversities, and is .68 in the presence of all four adversities.

Two conclusions can be drawn from these findings. First, adversities cumulatively increase the probability of high levels of behavior problems. Second, different single adversities and different combinations of adversities yield a differential probability of behavior problems. For example, for 12- to 17-year-olds, those with a parent who has poor mental health (.16 probability of behavior problems) have a 128% increase in the probability of behavior problems in comparison with those who have zero adversities (.07 probability of behavior problems). Children from poor families (.11 probability of behavior problems) have a 57% increase in the probability of behavior prob-

---

[3]Parent report of being in fair to poor physical health was measured by selection of the most extreme negative point on a single-item 3-point scale. For the entire NSAF data set, 4.8% scored as having fair to poor physical health.

[4]Levels of participation in activities or clubs and volunteering was assessed by adult report that the child participated in a sports team or club, took lessons after school, or participated in any adult-supervised organized activity and that the child participated in volunteer activities at least a few times per month. In the NSAF data set, 35.5% of children had this strength.

[5]Positive school engagement was assessed using a four-item scale developed by Connell and Bridges at the Institute for Research and Reform in Education in California. Questions assessed adult report of child interest in and willingness to do schoolwork. Possible range on this scale was 1 to 16, and a score of greater than 15 was considered by Connell and Bridges to indicate high school engagement; 38.1% of children in the NSAF scored as having this strength.

[6]The sum of six items that had previously been used by the National Health Interview was calculated. For children ages 6 to 11 a high level of behavior problems was defined as scoring above a cutoff point 2 standard deviations below the mean, the same definition used by the authors of the NSAF, a score that identified 7.8% of the NSAF sample. For adolescents ages 11 to 17, five items were used, and a cutoff point that identified 7.1% of the NSAF population was used to define high levels of behavior problems. One item from the original six items used by the NSAF was omitted from the adolescent behavior problem measure used in the current study because it referred to problems with school, thus overlapping conceptually with the school engagement scale.

TABLE 3.1

Predicted Probabilities for Developing Emotional or Behavioral Problems With Different Combinations of Risk Factors and Strengths With Data From NSAF

Number of risk factors	Presence of adversities				Probabilities of negative behavior problems							
	Poor parent mental health	Poor parent physical health	Family poverty	Single parent	No strengths present		Clubs or activities and volunteering		Positive school engagement		Both strengths	
					6–11	12–17	6–11	12–17	6–11	12–17	6–11	12–17
0					.06	.07	.05	.06	.01	.01	.01	.01
1	X				.18	.16	.15	.15	.04	.03	.03	.02
		X			.17	.20	.14	.18	.04	.03	.03	.03
			X		.10	.11	.08	.10	.02	.02	.01	.02
				X	.07	.11	.05	.10	.01	.02	.01	.01
2	X	X			.40	.40	.34	.37	.11	.09	.09	.08
	X		X		.25	.26	.21	.24	.06	.05	.05	.04
	X			X	.19	.25	.15	.23	.04	.05	.03	.04
		X	X		.24	.31	.20	.28	.06	.06	.04	.05
		X		X	.18	.29	.15	.27	.04	.06	.03	.05
			X	X	.10	.18	.08	.16	.02	.03	.02	.03
3	X	X	X		.51	.55	.45	.52	.16	.15	.13	.13
	X	X		X	.41	.54	.36	.50	.11	.14	.09	.13
	X		X	X	.26	.38	.22	.35	.06	.08	.05	.07
		X	X	X	.25	.43	.21	.40	.06	.10	.05	.09
4	X	X	X	X	.52	.68	.46	.65	.16	.23	.13	.21

Note. NSAF = National Survey of America's Families (Urban Institute, 1999). $N = 10{,}607$ for 6- to 11-year-olds and $N = 9{,}771$ for 12- to 17-year-olds. Probabilities shown for both 6- to 11-year-olds and 12- to 17-year-olds were computed with the following equations that are based on the results of the logistic regression model with this dataset (PPH = poor parent physical health, SP = single parent status, POV = poverty, PMH = parent mental health, CAV = involvement in clubs or activities, PSE = positive school engagement): Behavior problems (6–11 years) = $-2.6781 + 1.1208(\text{PPH}) + 0.0492(\text{SP}) + 0.4299(\text{POV}) + 1.1575(\text{PMH}) - 0.2432(\text{CAV}) - 1.7157(\text{PSE})$. Behavior problems (12–17 years) = $-2.6483 + 1.2365(\text{PPH}) + 0.5392(\text{SP}) + 0.5921(\text{POV}) + 1.0255(\text{PMH}) - 0.1368(\text{CAV}) - 1.9407(\text{PSE})$.

lems in comparison with those with zero adversities. Similarly, there is a wide range of problem outcomes across the different combinations of adversities. Illustratively, for 12- to 17-year-olds with zero strengths, the combination of poor parental mental and physical health is associated with a 40% probability of behavioral problems, whereas the combination of family poverty and single parent is associated with an 18% probability of behavior problems.

The effects of strengths can be seen by looking across the rows, which show the probability of behavior problems in the absence of either of the two strengths, in the presence of either strength alone, and in the presence of both strengths. Whereas each of the strengths has a statistically significant effect, positive engagement in school has the largest effect in reducing the probability of behavior problems. For example, as shown in Table 3.1, for 12- to 17-year-old children experiencing the dual adversities of poverty and single parent status, involvement in clubs or activities reduces the probability of behavior problems from .18 to .16, a drop of a little over 11%. However, the probability of child behavior problems is reduced from .18 to only .03 in the presence of the strength of positive engagement in school, a drop of 84%. The presence of both strengths affords no extra protection over and above positive school engagement.

National Longitudinal Study of Youth

The NLSY (Center for Human Resource Research, 1999) is a longitudinal study of a national probability sample of 6,284 women ages 14 through 21 who were interviewed yearly from 1979 to 1999. Starting in 1986, data were collected biannually to assess psychological characteristics of the children of the original NLSY women. For the current data analysis, measures were obtained from three interviews that occurred over a 5-year period (1992, 1994, and 1996). This enabled us to use the occurrence of adversities and strengths over the five years to predict the probability of behavior problems at the end of the 5-year period. A total of 1,504 children who had complete data on the variables were included in the analyses. They were between the ages of 10 and 14 in 1996. Because the original NLSY sample overly represented poor and minority respondents, all analyses were weighted (using the 1996 weights) to better reflect effects that were nationally representative.

Six adversities were assessed to provide at least one adversity across each level of the social ecology: individual (child physical health problems[7]),

---

[7]Child physical health problems were assessed with three items concerning whether the child had been limited in school attendance, schoolwork, or physical activity due to a physical condition. An affirmative answer to any of these items over the 5-year period was considered as indicating presence of a physical health problem; 6.6% were categorized as experiencing physical health problems.

microsystem (parental death,[8] parental divorce or separation,[9] family poverty,[10] parental physical health problems[11]) and macrosystem (living in a problem neighborhood[12]). Two strengths were assessed that reflected positive involvement in clubs or teams or volunteering,[13] and perceived scholastic competence.[14] These two strengths are conceptually similar to those assessed in the NSAF. An adversity or strength was counted if it was reported at any of the three interview times—1992, 1994, or 1996. Behavior problems were assessed at the 1996 time point with parent report on the Behavior Problem Index (Peterson & Zill, 1986).[15] The measures of adversities and strengths at any time over the 5-year period were used to predict behavior problems at the end of the 5-year period.

We analyzed the data using logistic regression. Each of the strengths and adversities was entered simultaneously to predict the dichotomous outcome of serious behavior problems. The results indicated that each of the adversities and strengths made a significant contribution to the prediction of behavior problems. Table 3.2 shows the predicted probability of behavior problems across levels of adversity and across levels of strength. The table only shows from zero to all combinations of three adversities, because less than 1% of the sample had any combination of four or more adversities during the 5-year period. The predicted probability of behavior problems increased markedly as the number of adversities increased. Illustratively, in the

---

[8]Because of low prevalence, parental death was considered present if ever experienced; 4.3% had experienced the death of a parent.

[9]Parental divorce or separation was considered present if divorce or separation occurred during the prior five years; 15.5% of the sample had experienced divorce in the five-year period.

[10]Family poverty was considered present if family income was below the official poverty level at any time during the prior five years; 38.9% of the sample was classified as being below the poverty level at some point during the 5-year period.

[11]Parental physical health problems were assessed by parent report of having a physical health condition at any time during the prior five years that limited the ability to work; 9.0% of the sample was classified as having parent health problems.

[12]Problem neighborhood was assessed with parent report on seven characteristics of the neighborhood: (a) people don't respect rules or laws, (b) crime and violence, (c) abandoned or run-down buildings, (d) not enough police protection, (e) parents don't supervise their children, (f) people don't care what goes on in neighborhood, and (g) lots of people can't find jobs. A cutoff point that identified the most problematic 5.7% of the sample was used to identify problem neighborhood, which involved rating six of the seven items as a big problem. Six percent of the population was selected because it approximately corresponds to U.S. Census reports of the percentage of the population living in neighborhoods in which 40% or more of the residents have incomes below the federal poverty level.

[13]Of the sample, 10.9% were classified as being involved in clubs or activities and volunteering at some point over the five years.

[14]Perceived scholastic competence was indicated by scores in the top 25% on the six items of the Harter Self-Perception Profile for Children scholastic competence scale (Harter, 1985). This cutoff point classified 39.9% of children in the sample as scoring high on scholastic competence at some point in the five years.

[15]The behavior problem index was developed using 28 items from the Achenbach Child Behavior Checklist (Achenbach & Edelbrock, 1983). The top 15% was used as the cutoff point for behavior problems to correspond with prior epidemiologic studies that found a median prevalence rate of child psychopathology of 12% for middle childhood and 15% for adolescents (Roberts, Attkisson, Rosenblatt, 1998). It should be noted that the prevalence of behavior problems is somewhat higher in this sample than in the general population, because the sample overrepresents younger parents and poor parents.

TABLE 3.2

Predicted Probabilities of Having Behavioral Problems With Different Combinations of Risk Factors and Strengths for Children Ages 10 to 14 Years (NLSY Data set)

	Presence of adversities						Probabilities of negative behavior problems			
Number of risk factors	Child health problem	Parent death	Divorce or separation	Poverty	Parent health problem	Poor neighborhood	Adversities only	Clubs and activities and volunteering	Perceived school competence	Both strengths
0							.26	.24	.17	.15
1	X						.33	.30	.22	.20
		X					.33	.30	.22	.20
			X				.40	.37	.28	.25
				X			.34	.32	.23	.21
					X		.40	.37	.27	.25
						X	.43	.40	.30	.28
2	X	X					.40	.37	.28	.25
	X		X				.47	.44	.34	.31
	X			X			.42	.38	.29	.27
	X				X		.47	.44	.34	.31
	X					X	.51	.47	.37	.34
		X	X				.47	.44	.34	.32
		X		X			.42	.39	.29	.27
		X			X		.47	.44	.34	.31
		X				X	.51	.48	.38	.35
			X	X			.49	.46	.36	.33
			X		X		.55	.52	.41	.38
			X			X	.58	.55	.45	.42
				X	X		.49	.46	.36	.33
				X		X	.53	.49	.39	.36

TABLE 3.2

								.58	.55	.45	.42
X	X	X				X		.55	.52	.42	.39
X	X	X	X					.49	.46	.36	.33
X	X	X					X	.55	.52	.42	.38
X	X	X				X		.59	.55	.45	.42
X	X		X	X			X	.57	.54	.43	.40
X	X		X	X				.62	.59	.49	.46
X	X		X				X	.66	.63	.52	.49
X	X			X		X		.57	.54	.43	.40
X	X			X		X	X	.60	.57	.47	.44
X	X					X		.65	.63	.52	.49
X	X		X		X	X		.57	.54	.44	.40
X	X		X	X	X			.63	.60	.49	.46
X	X		X	X	X	X	X	.66	.63	.53	.50
X	X		X			X		.57	.54	.43	.40
X			X	X	X	X		.60	.57	.47	.44
X		X	X	X	X	X	X	.66	.63	.53	.49
		X	X	X		X		.64	.61	.51	.48
		X	X	X		X	X	.67	.65	.54	.51
			X			X	X	.72	.69	.60	.57
				X		X	X	.67	.64	.54	.51

Note. NLSY = National Longitudinal Survey of Youth (Center for Human Resource Research, 1999). Probabilities were computed with the following equation that was based on the results of the logistic regression model with this dataset (CHP = child health problem, DP = parent death, D/S = divorce or separation, P = poverty, PHP = parent health problem, PN = poor neighborhood, CAV = clubs or activities and volunteering, PSC = perceived school competency): Behavior problems = −1.0383 + 0.3076(CHP) + 0.3196(PD) + 0.6181(D/S) + 0.3888(P) + 0.6147(PHP) + 0.7556(PN) + −0.1269 (CAV) + −0.5468(PSC).

absence of either strength, the probability of behavior problems is .26. It ranges from .33 to .43 in the presence of a single adversity, from .40 to .58 for any combination of two adversities, and from .49 to .72 for any combination of three adversities.

The effects of strengths on reducing the probability of behavior problems can be seen by looking across the rows to the columns labeled zero strengths, involvement in clubs or activities, perceived school competence, and presence of both strengths. Each strength has a significant effect in reducing the effects of adversities, but similar to the findings with the NSAF sample, perceived school competence had the more substantial effect. For example, for children with the adversities of parental divorce or separation and family poverty, the probability of behavior problems is reduced from .49 to .46 for children with high activity involvement, a drop of only 6.2%, and from .49 to .36 for children who perceive high competence in school, a drop of 26%. As in the NSAF data set, the presence of two strengths provides little additional protection over the effects of perceived school competence.

Summary of Findings

The analyses from these two national samples provide evidence that the presence of strengths reduces the probability of serious levels of behavior problems across the levels of exposure to adversity. However, these analyses do not speak to the theoretical mechanisms that might be responsible for these effects. Luthar et al. (2000) proposed that one theoretical theme that has guided research on resilience is that there are multiple levels of influence on the child's adjustment and reciprocal associations among these diverse influences. Hobfoll (1998) proposed a theoretical framework for how strengths and adversities affect problem outcomes through their influence on valued resources. We agree with these frameworks and below present an integrative model of how strengths protect against adversities through their influence on basic motivational systems. (See Sandler, 2001, for a more detailed presentation of this framework.)

CONCEPTUAL FRAMEWORK FOR ADVERSITIES AND STRENGTHS

We propose that adversities are multilevel constructs that can be characterized in terms of both their quality and their ecology. Strengths are also multilevel constructs that reduce the negative effects of adversities by affecting the quality or ecology of people's encounters with adversity.

Quality of Adversities and Strengths

Quality of adversities refers to relations of the person with his or her environment in which basic human needs, motivations, and goals are not satisfied and in which competencies to carry out valued social roles are not developed. Theorists have proposed that threat or loss of valued goals or resources leads to a state of negative emotional arousal or stress (Hobfoll, 1998; Lazarus, 1991). Although individuals have their own unique hierarchy of goals, four goals that appear prominently across motivational and developmental theories are (a) satisfying the need for safety and biological integrity, (b) obtaining a sense of control over the environment, (c) having secure positive and supportive human relations, and (d) maintaining a belief in one's own self-worth and autonomy (see review by Sandler, 2001; see also Skinner & Wellborn, 1994, for an elegant presentation of how basic needs are affected by adversities). Unfortunately, satisfaction of the basic needs of physical safety, shelter, and food cannot be taken for granted. They are threatened by the continued presence of high rates of poverty in U.S. society. Thirty-three percent of children who live in poor neighborhoods report being threatened with serious physical harm (Kliewer, Lepore, Oskin, & Johnson, 1998), and 4.2% of all children in the United States report going hungry (Food and Nutrition Service, 1997).

Need for control refers to a primary motivation to be effective in bringing about change in the environment. Being powerless to control events in one's life leads to a sense of distress and depression and exacerbates the effects of exposure to stress (Folkman, 1984). Having secure social relations within a caring social network is related to lower rates of a wide range of physical and mental health problems (Baumeister & Leary, 1995). Adversities may threaten self-esteem and thereby lead to the development of mental health problems (Kaplan, 1983) by either directly devaluing the individual or disrupting esteem-supporting social relations or esteem-enhancing activities.

Adverse conditions can also interfere with the development of age- and culturally appropriate competencies that enable fulfillment of important social roles (Masten & Coatsworth, 1998). For example, adversities may interfere with engagement in school by disrupting parent support for school functioning, distracting a child from school tasks, or involving the child in competing activities of higher salience. It is notable that competencies may be valued differentially by different cultures, so that, for example, school success may be punished by peers in inner-city neighborhoods but rewarded by peers in middle-class neighborhoods.

Strengths of individuals, families, and communities protect against the effects of adversities by promoting the satisfaction of basic needs and the development of competencies. For example, individual characteristics of children such as talents, academic abilities, or social skills may lead to success experiences that promote their sense of control and positive self-worth. At the family level, effective parenting may provide a sense of stability and security of social ties even when the family system is disrupted by divorce or the death of a parent. At the community level, social networks that provide mutual aid and support in adult monitoring and supervision of neighborhood youths may help provide a sense of safety and prevent delinquency in high-risk neighborhoods (Sampson, Raudenbush, & Earls, 1997).

Successful functioning in key social roles embeds children in a web of relations and routine activities through which their needs for a sense of worth, control, and social relatedness are satisfied. The developmental tasks and associated competencies across the life span have been described most recently by Masten and Coatsworth (1998), who gave them a central place in their conceptualization of resilience. During the school years of middle childhood and adolescence, competencies include achieving success at school, having friendships with peers, following rules for moral behavior, and developing one's unique skills and talents. In Masten and Coatsworth's model, *resilience* refers to success in developing these competencies despite adverse conditions.

Ecology of Adversity and Strengths

Adversities occur within different settings and in the context of different social roles. They also have a temporal dimension in that they occur over time. Finally, adversities have a dynamic quality; they may influence the occurrence and persistence of other adversities. We use the phrase *ecological properties of adversities* to refer to the place in which adversities occur, the time span over which they occur, and the dynamic relations between them.

Adversities may be characterized at multiple levels of the social ecology; individuals are nested within microsystems, which are nested within macrosystems. Individual-level adversities are those that affect children directly, such as being the victim of abuse or violence or having a physical illness or disability. Microsystem adversities affect the proximal settings in which children live and develop. Primary microsystems for children are the family, the classroom, the peer group, the work environment, or structured activity-oriented groups such as clubs or youth groups. Microsystem adversities include disruptions in the structure of the family, including parental divorce, economic strain, or parental mental illness; in the school, adversities include violence, overly punitive discipline, nonsupportive teachers, or understimulating classrooms. Macrosystem adversities are those that affect communities or cultures and include factors such as neighborhood-level poverty, crime, or disorganization; wars or civil unrest; and societal-level racism, sexism, or homophobia.

The second ecological property of adversities is that they occur over time. One of the classic distinctions in the conceptualization of life stress is between acute changes and chronic conditions. For several decades, research on the effects of life stress has focused on acute changes, with negative changes seen as the critical feature of stress that leads to negative health, mental health, and other social adaptation outcomes. Recently, however, increased attention has been given to ongoing stressful conditions, chronic stressors, and role strains (Gersten, Langner, Eisenberg, & Simcha-Fagan, 1977; Gottlieb, 1997). Chronic adverse conditions can be described in terms of ongoing difficulties in carrying out key social roles such as friend, student, or family member (Pearlin, 1983). Chronic adverse conditions can also be conceptualized in non-role-related terms, such as ongoing difficulties of living in dangerous neighborhoods, being poor, or living in a household with a mentally disordered parent.

The dynamic relations between adversities can be seen in the effects of adversities at one level on the occurrence of adversities at other levels and in the effects of chronic and acute adversities on each other. For example, a child's internalizing problems, conduct problems, and lack of planning ability predict increases in levels of family conflict (Roosa, Beals, Sandler, & Pillow, 1990) and selection of deviant peers and deviant spouses (Rutter, Champion, Quinton, Maughan, & Pickles, 1995). Similarly, living in a poor neighborhood is associated with exposure to more adversities in the microsystem of the school (Allison et al., 1999) and to a high rate of victimization and witnessing of violence (Kliewer et al., 1998). Occurrences of chronic and acute adversities mutually influence each other. Acute changes can lead to chronic adverse conditions or a chain of other adversities. For example, parental divorce can lead to a chronic decrease in economic well-being of the parents, increased parental distress, and children's subsequent exposure to inconsistent, harsh, and inept parenting (Simons & Associates, 1996). Similarly, ongoing chronic adversities can lead to a chain of negative changes that lead to additional chronic adversities. Rutter (1989) described a chain of adversities over time in which poor school experiences lead to leaving school early, which leads to a history of low-skill occupations and a poor work history. The cycle of acute and chronic adversities over the life course is self-reinforcing and may lead to negative effects on the developing person, which further perpetuates a cycle of adversity.

Strengths affect the ecology of adversity by reducing the frequency or duration of the occurrence of adversities. Strengths can reduce the likelihood that adversities at one ecological level influence the occurrence of adversity at another level. For example, in terms of individual-level strengths, Rutter (1989) found that for children reared in institutional placements, being more planful was associated with marrying a stable marital partner, which is related to lower exposure to later adversities. At the microsystem level, effective parents living in high-crime neighborhoods might use highly controlling strategies to prevent their children's exposure to neighborhood violence. At the macrosystem level, communities with a high level of collective efficacy monitor and control antisocial activities and thus reduce the exposure of individual children to threats or violence (see chap. 18, this volume; Sampson et al., 1997).

Strengths can also affect the dynamic relations between acute and chronic adversities. For example, although the acute adversity of parental divorce can lead to the chronic adversities of prolonged interparental conflict, effective parenting following divorce may reduce children's exposure to ongoing conflict between the parents. Similarly, court systems may distribute financial resources between the parents following divorce in a way that lowers the likelihood that children will live in conditions of chronic poverty.

PUBLIC POLICIES PROVIDE RESOURCES TO BUILD STRENGTHS AT MULTIPLE LEVELS

The thesis of this volume is that strengths are not immutable entities; they can be nurtured, supported, and sustained by well-informed public policies. As shown in Figure 3.1, public policies can provide resources that promote the development of enduring individual, family, and community strengths and that counteract the effects of adversities. We propose four pathways by which public policies may promote strengths and reduce the negative effects of adversities: (a) positive development, (b) prevention, (c) protection, and (d) counteraction.

Positive Development

First, policies that promote positive early development will prevent future problems because they increase the strengths and resources of individual, family, or community systems that are self-sustaining (Path A of Figure 3.1) over time. From a transactional perspective, individuals, microsystems, and macrosystems can be seen as organized self-regulating systems that also regulate each other over time (Sameroff & Fiese, 2000). Adversities disorganize these systems or threaten their ability to sustain themselves. Strengths are conceptualized as characteristics of these systems that facilitate healthy and sustainable satisfaction of needs and achievement of developmentally and culturally appropriate competencies. These organized systems have a degree of stability over time, so that strong individuals, families, and communities adapt to new conditions in ways that continue to support the healthy satisfaction of needs and development of new competencies.

Prevention

Second, policies that promote strengths should prevent the occurrence of future adversities (Path B of Figure 3.1). For example, at the individual level, policies that help children achieve early cognitive competencies such as reading should enable them to deal more effectively with academic demands at school and avoid stressors resulting from school failure. At the microsystem level, policies that protect women who are victims of domestic

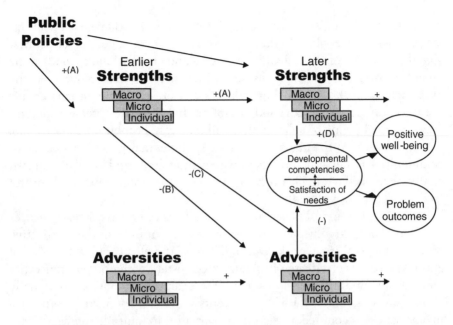

Figure 3.1. Alternative pathways from public policies to promote strengths and reduce problem outcomes: positive development (A), prevention of adversities (B), protection from adversities (C), promotion of needs and competencies and counteraction against adversities (D).

violence prevent their future victimization (see chap. 6, this volume). At the macrosystem level, court policies concerning child support affect whether children of divorce grow up in conditions of poverty and can enhance or reduce interparental conflict.

Protection

Third, policies can build strengths that protect by reducing the negative effects of adversities to which children are exposed (Path C of Figure 3.1). At the individual level, school policies may provide coping programs to help children cope more effectively with the stress of parental divorce. At the family level, expansion of mental health services for depressed parents may enable their children to better understand the disorder and cope more effectively. At a macrosystem level, policies that promote the strengths of minority cultures can enable children of poverty to learn a structure of meaning and of cultural rituals that protects against the negative effects of discrimination and societal racism.

Counteraction

Fourth, policies can counteract the negative effects of adversities (Path D of Figure 3.1) by directly promoting the satisfaction of basic needs and development of competencies. At the individual level, policies that counter-act peer rejection enable children to have success experiences in school that give them a sense of control and self-esteem and enable them to take on the socially reinforcing role of good student (see chap. 14, this volume). At the microsystem level, policies that reduce stress on divorcing parents enable them to provide the support and discipline that directly increase children's security of belonging to a family that will take care of their needs (see chap. 4, this volume). At the macrosystem level, policies may provide resources for communities to develop settings in which the talents and skills of children can be developed to enable them to have a sense of competence and control (see chap. 11, this volume).

Finally, it is useful to reconsider the effects of positive school engage-ment and youth involvement in community activities from the perspective of our conceptual framework. Our findings on the effects of positive school engagement and activity involvement are consistent with findings from other correlational and intervention studies. For example, a study of a nationally representative sample of 11,572 adolescents found that connectedness to fam-ily and school accounted for significant variance in multiple sources of ado-lescent morbidity, including emotional distress, suicidality, violence, and substance use (Resnick et al., 1997). Interventions to improve academic achievement have reported a reduction in behavior problems (Fantuzzo, King, & Heller, 1992; Kellam, Mayer, Rebok, & Hawkins, 1998). Positive engage-ment in school is an important social role that can provide satisfaction of needs for control, social bonding, and esteem as well as competencies neces-sary for later occupational success. Social policies that promote school suc-cess, particularly under conditions of adversity, may be particularly critical for preventing problem outcomes (see chap. 12, this volume).

The effects of involvement in volunteer activities or clubs were small but still notable. There is relatively little research on the effects on behavior problems of involving children and adolescents in clubs or volunteer activi-ties. One study that does provide important information on the effects of involving youths in volunteer activities is the evaluation of a national imple-mentation of the Teen Outreach Program (National Research Council, 1987). This program was designed to involve students in volunteer activities in their community and to link the volunteer activity to classroom-based discussions on human development and life decision making. Using a quasi-experimen-tal design, the program was found to reduce student school suspensions, school dropout, and pregnancy. Also, consistent with our theoretical perspective, Allen, Kuperminc, Philliber, and Herre (1994) found that the degree to which teen outreach programs promoted a sense of autonomy and relatedness was related to improvement in problem behaviors of the adolescents. The mea-sures of involvement in activities and volunteering used in the current study were rather crude, simply assessing reported involvement, and it may be that those activities that are more successful in satisfying basic needs of children have larger effects in reducing problem behavior. Further information on how activity involvement promotes satisfaction of needs for control, self-esteem, and relatedness may provide direction for understanding how to strengthen the positive effects of these programs.

The current chapter is intended to provide a conceptual framework and empirical support for the general thesis that the promotion of strengths can lead to a reduction of problem outcomes. However, this chapter does not address the ways in which adversities and strengths affect outcomes for children and families exposed to the specific adversities that are the subject of specific public policies (e.g., parental divorce, poverty, teenage pregnancy). Each specific adversity has its own characteristic configuration of acute and ongoing conditions that threaten satisfaction of basic human needs and its own unique opportunities in which promoting strengths may decrease the likelihood of negative outcomes. The chapters that follow describe the important strengths that protect children in a broad range of adverse situations and the public policy issues that are critical for promoting these strengths.

REFERENCES

Achenbach, T. M., & Edelbrock, C. S. (1983). *Manual for the child behavior checklist and revised child behavior profile.* Burlington, VT: Queen City Printers.

Allen, J. P., Kuperminc, G., Philliber, S., & Herre, K. (1994). Programmatic prevention of adolescent problem behaviors: The role of autonomy, relatedness, and volunteer service in Teen Outreach Program. *American Journal of Community Psychology, 22,* 617–638.

Allison, K. W., Burton, L., Marshall, S., Perez-Febles, A., Yarrington, J., Kirsh, L. B., & Merriwether-DeVries, C. (1999). Life experiences among urban adolescents: Examining the role of context. *Child Development, 70,* 1017–1029.

Baumeister, R. F., & Leary, M. R. (1995). The need to belong: Desire for interpersonal attachments as a fundamental human motivation. *Psychological Bulletin, 117,* 497–529.

Center for Human Resource Research. (1999). *NLS Handbook 1999: The National Longitudinal Surveys of Labor Market Experience.* Columbus: Ohio State University.

Fantuzzo, J. W., King, J. A., & Heller, L. R. (1992). Effects of reciprocal peer tutoring on mathematics and school adjustment: A component analysis. *Journal of Educational Psychology, 84,* 331–339.

Folkman, S. (1984). Personal control and stress and coping processes: A theoretical analysis. *Journal of Personality and Social Psychology, 46,* 839–852.

Food and Nutrition Service. (1997). *Household food security in the United States in 1995.* Washington, DC: Food and Nutrition Service.

Furstenberg, F. F., Jr., Cook, T., Eccles, J., Elder, G. H., & Sameroff, A. J. (1999). *Urban families and academic success.* Chicago: University of Chicago Press.

Gersten, J. C., Langner, T. S., Eisenberg, J. G., & Simcha-Fagan, O. (1977). An evaluation of the etiological role of stressful life-change events in psychological disorder. *Journal of Health and Social Behavior, 18*, 65–83.

Gottlieb, B. (1997). *Coping with chronic stress*. New York: Plenum Press.

Harter, S. (1985). *Manual for the Self-Perception Profile for Children*. Denver, CO: University of Denver.

Hobfoll, S. E. (1998). Stress, culture and community. *The psychology and philosophy of stress*. New York: Plenum Press.

Kaplan, H. B. (1983). Psychological distress in sociological context: Toward a general theory of psychological stress. In H. B. Kaplan (Ed.), *Psychosocial stress: Trends in theory and research* (pp. 195–264). New York: Academic Press.

Kellam, S. G., Mayer, L. S., Rebok, G. W., & Hawkins, W. E. (1998). Effects of improving academic achievement on aggressive behavior and of improving aggressive behavior on achievement through two preventive interventions: An investigation of causal paths. In B. S. Dohrenwend (Ed.), *Adversity, stress and psychopathology* (pp. 486–505). New York: Oxford University Press.

Kliewer, W., Lepore, S., Oskin, D., & Johnson, P. D. (1998). The role of social and cognitive processes in children's adjustment to community violence. *Journal of Consulting and Clinical Psychology, 66*, 199–209.

Lazarus, R. S. (1991). *Emotion and adaptation*. New York: Oxford University Press.

Luthar, S., Cicchetti, D., & Becker, B. (2000). The construct of resilience: A critical evaluation and guidelines for future work. *Child Development, 71*, 543–562.

Masten, A. S., & Coatsworth, J. D. (1998). The development of competence in favorable and unfavorable environments. *American Psychologist, 53*, 205–220.

National Research Council. (1987). *Risking the future: Adolescent sexuality, pregnancy, and childbearing*. Washington, DC: National Academy Press.

Pearlin, L. (1983). Role strains and personal stress. In H. B. Kaplan (Ed.), *Psychosocial stress* (pp. 3–32). New York: Academic Press.

Peterson, J. L., & Zill, N. (1986). Marital disruptions, parent-child relationships, and behavior problems in children. *Journal of Marriage and the Family, 48*, 295–307.

Resnick, M. D., Bearman, P. S., Blum, R. M., Bauman, K. E., Harris, K. M., Jones, J., et al. (1997). Protecting adolescents from harm: Findings from the National Longitudinal Study of Adolescent Health. *Journal of the American Medical Association, 278*, 823–832.

Roberts, R. E., Attkisson, C., & Rosenblatt, A. (1998). Prevalence of psychopathology among children and adolescents. *American Journal of Psychiatry, 155*, 715–725.

Roosa, M. W., Beals, J., Sandler, I. N., & Pillow, D. R. (1990). The role of risk and protective factors in predicting symptomatology in adolescent self-identified children of alcoholic parents. *American Journal of Community Psychology, 18*, 725–741.

Rutter, M. (1979). Protective factors in children's responses to stress. In M. W. Kent & J. E. Rolf (Eds.), *Primary prevention of psychopathology: Vol. 3. Social competence in children* (pp. 49–74). Hanover, NH: University Press of New England.

Rutter, M. (1989). Pathways from childhood to adult life. *Journal of Child Psychology and Psychiatry, 30*, 23–51.

Rutter, M., Champion, L., Quinton, D., Maughan, B., & Pickles, A. (1995). Understanding individual differences in environmental-risk exposure. In P. Moen, G. H. Elder, & K. Lüscher (Eds.), *Examining lives in context: Perspectives on the ecology of human development* (pp. 61–93). Washington, DC: American Psychological Association.

Sameroff, A. J., & Fiese, B. H. (2000). Transactional regulation: The developmental ecology of early intervention. In J. P. Shonkoff & S. J. Meisels (Eds.), *Handbook of early childhood intervention* (2nd ed., pp. 135–160). New York: Cambridge University Press.

Sampson, R. J., Raudenbush, S., & Earls, F. (1997, August). Neighborhoods and violent crime: A multilevel study of collective efficacy. *Science, 277*, 918–924.

Sandler, I. N. (2001). Quality and ecology of adversity as common mechanisms of risk and resilience. *American Journal of Community Psychology, 29*, 19–63.

Simons, R. L., & Associates. (1996). *Understanding differences between divorced and intact families: Stress, interaction and child outcome.* Thousand Oaks, CA: Sage.

Skinner, E., & Wellborn, J. G. (1994). Coping during childhood and adolescence: A motivational perspective. In D. Featherman, R. Lerner, & M. Perlmutter (Eds.), *Life-span development and behavior* (pp. 91–133). Hillsdale, NJ: Erlbaum.

Stewart, A. L., Hays, R., & Ware, J. E. (1988). The MOS Short-Form General Health Survey, reliability and validity in a patient. *Medical Care, 26*, 724–735.

Urban Institute. (1999). *National Survey of America's Families—1997.* [Downloadable public-use data set]. Urban Institute and Child Trends [Producers and distributors]. Retrieved June 23, 2003, from http://www.urban.org/content/Research/Databases/Databases.htm

Werner, E. E. (2000). Protective factors and individual resilience. In J. P. Shonkoff & S. J. Meisels (Eds.), *Handbook of early childhood intervention* (2nd ed., pp. 115–135). New York: Cambridge University Press.

Yoshikawa, H. (1994). Prevention as cumulative protection: Effects of early family support and education on chronic delinquency and its risks. *Psychological Bulletin, 115*, 28–54.

II

OVERCOMING ADVERSE CIRCUMSTANCES AFFECTING THE INDIVIDUAL AND THE FAMILY

4

STRENGTHS-BUILDING PUBLIC POLICY FOR CHILDREN OF DIVORCE

SANFORD L. BRAVER, KATHLEEN N. HIPKE, IRA M. ELLMAN,
AND IRWIN N. SANDLER

not much in this chapter except "high degree of variability"... in outcomes

Instead of focusing on the problems associated with divorce, this chapter de-lineates a strengths-based model of the relations among divorce policies, mediating factors, and children's outcomes. Little research has linked specific divorce policies to child well-being following divorce. Based on an extensive review of the literature, several factors—such as children's positive coping skills, low parental conflict, high warmth and consistency of the parents, and the quality of the contact with the noncustodial parent—appear to mediate the effects of divorce. The chapter illustrates that policies that are designed to influence these mediators to maximize strengths and minimize risks will lead to the most positive child outcomes and concludes with a public health model for integrating research and policy.

* * *

The divorce or marital separation of their parents is one of the most common potentially adverse conditions that children in America experience today.[1] Currently, over 40% of children are expected to live in a di-

---

This research was supported by National Institute of Mental Health grant P30 MH439246-16.
[1]A related adverse circumstance is nonmarital childbirth, which is almost as common (35.8 % versus 37.0% of children living in divorced homes; Bureau of the Census, 1996) and perhaps even more toxic. This chapter is confined to children whose parents were once legally married and subsequently experienced divorce.

vorced home before the age of 16 (Cherlin, 1992), more than double the proportion 30 years ago (Shiono & Quinn, 1994). As divorce has become such a normative transition for children, a substantial literature examining the effects of divorce on children's well-being has accumulated.

Using meta-analysis to quantitatively summarize the findings of nearly 100 empirical studies that compared the well-being of children from divorced and nondivorced homes, Amato and Keith (1991a) concluded that children who experience marital dissolution are significantly more likely to exhibit a variety of behavioral, internalizing (i.e., depression, anxiety), social, and academic problems. Although negative effects on well-being are found for children ranging in age from preschool to college age (Amato & Keith, 1991a), the manifestation of adjustment problems differs depending on a child's age or developmental level. Wallerstein (1983) delineated patterns of postdivorce reactions from four age groups: preschool, early school-age (6 to 8 years), older school-age (9 to 12 years), and adolescents. Fear of parental abandonment, self-blame for the divorce, and feelings of rejection were found most frequently among the youngest groups and reactions of grief, anxiety, and aggressive behavior following divorce were common. Older children reported more feelings of anger toward parents, academic problems, and changes in peer and social relationships.

Some of the negative outcomes found in children from divorced homes can be accounted for by the fact that many children in families that eventually divorce are already showing maladjustment years prior to marital disruption, calling into question whether the adversity the children are dealing with is actually the divorce per se (e.g., Furstenberg & Teitler, 1994). However, divorce has been shown to contribute to the risk of maladjustment (e.g., Chase-Lansdale, Cherlin, & Kiernan, 1995). Moreover, as children of divorce mature, the consequences carry heavier personal and societal costs. Adolescents from divorced homes are at elevated risk for dropping out of high school, becoming pregnant, and abusing substances (Furstenberg & Teitler, 1994; McLanahan & Sandefur, 1994). Disruptions to healthy development during adolescence, in turn, predict psychological maladjustment in young adulthood (Chase-Lansdale et al., 1995). Meta-analytic findings comparing young adults from divorced and married-parent homes show that the former exhibit more depression; have lower levels of marital quality, physical health, and life satisfaction; and achieve lower levels of educational, financial, and occupational status (Amato & Keith, 1991b).

The findings reviewed thus far focus on the problems and deficiencies of children from divorced homes as compared to children in married-parent families: a deficits model. The aim of this chapter is to develop an alternative, strengths-based, approach. Such a perspective, in contrast, focuses on positive outcomes and resiliencies in children in adverse circumstances. A much narrower empirical literature has investigated such competencies and strengths among children of divorce as compared to their peers. Findings have focused on enhanced maturity (Kurdek & Siesky, 1980), increased self-esteem if the child has coped effectively (e.g., Slater, Stewart, & Linn, 1983), and enhanced empathy and perspective taking (Hetherington, 1998).

Another aspect of the literature, however, provides even stronger support for a strengths-based approach: the very high degree of variability found in responses of children and families to divorce. Although some children of divorce experience serious and ongoing problems, many appear to show no deficits whatsoever relative to their peers from married-parent households (Amato & Keith, 1991a, 1991b). The diversity of responses is vast, suggesting that the resources children have available to them to cope with marital dissolution condition the outcome. Fortunately, a rather voluminous literature has investigated various features of the children, their parents, and the environment in which they function that correlate with their postdivorce adaptation. The focus of a strengths-based approach in evaluating this literature is to identify resources that enhance children's resilience in dealing with the stress of their parents' divorce, especially factors that can be facilitated by public policies. We conclude the chapter with a proposal for a public health model, a comprehensive perspective with which to view and tie together strengths-building policy. First, however, we address the issue of the legal context of divorce and the definition of the "child's best interests."

THE LEGAL CONTEXT SURROUNDING DIVORCE AND DEFINITION OF "CHILD'S BEST INTERESTS"

Perhaps more than almost any of the other adversities chronicled in this volume, the process of divorce occurs virtually entirely within the context of the legal system; thus, many of the policies to be considered are explicitly legal policies. Existing statutes and case law or court, government, and legal policies concern almost every aspect of divorce, including custody, visitation or "access," child support, and so forth, as well as the circumstances under which a divorce can even be obtained at all.

It is important to note that the standard modern policymakers almost invariably adopt for existing child-relevant divorce policies is whether they promote the "child's best interests," rather than parental rights, justice for the parents, or other standards. Thus, policymakers already appear to implicitly weigh policies against their inevitable impact on the child's adjustment. However, this standard is only vaguely defined in the legal literature, and judges are desirably permitted considerable leeway. To avoid this definitional vagueness, the focus here will be on empirically investigated indicators of both child maladjustment, such as children's mental health problems, and developmental competence (Masten & Coatsworth, 1998), such as indicators of success in developmental tasks like school or employment. We thus operationally define *the child's best interests* as positive outcomes on any of these measures, a far narrower definition than that of the law.[2]

The conceptual model we use to summarize the literature is displayed in Figure 4.1. As noted, we propose that policies will have an impact on child outcomes by altering various "mediating factors." The child outcome variables we consider (those that have been empirically studied) are in the bottom box in Figure 4.1.

The top box indicates the various substantive domains about which policy making related to divorce has taken place. The most obvious and far-reaching domains concern parent–child contact issues, including custody, both legal (i.e., decision-making authority regarding issues such as schooling, medical care, and religion for the child) and physical (i.e., where the child primarily lives), and the access or visitation schedule between the child and the nonresidential parent. A relatively new but hotly debated issue (Warshak, 2000) concerns the ability of a parent to relocate at will with the child away from the other parent. Next in prominence are the financial issues: child support amount and collection policies, as well as remaining financial matters (such as who pays for the child's medical and dental needs, child care, and college expenses), alimony, and division of assets and debts. Another policy issue, which will not be discussed here, concerns the parents' ease or difficulty in obtaining a legal divorce in the first place (the grounds for divorce, no fault).

The remaining areas of policy debate concern the process of dissolution. Currently an ever-growing menu of dispute resolution procedures is being offered as an alternative or supplement to traditional litigation or legal practice. One of the oldest of these is mediation, in which a trained neutral third party attempts to help couples arrive at a mutually acceptable compromise.

A more recent but very fast growing program is to offer, or even require, divorcing parents to participate in a short education program (usually about 4 hours) that instructs them on how to minimize the detrimental effects of the divorce on their children (Braver, Salem, Pearson, & DeLuse, 1996; Geasler & Blaisure, 1999). Such programs typically attempt to teach parenting skills, the value of shielding the child from parental conflict, and the importance of emotional and financial support from both parents. Two relatively new options feature expanded use of mental health professionals. Custody evaluations (e.g., Ackerman, 1995) allow such experts to make nonbinding recommendations to the parties and the court concerning custody and access

---

[2]Even though the child's interests should remain the most important consideration, both the decision-making process and the substantive rules must also take into account other values, such as fairness to the parents and privacy interests. This chapter does not discuss how such concerns *should* be weighed when considering measures that would advance the child's interests, although such fundamental policy choices are important in fashioning the law. We consider only the more circumscribed mission of describing how the child's strengths and interests, narrowly defined, might be advanced and built on by changes in legal policy.

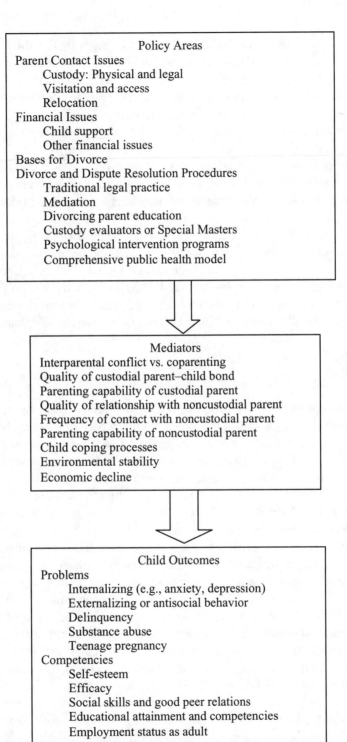

Figure 4.1. Conceptual model linking policy substantive domains, mediating factors, and child outcome variables.

after full psychological evaluation of the family. Although in the recent past each side could hire their own expert to "duel it out," current guidelines from the American Psychological Association (1994) discourage that practice, preferring instead only one evaluator, appointed by the court, whose code of ethics requires giving fair consideration to each side.

An even newer role for mental health professionals, in place in at least three states, is that of Special Master (also called Family Court Masters or Advisors or Family Coordinators), an ongoing advisor to the family appointed by the court. Such a professional consults with them on emerging parenting disputes and makes nonbinding recommendations after nonconfidential fact-finding.

Additionally, a number of longer (e.g., several weeks) psychological interventions have been designed and evaluated. Some of these, designed for children, are group therapy-like programs conducted in schools. Others, such as psychoeducational programs directed at parents, teach parenting, communication, and conflict resolution skills to enhance functioning in the postdivorce family (Braver, Griffin, Cookston, Sandler, & Williams, in press; Wolchik et al., 2002).

RESEARCH LINKING POLICIES TO CHILDREN'S OUTCOMES

There is surprisingly little research that directly links the majority of policy areas in the top box of Figure 4.1 to children's outcomes in the bottom box. For example, despite policy making based on the assumption that more and better child support payments result in better outcomes for children, there is little evidence supporting the assumption (e.g., McLanahan, Seltzer, Hanson, & Thompson, 1994). A similar paucity of research applies to policies concerning visitation and access, relocation, all financial policies, and custody evaluators or Special Masters.

A comparatively greater number of studies purport to compare the impact of various custody arrangements on children's adjustment. For example, a meta-analysis of 31 empirical evaluations comparing joint to maternal physical custody (Bauserman, 2002) found that the preponderance of these findings clearly favor joint custody. However, most of the research on custody, as well as on child support, faces the severe difficulty of drawing clear conclusions from correlational data. For example, although McLanahan and Sandefur (1994) found that higher child support payments were associated with better outcomes for children, substantial doubt remains about the causal direction: Is more child support actually the cause of the better child outcomes? Or, for example, do better-adjusted children elicit higher payments as a more worthwhile "investment"? Or families with less interparental conflict might both pay more child support and have better adjusted children. Analogous arguments can be made to question most of the custody findings. As a result, firm conclusions about the impact of the policies are rarely warranted from any extant data.

Two policies have been evaluated much more conclusively in randomized experiments instead of or in addition to purely correlational studies. First, many of the longer psychological intervention programs for children and parents have been shown effective in improving children's outcomes. In addition, mediation has been found to be effective in reducing court hearings (e.g., Pearson & Thoennes, 1984) and increasing parental satisfaction with the divorce process (Emery, Matthews, & Wyer, 1991), although it has not been found to improve children's mental health (Emery, 1994).

Additionally, a few of the policy issues have been studied using quasi-experimental methods. For example, legal (not physical) custody was evaluated using sophisticated statistical modeling techniques that ruled out most other interpretations, leaving the conclusion that joint legal custody typically does lead to better adjusted children than sole maternal legal custody (Gunnoe & Braver, 2001).

Mediating Factors

In the absence of evidence directly linking policies to child outcomes, in the next section we focus instead on a number of the factors that have been well researched in connection to child outcomes. The bulk of the literature on children and divorce has related child outcomes to mediating factors (see middle box in Figure 4.1). These mediating factors represent the resources children have available to them as they navigate the divorce process and include the quality of family relationships (i.e., parents' relationships with each other and with their children), the children's own intrapersonal strengths and coping skills, environmental stability, and economic matters. The review of these resources is organized in roughly the order that research has most reliably related the factor to positive child outcomes.

Interparental Relationship

Interparental conflict has consistently been identified as perhaps the most detrimental aspect of divorce for children's well-being, being related to behavioral and emotional problems as well as deficits in social and academic competencies for children of all ages (e.g., Amato & Keith, 1991a). Although conflict usually begins long before parents actually divorce, it does not necessarily end with separation and, in fact, may increase around divorce-related issues such as child custody or support, the division of property, and visitation rights (Hetherington & Stanley-Hagan, 1999). It is easy to imagine that when parents are continually fighting, especially about matters that directly concern the child such as visitation or moral issues, the child is likely to feel emotionally threatened. Thus, efforts to shield children from postdivorce conflict, or at least from the most detrimental types of conflict (i.e., conflict that involves physical aggression, is about child-related issues, or goes unresolved), are important to the promotion of children's divorce adaptation (Grych & Fincham, 1990).

Children also benefit from parental cooperation around child rearing following divorce. "Coparenting" is not simply the absence of interparental conflict, but rather the act of working together to raise children through shared communication, parenting responsibilities, and decision making despite divorce (Whiteside, 1998). Studies consistently show that coparenting is linked to better psychological functioning, academic performance, social competence, and lower levels of externalizing and internalizing symptoms among school-age children and adolescents in divorced homes (e.g., Buchanan, Maccoby, & Dornbusch, 1991). Although not possible in some highly conflicted families, research suggests that with time, at least half of divorced families can achieve a reasonably cooperative parental alliance, marked by relatively high levels of cooperation and low levels of interparental conflict (Whiteside, 1998). Other families remain conflicted (i.e., low levels of cooperation, high levels of conflict) or disengaged (i.e., low levels of both cooperation and conflict) (Maccoby, Depner, & Mnookin, 1990; Whiteside, 1998). Clearly, strengths-based policies would be those that encourage these cooperative arrangements.

Custodial Parental Functioning and Relationship to Child

Because most children still reside primarily with their mothers following divorce, custodial mothers are in the prime position to provide children with critical support and guidance throughout the divorce process. The children of custodial mothers who provide high levels of postdivorce warmth, affection, and consistent discipline and supervision show fewer behavioral problems, perform better academically, and have more self-esteem and competencies than those in homes marked by lower quality parenting (see Hetherington, 1998; Wyman, Sandler, Wolchik, & Nelson, 2000). Moreover, psychoeducational programs designed to teach enhanced parenting skills to custodial mothers have demonstrated that their success in improving children's mental health and academic competence is accounted for by improvements in the quality of the mother–child relationship and discipline skills (Forgatch & DeGarmo, 1999; Wolchik et al., 2000). Because these interventions have been evaluated using randomized, experimental research designs, their findings provide strong causal evidence for the positive impact of postdivorce custodial parenting on children's well-being.

High-quality parenting is important to the development of all children and adolescents, facilitating the development of self-confidence, competence, and responsibility in children (Baumrind, 1989). In divorced families, the sense of relatedness provided by a strong mother–child bond may also reduce children's divorce-related fears and facilitate their acquisition of age-appropriate competencies despite the disruptive nature of divorce in their lives (Wyman et al., 2000). For example, an engaged, supportive mother could help a child keep up with his or her schoolwork in the midst of the father's move out of the family home, a change in residence, or other stressful divorce-related transition.

During a period when high-quality parenting is so important to children, however, many newly divorced mothers are coping with feelings of stress, loneliness, depression, and "task overload" as they manage child rearing and work and financial responsibilities alone (Hetherington & Stanley-Hagan, 1999). Although successfully navigating this process can eventually lead to enhanced confidence and emotional well-being (Hetherington & Stanley-Hagan, 1999), disruptions to quality parenting typically occur in the first few years following divorce (Forgatch & DeGarmo, 1999; Hetherington, 1998). Parenting eventually restabilizes for many, albeit at an average level of quality lower than in nondivorced families (Forgatch & DeGarmo, 1999; Hetherington, 1989). In addition, the presence of social support, such as when a mother enters into a supportive, intimate relationship with a new partner, can improve mothers' emotional well-being and capacity to provide responsive parenting (Forgatch & DeGarmo, 1999). For others, characteristics that predate divorce, like antisocial personality (which is found more frequently among divorced relative to nondivorced mothers), make ongoing parent–child relationship problems, and consequently child adjustment problems, more likely (e.g., Simons, 1996). Thus, policies that affect parenting could be useful to families coping with both short- and long-term custodial parent–child relationship issues.

Noncustodial Fathers

Because few children reside in father-headed households, divorce usually results in reduced contact with fathers. A recent synthesis of the literature, however, demonstrates that for children ranging in age from preschool to young adulthood, the quality of parenting by noncustodial fathers and of father–child relationships, rather than the frequency of contact, is predictive of children's academic success and degree of behavioral disturbance (Amato & Gilbreth, 1999). High-quality fathering probably serves a function in children's adaptation to divorce similar to that described for mothering. In addition, high-quality father–child relationships may elicit higher child support payments, alleviating financial difficulties that may decrease child adaptation, and reduce the task overload of custodial mothers, thereby indirectly improving mother–child relationships (Wyman et al., 2000).

Child Characteristics

Divorce is wrought with emotion for children and presents a myriad of changes over which children have little control (Sandler, Wolchik, & Braver,

1988). Thus, the most resilient children are those who have the internal resources to effectively modulate their experience of these changes. For example, children who are low in negative emotional reactivity (Lengua, West, & Sandler, 1998), feel they understand why things happen in their environment (Sandler, Kim-Bae, & MacKinnon, 2000), and do not interpret stressful events in a negatively biased manner (Mazur, Wolchik, Virdin, Sandler, & West, 1999) have fewer behavior problems, less anxiety, and higher self-esteem than children without these dispositional qualities.

The way children think about and cope with divorce has implications for their adjustment (see Wyman et al., 2000). For example, a fear of abandonment by one's parents is associated with anxiety and other adjustment problems (Kurdek & Berg, 1987; Wolchik et al., 1993). Children who use active coping strategies, such as problem solving and positive thinking, develop an increased sense of efficacy or success regarding their ability to handle difficult situations and exhibit fewer mental health problems (Sandler, Tein, Mehta, Wolchik, & Ayers, 2000). Experimental evaluations of programs that teach children adaptive ways to think about and cope with divorce show that such programs enhance children's mental health and competencies (see Emery, Kitzmann, & Waldron, 1999; Grych & Fincham, 1992; Wyman et al., 2000), further evidence that children's divorce-related cognitions and coping behaviors are important mediators of their adjustment. Although the majority of these interventions have been provided to children in middle-to-late childhood or early adolescence, Pedro-Carroll and Alpert-Gillis (1997) successfully worked with kindergarten and first-grade children in this manner, suggesting that even young children can be taught to regulate their feelings, thoughts, and coping behaviors.

Environmental Stability

In divorce, many children also face a number of changes in their environment, such as moving to a new house or school or participating less in extracurricular activities. In general, cross-sectional studies find that when the circumstances and changes that children are exposed to following marital disruption are less stressful, they exhibit fewer behavioral problems and internalizing symptoms (e.g., Sandler, Wolchik, Braver, & Fogas, 1991). Given that some change is inevitable, the maintenance of consistent positive events, such as spending regular leisure time with parents or friends, appears to promote child well-being (Sandler et al., 1991).

Economic Decline

Recent research (Braver, 1999; Braver & O'Connell, 1998) and policy changes have thrown into question the conventional wisdom about how much economic decline is typically experienced by the custodial household. Economic decline is generally adversely related to children's adjustment. This is likely due to its negative impact on custodial mothers' emotional well-being (Braver, Gonzalez, Wolchik, & Sandler, 1989) and parenting (Simons, 1996) and to the fact that forcing moves into less affluent neighborhoods diminishes access to quality schools and services and disrupts children's social networks (e.g., Grych & Fincham, 1997; McLanahan, 1999; McLanahan & Sandefur, 1994). Available studies also suggest that economic hardship accounts more directly for some of children's long-term postdivorce difficulties, such as risk of high school dropout and teenage pregnancy (McLanahan, 1999).

POLICIES' PLAUSIBLE IMPACT ON MEDIATING FACTORS

We speculate in this section about the likely effects of various policies on the mediators that have been clearly related to child outcomes. Generally, these discussions highlight questions and issues to be considered and weighed by the decision maker in each case, rather than one-size-fits-all recommendations.

Custody

The evidence rather strongly suggests a direct link between joint legal custody and child well-being, as well as a favorable effect on the mediating factor of promoting more beneficial contact with the noncustodial father (Braver & O'Connell, 1998; Gunnoe & Braver, 2001). However, the effect of physical custody on child well-being is less clear. In addition, there is little in the research to definitively conclude that one form of physical custody has a generally better impact on the mediators of children's well-being than another (e.g., Lamb, Sternberg, & Thompson, 1997).

Currently, most states have a list of criteria for the court or others to use that guide physical custody placements. Based on the literature of mediating factors reviewed in this chapter, this list should weigh the arrangements that are most likely to (in order of importance) minimize conflict or shield the child from conflict; result in positive coparenting; expose the child to the least disrupted or most effective parent, promote the child's feeling of closeness to and high-quality parenting from the nonprimary parent, minimize environmental changes (e.g., replacing the primary parent, moving to a new house or school, or relocating to a new geographic locale), and result in the least economic decline. It is worth noting that the list comports only roughly with the typical state's list, and it is important to recognize that many of these goals may be in conflict with one another. For any given family, an arrangement might well favorably influence one mediating factor (such as giving custody to the parent with the highest level of parental effectiveness) while simultaneously influencing another unfavorably (for example, minimizing the contact with the noncustodial parent). Each family has its own unique dynamics that require an individual weighing of the impact of different custody options on the mediating factors.

Visitation and Access

Much of what applies to custody applies equally well to access arrangements. There seems no consensus in the literature that one arrangement is to be generally preferred over another. Instead, arrangements should be sought that promote strong relationships with both parents (Kelly & Lamb, 2000; Warshak, 2000) while shielding the child from conflict. Means should be sought that provide both parents with incentives for cooperation rather than conflict, while simultaneously promoting enough access for the child to have a beneficial relationship with the noncustodial parent.

Relocation

Because there is no research that directly evaluates the effect of relocation on child well-being, policymakers are faced with the task of weighing the competing effects on the mediating factors (Rotman, Tomkins, Schwartz, & Samuels, 2000). Mitigating against permitting moves away is the negative impact on the relationship with the nonmoving parent and the disruption to environmental stability (Warshak, 2000). Mitigating toward it is the potential to minimize conflict and the prospects of enhancing the quality of the relationship with the custodial parent or of greater economic prosperity if the move is for a better job (Wallerstein & Tanke, 1996). It appears that courts have largely decided this issue not solely on the basis of the child's best interests, but also on the basis of the moving parent's rights and interests.

Child Financial Support

There is little in the way of direct convincing evidence that child support payments improve child adjustment, although better financial circumstances have been shown to result in higher quality custodial parenting and, of course, less economic decline to the child. Concern over setting the level too high now appears warranted, however, based on recent findings concerning comparative standard of living (Braver, 1999). It has been noted that concern over such an inequity and "being treated as little more than a wallet" contribute to noncustodial parents' disengagement (Braver & O'Connell, 1998), which can in turn diminish the benefits of a quality noncustodial parent–child relationship.

Divorce and Dispute Resolution Procedures

Children from families with low levels of marital conflict are almost never better off if their parents divorce, while those in highly conflicted families are better off divorcing if and only if the divorce will diminish the conflict, which it very frequently does not (Hetherington & Stanley-Hagan, 1999). The challenge for policy is how to develop postdivorce arrangements that reliably lower conflict for those who were formerly conflicted. Toward this end, efforts to develop policies that de-escalate or shield children from conflict, which mediation and parent education programs do (Emery, 1994; Kramer, Arbuthnot, Gordon, Rousis, & Hoza, 1998), should be continued.

A PROPOSAL FOR A COMPREHENSIVE STRENGTHS-BASED APPROACH: THE PUBLIC HEALTH MODEL

In this section, we develop a new proposal for a program to promote better child functioning after divorce by building on the favorable elements of policies currently in practice. Current thinking construes family dissolution not as a monolithic event, but rather as putting into motion a series of smaller events, some of which are deleterious but others of which are beneficial to children (as well as adults; Sandler, Wolchik, & Braver, 1988). The key to strengths-building policy development in this area is to maximize the events that positively modify the mediating factors discussed above while minimizing the events that negatively modify those factors. A public health model provides a useful way to conceptualize this alternative approach.

Divorce is clearly a public health problem for children, a pervasive part of our culture that is associated with negative health outcomes. Research has now elucidated several mediating factors that account for variability in children's postdivorce adaptation. When an individual or family acquires many other public health disorders, such as a low-birthweight child, diabetes, or AIDS, a public health nurse is often assigned who makes home visits, informs and educates the victims about warning signs and possible progressions and ameliorative or preventive practices, assists in the proper use of such practices, commiserates and provides social support, determines what additional resources are necessary, and connects the family with these resources. Some aspects of this work involve "universal" services (e.g., the assignment of the home health nurse, the educational elements), which are minimally intrusive and thought to be uniformly helpful with no undesirable side effects, whereas other aspects involve more intensive and specialized "selected" or "indicated" services.

We envision an analogous approach to divorce following from the public health orientation. The primary goal of the system would be to prevent the public health problems for children that often accompany parental divorce by systematic intervention with the mediating factors that research has shown predict their trajectory. Some elements of a public health model already exist in current practice, such as parent education programs designed to improve parenting quality and shield children from conflict; our proposal extends these elements into a more comprehensive system. The key elements of such a public health approach include the divorce transition guide, early intervention, universal interventions, and more specialized interventions.

Divorce Transition Guide

A divorce transition guide (DTG), analogous to the public health nurse, would be assigned to each family. The mission of the DTG would be to assist the family in achieving forms and arrangements that are functional in the long term as it proceeds through the multiple transitions of divorce. Because all divorcing families come to the attention of the court, and because the court has considerable power to compel behaviors of the parties, the DTG would ideally be affiliated with the court. The DTG should be knowledgeable about the mediating factors important to children's well-being and work with the family to improve these factors. When the DTG confronts inevitable points of conflict—where the parents each want something distinctly different—they could either refer the family to mediation or themselves guide the family to resolutions in as nonadversarial a fashion as possible.

Early Intervention

The earlier the approach by the DTG, the better the prospects for strengths building. This intervention may happen even before the family comes to the attention of the legal system. Analysis of one of our own data sets revealed that 72% of families reported that either the husband or wife or both spouses had obtained "professional therapy for marital issues prior to the final separation." Thus, marital counselors could inform the couple that if a decision is made to dissolve the marriage, they should immediately recontact the counselor for a referral to a DTG or contact the DTG themselves.

Presently, almost all services are conducted on a reactive basis: One or both parents must actively seek (and pay for) them. The proposed system, in contrast, is proactive: Services are actively brought to the attention of the couple, rather than waiting for them to request them.

Some Universal Interventions

Some services and programs are likely appropriate for virtually all divorcing families. Parental divorce education programs could be continued on a more or less mandatory universal basis because of their favorable impact on such mediating factors as custodial parent effectiveness, conflict levels, and financial and emotional support of both parents. Education could be expanded to include more information about legal matters such as how child support works, common custody and access arrangements, and so on. Because children are so often misinformed about what their new life will be like, consideration should also be given to some universal short child psychoeducational programs.

More Intensive Services and Intervention Programs

A menu of other, more intensive services and intervention programs should be made available for those families who need and can benefit from them. At Arizona State University, for example, we tailor individual psychoeducational programs for custodial mothers (New Beginnings) and noncustodial fathers (Dads for Life). These programs are designed to strengthen mediating factors, including interparental conflict reduction, increased parenting skill, increased noncustodial parent-child contact, and payment of child support to protect economic well-being. Coping programs for children (such as our Kids Cope With Divorce) should be available.

The use of Special Masters to help resolve ongoing disagreements would be helpful to a great many families. Specialized programs for particularly troubled families would include domestic violence diversion programs and supervised visitation if a parent has a confirmed history of physical or sexual child abuse.

As-Needed Services

A menu of services to be selected on an as-needed, case-by-case basis should be available to families in consultation with the DTG. For maximum effectiveness, these programs and services should be chosen by the family after they have reviewed all options in the light of their own values. The role of the DTG should be to (a) develop a resource list of services available, (b) develop systems to help people review their options and decide what services are most appropriate for them, (c) identify who is at risk for negative outcomes, and (d) evaluate the new system and develop correctives.

Follow-Up

Continuous follow-up, case management, or monitoring is needed to address postdecree problems as they develop. Because it is clear that divorce requires almost continuous developmental adjustments from the family members, an effective DTG program would, like a public health nurse, regularly assess the family's status and problems and provide correctives as needed. As crisis times recede, this monitoring would become more sporadic but would always be available to any family member upon request.

A number of features of such a program are far less clear and require further consideration. Among them are the following:

- What training should the DTG have (e.g., legal, mental health)?
- What is the role of the family law attorney in such a system? How will the traditional role and training of the legal specialist be meshed with the other services? Because the focus is on what will help the child, how will the rights and interests of the parents be protected?
- How will the services be funded (e.g., public monies or by the couple)? If the latter, how will inability to pay be factored in?
- Are utterances of the parties to DTGs admissible or protected by confidentiality privileges?

CONCLUSION

Families, even those experiencing divorce, have many resources to draw on to promote better outcomes for all family members, especially the children. The goal of policy should be a seamless meshing with those resources and services already in place that facilitate healthy resolution and development. It is our hope that this chapter will stimulate a debate about these issues and facilitate consideration of a comprehensive public health approach.

REFERENCES

Ackerman, M. J. (1995). *Clinician's guide to child custody evaluations*. New York: Wiley.

Amato, P. R., & Gilbreth, J. G. (1999). Nonresident fathers and children's well-being: A meta-analysis. *Journal of Marriage and the Family, 61*, 557–573.

Amato, P. R., & Keith, B. (1991a). Consequences of parental divorce for the well-being of children: A meta-analysis. *Psychological Bulletin, 110*, 26–46.

Amato, P. R., & Keith, B. (1991b). Parental divorce and adult well-being: A meta-analysis. *Journal of Marriage and the Family, 53*, 43–58.

American Psychological Association. (1994). Guidelines for child custody evaluations in divorce proceedings. *American Psychologist, 49*, 677–680.

Baumrind, D. (1989). Rearing competent children. In W. Damon (Ed.), *Child development today and tomorrow* (pp. 349–378). San Francisco: Jossey-Bass.

Bauserman, R. (2002). Child adjustment in joint-custody versus sole-custody arrangements: A meta-analytic review. *Journal of Family Psychology, 16*(1), 91–102.

Braver, S. L. (1999). The gender gap in standard of living after divorce: Vanishingly small? *Family Law Quarterly, 33*(1), 111–134.

Braver, S. L., Gonzalez, N., Wolchik, S. A., & Sandler, I. N. (1989). Economic hardship and psychological distress in custodial mothers. *Journal of Divorce, 12*, 19–34.

Braver, S. L., Griffin, W. A., Cookston, J. T., Sandler, I. N., & Williams, J. (in press). Promoting better fathering among divorced nonresident fathers. In W. M. Pinsof & J. Lebow (Eds.), *Family psychology: The art of the science*. New York: Oxford.

Braver, S. L., & O'Connell, D. (1998). *Divorced dads: Shattering the myths*. New York: Tarcher/Putnam.

Braver, S. L., Salem, P., Pearson, J., & DeLuse, S. R. (1996). The content of divorce education programs: Results of a survey. *Family and Conciliation Courts Review*, 34(1), 41–59.

Buchanan, C. M., Maccoby, E. E., & Dornbusch, S. M. (1991). Caught between parents: Adolescents' experience in divorced homes. *Child Development, 62*, 1008–1029.

Bureau of the Census. (1996). *Marital status and living arrangements, March 1994, Table E* (Current Population Reports Series P20-484). Washington, DC: Author.

Chase-Lansdale, P. L., Cherlin, A. J., & Kiernan, K. E. (1995). The long-term effects of parental divorce on the mental health of young adults: A developmental perspective. *Child Development, 66*, 1614–1634.

Cherlin, A. J. (1992). *Marriage, divorce and remarriage*. Cambridge, MA: Harvard University Press.

Emery, R. E. (1994). *Renegotiating family relationships: Divorce, child custody and mediation*. New York: Guilford Press.

Emery, R. E., Kitzmann, K. M., & Waldron, M. (1999). Psychological interventions for separated and divorced families. In E. M. Hetherington (Ed.), *Coping with divorce, single parenting and remarriage: A risk and resiliency perspective* (pp. 323–344). Mahwah, NJ: Erlbaum.

Emery, R. E., Matthews, S. G., & Wyer, M. M. (1991). Child custody mediation and litigation: Further evidence on the differing views of mothers and fathers. *Journal of Consulting and Clinical Psychology, 59*, 410–418.

Forgatch, M. S., & DeGarmo, D. S. (1999). Parenting through change: An effective prevention program for single mothers. *Journal of Consulting and Clinical Psychology, 67*, 711–724.

Furstenberg, F. F., & Teitler, J. O. (1994). Reconsidering the effects of marital disruption. *Journal of Family Issues, 15*, 173–190.

Geasler, M. J., & Blaisure, K. R. (1999). 1998 nationwide survey of court-connected divorce education programs. *Family and Conciliation Courts Review, 37*, 36–63.

Grych, J. H., & Fincham, F. D. (1990). Marital conflict and children's adjustment: A cognitive-contextual framework. *Psychological Bulletin, 108*, 267–290.

Grych, J. H., & Fincham, F. D. (1992). Interventions for children of divorce: Toward greater integration of research and action. *Psychological Bulletin, 111*, 434–454.

Grych, J. H., & Fincham, F. D. (1997). Children's adaptation to divorce: From description to explanation. In S. A. Wolchik & I. N. Sandler (Eds.), *Handbook of children's coping: Linking theory and intervention. Issues in clinical child psychology* (pp. 159–193). New York: Kluwer.

Gunnoe, M. L., & Braver, S. L. (2001). The effects of joint legal custody on mothers, fathers, and children controlling for factors that predispose a sole maternal versus joint legal award. *Law and Human Behavior, 25,* 25–43.

Hetherington, E. M. (1998). What matters? What does not? Five perspectives on the association between marital transitions and children's adjustment. *American Psychologist, 53,* 167–184.

Hetherington, E. M., & Stanley-Hagan, M. (1999). The adjustment of children with divorced parents: A risk and resiliency perspective. *Journal of Child Psychology and Psychiatry and Allied Disciplines, 40,* 129–140.

Kelly, J. B., & Lamb, M. E. (2000). Using child development research to make appropriate custody and access decisions for young children. *Family and Conciliation Courts Review, 38,* 297–311.

Kramer, K. M., Arbuthnot, J., Gordon, D. A., Rousis, N. J., & Hoza, J. (1998). Effects of skills-based versus information-based divorce education programs on domestic violence and parental communication. *Family and Conciliation Courts Review, 36,* 9–31.

Kurdek, L. A., & Berg, B. (1987). Children's beliefs about parental divorce scale: Psychometric characteristics and concurrent validity. *Journal of Consulting and Clinical Psychology, 55,* 712–718.

Kurdek, L. A., & Siesky, A. E. (1980). Effects of divorce on children: The relationship between parent and child perspectives. *Journal of Divorce, 4,* 85–99.

Lamb, M. E., Sternberg, K. J., & Thompson, R. A. (1997). The effects of divorce and custody arrangements on children's behavior, development and adjustment. *Family and Conciliation Courts Review, 35,* 393–404.

Lengua, L. J., West, S. G., & Sandler, I. N. (1998). Temperament as a predictor of symptomatology in children: Addressing contamination of measures. *Child Development, 69,* 164–181.

Maccoby, E. E., Depner, C. E., & Mnookin, R. H. (1990). Coparenting in the second year after divorce. *Journal of Marriage and the Family, 52,* 141–155.

Masten, A. S., & Coatsworth, D. J. (1998). The development of competence in favorable and unfavorable environments: Lessons from research on successful children. *American Psychologist, 53,* 205–220.

Mazur, E., Wolchik, S. A., Virdin, L., Sandler, I. N., & West, S. G. (1999). Cognitive mediators of children's adjustment to stressful divorce events: The role of negative cognitive errors and positive illusions. *Child Development, 70,* 231–245.

McLanahan, S. S. (1999). Father absence and the welfare of children. In E. M. Hetherington (Ed.), *Coping with divorce, single parenting and remarriage: A risk and resiliency perspective* (pp. 117–145). Mahwah, NJ: Erlbaum.

McLanahan, S. S., & Sandefur, D. (1994). *Growing up with a single parent: What hurts, what helps.* Cambridge, MA: Harvard University Press.

McLanahan, S. S., Seltzer, J. A., Hanson, T. L., & Thompson, E. (1994). Child support enforcement and child well-being: Greater security or greater conflict?

In I. Garfinkel, S. S. McLanahan, & P. K. Roberts (Eds.), *Child support and child well-being* (pp. 239–254). Washington DC: Urban Institute Press.

Pearson, J., & Thoennes, N. (1984). A preliminary portrait of client reactions to three court mediation programs. *Mediation Quarterly, 3,* 21–40.

Pedro-Carroll, J. L., & Alpert-Gillis, L. J. (1997). Preventive interventions for children of divorce: A developmental model for 5 and 6 year old children. *Journal of Primary Prevention, 18,* 5–23.

Rotman, A. S., Tompkins, R., Schwartz, L. L., & Samuels, M. D. (2000). Reconciling parents' and children's interests in relocation: In whose best interest? *Family and Conciliation Courts Review, 38,* 341–367.

Sandler, I. N., Kim-Bae, L., & MacKinnon, D. (2000). Coping and negative appraisal as mediators between control beliefs and psychological symptoms in children of divorce. *Journal of Clinical Child Psychology, 29,* 336–347.

Sandler, I. N., Tein, J.-Y., Mehta, P., Wolchik, S. A., & Ayers, T. (2000). Coping efficacy and psychological problems of children of divorce. *Child Development, 71,* 1097–1118.

Sandler, I. N., Wolchik, S. A., & Braver, S. L. (1988). The stressors of children's postdivorce environments. In S. A. Wolchik & P. Karoly (Eds.), *Children of divorce: Empirical perspectives on adjustment* (pp. 111–143). New York: Gardner.

Sandler, I. N., Wolchik, S. A., Braver, S. L., & Fogas, B. (1991). Stability and quality of life events and psychological symptomatology in children of divorce. *American Journal of Community Psychology, 19,* 501–520.

Shiono, P. H., & Quinn, L. S. (1994). Epidemiology of divorce. *Future of Children, 4,* 15–28.

Simons, R. L. (1996). *Understanding the differences between divorced and intact families: Stress, interaction and child outcome.* Thousand Oaks, CA: Sage.

Slater, E. J., Stewart, K. J., & Linn, M. W. (1983). The effects of family disruption on adolescent males and females. *Adolescence, 18,* 931–942.

Wallerstein, J. S. (1983). Children of divorce: Stress and developmental tasks. In N. Garmezy & M. Rutter (Eds.), *Stress, coping, and development in children* (pp. 265–302). New York: McGraw-Hill.

Wallerstein, J. S., & Tanke, T. J. (1996). To move or not to move: Psychological and legal considerations in the relocation of children following divorce. *Family Law Quarterly, 30,* 305–332.

Warshak, R. A. (2000). Social science and children's best interests in relocation cases: *Burgess* revisited. *Law Quarterly, 34,* 83–113.

Whiteside, M. F. (1998). The parental alliance following divorce: An overview. *Journal of Marital and Family Therapy, 24,* 3–24.

Wolchik, S. A., Ramirez, R., Sandler, I. N., Fisher, J. L., Organista, P. B., & Brown, C. (1993). Inner-city, poor children of divorce: Negative divorce-related events, problematic beliefs and adjustment problems. *Journal of Divorce and Remarriage, 19,* 1–20.

Wolchik, S. A., Sandler, I. N., Millsap, R. E., Plummer, B. A., Greene, S. M., Anderson, E. R., et al. (2002). Six-year follow-up of a randomized, controlled trial of preventive interventions for children of divorce. *Journal of the American Medical Association, 288*, 1874–1881.

Wolchik, S. A., West, S. G., Sandler, I. N., Tein, J.-Y., Coatsworth, D., Lengua, L., et al. (2000). An experimental evaluation of theory-based single-component and dual-component programs. *Journal of Consulting and Clinical Psychology, 68*, 843–856.

Wyman, P. A., Sandler, I. N., Wolchik, S. A., & Nelson, K. A. (2000). Resilience as cumulative competence promotion and stress protection: Theory and intervention. In D. Cicchetti, J. Rappaport, I. N. Sandler, & R. P. Weissberg (Eds.), *The promotion of wellness in children and adolescents* (pp. 133–184). Thousand Oaks, CA: Sage.

5

RESILIENT OUTCOMES IN ABUSED AND NEGLECTED CHILDREN: BASES FOR STRENGTHS-BASED INTERVENTION AND PREVENTION POLICIES

PENELOPE K. TRICKETT, DAWN A. KURTZ,
AND KARABELLE PIZZIGATI

" Degree of variability of impact... "

Although all forms of abuse and neglect result in adverse developmental consequences for children and adolescents, the nature and magnitude of this impact are quite variable. In this chapter the authors summarize the research on protective factors that influence adaptation among maltreated children. This research suggests that individual factors, peer and familial factors, and social resources may influence positive adaptation. The chapter underscores the extremely limited knowledge base on strengths-based research with abused and neglected children and adolescents. Recommendations are made for social policies that identify strengths among these children, that increase capacity for providing resources that promote prevention rather than remediation, and that increase parent and youth involvement in program and policy development at all levels.

* * *

Society has been aware of the existence of child neglect since the earliest years of the 20th century. On the other hand, societal awareness of the frequency of physical and sexual abuse of children has been more recent—within the last 30 years. Awareness of physical abuse came about in the 1960s, when doctors "discovered" that children were being physically injured by parents and then coined the phrase "battered child syndrome" (Kempe, Silverman, Steele, Droegemueller, & Silver, 1962). About a decade after that, there was recognition of the frequency of the existence of sexual abuse, which had previously been considered an extremely rare phenomenon.

Out of this awareness came federal legislation, in 1974, in the form of the Child Abuse Prevention and Treatment Act and the establishment of the National Center on Child Abuse and Neglect (NCCAN). NCCAN has sponsored three national incidence studies, published in 1981 (Burgdorf, 1980), 1988 (NCCAN, 1988), and 1996 (NCCAN, 1996), which indicated that a startlingly high number of children in America were the victims of abuse and neglect (or, more accurately, were known to authorities to have been victims of abuse or neglect or both) and that the numbers of known cases of maltreatment, and especially abuse, increased dramatically over the decade and a half between the first and third incidence studies.

As Table 5.1 indicates, the *Third Study of National Incidence and Prevalence of Child Abuse and Neglect* (NCCAN, 1996) found that using the more stringent "harm standard" (i.e., evidence that the child had been harmed by the maltreatment), the annual incidence of child abuse and neglect was over 1½ million children (a rate of 23.1 per 1,000). Using the less stringent "endangerment" standard (i.e., evidence that the child had been harmed or was in danger of being harmed), the accrued incidence of all forms of abuse and neglect was almost 3 million annually (a rate of 41.9 per 1,000). This table also indicates the percentage of maltreated children labeled as physically abused, sexually abused, emotionally abused, and neglected. The majority of maltreated children were neglected, and the increase in cases when using the endangerment standard compared with the harm standard is primarily in the emotional abuse and neglect categories. The number of children known to be physically abused doubled from the first incidence study (Burgdorf, 1980) to the third (NCCAN, 1996). For sexual abuse, the increase in identified cases from the first to the third study was 600%. The other types of maltreatment also increased, but by much smaller amounts.

As Figure 5.1 indicates, the third incidence study (NCCAN, 1996) also indicated that the rates of different forms of maltreatment all rise from birth through early childhood until about age 5 or 6 (probably reflecting the importance of school entry for detection of child maltreatment), and then remain relatively steady throughout childhood and adolescence. Thus, despite the stereotype of the abused and especially the neglected child as an infant or very young child, the rates of reported maltreatment are higher during middle childhood and adolescence than during infancy and early childhood. Other important information coming from this study includes the following:

TABLE 5.1
Incidence of Child Maltreatment

Type of maltreatment	Harm standard	Endangerment standard
All maltreatment	1,553,800	2,815,600
	(23.1/1000)	(41.9/1000)
Abuse		
Physical	25%	22%
Sexual	14%	11%
Emotional	13%	19%
Neglect	56%	70%

Note. Data are from National Center of Child Abuse and Neglect (1996).

- With the exception of sexual abuse, where rates are about three times greater for girls than boys, no gender differences were found. That is, boys and girls were equally likely to be reported as neglected or abused.
- Although child abuse and neglect occurred among all social classes, abuse and especially neglect occurred with greater frequency among lower social class families, whether indexed by education and occupational level or by income.
- No ethnic group is overrepresented in incidence rates when the coincidence of ethnic minority status and poverty is taken into account.

STATE OF THE RESEARCH

Research on the developmental impact of child abuse and neglect has proliferated in recent years, as a number of reviews attest (e.g., Ammerman, Cassis, Hersen, & Van Hasselt, 1986; Beitchman, Zucker, Hood, daCosta, & Akman, 1991; Kendall-Tackett, Williams, & Finkelhor, 1993; Trickett & McBride-Chang, 1995; Widom, 1989). With a very few notable exceptions, this research has consisted of two basic designs, each of which has some inherent limitations. First, short-term or acute impact has been assessed using cross-sectional designs in samples of children and adolescents after maltreatment has been officially identified or disclosed. Second, long-term impact has been assessed using retrospective designs in samples of adults who reported themselves to have been abused as children. There have been very few longitudinal studies that have examined maltreatment in samples of children or adolescents over time.

There are particular difficulties with cross-sectional designs in the area of child maltreatment because aspects of the maltreatment can easily be confounded with the age or developmental stage of the research participants. For example, the type of maltreatment, its frequency or duration, and many

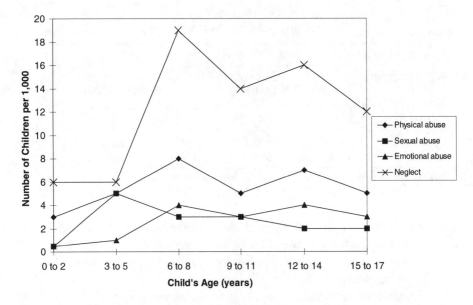

Figure 5.1. Rates of child abuse and neglect under the harm standard, by age. Adapted from *Third study of national incidence and prevalence of child abuse and neglect (preliminary findings)* (p. 16), by National Center of Child Abuse and Neglect, 1996, Washington, DC: U.S. Department of Health and Human Services.

other characteristics are likely to differ depending on whether the child was 3 or 8 or 12 years old, and a cross-sectional design usually does not allow one to disentangle these factors.

Retrospective designs also have some inherent limitations. The most serious problem concerns the distortions of memory that can occur with the passage of time and with experience (see Brewin, Andrews, & Gotlib, 1993, for a recent review of the limits of retrospective reports). A second problem with the use of retrospective designs in studies of the impact of child maltreatment on adults is that the information used to classify a research participant as maltreated is based entirely on that person's memory and perceptions, which is quite different from the way this classification takes place in the studies involving children. In these latter studies, samples almost always come from an agency (such as a county child protective services agency) that determines the presence of maltreatment based on a number of sources of evidence including, but not limited to, self-report.

Besides these limitations of the research designs used, the extant research on child abuse and neglect has other shortcomings, which are described in detail in Trickett and McBride-Chang (1995) and elsewhere. Of particular importance here are two. First, many studies on abuse and neglect have had no meaningful comparison (control) groups or variables. Outcomes of maltreatment can be associated with poverty and related factors, but results from studies without appropriate comparison groups provide no basis for distinguishing between effects associated with the maltreatment and effects brought on by other influences such as poverty and its concomitants (see Trickett, Aber, Carlson, & Cicchetti, 1991).

A second problem with the extant research is that the definition of the abuse or neglect experienced by the research participants has been inconsistent and too sketchy to allow the reader to understand what it is, exactly, that the child experienced. That is, groups of research participants are often described as "neglected" or "sexually abused" with no further details. Neglect, in particular, has so many variants that a one-word label only is more obfuscating than clarifying. Many samples are described as "maltreated"—that is, as having experienced more than one form of maltreatment (physical abuse, sexual abuse, emotional abuse, or neglect) or different forms of maltreatment. The proportion of physically abused and neglected children tends to vary in these studies, as does the inclusion or exclusion of sexually abused children. As a result, it is often impossible to determine how comparable one "maltreated" sample is to another.

Even given these shortcomings, the research reviews make quite evident that all the forms of abuse and neglect often result in adverse effects on the development and adjustment of children and adolescents. These effects include problems of aggression and undercontrol, as well as problems of depression and social withdrawal. They include problems with relationships with parents, other adults, and peers. Academic performance is often adversely affected, as well, especially in samples of neglected and physically abused children. All these forms of maltreatment are associated with behavior problems and psychopathology from early childhood through adolescence and, in some cases, into adulthood, as well as with social deviancy (e.g., delinquency) beginning in early adolescence. The current knowledge about the nature of these problems remains at what might be called a "generic" level. That is, the different forms of abuse and neglect have all been found to result in any of the problems listed. The only "specific" relationship yet identified is that sexually abused children, unlike victims of other types of maltreatment, tend to exhibit problems involving sexual acting out (Trickett, Allen, Schellenbach, & Zigler, 1998).

What is also clear from these reviews of research on the impact of abuse and neglect and from the individual research studies themselves is the degree of variability of impact. That is, even though much research shows "main effects" between an abuse group and a comparison group, the nature and strength of these effects is quite variable. This variability manifests itself in a number of ways—especially the percentage of different samples that manifest a problem and the heterogeneity of severity of a problem within a sample. For example, Putnam, Helmers, and Trickett (1993) found a mean difference in dissociation level between sexually abused and nonabused girls. There was also significantly greater scatter (variance) in the dissociation scores for the abuse group as compared with the nonabuse group. Kendall-Tackett et al. (1993) noted the variability from study to study in the percentage of a sample that manifests a particular problem. And many (e.g., Conte & Schuerman, 1987) have noted that even when an abuse group shows a significantly higher percentage with a certain problem or diagnosis (e.g., depression) as compared with a control group, it is still true that usually the majority of neither group manifests that problem (e.g., 40% of sexually abused girls receive a diagnosis of major depression; thus, 60% do not).

The between-group variation in reported percentages can be accounted for, in part, by differences in sample selection and in the measures used in different studies. Some of the differences both within and between studies may be due to developmental effects, although this has rarely been the focus of research. It also seems likely that some of this variability may be due to important variations in the nature and severity of the abuse and neglect experienced by different individuals. For example, we are finding, in a longitudinal study of a sample of girls who were sexually abused by a family member, that characteristics of the abuse including who the perpetrator was, whether or not the abuse included penetration or violence, and whether there were multiple perpetrators are important predictors of different aspects of later development (see Noll, Trickett, & Putnam, 2000; Trickett, Noll, Reiffman, & Putnam, 2001; Trickett, Reiffman, Horowitz, & Putnam, 1997).

RESEARCH ON RESILIENCE

Another possibility is that this variability indicates that some maltreated children are resilient—that is, to use Masten and Wright's (1998) definition, show "successful adaptation or development during or following adverse conditions" (p. 10), in this case child abuse or neglect or both. Very recently, a number of research studies have directly examined this notion. We identified 11 studies that have explicitly examined resilient outcomes or protective factors in abused and neglected children; these are summarized in Table 5.2. Of these studies, four had samples of "maltreated" children or adolescents, and the remaining seven studies had samples of sexually abused individuals.

As can be seen in Table 5.2, these 11 studies took varying approaches in defining and examining resilience and protective factors. Four of the studies did not explicitly define or discuss resilience or resilient outcomes (Lam & Grossman, 1997; Lynskey & Fergusson, 1997; Moran & Eckenrode, 1992; Tremblay, Hebert, & Piche, 1999). Rather, they focused on the role of protective factors as mediators of the impact of abuse and neglect on development. The other seven defined resilience either as absence of pathology or symptoms (Feinauer & Stuart, 1996; Kaufman, Cook, Arny, Jones, & Pittinsky, 1994) or as successful adaptation (Cicchetti & Rogosch, 1997; Herrenkohl, Herrenkohl, & Egolf, 1994; Himelein & McElrath, 1996) or

TABLE 5.2
Summary of Studies Investigating Resilience in Abused and Neglected Samples

Study	Definition of resilience	Sample characteristics	Study design	Outcomes
Cicchetti & Rogosch (1997); see also Cicchetti, Rogosch, Lynch, & Holt (1993)	High adaptive functioning in four or more areas (out of a possible seven)	N = 213 children attending a summer day camp over three summers Time 1: 6–11 years of age; 62% boys; 62% African American, 13% Hispanic, 19% Caucasian; 113 maltreated, 80 nonmaltreated 73% of maltreated children experienced multiple forms of maltreatment (mean = 2.11 types)	Longitudinal Used a comparison group recruited from AFDC; no statistical differences except that there were slightly fewer minorities in maltreated group (76% vs. 89%)	A higher percentage of nonmaltreated than maltreated children were found to be resilient. For maltreated children, positive self-esteem, ego resilience, and ego overcontrol predicted resilient functioning.
Feinauer & Stuart (1996)	Current lack of trauma symptoms	N = 276 female, sexually abused participants Mean age 37, married 12 years, middle class, majority Mormon No details on nature of sexual abuse	Retrospective No nonabused comparison group	Subjects who blamed self, fate, or both self and fate had higher trauma symptom counts. Subjects who blamed the perpetrator had fewer trauma symptoms. Severity of abuse was associated with lower resilience.
Herrenkohl, Herrenkohl, & Egolf (1994)	Higher functioning in elementary school in cognitive and academic, social, and emotional domains (top 40% of total sample) plus maltreated but considered resilient	Sample drawn from larger study with 457 children in 1976 (ages 1.5 to 6 years), 345 at follow-up in 1980–82 (elementary school age) and 1990–92 (ages 15–21) Gender breakdown not provided 105 abused, 86 neglected children from families receiving services for abuse and neglect, not otherwise defined	Longitudinal Compared resilient maltreated sample with middle- and low-functioning maltreated children	Those defined as resilient in elementary school were more likely to graduate from high school (61%) than maltreated children defined as middle functioning (42%) or low functioning (35%). Predictors of success over time included intellectual capacity and stable caretaking. Chronicity of maltreatment was associated with low resilience.

continues

TABLE 5.2 (Continued)

Study	Definition of resilience	Sample characteristics	Study design	Outcomes
Himelein & McElrath (1996)	Healthy adjustment following a history of child sexual abuse	$N = 180$ female college freshman at a southeastern public university Mean age 18.1; 94% White 45 reported sexual abuse, defined as sexual experience, involving contact prior to age 15 with a perpetrator who was at least 5 years older	Retrospective Included a comparison group (the 129 non-sexually abused girls) No differences in age, family income, race, or marital status for the two groups	Sexual abuse victims and nonvictims did not differ in overall adjustment; greater perceptions of internal control and higher levels of unrealistic optimism were strongly related to better adjustment. Regardless of abuse history, believing in one's personal ability to control future events and believing that those events will be more positive than negative were associated with healthy adjustment.
Kaufman, Cook, Arny, Jones, & Pittinsky (1994)	Absence of pathology (using cutoff scores used in previous studies to discriminate between clinical and nonclincal populations)	$N = 56$ elementary-age (1st–6th grade), maltreated children (29 girls, 27 boys) Mean age 9 years, 7 months (7–12); 58% Caucasian, 14% African American, 28% Hispanic; 59% single-parent household; 43% welfare recipients Maltreatment included physical and sexual abuse, neglect, and/or emotional maltreatment—84% had more than 1 type	Cross-sectional No comparison group	Wide variation was found in number of children classified as resilient when comparing individual measures within and across domains (range 21%–64%, depending on measure and informant).
Lam & Grossman (1997)	Not explicitly defined Participants divided into four groups based on high and	$N = 264$ female undergraduates (mostly freshman) from a northeastern, urban university Mean age 18.8 (17–25, 46), mostly	Retrospective Comparison group was the 216 participants with no	Composite index of protective factors, including indexes of peer and family support, secure attachment, self-efficacy, and internal locus of control

TABLE 5.2

	Definition	Sample	Design	Findings
	low scores on the Child Abuse and Trauma Scale and on the composite index of protective factors	single, White, diverse in faith, middle class 48 reported child sexual abuse (i.e., had a traumatic sexual experience as a child or revealed that their relationship with parents involved a sexual experience)	self-reported history of sexual abuse No differences between the two groups except more abused women were employed	were associated with depression, symptoms, and social adjustment for total sample. Sexual abuse victims and nonvictims did not differ in overall functioning. Protective factors were more beneficial for participants with sexual abuse than for those without.
Liem, James, O'Toole, & Boudewyn (1997)	Positive self-worth and absence of depression following a history of child sexual abuse	Sample drawn from larger group of 687 undergraduates (253 males, 434 females) ages 16–65 from urban commuter college campuses in the northeast 66% Caucasian, rest ethnic minority; 52% Catholic; 72% single 145 (16% men, 24% women) reported sexual abuse histories—unwanted sexual contact before 14 involving a 5-year age difference or overt coercion)	Retrospective Resilient abused participants (n = 40) compared with nonresilient abused participants (n = 105)	Resilient group had more internal vs. external attributional styles, were less likely to blame themselves for the abuse, were less likely to be chronically self-destructive, reported less stressful family environments during childhood, and were more likely to have sought therapy. Male participants with a history of childhood sexual abuse were more likely to be considered resilient than female participants (50% vs. 20%). Physical force was associated with low resilience.
Lynskey & Fergusson (1997)	Resilience not specifically discussed but implicitly defined as no adjustment problems or	N = 1,265 children born in New Zealand in 1977 (approximately 80% female) interviewed at age 18 about sexual abuse, defined as unwanted sexual activity before age 16 (N = 1025)	Retrospective accounts of sexual abuse within a longitudinal study Comparison group was nonabused	The abuse group had significantly more diagnoses and adjustment difficulties than the nonabused group; 26 abused participants did not meet criteria for any adjustment difficulties. Decreasing paternal care and

continues

TABLE 5.2 (Continued)

Study	Definition of resilience	Sample characteristics	Study design	Outcomes
	psychiatric diagnoses at age 18 in participants who were sexually abused as children	Sexually abused participants ($n = 107$) were divided into three groups: noncontact ($n = 24$), contact ($n = 47$), and intercourse ($n = 36$) Sexual abuse	participants ($n = 918$).	affiliation with delinquent or substance using peers at age 16 were associated with increased adjustment difficulties in sexually abused participants at age 18. However, after controlling for affiliations with delinquent or substance-using peers and paternal care, sexual abuse did not predict adjustment difficulties. Severity of abuse and younger age at onset of abuse were related to increase in rates of adjustment difficulties.
Moran & Eckenrode (1992)	Resilience not specifically examined; rather, protective personality characteristics were examined, such as locus of control orientation and self-esteem	$N = 33$ maltreated, lower middle class adolescent females ages 12–18; 11 neglected, 13 sexually abused, 4 physically abused, 5 physically and sexually abused (identified via four social service agencies)	Cross-sectional Used comparison group of 112 nonmaltreated females ages 12–18 Comparison group from higher socioeconomic status	Self-esteem and locus of control for good events interacted with maltreatment status to affect depression. Maltreated adolescents with low self-esteem who did not take responsibility for good events reported the highest levels of depression. Long-term maltreatment was associated with significantly lower levels of self-esteem, lower levels of internal locus of control for good events, and greater depression.

TABLE 5.2

Study	Resilience operationalization	Sample	Design	Results
Spaccarelli & Kim (1995)	Absence of clinical levels of symptomatology and maintenance of age-normative levels of social competence	$N = 43$ 10–17-year-old (mean = 14) sexually abused girls. 74% Caucasian, 19% Hispanic, 5% Black; middle to low socioeconomic status. 70% had at least one type of "invasive" abuse (anal, vaginal, or oral copulation), 21% experienced fondling, 9% experienced noncontact abuse	Cross-sectional. No comparison group	Classification as resilient varied depending on measure (depression, social competence, or combination) and rater (self-report vs. parent report). Resilient participants reported higher parental support, lower abuse stress, and lower aggressive coping than nonresilient participants.
Tremblay, Hebert, & Piche (1999)	Resilience not specifically examined; rather, coping strategies and peer and family support as protective factors were examined	$N = 50$ children (39 girls, 11 boys) referred to a clinic for evaluation of alleged sexual abuse. Ages 7–17 (mean 9.2); 96% Caucasian (Canadian sample); 48% from single-parent families; average parental education level 10–11 years. 72% considered very serious abuse, 22% serious, and 6% least serious (using severity criteria proposed by Russell). 52% of the perpetrators immediate family, 14% extended (Russell, 1983)	Cross-sectional. No comparison group	Avoidant coping strategies were related to internalizing and externalizing problems. Children who perceived more family support positively evaluated their global self-worth and exhibited fewer externalizing problems. Perpetrator closeness was associated with internalizing problems.

Note. AFDC = Aid to Families With Dependent Children.

both (Liem, James, O'Toole, & Boudewyn, 1997; Spaccarelli & Kim, 1995). Only two (Cicchetti & Rogosch, 1997; Herrenkohl et al., 1994) explicitly included, in their definition of resilience, competence in more than one domain (e.g., social, cognitive, emotional). Thus, in this sample of 11 studies there are important differences in definitions of resilience and, at times, vagueness of definition. Two of the studies (Kaufman et al., 1994; Spaccarelli & Kim, 1995) include analyses that make clear that the operational definitions of resilience, the domain examined, and the reporter (e.g., self or parent) all make a difference in whether members of a sample were considered resilient or not.

The research designs of these 11 studies are of three types:

1. Four are cross-sectional studies with samples of maltreated or abused children and adolescents or both obtained from protective service or treatment agencies.
2. Three are longitudinal studies of maltreated adolescents or children based on information of abuse from agency reports in two studies and from retrospective self-reports in one.
3. Four are cross-sectional, retrospective studies with samples of older adolescents or adults where abuse status is based on self-report. It is important to consider that two of these samples were drawn from college populations. One could argue that such a sampling strategy would result in oversampling of resilient individuals—that is, of abused individuals who were coping well enough to attend college.

Although the studies summarized in Table 5.2 are small in number and contain some of the definitional and sampling problems frequently seen in other maltreatment research, they show some consistency of findings that suggest fruitful areas to consider in efforts to understand resilience in maltreated children.

One group of factors associated with resilient outcomes is personality traits or other individual difference factors. These include positive self-esteem (Cicchetti & Rogosch, 1997; Moran & Eckenrode, 1992), ego resilience and ego control (Cicchetti & Rogosch, 1997), lack of self-blame (Feinauer & Stuart, 1996; Liem et al., 1997), adaptive coping styles (nonavoidant and nonaggressive; Spaccarelli & Kim, 1995; Tremblay et al., 1999), internal locus of control (Himelein & McElrath, 1996; Liem et al., 1997; Moran & Eckenrode, 1992), optimism (Himelein & McElrath, 1996), and intellectual capacity (Herrenkohl et al., 1994). Other factors associated with resilient outcomes are family, peer, and social resources, including less stressful family environments (Liem et al., 1997), stable caretaking (Herrenkohl et al., 1994), parental support (Spaccarelli & Kim, 1995;

Tremblay et al., 1999) and particularly paternal presence and support (Lynskey & Fergusson, 1997), affiliation with nondeviant peers (Lynskey & Fergusson, 1997), and therapy experience (Liem et al., 1997).

These studies also indicate that worse maltreatment experiences, as represented by severity (Feinauer & Stuart, 1996; Lynskey & Fergusson, 1997), long duration or chronicity (Herrenkohl et al., 1994; Moran & Eckenrode, 1992), physical force (accompanying sexual abuse; Liem et al., 1997), younger age at onset (Lynskey & Fergusson, 1997), and closeness to the perpetrator (Tremblay et al., 1999), are associated with less resilient outcomes.

The findings of these 11 resilience studies are not especially surprising—they support and are supported by much other research on children's resilience to a number of different adverse conditions. In brief, they suggest that intraindividual characteristics such as good coping skills, intellectual capacity, good interpersonal resources, and social supports are predictive of better developmental outcomes for abused and neglected children. The finding that characteristics of the maltreatment, such as long duration or chronicity, are associated with differential developmental outcomes is also supported by other research (see Trickett et al., 1997, for a brief review).

It is important to recognize that these 11 studies provide a very limited knowledge base. The factors that have been investigated are most often at the individual level of analysis—little is known about protective factors at the familial and community levels of analysis, even though these are important systems mediating the impact of maltreatment. Almost all of these 11 studies have samples of school-age or older children or adolescents; very little is known about resilience in young children. And as noted earlier, there are limits as well to the research designs used in the studies—almost all are cross-sectional, and many are retrospective. Even so, taken together, this evidence suggests useful approaches that could be the foci of educational or therapeutic interventions or services designed to forestall or prevent later maladaptive development of abused and neglected youth.

BUILDING BRIDGES AMONG RESEARCH, PRACTICE, AND POLICY

There have been few direct policy initiatives that specifically focus on strengths-based approaches to the prevention and treatment of child abuse and neglect. However, progress has been made in policy pronouncements and investments that target prevention, early intervention, family support, and other related efforts. These kinds of initiatives often have the underlying view of enhancing the skills, capacities, and resources of individuals and families that the research reviewed in this chapter suggests are important in reducing harm and promoting healthy development.

Among the key themes slowly but increasingly reflected are that policies and program services

- view children, parents, and communities as having strengths that can and should be tapped and enhanced, not merely as entities that need fixing;
- work through education, training, counseling, and other means to increase individual, family, and community capacities and success to enable them to avert problems and to solve their own problems more effectively;
- recognize the importance of involving those who receive services in designing and refining those services (e.g., the value of parent involvement and youth involvement); and
- have sufficient funding and links to other community resources to get the job done.

Drawing the connections among the lessons from research and policy formulation is not easy. Public policies and their making tend to be broad in concept and in application and generally have little in their design and process to address directly either widely varying strengths or problems. By contrast, clinical practice and decision making demand case-by-case analysis to identify and take into account individual differences. So does research that documents individual and group similarities and differences. However, the literature in this area, although growing, remains very modest. The differences in approaches and the still limited weight of evidence have not as yet been able to transcend the generic problems associated with translating good social science research findings into good public policies.

National policies affecting child welfare funding, administration, and practice have neither well nor consistently supported clear direction to the field or needed best practices. There has been and continues to be wide variability across the country in definitions, programmatic emphasis, administrative authorities, and resources allocated.

Furthermore, federal policy making has focused principally on intervention to protect and support children who have suffered abuse and neglect. More recent policies have devoted some attention—although still modest—to prevention. That attention includes some greater emphasis on risk factors that may place children in jeopardy in the first place and the strengths that they, their families, and their communities may have to address the issues before and after the fact.

The U.S. Advisory Board of Child Abuse and Neglect concluded in 1990 that child abuse and neglect constitute a national emergency. Several policy changes have occurred since then, but program and fiscal supports still remain largely uncoordinated and heavily focused on dealing with the results of abuse and neglect rather than preventing harm from happening in the first instance.

Limited Strengths-Based Focus in Federal Child Protection and Child Welfare Services

Several federal programs and activities in the area of child protection promote and support elements of strengths-based strategies directly or indirectly with the themes of prevention, early intervention, and family support. Although few discrete funding resources exist that are specifically designed to support strengths-based efforts, many of the varied federal funding streams allow, and even encourage, the use of funds for an array of strengths-based efforts along with many other functions requiring support. Home visitation programs, which provide home-based services to support and strengthen parental and family functioning and certain models of which have demonstrated success in preventing harm and enhancing healthy development for children and families (Daro & Harding, 1999; Olds et al., 1999), have generated increased attention in research, program, and policy arenas over the last 15 years. In part because of the research, along with communication and connections with the policy world, several types of home visitation programs have taken hold and received funding from an array of federal, state, and local sources.

The Child Abuse Prevention and Treatment Act (CAPTA), first authorized in 1974 and amended most recently in June 2003 as Title I of Keeping Children and Families Safe Act (P.L. 108-36), supports grant programs to identify, prevent, and treat child abuse and neglect and to conduct and disseminate research on the issues. This discretionary program, however, has received but a small fraction of the resources expended on child welfare and children's services in general.

In 1996, amendments to CAPTA changed the federal infrastructure that administers the programs. The amendments abolished the National Center on Child Abuse and Neglect (NCCAN) and integrated some of its functions into a newly established Office of Child Abuse and Neglect (OCAN). Some activities, formerly under NCCAN, now fall to other divisions within the Administration on Children, Youth, and Families in the U.S. Department of Health and Human Services. This change has generated mixed reviews with concerns about potential limitations on current and future coordinated research and development efforts that have a big role in informing programs and policy. Funding for CAPTA programs has remained relatively constant, far below what experts estimate is needed to address child abuse and neglect.

In 1980, the Adoption Assistance and Child Welfare Amendments (P.L. 96-272) made significant changes in national policy supporting services to abused and neglected children. The 1980 law, under Title IV-E of the Social Security Act, guaranteed federal support to states to provide foster care for children who could not remain safely in their homes. The Title IV-E program, then and now, emphasizes protection, safety, removal, and support for care, not child and family development.

However, P.L. 96-272, importantly, also authorized 75% matching grants to states for services to protect children and provide support to families (Title IV-B, Child Welfare Services). Increasingly, those support services have some grounding in child and family development and seek to help families gain and enhance their skills and resources to take care of themselves. Unfortunately, although critical support to care for children in foster care has increased as the need has grown, the funding for equally critical preventive and supportive services has fallen far short of what was originally intended and needed. As a result, vital supports to address both the serious consequences of abuse and neglect, as well as key interventions that could have strengthened families and averted harm, remain shortchanged.

Authorized early in 1993 and beginning in FY 1994, the Family Preservation and Support Services Program created a new part under Title IV-B. This initiative provided new funding (approximately $1 billion over 5 years) and expanded options for services to assist families and children in at-risk situations and to help in circumstances where abuse and neglect had occurred. States already had authority to use funding under Title IV-B, Part I, the Child Welfare Services Program, for family support and preservation efforts. However, few states used a significant amount of their Title IV-B resources in this way because of inadequate funding and differing priorities (Committee on Ways and Means, 1998).

In 1997, the Family Preservation and Support Services program was renamed Promoting Safe and Stable Families and modified with the passage of the Adoption and Safe Families Act, P.L. 105-89.[1] This expanded program supports services for children and families, including extended and adoptive families, who are at risk or in crisis. Services include programs to help reunite children with their biological families, if appropriate, or to place them with adoptive families or in other permanent living arrangements; programs to prevent placement of children in foster care, including intensive family preservation services; programs to provide follow-up services to families after a child has been returned from foster care; and respite care to provide temporary relief for parents and other caregivers.

The small Children's Advocacy Centers program,[2] authorized in 1992, supports a multidisciplinary approach to address child abuse within a safe community-based setting. The program attends to child victims, provides support to them and nonoffending family members, and brings the child and family together in one place with the all the community agencies that are involved—from investigation to medical and social support services. By de-

---

[1]The Adoption and Safe Families Act of 1997 (P.L. 105-89) makes changes and clarifications in a wide range of policies established under the Adoption Assistance and Child Welfare Act of 1980 (P.L. 96-272) and authorized under Titles IV-B and IV-E of the Social Security Act. The principal themes of the 1997 law are to enhance child safety, permanency, and well-being. Provisions of these laws are codified in 42 U.S.C. §§620-629, 670-676.

[2]The Children's Advocacy Center program was included in the Juvenile Justice and Delinquency Prevention Amendments of 1992 (P.L. 102-586; 42 U.S.C. §13001).

sign, this program helps to avert additional trauma to the child, providing support to the child and family as they begin healing and rebuilding.

The Social Services Block Grant (SSBG)[3] has provided another important and flexible funding tool for states to support a variety of social services, including child protection, prevention, early intervention, and other services. Except for funds that states might transfer from their welfare allocations (TANF funds) into their SSBG accounts, SSBG does not have federal eligibility requirements. States have typically used the funds to serve low-income individuals and families and in FY 1998 used more than a quarter of their SSBG allocation to provide child protection and child abuse prevention and treatment services. This key funding source has suffered enormous threats and actual cuts over the last several years; funding for Title XX has been reduced from $2.8 billion to $1.7 billion for FY 2002, and the threats have remained constant and likely will intensify in this and other areas as the larger budget pictures worsen.

The Evolution of Child Welfare Services to Adolescents and Young Adults

Federal programs that invest in youths have reflected a growing acknowledgment of youth development and the value of strengths-based interventions to effect positive changes in the lives of young people and their communities. In the area of child protection and child welfare, the federal independent living program,[4] established in 1986 and recently reshaped by the Foster Care Independence Act of 1999,[5] was created to assist young people aging out of foster care in gaining skills and developing supports to help them make a successful transition to adulthood.

Federal Programs Serving Youths Increase Attention to Youth Development

Beyond the formal range of child protection and child welfare policy, elements of youth development have taken a small hold in other areas of federal policy, mainly in youth services and education programs that support prevention, early intervention, volunteer service, mentoring and leadership development, and other activities. AmeriCorps,[6] for example, supports a net-

---

[3]In 1981 the Omnibus Budget Reconciliation Act (P.L. 97-35) ammended title XX of the Social Security Act to establish the Social Services Block Grant Program, under which grants are allocated to the 50 states, the District of Columbia, and other eligible jurisdictions, on the basis of population. Provisions are codified in 42 U.S.C.A. § 1397a–f.
[4]The Independent Living Program was first authorized in 1986 under Title IV-E of the Social Security Act (P.L. 99-272; 42 U.S.C. §677).
[5]Title I of the Foster Care Independence Act of 1999 (P.L. 106-169; 42 U.S.C. §677).
[6]AmeriCorps was authorized in the National and Community Service Trust Act in 1993 to support community service programs for individuals age 17 and older, who receive an annual living allowance

work of community service programs that address educational, public safety, human, or environmental needs through services that provide a direct benefit to the community and have children and youths as priorities for services. Young adults participate and strengthen their own capabilities at the same time they are involved in work that enhances opportunities for the children and youths in the communities they serve.

The Youthbuild[7] program provides another example of incorporating elements of youth development and strengths-based work into federal youth policy and programming. Youthbuild provides disadvantaged high school youths who have dropped out of school with education and employment skills training through rehabilitating and building housing for low-income and homeless people. The program also provides leadership development to assist the youths in becoming knowledgeable about and involved in decision making regarding programming and policies, as well as in developing entrepreneurial skills. Such positive youth development models have increased, and elements have been explicitly or implicitly included in a number of federal programs. However, they remain the exception and still far from the predominant view of youths in policy making affecting them (Rollin, 2000).

Over the last few years, there have been promising developments on this front. Congressional interest in youth issues received renewed attention with particular emphasis on supporting efforts aimed at assisting youths in growing up safely and achieving their potential. The Younger Americans Act, first introduced late in the 106th Congress by a bipartisan group of members of the House of Representatives led by Representatives George Miller (CA) and Marge Roukema (NJ), was reintroduced on the first day of the 107th Congress in 2001. Early in the 108th Congress, the proposal was reintroduced again, this time as Title IX of the Leave No Child Behind Act of 2003, designated as H. R. 936 in the House of Representatives and S. 448 in the Senate. Representative George Miller (CA) and Senator Christopher Dodd (CT) were leading sponsors of the comprehensive bill in their respective chambers. This proposal would authorize significant new resources ($5.75 billion over 5 years) to fund community-based activities that support and build on the strengths of youths by providing young people ages 10 to 19 access to five core youth development resources:

1. ongoing relationships with a caring adult,
2. safe places with structured activities,
3. access to services that promote healthy lifestyles,
4. opportunities to acquire marketable skills, and
5. opportunities for community service and civic participation.

---

and are eligible to receive an educational award on successful completion of service (P.L. 103-82; 42 U.S.C. 12501 et seq.).
[7]The Youthbuild program was authorized as subtitle D of the Housing and Community Development Act of 1992 (P.L. 102-550; 42 U.S.C. 1437aaa note et seq.).

Although activities supported under the act could reach all sectors of the youth community, the act targets young people who face greater risks and challenges. These include youths placed in correctional facilities and other out-of-home residential settings; youths who live in areas with high concentrations of poverty; youths living in rural areas; and youths at higher risk because of a history of abuse, neglect, or disconnection from family or school (Child Welfare League of America, 2001).

In sum, there are a number of programs in place that build on the competence, skills, and social resources of youths and families (especially families of young children). Although these are often not specifically targeted to abused and neglected children, they are available to them and other at-risk youths and families. Similarly, although not necessarily labeled "prevention programs," often objectives of these programs can be considered prevention— at least as secondary prevention of long-term maladaptive outcomes of child maltreatment. Unfortunately, but not surprisingly, these programs make little use of existing research knowledge on resilient outcomes for children and youths who have experienced maltreatment or other forms of adversity.

We know from the history of programs such as Head Start that basing program development on research knowledge about development and even research knowledge on effectiveness (Lee, Brooks-Gunn, & Schnur, 1988) is not sufficient to guarantee funding at adequate levels. Nonetheless, increasing such research knowledge and improving links between the researchers and the program and policy developers improve efforts to provide the needed services to children and youths.

RECOMMENDATIONS FOR IMPROVING BRIDGE-BUILDING BETWEEN RESEARCH, PROGRAMS, AND POLICY

First and foremost, it is critical that the identification of and communication about policy implications of research be increased in both the research and policy communities. This book constitutes an important step. A number of professional organizations (including, especially, the American Psychological Association and the Child Welfare League of America) devote a lot of energy and resources to this goal. But more could be done, and other innovative approaches need to be considered.

Second, there are a number of research topics and questions that are closely and clearly linked to policy and program development that could be emphasized. These include examining and improving approaches to early needs assessment of abused and neglected children in order to tailor and individualize interventions that can reinforce and build on the skills and competencies of children and their families. That is, research needs to be done to improve needs assessment so it can better pinpoint the individual strengths, competencies, *and* problems of children and families to guide the development of programs that can be sensitive to varying needs. And, directly related, there should be an increase in quality program evaluations that assess the value in terms of both successful outcomes and cost-effectiveness of strengths-based interventions (Tolan & Brown, 1998).

There is truly a great need to continue and to expand research that addresses basic questions of how different forms of child abuse and neglect affect the development of children who vary in many ways (including age and gender, ethnicity, culture, and other aspects of social context). What is needed are theory-based, multivariate approaches with a developmental, long-term, or longitudinal perspective. Such research must pay keen attention to explicitly defining and describing the nature of the abuse and neglect experienced by the child and focus on broad outcomes including not only psychopathology and problems but competencies and strengths as well.

On the policy front, there also is an enormous need to assess how well or poorly existing and proposed programs and policies support, attend to, and build on the strengths of children and families. Ideally, this focus should apply while programs and policies are on the drawing board, not after the fact, and both the research and policy making communities have substantial roles to play in structuring that work responsibly.

And, finally, to expand needed research, to communicate it, and to apply it well, students and professionals in the various human sciences and services fields need adequate preparation and support to understand the importance of building bridges and to gain the skills to do the work well.

REFERENCES

Adoption Assistance and Child Welfare Amendments of 1980 (P. L. 96-272), 42 U. S. C. §§ 620–628, 670–679.

Ammerman, R. T., Cassis, J. E., Hersen, M., & Van Hasselt, V. B. (1986). Consequences of physical abuse and neglect in children. *Clinical Psychology Review*, 6, 291–310.

Beitchman, J. H., Zucker, K. J., Hood, J. E., daCosta, G. A., & Akman, D. (1991). A review of the short-term effects of child sexual abuse. *Child Abuse and Neglect*, 15, 537–556.

Brewin, C. R., Andrews, B., & Gotlib, I. H. (1993). Psychopathology and early experience: An appraisal of retrospective reports. *Psychological Bulletin*, 113, 82–98.

Burgdorf, K. (1980). *Recognition and reporting of child maltreatment: Summary findings from the National Study of the Incidence and Severity of Child Abuse and Neglect.* Washington, DC: National Center for Child Abuse and Neglect, U.S. Department of Health and Human Services.

Child Abuse Prevention and Treatment Act of 1974, as amended (P.L. 108-36), 42 U. S. C. §§5101 et seq.

Child Welfare League of America (2001). *CWLA legislative agenda*. Washington, DC: Author.

Cicchetti, D., & Rogosch, F. A. (1997). The role of self-organization in the promotion of resilience in maltreated children. *Development and Psychopathology, 9,* 797–815.

Cicchetti, D., Rogosch, F. A., Lynch, M., & Holt, K. D. (1993). Resilience in maltreated children: Processes leading to adaptive outcome. *Development & Psychopathology, 2,* 629–647.

Committee on Ways and Means, U.S. House of Representatives. (1998). *1998 green book*. Washington, DC: U.S. Government Printing Office.

Conte, J. R., & Schuerman, J. R. (1987). Factors associated with an increased impact of child sexual abuse. *Child Abuse & Neglect, 11,* 201–211.

Daro, D. A., & Harding, M. A. (1999). Healthy Families America: Using research to enhance practice. *Future of Children, 9,* 152–176.

Feinauer, L. L., & Stuart, D. A. (1996). Blame and resilience in women sexually abused as children. *American Journal of Family Therapy, 24,* 31–40.

Herrenkohl, E. C., Herrenkohl, R. C., & Egolf, B. (1994). Resilient early school-age children from maltreating homes: Outcomes in late adolescence. *American Journal of Orthopsychiatry, 64,* 301–309.

Himelein, M. J., & McElrath, J. V. (1996). Resilient child sexual abuse survivors: Cognitive coping and illusion. *Child Abuse & Neglect, 20,* 747–758.

Kaufman, J., Cook, A., Arny, L., Jones, B., & Pittinsky, T. (1994). Problems defining resiliency: Illustrations from the study of maltreated children. *Development & Psychopathology, 6,* 215–229.

Kempe, C. H., Silverman, F. N., Steele, B. F., Droegemueller, W., & Silver, H. K. (1962). The battered child syndrome. *Journal of the American Medical Association, 181,* 17–24.

Kendall-Tackett, K. A., Williams, L. M., & Finkelhor, D. (1993). Impact of sexual abuse on children: A review and synthesis of recent empirical studies. *Psychological Bulletin, 113,* 164–180.

Lam, J., & Grossman, F. K. (1997). Resiliency and adult adaptation in women with and without self-reported histories of childhood sexual abuse. *Journal of Traumatic Stress, 10,* 175–196.

Lee, V., Brooks-Gunn, J., & Schnur, E. (1988). Does Head Start work? A 1-year follow-up comparison of disadvantaged children attending Head Start, no preschool, and other preschool programs. *Development Psychology, 24,* 210–222.

Liem, J. H., James, J. B., O'Toole, J. G., & Boudewyn, A. C. (1997). Assessing resilience in adults with histories of childhood sexual abuse. *American Journal of Orthopsychiatry, 67,* 594–606.

Lynskey, M. T., & Fergusson, D. M. (1997). Factors protecting against the development of adjustment difficulties in young adults exposed to childhood sexual abuse. *Child Abuse & Neglect, 21,* 1177–1190.

Masten, A. S., & Wright, M. O. (1998). Cumulative risk and protection models of child maltreatment. *Journal of Aggression, Maltreatment, and Trauma, 2,* 7–30.

Moran, P. B., & Eckenrode, J. (1992). Protective personality characteristics among adolescent victims of maltreatment. *Child Abuse & Neglect, 16,* 743–754.

National Center of Child Abuse and Neglect. (1988). *Study of national incidence and prevalence of child abuse and neglect, 1988.* Washington, DC: U. S. Department of Health and Human Services.

National Center of Child Abuse and Neglect. (1996). *Third study of national incidence and prevalence of child abuse and neglect (preliminary findings).* Washington, DC: U.S. Department of Health and Human Services.

Noll, J. G., Trickett, P. K., & Putnam, F. W. (2000). A prospective investigation of the impact of childhood sexual abuse on sexuality in adolescence and early adulthood. *Journal of Consulting and Clinical Psychology, 71,* 575–586.

Olds, D. L., Henderson, C. R., Jr., Kitzman, H. J., Eckenrode, J. J., Cole, R. E., & Tatelbaum, R. C. (1999). Prenatal and infancy home visitation by nurses: Recent findings. *Future of Children, 9,* 44–65.

Putnam, F. W., Helmers, K., & Trickett, P. K. (1993). Development, reliability, and validation of a child dissociation scale. *Child Abuse & Neglect, 17,* 731–740.

Rollin, M. (2000). Youth policy approaches: Where we've come from . . . where we're going. *Community Youth Development, 1*(1), 47–51.

Russell, D. E. (1983). The incidence and prevalence of intrafamilial and extrafamilial sexual abuse of female children. *Child Abuse & Neglect, 7,* 133–146.

Spaccarelli, S., & Kim, S. (1995). Resilience criteria and factors associated with resilience in sexually abused girls. *Child Abuse & Neglect, 19,* 1171–1182.

Tolan, P. H., & Brown, H. (1998). Evaluation research on violence interventions: Issues and strategies for design. In P. K. Trickett & C. J. Schellenbach (Eds.), *Violence against children in the family and the community* (pp. 439–464). Washington, DC: American Psychological Association.

Tremblay, C., Hebert, M., & Piche, C. (1999). Coping strategies and social support as mediators of consequences in child sexual abuse victims. *Child Abuse & Neglect, 23,* 929–945.

Trickett, P. K., Aber, J. L., Carlson, V., & Cicchetti, D. (1991). Relationship of socioeconomic status to the etiology and development sequelae of physical child abuse. *Developmental Psychology, 27,* 148–158.

Trickett, P. K., Allen, L., Schellenbach, C. J., & Zigler, E. F. (1998). Integrating and advancing the knowledge base for intervention and prevention. In P. K. Trickett & C. J. Schellenbach (Eds.), *Violence against children in the family and the community* (pp. 419–438). Washington, DC: American Psychological Association.

Trickett, P. K., & McBride-Chang, C. (1995). The developmental impact of different forms of child abuse and neglect. *Developmental Review, 15,* 311–337.

Trickett, P. K., Noll, J. G., Reiffman, A., & Putnam, F. W. (2001). Variants of intrafamilial sexual abuse experience: Implications for long term development. *Development and Psychopathology, 13,* 1001–1019.

Trickett, P. K., Reiffman, A., Horowitz, L. A., & Putnam, F. W. (1997). Characteristics of sexual abuse in a sample of girls and female adolescents. In D. Cicchetti

& S. L. Toth (Eds.), *Rochester Symposium on Developmental Process* (pp. 289–314). Rochester, NY: University of Rochester Press.

U.S. Advisory Board on Child Abuse and Neglect. (1990). *Child abuse and neglect: Critical first steps in response to a national emergency.* Washington, DC: U.S. Government Printing Office.

Widom, C. S. (1989). Does violence beget violence? A critical examination of the literature. *Psychological Bulletin, 108,* 3–28.

6

THE STRENGTHS, COMPETENCE, AND RESILIENCE OF WOMEN FACING DOMESTIC VIOLENCE: HOW CAN RESEARCH AND POLICY SUPPORT THEM?

SARAH L. COOK, JENNIFER L. WOOLARD, AND
HARRIET C. MCCOLLUM

Instead of presenting women experiencing violent relationships as "victims" of battering, this chapter reviews their help-seeking efforts and the obstacles they confront in their efforts to protect themselves and their children. This reframing of how we understand the nature of this problem is essential to a strengths-based approach. The authors discuss obstacles to leaving violent relationships that are embedded, for example, in inadequate resources, police attitudes in responding to domestic violence, and policies that create particular risks for immigrant women. They suggest policies that capitalize on women's strengths as active help seekers and focus on identifying and correcting system-level obstacles to create safe and effective exits for women who experience domestic violence.

* * *

Debate surrounds the nature and scope of violence in families, how to prevent it, and when to intervene. One enduring point of agreement, however, is that violence in families is a multidimensional problem that exacts a tremendous toll on society. Although families can provide warm, wonderful, and secure places to grow and develop, violence within them creates adverse environments that impede health, well-being, and development. This chapter integrates social science research with policy perspectives to show how public policies can foster strength, competence, and resilience in women who seek safety for themselves and their children from violent and abusive relationships.

NATURE AND SCOPE OF VIOLENCE WITHIN FAMILIES

In the United States, families use violence and inflict injury at an alarming rate. The National Family Violence Survey (NFVS) estimated that approximately one out of every six couples experiences a physical assault each year—a rate equivalent to 8.7 million couples (Straus & Gelles, 1990). Forty percent of these assaults have the potential to cause injury. Similar estimates of psychological abuse and coercion (e.g., intimidation, deprivation, social isolation, and limited mobility) are difficult to identify but often co-occur with physical and sexual violence. The NFVS estimated that parents abuse 6.9 million children annually. Retrospective studies of adults' recollections suggest that between 11% and 20% witnessed violent partner incidents as children (Wolak & Finkelhor, 1998). From a child's perspective, violence in the family is pandemic.

Women are six times more likely than men to experience violent victimization by an intimate partner (Bureau of Justice Statistics, 1995). According to the National Violence Against Women Survey, women are also more likely than men to be stalked by a current or former partner and report more frequent and longer lasting victimization, more time lost from work, and greater use of medical, mental health, and justice system services than men (Tjaden & Thoennes, 2000). Finally, women are far more likely than men to be seriously injured (Straus & Gelles, 1990) or killed by an intimate partner (Browne, Williams, & Dutton, 1999).

Economic losses due to domestic violence are estimated to reach $67 million annually (Miller, Cohen, & Wiersema, 1996). The World Bank estimated that gender-based victimization accounts for almost 1 in every 5 healthy years of life lost to women ages 15 to 44 in countries with established market economies (Koss, Heise, & Russo, 1994). When measured in disability-adjusted life years, the health burden of violence against women is comparable to threats posed by other leading diseases such as HIV, cancer, and cardiovascular disease (Koss et al., 1994).

Mothers' safety is fundamental to children's safety. Although women's roles in contemporary society have changed greatly, they remain primary caretakers of children. Almost 60% of women between the ages of 15 and 44 have at least one child (U.S. Bureau of the Census, 1990). Children suffer immediate and long-term consequences as witnesses to violence toward their mothers, as reluctant participants in violence trying to protect their mothers, as unwitting targets of abusive or violent behavior (Wolak & Finkelhor, 1998), or as targets used by perpetrators to retaliate against or coerce mothers. Abused mothers find themselves doubly jeopardized. Not only do they suffer the physical, emotional, social, and economic consequences of intimate violence, they are held responsible for the safety and protection of their children. Perpetrators, who may also be fathers, are often not held accountable.

Society is also rightfully concerned about whether children exposed to family violence become abusive adults. Abusive adulthoods are not inevitable. Most escape the "cycle of violence"; however, exposure to domestic violence is a risk factor for perpetrating later abusive behavior and is linked to health consequences. Household dysfunction, such as domestic violence, is linked to multiple risk factors for leading causes of death in adults, such as heart disease, cancer, and chronic lung disease (see also chap. 6, this volume; Felitti et al., 1998). Family violence is also associated with teenage pregnancy (Leadbeater & Way, 2001), substance use (Kilpatrick, Acierno, Resnick, Saunders, & Best, 1997; Lipsey, Wilson, Cohen, & Derzon, 1997), welfare dependency, and unemployment (Browne, Salomon, & Bassuk, 1999; Lloyd, 1997)—all of which directly or indirectly affect children. If family violence is reduced or prevented, these other deeply entrenched problems may be ameliorated.

The nature and scope of family violence are difficult to understand. Many ask, "Why don't women leave abusive relationships?" In reality, many women do leave abusive relationships, and many try to leave numerous times (Choice & Lamke, 1997). Ironically, when women seek safety, they often become more fearful for their lives than when they were with their partners (Sullivan & Bybee, 1999). In this chapter, our overarching goal is to show that even in the face of insurmountable odds, society can help women and their children live in safety through thoughtful, deliberate, and research-based public policy. We have three specific aims. First, we briefly review the history of federal policy related to family violence to understand the current context of policy making and to evaluate how research can best inform policy. Second, we review cutting-edge, multidisciplinary research that highlights how victimized women mobilize resources to leave violent partners and identify obstacles that they face as they attempt to seek help generally and specifically through the criminal justice system. Finally, we make three broad policy recommendations that can be considered "best bets" for helping women. These recommendations capitalize on women's strengths and facilitate their help seeking; they target systems, such as the criminal justice and social service systems, and advocate for consistent and effective implementation of reforms.

A HISTORICAL LOOK AT FAMILY VIOLENCE POLICY

Public policies are shaped, in part, by the social and political climates that surround social problems. In the past, federal, state, and local governments set policies on violence against women by simply ignoring the problem. Society's emphasis on individual rights and family privacy ensured that government remained relatively uninvolved in family matters, except in extreme cases of child abuse and neglect. Moreover, early research reified male violence against women as a "women's issue" by focusing narrowly on poor mental health precursors or outcomes of victimization. Thus, the history of the domestic violence advocacy movement in the United States has been marked by a struggle for recognition and empowerment through grassroots advocates supporting women who were at best ignored and at worst endangered by the criminal justice system. The movement had to overcome barriers to establish violence against women as a social problem in the national consciousness and to press for social and political changes.

Social and state-level legal reforms proceeded unevenly until advocates won a major victory in 1994. The National Task Force on the Violence Against Women Act organized advocacy efforts that led to the passage of the first major federal policy on violence against women. Enacted into law as part of the Omnibus Crime Control Act of 1994, the Violence Against Women Act of 1994 (P.L. 103-322; VAWA) reframed violence against women as a criminal justice problem. This far-reaching legislation has promoted a progressive context for criminal justice reform. The bill allotted new monies for women's shelters and court services and training for law enforcement, prosecution, and judicial staff to improve apprehension, arrest, and prosecution rates. It also mandated interstate cooperation to guarantee orders of protection for women who cross state lines. VAWA's STOP (Services, Training, Officers, and Prosecutors) grant program funded victim services and the development of new law enforcement and prosecution strategies. Many states capitalized on STOP grants and other provisions to augment existing state-supported reform efforts. For example, the Virginia Commission on Family Violence Prevention analyzed state family violence laws and recommended broad changes in victim safety and protection that were implemented in 1997.

Reform will continue. In 2000, Congress reauthorized VAWA, and the National Task Force is already planning for future legislative needs. The policy making process is intentionally slow and deliberate, allowing multiple points of influence. Whether social science research will be useful depends on where and how an impact on policy making is needed (Weiss, 1979). The answer to "where?" lies across systems at all levels of government that should respond (i.e., criminal justice, health, mental health, education, labor, and economic systems). The answer to "how?" is threefold: by defining the problem's nature and scope, by developing policy responses, and by identifying effective implementation methods. The National Research Council's panel report *Under-*

standing Violence Against Women (Crowell & Burgess, 1996) further underscores the need for research at each point along the process.

When problems require the involvement of multiple systems and authority for policy decisions is diffuse and decentralized, as is the case with
family violence, the most effective way to influence policy may be through
strategically disseminating knowledge about the nature and scope of the problems (Weiss, 1979). Cutting-edge research on "battered women" and help
seeking redefines the problem from protecting helpless victims to supporting
agentic women who strive to escape violence in the face of numerous obstacles. As policy develops, research that identifies appropriate targets for
intervention is critical. For example, a growing body of research illustrates
the need for policies that target deficits in the justice system instead of targeting assumed deficits in women "who stay." Information on best practices
for consistent and effective practice is needed for policy implementation.

REFRAMING THE PROBLEM: FROM
HELPLESSNESS TO HELP SEEKING

As social activism around the battered women's movement develops,
so too does theoretical work that shapes policy and intervention strategies.
In the past, theories focused on the impact of a battering relationship and
offered deficits-based explanations of why women remained in violent relationships. This approach provided valuable insights into the dynamics of
violence against women, but it portrayed victims as having learned helplessness or as passive and unable to cope and led to paternalistic responses focused on convincing women to leave. This criticism is not intended to minimize the potentially devastating physical and emotional effects of violent
relationships, but instead to reorient researchers and policy makers toward
strategies that women can use to protect themselves while negotiating a path
toward a violence-free existence.

New research on "what prevents her from leaving" has moved away
from investigation of individual deficits toward assessment of the match or
mismatch between help seeking, the needs of victims, and the resources available to them. Studies have begun to investigate critical dimensions of women's
help seeking, including sources and dimensions of help seeking and the strategies they use to leave violent relationships.

What Is Help Seeking?

Help seeking comprises a divergent set of activities that include reporting abuse to formal or informal sources, stabilizing an unpredictably violent
partner, minimizing the impact of violence, protecting children, and leaving
the relationship. When interpreted in light of helping women to survive,

individual acts such as traumatic stress reactions, covering up for the batterer, minimizing incidents that trigger abuse, or even remaining in abusive relationships are understood as effective coping. Externally focused activities may include making phone calls to family and friends (informal sources) for advice and emotional and instrumental support, seeking legal action through formal help sources such as attorneys or advocacy organizations, or seeking medical care.

How Many Women Seek Help?

Domestic violence is complex and creates a complicated interpersonal context for help seeking. Beyond the emotional attachments of romantic relationships, domestically violent relationships can also result in partner control of finances, social isolation, fears for the custody and safety of children, and further risk of abuse when ending the relationship. These characteristics can limit women's access to resources. Research confirms, however, that women in violent relationships are active help seekers. In a National Institute of Justice Spouse Assault Replication project in Charlotte, North Carolina, involving 419 women, 98% had called the police and at least one other source for help (Hutchison & Hirschel, 1998).

Where Do Women Seek Help?

There are a number of entry points through which women seek help. In addition to relying on their own resources, women seek help from a variety of formal and informal sources. Shelters and other advocacy organizations work with women to provide a number of services to victims of domestic violence. Other formal institutions that provide resources include the criminal justice system, health and mental health care providers, social service agencies, the workplace, and faith-based organizations. In an advocacy intervention study of 278 women residing in shelters for women who had experienced partner violence, between half and three fourths attempted to obtain resources related to education, legal assistance, employment, child care, housing, transportation, financial assistance, and health care (Sullivan & Bybee, 1999). The justice system is the most frequently accessed source (Hutchison & Hirschel, 1998). Informal sources also play an important role in women's lives (including neighbors, friends, and community businesses such as hair salons). Finally, women also rely on themselves and other family members for support (Tan, Basta, Sullivan, & Davidson, 1995).

Dimensions of Help Seeking

Help seeking is not unidimensional. Research has moved away from descriptive questions (Do battered women seek help?) to investigate more complex questions regarding the onset, diversity, persistence, and obstacles that characterize help seeking. When, where, and how do battered women seek help? Although a minority never seek help, the majority of court-involved women seek help from a diverse set of sources. Hutchison and Hirschel (1998) reported that whereas just under a fifth of their sample sought help from one source, slightly more than one third used two to three sources, one fourth used between five and six sources, and almost one woman in six used more than six sources. Indeed, it may be not persistence in obtaining help from a single source, but instead persistence with multiple sources of assistance, that is necessary. Both the number and diversity of contacts may be related to success in ending violence.

The relation between demographic factors and help seeking is complex. In general, help seeking is more likely when abuse is frequent and severe, when the victim and batterer have children in common, and when they are married (Berk, Berk, Newton, & Loseke, 1984; Hutchison & Hirschel, 1998; Johnson, 1990). However, the utility of these predictors may depend on the type of help sought. For example, abuse severity predicts greater diversity of help contacts (Gondolf & Fisher, 1988) and likelihood of calling the police (Johnson, 1990) but less persistence in obtaining a restraining order (Fernandez, Iwamoto, & Muscat, 1997). In addition, although married women are more likely to seek help generally, they are less likely to use the police than cohabiting women (Hutchison & Hirschel, 1994).

Ensuring That Help-Seeking Efforts Are Successful

Identifying when and why women stop seeking help is critical for identifying the personal and institutional barriers facing women who experience partner violence. Opportune times for support and change require a convergence of personal factors and external events, many of which are beyond the woman's control. Conceptualizing help seeking as a process that changes over time highlights the match or mismatch between women's needs and available resources. For example, the fluidity of relationships means that women may experience various stages of "togetherness" with their partners (Campbell, Rose, Kup, & Nedd, 1998). Turning points in the relationship, such as first assaults, when abuse becomes severe, or when it threatens children's health or safety, may trigger women's help seeking. Conversely, the availability of support may be necessary but not sufficient if situational characteristics preclude access at a given time. For example, women who made the decision to prosecute their abuser and who saw support from prosecutors and court advocates as very helpful still faced obstacles throughout proceedings due to lack of transportation or child care (Goodman, Bennett, & Dutton, 1999).

Accumulating research establishes that help-seeking behaviors are a function of both actual and perceived availability of resources. Hutchison and Hirschel (1998) highlighted discrepancies between cohabiting and married women's help-seeking patterns. They suggested that cohabiting women may perceive that they are not eligible for some types of help or that they would be viewed negatively by help sources because they are not married. Utilization of support systems also depends on their perceived and actual effectiveness and on the degree to which women trust the systems. Leadbeater and Way (2001) pointed out an apparent paradox—as battered women move toward self-sufficiency and control, their experiences of interpersonal violence may leave them less likely to trust others and rely on them for help. When combined with the complicated procedures and demands of some formal help systems such as the justice system, fear for one's safety, conflict over the ending of a relationship, and lack of social support can impede obtaining needed resources (Bennett, Goodman, & Dutton, 1999).

Difficulties getting essential financial assistance, securing a safe home, and identifying useful counseling have been identified as factors that contribute to women feeling revictimized or to returning to the abusive relationship (Newman, 1993). Communities must ensure that women's help-seeking overtures meet with positive responses. Sullivan and colleagues developed and tested a client-centered, participant-directed, and cost-effective advocacy intervention for women in shelters that aimed to enhance women's help-seeking behavior by transferring advocacy skills and knowledge from advocates to women and holding the community responsible for the delivery and distribution of resources to victims of violence (Sullivan, Campbell, Angelique, Eby, & Davidson, 1994). When compared to a control condition, women who worked with advocates (trained paraprofessionals) experienced fewer difficulties obtaining resources (Sullivan & Bybee, 1999). Moreover, women who received advocacy services were more effective when they wanted to end abusive relationships, experienced less physical violence, increased their quality of life, perceived higher levels of social support, and had fewer depressive symptoms than women who did not receive advocacy services. The intervention was also successful in reducing violence by original partners and new partners. Especially impressive is that intervention effects were also apparent 2 years later.

The timing of interventions is critical. Leaving an abusive relationship is not a discrete event—it is often a long and arduous process that begins with surviving the abuse, preparing to leave, and managing the initial crisis of leaving (Wuest & Merritt-Gray, 1999). Women interviewed in a criminal justice setting reported making at least two previous attempts to leave before they were successful (Dutton, Goodman, & Bennett, 1999). Among those who had left, the average number of attempts was 3.3 (Dutton et al., 1999). The struggle to maintain the separation requires sustained support (Wuest & Merritt-Gray, 1999). Sullivan et al.'s (1994) advocacy intervention demonstrates a method of providing the type of help that can sustain safety.

The cultural sensitivity of resources available and acculturation or immigration history can also affect help seeking. West, Kantor, and Jasinski

(1998) found that Latina women sought less help from informal and formal sources than Anglos. In combination with preliminary studies of Vietnamese women (Bui & Morash, 1999), these findings suggest that greater help seeking is associated with greater acculturation. However, because so few studies have explored help seeking in immigrant and ethnic minority groups, further research on the role of culture in help seeking is needed.

Systems that are supposed to help sometimes respond with harsh consequences to help seeking, including the deportation of immigrant women (Weissman, 2000); "pinklining," or the practice of denying or canceling health, auto, life, and home insurance for women who have sought help through health care or law enforcement agencies (Fromson & Durborow, 1998); removal of children from the home because of allegations of abuse and neglect (Whitney & Davis, 1999); loss of employment or housing (Browne, Salomon, et al., 1999); and sometimes arrest (Hamberger & Potente, 1994). Systematic data are not available on the scope of these consequences, but some have attracted enough attention to warrant policy responses at the state and federal levels. For example, the Battered Immigrant Women's Act of 1994 (part of Violence Against Women Act of 1994, P.L. 103-322) attempted to provide security to immigrant women. Although the bill's strength was limited in ensuing immigration legislation, new provisions in VAWA 2000 restore and further strengthen protections to immigrant women. Following attention from federal legislators in 1994, states aggressively pursued legislation to curb discriminatory insurance practices. In early 2000, Georgia became the 33rd state to ban pinklining.

Perhaps the greatest policy dilemma is the need to coordinate child protection and domestic violence policies. Although conclusive data on the overlap between child abuse and neglect and domestic violence are not available, anecdotal data and preliminary studies suggest that these problems frequently co-occur to a great extent (Edleson, 1999; Magen, 2000; Murphy & Potthast, 1999). Because separate institutions respond to reports of child abuse and domestic violence, policy changes directed at one institution can affect the other, but rarely are these indirect impacts considered. For example, the Adoption and Safe Families Act of 1997 (AFSA) was passed in response to the perception that family preservation efforts endanger children. To hedge against harm from keeping dangerous families intact, AFSA encourages states to quickly rule out parents as caretakers and create permanent plans for children in custody. But if child protection systems hold mothers responsible for protection of their children and at the same time fail to assess the role of domestic violence and help mothers gain safety, they risk unnecessarily removing children. Systematic efforts to detect co-occurring domestic violence in child protection cases can limit this risk. When systematic screening was used in child protection cases across all five boroughs of New York City, the detection of domestic violence increased by 300% (Magen, 2000). However, efforts cannot stop at detection. States, with advocates, need to carefully review child protective service policies so that social workers can intervene appropriately to support families through transitions to safety. For example, through the development of a statewide, multidisciplinary assessment and intensive family-based service called the Family Life Center, Massachusetts has worked to address the intersection of domestic violence and child abuse for over a decade (Whitney & Davis, 1999), but few states have followed. Empirical research to support best practices also lags behind practice.

TARGETING INTERVENTIONS TO ENSURE CONSISTENT AND EFFECTIVE POLICY IMPLEMENTATION

In this section, we use research on women's active use of the criminal and civil justice systems to examine the ways in which policy has both facilitated and undermined their efforts to end abusive relationships. The justice system is widely used by victims, but it has some of the lowest ratings of helpfulness and effectiveness (see Gordon, 1996), and it is the primary target of grassroots advocacy, policy reform, and research. Recent policy initiatives in the areas of arrest, civil protection orders, no-drop prosecution, and domestic violence courts aim to make the justice system's response to domestic violence systematic to minimize discrepancies between domestic violence and similar crimes committed by nonintimates. These policies have nonetheless been inconsistently implemented (Websdale & Johnson, 1998) and have generated some unintended consequences such as victim arrest (Buzawa, Hotaling, & Klein, 1998; Davis & Smith, 1995) and dissension in the advocacy community.

Law enforcement and prosecution responses can be critical to victims' willingness to pursue legal intervention. Because the justice system is reactive, research has focused on barriers to and predictors of initial and persistent use of justice system remedies. Barriers include situational and practical factors (e.g., lack of child care, transportation, access to telephone). Fleury, Sullivan, Bybee, and Davidson (1998) found that two thirds of victims in a shelter reported that rather than choosing not to contact police, in a number of circumstances they were prevented from calling the police. Approximately one third of the sample said that they did not have access to a telephone. The confusing and frustrating nature of the criminal and civil systems, women's conflict over the potential incarceration of their partners, and fear of retaliation if prosecution is pursued pose additional threats to sustained cooperation with legal processes (Bennett et al., 1999). On the other hand, factors that predict persistence in the system include marital status, presence of children in common with the abuser, severity of violence, and social support (Bennett et al., 1999; Dutton et al., 1999; Fleury et al., 1998; Goodman et al., 1999; Hutchison & Hirschel, 1998). Two ways women seek help from law enforcement are arrest and civil protection policies; these processes often shape victims' first experiences in the justice system.

Arrest Policies

The major policy initiative in most states has been the implementation of mandatory or proarrest policies, which direct law enforcement officers to arrest the primary aggressor in situations of domestic violence. These policies structure the initial contact between law enforcement and victims and establish a critical gateway for subsequent help seeking. Mandatory arrest can facilitate victims' help seeking if it is accompanied by positive interaction with law enforcement and if the interaction establishes a link to other resources such as advocacy or protective orders. Of victims who initiated contact with the criminal justice system themselves (90% of the sample), only half felt that they were encouraged by law enforcement or prosecuting attorneys to pursue criminal cases (Fischer & Rose, 1995). Frequently, women perceive that police minimize their injury, do not believe them, or want them to drop the complaint (Erez & Belknap, 1998). Research is needed on how well and under what conditions various arrest policies are effective in ending the violence.

Feder (1997) examined whether arrest policies are associated with police behaviors and attitudes. In a study of almost 300 law enforcement officers within a police department noted for a proarrest enforcement stand in domestic assault, only 79% believed in the utility of arrest, although nearly 90% believed that responding to domestic violence calls is a legitimate part of a police officer's job. Yet these police reported that they would be more likely to arrest when a husband slaps his wife because he is drunk than in other situations (e.g., if she disobeyed him, if he was laid off, or if she insulted him in front of his friends). In fact, only 41% indicated that they would arrest in each of these latter scenarios, and 18% indicated that they would not arrest in any of these situations. Reported likelihood to arrest was also associated with whether officers held egalitarian attitudes toward women, had accurate knowledge of the domestic violence arrest policy, and believed that police intervention in domestic violence was appropriate and effective (Blount et al., cited in Feder, 1997). These data contrast with similar data collected in the 1980s before the widespread adoption of proarrest policies documenting that police often believed that domestic violence was a private aspect of family life and that police involvement was not legitimate (Robinson, 2000).

Events after the arrest are also important. In a study of police decision making, police officers reported that they would rarely refer women who appeared to have substance abuse problems (e.g., alcohol dependence) or mental health problems (e.g., posttraumatic stress disorder) to either outpatient mental health centers or women's shelters (Stalans & Finn, 1995). Without appropriate referrals at the point of police intervention, the opportunity to prevent future abuse may be lost. These missed opportunities become even more critical in light of studies that documented an increased risk of recidivism for offenders who had a minimal stake in society (i.e., who were not married to their victims and unemployed; Sherman, Smith, Schmidt, & Rogan, 1992). Moreover, recidivism could discourage victims from calling police again.

Protection Orders

A significant development in civil protection sprang from a VAWA provision that created new offenses for interstate domestic violence and extended "full faith and credit" to protection orders. Full faith and credit ensures that states honor protection orders issued in any other state. Protection orders can offer women protection from further abuse during the critical period of initial separation and can enhance sustained safety. Victims of violence must be guaranteed safety while they wait for trial dates, when they travel to employment opportunities, and when they establish new homes. In short, the safety offered by protection orders should accompany victims wherever they are. In an archival study (Carlson, Harris, & Holden, 1999) of court records from 210 couples in which women successfully petitioned for temporary or permanent (1 year in duration) protection orders, the number of women who reported physical violence during a follow-up period decreased 66%. When a protection order was combined with arrest, the number of women who reported no further abuse increased to 71%.

The effectiveness of protection orders, however, has always been tempered by inconsistent implementation. Although the full faith and credit provision is promising, it has not solved all problems. For example, low levels of enforcement, the need for women to register out-of-state orders and have them validated in asylum states, the lack of central registries, selective honoring of orders, concerns about liability for false arrest, and other barriers prevent full interstate cooperation (Websdale & Johnson, 1998). These factors are complex because they are manifest differently in each state and require a combination of legal and behavioral solutions. The Virginia Commission on Family Violence Prevention, with a diverse group of service providers, Supreme Court personnel, and advocates, developed a centralized registry of protection orders that virtually guarantees that all orders issued in Virginia are implemented. The majority of states have yet to take this first critical step toward compliance with the full faith and credit provision.

POLICY RECOMMENDATIONS

Women who have experienced violence at the hands of their intimate partners face complex dilemmas and limited choices, many of which exact acute losses in exchange for safety. Envisioning options at the point women are able to leave an abusive relationship brings these dilemmas into focus. They are likely to be living with their abuser, who may also be the father of their children. They have established a home with the batterer and accumulated possessions and other personally meaningful items. They may have established relationships with their community through friendships with neighbors, church membership, children's school and athletic activities, and local businesses such as banks and shops convenient to their home. When women make the decision to leave a violent relationship, law enforcement is usually involved. At this point they often must leave their homes, neighborhoods, and possessions for the interim safety of a shelter. Children face similar losses of connections and may feel anger and resentment.

We must also recognize that most women who are involved in abusive relationships did not enter the relationship recognizing it as abusive (perhaps because initially it was not abusive). Most entered the relationship because they were attracted to their partner and found the relationship satisfying. Women who experience abuse do not necessarily want their partner arrested, prosecuted, and incarcerated. They may not want the relationship to end. Their prime motivation for seeking help is to end the violence. A law enforcement response may not be consistent with these wishes but may be a critical and necessary part of a broader community response. Nevertheless, a singular focus on the criminal justice response ignores the complexity of domestic violence and is often in tension with the wishes of victims. Recent national and state legislative and policy reforms have created criminal justice responses that are more comprehensive than ever before. These reforms send a clear message: Violence between family members is unacceptable and will be treated as a crime. Although this is the advance that advocates have been working toward for decades, the pendulum could swing too far in this direction and underemphasize other necessary resources.

The justice system, by design, is slow, deliberate, and cumbersome. Prosecution, if and when pursued, often begins weeks or months after violent episodes. Most states treat first offenses as misdemeanors, and even with conviction, the perpetrator is likely to spend very little time in jail. However, law enforcement intervention, whether it results in arrest (with or without incarceration) or a protection order, is valuable because it allows the woman time and safety to seek broader services that will help her re-establish financial security, a home, and meaningful interpersonal and community relationships for herself and her children (Fischer, 1998). Without concomitant family and community support, victims of violence may give up and return to the relationship even when the danger of violence is still present.

In the context of the dilemmas and choices victims face, and mindful of recent policy advances at the state and federal levels and evidence that victims actively seek help, we offer three broad policy recommendations that promote women's competence, strength, and resilience:

1. Policies must capitalize on women's strengths as active help seekers and increase the number, diversity, and responsiveness of intervention points.
2. Policies must focus on system-level interventions.
3. Intervention goals must emphasize effective and consistent implementation.

1. Capitalize on Women's Strengths and Increase Intervention Points

A single response by a single agency will not stop domestic violence. Instead, resources must ensure a comprehensive array of programs designed to work with the entire family. At a minimum, these services must include emergency support services and counseling for victims, short-term financial and housing support for victims and their children, long-term financial and employment counseling services, batterer intervention programs, and child assessment and counseling programs.

Policies must encourage a broad spectrum of agencies and organizations across the public and private sectors to consider themselves potential sources of help and focus on ways that they can identify and assist victims of domestic violence. Movement beyond usual beliefs that particular problems belong only to specific sectors (private versus public) or service areas (law enforcement or social services) is needed to ensure that help is available when women seek it and wherever they seek it. For example, some have proposed providing incentives to the corporations that educate employees and management and human resources staff to recognize and assist women experiencing violence. These provisions should become an integral part of future legislation and be expanded at state and local levels.

2. Focus on System-Level Interventions

Explanations of system failure are often easily dismissed with case-level explanations ("She really didn't want to leave; her boyfriend has a lot of control over her"). A system-level approach focuses on common problems faced by women from a variety of backgrounds in their attempts to escape violence. Policies must direct institutions to identify impediments to help seeking and provide resources to reduce them. Particular attention should be paid to barriers specific to immigrant and ethnic minority women. Future potential funding could be dependent on demonstrating successful interventions that reduce obstacles.

Policies must identify and prohibit the negative consequences of help seeking. Policies must anticipate, acknowledge, and resolve unintended consequences of help seeking that may prevent women from persisting. Although sometimes it is difficult to foretell the nature of these consequences, systems must respond quickly and alter their responses.

Policies must encourage, and mandate when necessary, collaboration among systems which are likely to be involved with families facing domestic violence. State and local commissions or coordinating councils are a promising mechanism for developing collaborative processes. Successful collaborative relationships require more than good will on the part of participants, however, and policies must provide the human and fiscal resources that allow collaboratives to grow and mature.

Policies must emphasize that interventions must be systematically and rigorously evaluated by collaborative partnerships between university-based researchers and community and faith-based service and advocacy organizations. Results of intervention studies should be widely disseminated within advocacy, service, and research communities with the goal of identifying best practice models. Intervention evaluation should focus on identifying the critical core components of effective interventions.

Policies should fund studies of technology transfer so that successful system-level interventions can be implemented with fidelity in multiple locales. The role for research does not end when successful interventions are identified. The process of bringing demonstration projects to scale in multiple communities under widely different conditions must also be supported and evaluated.

Policies must continue federal funding for research on individual, system-level, and cultural factors that inhibit as well as facilitate help seeking, including the nature and scope of negative consequences. Congruent with the strengths-building approach of this volume, a focus on factors that facilitate help seeking is necessary, keeping in mind that factors that facilitate may not necessarily be the converse of those that debilitate.

3. Emphasize Effective and Consistent Implementation

Responses to domestic violence must be implemented consistently to engender trust in their effectiveness. Flexibility is a key component of effective responses to the changing circumstances of domestic violence because geographic and jurisdictional variations exist. When women attempt to access help, the response should not depend primarily on the beliefs of individual officers, lawyers, or program advocates.

Policies should emphasize training on new and existing policy developments for staff at all levels within institutions and organizations likely to encounter women seeking help. This recommendation is critically related to increasing the number of effective intervention points for women seeking safety.

Policies should encourage interdisciplinary and interagency or interorganizational training. Child protection and domestic violence agencies should be cross trained, as should educational, civil, and criminal justice agencies.

CONCLUSION

Policy has made tremendous progress in placing family violence in the national consciousness. Momentum generated by recent legislative and policy reforms provides an opportunity to reconceptualize the common understanding of victims of family violence from helpless to help seeking, disenfranchised to empowered, passive to active. Policy makers and researchers must not perpetuate stereotypes of helpless, battered women by creating social circumstances that place the burden of securing safety solely on the women themselves. Strengths-based policy initiatives informed by empirical research can create a context in which women can identify, develop, and exercise their own competencies to seek safety from abusive environments for themselves and their children.

REFERENCES

Adoption and Safe Families Act of 1997, P. L. 105-89, 111 Stat. 2115.

Bennett, L., Goodman, L., & Dutton, M. A. (1999). Systemic obstacles to the criminal prosecution of a battering partner: A victim perspective. *Journal of Interpersonal Violence, 14*, 761–772.

Berk, R. A., Berk, S. F., Newton, P. J., & Loseke, D. R. (1984). Cops on call: Summoning the police to the scene of spousal violence. *Law and Society Review, 18*, 479–498.

Browne, A., Salomon, A., & Bassuk, S. S. (1999). The impact of recent partner violence on poor women's capacity to maintain work. *Violence Against Women, 5*, 393–426.

Browne, A., Williams, K. R., & Dutton, D. G. (1999). Homicide between intimate partners: A 20-year review. In M. D. Smith & M. A. Zahn (Eds.), *Homicide: A sourcebook of social research* (pp. 149–164). Thousand Oaks, CA: Sage.

Bui, H. N., & Morash, M. (1999). Domestic violence in the Vietnamese immigrant community: An exploratory study. *Violence Against Women, 5*, 769–795.

Bureau of Justice Statistics. (1995). *Violence against women: Estimates from the redesigned survey*. Washington, DC: Office of Justice Programs, U.S. Department of Justice.

Buzawa, E., Hotaling, G., & Klein, A. (1998). What happens when a reform works? The need to study unanticipated consequences of mandatory processing of domestic violence. *Journal of Police and Criminal Psychology, 13*, 43–54.

Campbell, J. C., Rose, L., Kup, J., & Nedd, D. (1998). Voices of strength and resistance: A contextual and longitudinal analysis of women's responses to battering. *Journal of Interpersonal Violence, 13*, 743–762.

Carlson, M. J., Harris, S. D., & Holden, G. W. (1999). Protective orders and domestic violence: Risk factors for re-abuse. *Journal of Family Violence, 14*, 205–226.

Choice, P., & Lamke, L. (1997). A conceptual approach to understanding abused women's stay/leave decisions. *Journal of Family Issues, 18,* 290–314.

Crowell, N. A., & Burgess, A. W. (1996). *Understanding violence against women.* Washington, DC: National Academy of Sciences.

Davis, R. C., & Smith, B. (1995). Domestic violence reforms: Empty promises or fulfilled expectations? *Crime & Delinquency, 41,* 541–552.

Dutton, M. A., Goodman, L. A., & Bennett, L. (1999). Court-involved battered women's responses to violence: The role of psychological, physical, and sexual abuse. *Violence and Victims, 14,* 89–104.

Edleson, J. L. (1999). The overlap between child maltreatment and woman battering. *Violence Against Women, 5,* 134–154.

Erez, E., & Belknap, J. (1998). In their own words: Battered women's assessment of the criminal processing system's responses. *Violence and Victims, 13,* 251–268.

Feder, L. (1997). Domestic violence and police response in a pro-arrest jurisdiction. *Women & Criminal Justice, 8,* 79–98.

Felitti, V. J., Anda, R. F., Nordenberg, D., Williamson, D. F., Spitz, A. M., Edwards, V., et al. (1998). Relationship of childhood abuse and household dysfunction to many of the leading causes of death in adults. *American Journal of Preventive Medicine, 4,* 245–258.

Fernandez, M., Iwamoto, K., & Muscat, B. (1997). Dependence and severity of abuse: Impact on women's persistence in utilizing the court system as protection against domestic violence. *Women & Criminal Justice, 9,* 63.

Fischer, K. (1998, August). Rethinking empowerment goals in domestic violence legal intervention. In K. Fischer (Ed.), *Addressing violence against women— Contributions of community psychology.* San Francisco: 106th Annual Convention of the American Psychological Association.

Fischer, K., & Rose, M. (1995). When "enough is enough": Battered women's decision making around court orders of protection. *Crime & Delinquency, 41,* 414–429.

Fleury, R. E., Sullivan, C. M., Bybee, D. I., & Davidson, W. S. (1998). "Why don't they just call the cops?": Reasons for differential police contact among women with abusive partners. *Violence and Victims, 13,* 333–346.

Fromson, T., & Durborow, N. (1998). *Insurance discrimination against victims of domestic violence.* Philadelphia: Pennsylvania Coalition Against Domestic Violence and the Women's Law Project.

Gondolf, E. W., & Fisher, E. R. (1988). *Battered women as survivors: An alternative to treating learned helplessness.* Lexington, MA: Lexington Books.

Goodman, L. A., Bennett, L., & Dutton, M. A. (1999). Obstacles women face in cooperating with the prosecution of their batterers: The role of social support. *Violence and Victims, 14,* 427–444.

Gordon, J. S. (1996). Community services for abused women: A review of perceived usefulness and efficacy. *Journal of Family Violence, 11,* 315–329.

Hamberger, L. K., & Potente, T. (1994). Counseling heterosexual women arrested for domestic violence: Implications for theory and practice. *Violence and Victims, 9*, 125–137.

Hutchison, I. W., & Hirschel, J. D. (1994). Family violence and police utilization. *Violence and Victims, 9*, 299–313.

Hutchison, I. W., & Hirschel, J. D. (1998). Abused women: Help seeking strategies and police utilization. *Violence Against Women, 4*, 436–456.

Johnson, I. M. (1990). A loglinear analysis of abused wives' decisions to call the police in domestic-violence disputes. *Journal of Criminal Justice, 18*, 147–159.

Kilpatrick, D. G., Acierno, R., Resnick, H. S., Saunders, B. E., & Best, C. L. (1997). A 2-year longitudinal analysis of the relationships between violent assault and substance use in women. *Journal of Consulting and Clinical Psychology, 65*, 834–847.

Koss, M. P., Heise, L., & Russo, N. F. (1994). The global health burden of rape. *Psychology of Women Quarterly, 18*, 509–537.

Leadbeater, B. J., & Way, N. (2001). *Growing up fast: Transitions to early adulthood for inner city adolescent mothers*. Mahwah, NJ: Erlbaum.

Lipsey, M. W., Wilson, D. B., Cohen, M. A., & Derzon, J. H. (1997). Is there a causal relationship between alcohol use and violence? A synthesis of evidence. *Recent Developments in Alcoholism, 13*, 245–282.

Lloyd, S. (1997). The effects of domestic violence on women's employment. *Law & Policy, 19*, 139–167.

Magen, R. H. (2000). Domestic violence in child welfare preventative services: Results from an intake screening questionnaire. *Children and Youth Services Review, 22*, 251–274.

Miller, T. R., Cohen, M. A., & Wiersema, B. (1996). *Victim costs and consequences: A new look* (Publication no. NCJ 155282). Washington, DC: National Institute of Justice.

Murphy, J. C., & Potthast, M. J. (1999). Domestic violence, substance abuse, and child welfare: The legal system response. *Journal of Health Care Law & Policy, 3*, 88–126.

Newman, K. (1993). Giving up: Shelter experiences of battered women. *Public Health Nursing, 10*, 108–113.

Robinson, A. L. (2000). The effect of a domestic violence policy change on police officers' schemata. *Criminal Justice and Behavior, 27*, 600–624.

Sherman, L. W., Smith, D. A., Schmidt, J. D., & Rogan, D. P. (1992). Crime, punishment, and stake in conformity: Legal and informal control of domestic violence. *American Sociological Review, 57*, 680–690.

Stalans, L. J., & Finn, M. A. (1995). How novice and experienced officers interpret wife assaults: Normative and efficiency frames. *Law and Society Review, 29*, 287–321.

Straus, M. A., & Gelles, R. J. (1990). How violent are American families? Estimates from the National Family Violence Resurvey and other studies. In M. A. Straus

& R. J. Gelles (Eds.), *Physical violence in American families: Risk factors and adaptations to violence in 8,145 families* (pp. 95–112). New Brunswick, NJ: Transaction Publishers.

Sullivan, C. M., & Bybee, D. I. (1999). Reducing violence using community-based advocacy for women with abusive partners. *Journal of Consulting and Clinical Psychology, 67,* 43–53.

Sullivan, C. M., Campbell, R., Angelique, H., Eby, K. K., & Davidson, W. S. (1994). An advocacy intervention program for women with abusive partners: Six-month follow-up. *American Journal of Community Psychology, 22,* 101–122.

Tan, C., Basta, J., Sullivan, C. M., & Davidson, W. S. (1995). The role of social support in the lives of women exiting domestic violence shelters: An experimental study. *Journal of Interpersonal Violence, 10,* 437–451.

Tjaden, P., & Thoennes, N. (2000). Prevalence and consequences of male-to-female and female-to-male intimate partner violence as measured by the National Violence Against Women Survey. *Violence Against Women, 6,* 142–161.

U.S. Bureau of the Census. (1990). *Statistical abstract of the United States: 1990* (110th ed.). Washington, DC: U.S. Government Printing Office.

Violence Against Women Act of 1994, 42 U.S.C.A. §13981 et seq. (West, 1994).

Websdale, N., & Johnson, B. (1998). Have faith, will travel: Implementing full faith and credit under the 1994 Violence Against Women Act. *Women and Criminal Justice, 9,* 1–45.

Weiss, J. A. (1979). Access to influence: Some effects of policy sector on the use of social science. *American Behavioral Scientist, 22,* 437–458.

Weissman, D. M. (2000, Spring). Addressing domestic violence in immigrant communities. *Popular Government,* pp. 13–18.

West, C. M., Kantor, G. K., & Jasinski, J. L. (1998). Sociodemographic predictors and cultural barriers to help-seeking behavior by Latina and Anglo American battered women. *Violence and Victims, 13,* 361–375.

Whitney, P., & Davis, L. (1999). Child abuse and domestic violence in Massachusetts: Can practice be integrated in a public child welfare setting? *Child Maltreatment, 4,* 158–166.

Wolak, J., & Finkelhor, D. (1998). Children exposed to partner violence. In J. L. Jasinski & L. M. Williams (Eds.), *Partner violence: A comprehensive review of 20 years of research* (pp. 73–113). Thousand Oaks, CA: Sage.

Wuest, J., & Merritt-Gray, M. (1999). Not going back: Sustaining the separation in the process of leaving abusive relationships. *Violence Against Women, 5,* 110–133.

7

ENHANCING THE DEVELOPMENTAL OUTCOMES OF ADOLESCENT PARENTS AND THEIR CHILDREN

CYNTHIA J. SCHELLENBACH, BONNIE J. LEADBEATER, AND KRISTIN ANDERSON MOORE

Although past research has focused on the negative outcomes of teenage parenting, this chapter reviews findings from recent longitudinal studies and presents a model of risks and protective factors that explain the diversity of developmental outcomes for adolescent mothers and their children. The chapter highlights the individual, family, and community strengths that support positive outcomes. Taking a developmental perspective, it addresses both the strengths of the foundations in place before a pregnancy and the quality of supports that are available once a child is born to a teenager. Recommendations for policy focus on helping young mothers to meet the developmentally appropriate challenges of adolescence—for example, through efforts to support self-sufficiency for older adolescent mothers and to facilitate school engagement for younger ones. Long-term programming approaches that seek to influence girls' aspirations before they become pregnant and continue to support their development as adolescents and as parents after a pregnancy may also be important.

* * *

Although the teen birthrate in the United States fell in 2000 to the lowest rate ever recorded, 48.7 births per 1,000 young women ages 15 to 19

(National Center for Health Statistics, 2000), it remains higher than the rate in any other industrialized democracy (Singh & Darroch, 2000). The good news is that the teen birthrate is now declining in all states; the states with the lowest teen birthrates have recently achieved rates comparable to several other industrialized democracies. Thus, with 26 births per 1,000 young women ages 15 to 19 in 1999, Vermont had the lowest teen birthrate in the United States, similar to those of England and Wales at 28 and Canada at 24, though still much higher than Japan at 4 or France at 10. On the other hand, teen birthrates in the states with the highest birthrates are many times higher than in other industrialized democracies. For example, Arizona, Arkansas, Texas, and Mississippi all have rates of 70 or higher.

A similar situation exists regarding racial and ethnic differences in birthrates. The rate for non-Hispanic White teens (33 in 2,000) is now similar to the rate in several other nations. At 84 in 1999, the rate for non-Hispanic Black teens is high but declined dramatically during the 1990s, falling from 116 per 1,000 in 1991. Among Hispanics, the rate peaked in 1994 at 107 and had fallen to 94 in 2000. Thus, despite encouraging declines, rates remain very high. Moreover, because the number of adolescents in the United States is increasing, declines in the teen birthrate are not resulting in comparable declines in the number of births to teens. In 2000, nearly half a million babies were born to teen mothers. Of these, more than 165,000 babies had mothers age 17 or younger (Child Trends, 2001), an age group considerably less ready to meet the social, economic, and psychological demands of parenting than adults parents or even parents in their late teens.

Research on the developmental impact of adolescent pregnancy and parenting has proliferated. Reviews of this research illuminate the risks of adolescent parenting for mothers and their children but also point to the lack of integrative, developmental evidence on which to base policy and program efforts to reduce these risks (Coley & Chase-Landsdale, 1998). Moreover, there is only limited consideration of the diversity of outcomes for adolescent mothers and their children, including the possibility of positive outcomes and a tendency to focus on short-term outcomes for individuals rather than longer term developmental outcomes for young mothers, or even young couples, and their children.

The purpose of the chapter is first to review the research indicating diversity in outcomes for adolescent mothers and their children and to propose a strengths-based conceptual model that reflects this diversity. This process-oriented model highlights risk and protective factors (at individual, family, and community levels of analysis) that predict diversity in outcomes for adolescent mothers and their children. The second purpose is to use the proposed model to integrate risk and protective factors that are empirically associated with resilient outcomes for young mothers and their children. Finally, the model is used as a foundation to guide strengths-based policies that enhance resilient outcomes.

DIVERSITY OF OUTCOMES FOR ADOLESCENT
MOTHERS AND THEIR CHILDREN

Research has emphasized the negative correlates that precede and stem from early pregnancy and parenting. Adolescent girls with poor school performance and limited aspirations for the future are at greater risk for pregnancy than their higher achieving peers (Maynard, 1998; Moore, Miller, Glei, & Morrison, 1995). Adolescent pregnancy has also been associated with a host of risk-taking behaviors among adolescents such as alcohol and drug use, early sexual activity, and poor problem-solving ability (Moore et al., 1995). Higher rates of community levels of poverty, unemployment, and single-parent, mother-headed homes are also associated with higher rates of teenage pregnancy (Wilson, 1995). Following the birth, adolescent mothers are also more likely to fail to graduate from high school, have reduced employment opportunities and income, and are overrepresented among welfare recipients (Coley & Chase-Lansdale, 1998).

However, evidence of individual differences among subgroups of adolescent mothers is accumulating. Within a high-risk sample of African American mothers, Miller-Johnson et al. (1999) found that girls who demonstrated stable patterns of aggression in childhood were more likely to become pregnant in early adolescence and more likely to have multiple births before 19 years of age. A second group of girls became pregnant in late adolescence but functioned competently in other domains of behavior. A third group of girls were characterized by parent reports of depressive symptoms, although the adolescents themselves did not corroborate this. Confirming the relationship between aggression and early pregnancies, Underwood and colleagues (1996) also found that half of the aggressive girls in a sample of lower income, African American girls became pregnant compared to 25% of girls rated as nonaggressive. Moreover, these highly aggressive girls were more likely to belong to social groups that accepted and encouraged early risk-taking behaviors.

Subgroup differences were also reported in longitudinal studies of adolescent mothers' academic achievement. Mothers who graduated from or returned to school differed on a number of variables from those who dropped out before the pregnancy, including school success before the pregnancy, depressive symptoms, life stress, and social supports (Leadbeater & Way, 2001). A longitudinal study of 233 teen mothers in a small town also identified resilient mothers as those who were older, on grade level for their age, and more socially competent and active when they became pregnant (Whitman, Borkowski, Keogh, & Weed, 2001).

Considerable research has shown more negative outcomes for adolescent mothers who are also depressed and for their children than for mothers who are not depressed (Hair, McGroder, Zaslow, Ahluwalia, & Moore, in press; Leadbeater, Bishop, & Raver, 1996; Leadbeater & Way, 2001). On the other hand, personal competence and career aspirations function as protective factors that predict long-term positive outcomes (Furstenberg, Brooks-Gunn, & Chase-Lansdale, 1989; Werner & Smith, 1992).

Clearly, more research is needed to illuminate the developmental foundations that allow for resilient and competent responses to stressful life events in all adolescents. However, the key roles of school success and of personal competence and prevention (or treatment) of aggression and depression in adolescent girls are already evident.

A DEVELOPMENTAL COMPETENCE MODEL OF ADOLESCENT PARENTING

Masten and Coatsworth (1998) defined *resilience* as "manifest competence in the context of significant challenges to adaptation or development" (p. 205). *Competence* is a pattern of effective adaptation in the environment, defined either broadly in terms of the achievement of developmental tasks or specifically in terms of domains of achievements. The competence model for adolescent mothers that is depicted in Figure 7.1 highlights the temporal trajectory (early to later adolescence) and social contexts of adolescent development that affect resilient outcomes. Having a baby as an adolescent is generally thought of as a negative turning point—one that essentially renames teenage girls as teenage mothers, abruptly and prematurely ending their adolescence. However, teen mothers vary in their capacity to move forward.

Developmentally appropriate indicators of competence vary for younger and older adolescents. For young adolescents, school engagement, academic achievement, positive peer relationships, and the development of positive aspirations for the future based on unique talents and abilities are all normative tasks. For older adolescents, the steps necessary for a successful transition to young adulthood include high school graduation, the pursuit of postsecondary training, and, for some, marriage and household formation.

Past research points to many of the individual, family, and community factors that support resilient outcomes. Individual competencies (such as psychosocial adjustment, sociability, high intellectual functioning, or parenting skills) operate as protective factors. Personal resources also include the cognitive and social adjustment of the mother, the mother's knowledge of child development and parenting, her educational achievement, and her physical health. Family resources prior to a pregnancy such as financial status, warmth, and educational expectations for the mother and community resources and support are also central to the healthy developmental outcomes of adolescent mothers and their children.

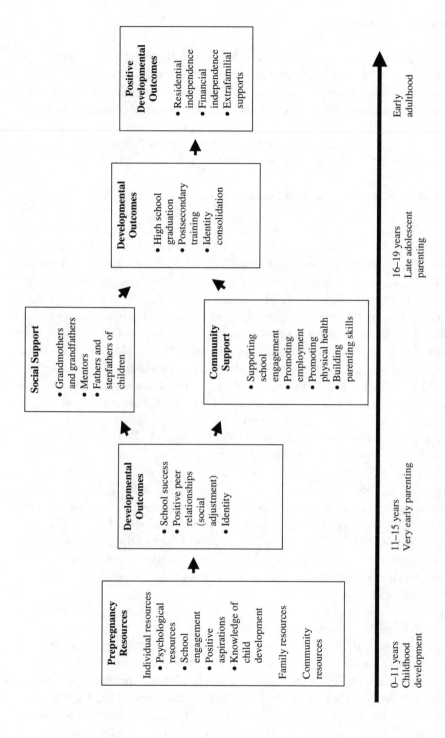

Figure 7.1. A developmental competence model of adolescent parenting.

Individual Resources

Having a baby as a teenager can be a critically transforming event, but this event alone neither erases past experiences nor definitively determines future ones. If competence is indicated by the pattern of effective adaptation in the environment, then researchers focused on resilience must turn to an examination of the psychological strengths of adolescent mothers (prior to and following the pregnancy) that help them confront the stresses not only of early parenting but also of adolescence.

Psychological Resources and Social Adjustment

Recent prospective research substantiates the relations between adolescent psychosocial adjustment before pregnancy and the quality of subsequent outcomes for the mothers or their children. Enduring characteristics of the adolescent, including personality attributes such as self-esteem, coping ability, and effective problem-solving ability, can have a critical influence on the quality of parenting exhibited by young mothers. In one study, pregnant adolescents showed higher scores on measures of problem-solving ability than a similar group of nonpregnant peers (Miller, Monson, & Norton, 1995). The normative activities of adolescence, such as experimentation with social roles, risk-taking behavior, and egocentrism, may also conflict with the requirements for optimal parenting of an infant. However, some young mothers respond to parenting demands by avoiding these normative risks of adolescence on behalf of their children (Leadbeater & Way, 2001).

On the other hand, the adjustment problems of adolescent mothers reflect the multiple sources of stress that they have experienced prior to or following the birth (Barth et al., 1983; Quint, Bos, & Polit, 1997). For example, research indicates that sexual abuse is a frequent precursor of early pregnancy (Miller et al., 1995; Moore et al., 1995). Research focused exclusively on individual deficits limits recognition of the multiple sources of stress (e.g., poverty, housing instability, family illnesses) that many young mothers confront. It also limits the capacity of policy and program efforts to alleviate these sources of stress.

School Engagement and Positive Aspirations

Aspirations and academic engagements before pregnancy are related to positive adjustment following birth (Leadbeater, 1996; Whitman et al., 2001). In an interview study by Camerena, Minor, Melmer, and Ferrie (1998), only a minority of mothers reported lowered aspirations or resignation following the birth (16%). Among the factors that differentiated adjustment were the positive involvement of fathers of the infants and the higher educational attainment of the fathers of the young mothers (the grandfathers). The educational expectations of parents also appear to have a strong influence on outcomes for teenage mothers (Way & Leadbeater, 1999).

Knowledge of Child Development

Research on knowledge of child development and parenting skills among young mothers has focused primarily on deficits in knowledge and understanding among adolescent mothers compared to adult mothers. However, recent research suggests that young mothers' general knowledge base may differ from their knowledge about and specific expectations of their own infants. Crnic, Greenberg, and Slough (1986) found no differences between the general knowledge base concerning developmental milestones held by younger and older mothers. However, a small subgroup of the younger mothers reported perceptions of their own infants that were significantly better than their general knowledge base and than the expectations held by the older mothers. Mothers who perceive the parenting role as difficult and exceedingly stressful (whether adult or adolescent) can experience feelings of inadequacy that may lead to negative expectations for their infants.

Family Resources

Athough the families, mentors, male partners, and neighborhoods of adolescent parents are frequently exposed to the same adversities the teenage mothers are experiencing, the capacity of these social networks to support young mothers, or couples, and their children can have major consequences for the developmental outcomes of both.

Support from Grandparents

Popular opinion and even legislation are based on the assumption that the mothers of adolescent mothers are more competent parents than their adolescent daughters and that they can provide financial, housing, parenting, and child care support. However, research findings do not predict uniformly positive outcomes for adolescent mothers or their children as a result of the grandmothers' involvement. Cross-sectional research shows that grandmothers' support is associated with enhanced economic status, residential stability, child care availability, parenting skills, educational achievement, and psychological well-being among adolescent mothers (Trent & Harlan, 1994; Way & Leadbeater, 1999). However, the relations among grandmothers' involvement and adolescent mothers' outcomes are less consistent in longitudinal studies. Although more family support and coresidence with grandmothers had positive effects on the parenting styles of younger adolescent mothers, these family factors predicted *poorer* maternal warmth and responsiveness among older mothers (Black & Nitz, 1996; Chase-Lansdale et al.,

1994; Spieker & Bensley, 1994). Younger adolescents may be more willing to defer to the "wisdom" of their own mothers, and continued coresidence during young adulthood may reflect problems that older mothers are having with relationships, health, housing, or social capital. Conflict in the relationships among the grandmother, the adolescent mother, and the child has been shown to affect coparenting. Gee and Rhodes (1999) found that support from grandmothers decreased over time and strain increased, highlighting the importance of considering changes in the quality of these relationships. Relationship problems also interact with economic strain in predicting poorer psychological symptoms and social adjustment in adolescent mothers (Davis & Rhodes, 1996). With respect to educational outcomes, months of coresidence with the grandmother and perceived emotional support from the grandmother in the first year postpartum were also associated with poorer educational outcomes at a 6-year follow-up (Way & Leadbeater, 1999), and perceived support from family had little effect on the long-term economic outcomes of adolescent mothers in a Baltimore study (Furstenberg, Brooks-Gunn, & Morgan, 1987).

The presence of a grandfather in the home has been found to have positive effects on adolescent mothers' parenting, operating possibly through the grandfathers' role in alleviating economic strain or increasing nurturance toward the infant. Grandparents' displays of nurturance toward the infant may serve as a model to the adolescent mother or may act by increasing the manageability of the infant. Targeted programs that increase grandparents' capacities to support young mothers and their children during the transition to young adulthood could serve to build and sustain positive trajectories.

Relationships With Mentors

Rhodes and her colleagues (e.g., Rhodes, in press) found that natural mentors (e.g., female relatives of boyfriends, sisters, grandparents, aunts, uncles) were frequently nominated by young mothers and that those who named a natural mentor were less depressed than those who did not. The effects of assigned mentors or volunteer relationships may be less influential, particularly if these relationships are short term in nature. On the other hand, the presence of natural mentors may reflect the social competence of the teens even prior to pregnancy.

Biological Fathers and Stepfathers of the Children of Adolescent Mothers

There is little prospective research on the parenting skills, stresses, competencies, or problems of biological fathers who are or are not involved with their children (Federal Interagency Forum on Child and Family Statistics, 1998). Support from a male partner is positively related to residential stability, overall life satisfaction, psychological well-being, and social participation of adolescent mothers (Cooley & Unger, 1991; Spieker & Bensley, 1994). Although the economic contributions of noncustodial fathers are generally modest and irregular, qualitative studies of young, low-income fathers have found that many are strongly committed to their children and often provide noneconomic support, including acknowledging paternity, maintaining contact or emotional bonds with their children, providing child care, and giving clothes, diapers, and other material support (Furstenberg & Harris, 1993; Greene & Moore, 2000; Sullivan, 1989). Involvement of these fathers may be hampered more by their disadvantaged economic, educational, and residential circumstances than by their lack of concern for or commitment to their children (Leadbeater, Way, & Raden, 1996; Marsiglio, 1987; Watson, Rowe, & Jones, 1989).

Little research has focused on the reasons for stability or instability in the relationships of poor young couples. In one qualitative study of resilient relationships (Leadbeater & Way, 2001), the stability of these relationships reflected the following themes: a considered decision to marry rather than merely drifting or escaping into a relationship, extended family members who modeled what to avoid in a marriage, extended family members who offered material support and advice, the growth of self-respect and self-determination in the young women, and the flexible assignment of gender roles.

Father involvement appears to have positive effects for the children of adolescent mothers; however, findings are mixed. Cooley and Unger (1991) found that involvement of a male partner was associated with greater overall cognitive stimulation. This in turn was related to fewer problem behaviors and better academic achievement of the children of adolescent mothers at 6 to 7 years of age. Similar findings were reported for residential and nonresidential African American fathers in low-income urban families with very young children (Black, Dubowitz, & Starr, 1999). In other studies, father involvement did not enhance the child's outcomes, particularly when the parents were in conflict (Leadbeater, Way, & Raden, 1996; Zaslow et al., 1999). Following a small group of adolescent children born to adolescent mothers in the late 1950s, Furstenberg and Harris (1993) found that the few youths who had long-term relations with a resident biological father or stepfather were more likely to have entered college or to have found stable employment after high school, were less likely to have become teenage parents themselves or to have been in jail, and were less likely to report depressive symptoms. Early marriages or cohabitation were also associated with less maternal education for African American and White mothers and a higher incidence of repeat births (Manlove, Mariner, & Papillo, 2000).

Community Support

Teenage parents from poor communities often receive substandard education, are exposed to high rates of dropout among their siblings and peers, live in communities with few employed men, and may have difficulty obtaining physical and mental health care. Even finding a safe place to live may be difficult. The security deposit for an apartment is beyond the reach of many, and occupational options are often limited to low-wage jobs. Teen mothers also experience high levels of residential instability (Leadbeater & Way, 2001; Quint et al., 1997). Evidence for the effects of community support on outcomes for teen mothers and their children comes mainly from evaluations of programs designed to support their educational and employment outcomes, promote physical health, limit repeat pregnancies, and increase parenting skills. Findings of these evaluations demonstrate some success in influencing mother and child outcomes through home-based interventions and increased community resources that support school engagement and promote employment, health, and parenting skills.

INTERVENTION OUTCOMES

Supporting School Engagement and Promoting Employment

Comprehensive nurse home visitation programs have been shown to have a positive impact (Olds et al., 1999). One study followed mothers at social risk due to young age, single parenthood, or poverty who were involved in a home-based prevention program designed to promote a host of positive outcomes, including educational and occupational achievements, parenting, maternal and child physical health, and overall development. Work participation among the home-visited group increased by 83% in comparison to the control group, and the home-visited group reported a shorter period of welfare dependence (60 vs. 90 months) during the 15 years following birth.

In the broad-based social service programs for teen mothers on welfare launched in the late 1980s, short-term positive outcomes were reported, but long-term improvements were hard to sustain. These programs, including New Chance, the Learning, Earning and Parenting (LEAP) Program, and the Teen Parent Demonstration program combined case management with a broad array of services such as job and vocational training, support for educational attainment, and efforts to prevent subsequent pregnancy (Quint et al., 1997). Considerable outreach and penalties for noninvolvement were used to maintain fairly high participation rates. GED attainment increased in all three programs. The teen mothers were also more likely to be employed in LEAP and in the Teen Parent Demonstration, though not in New Chance. In addition, outcomes on maternal psychological well-being were not positive, and a short-term improvement in parenting disappeared by 42 months in the New Chance mothers (Granger & Cytron, 1999; Zaslow & Eldred, 1998). No positive effects on the children were found. In the New Chance project, the more disadvantaged mothers and those with depressive symptoms at baseline had children with more behavior problems than nonparticipants.

The poorer outcomes for New Chance mothers may reflect the fact that the program served many particularly high-risk mothers who had already dropped out of high school and enrolled in welfare (Granger & Cytron, 1999). In LEAP and the Teen Parent Demonstration, the positive impacts for mothers were concentrated among teen mothers who were still in school. In addition, results indicate that employment did not lift the mothers out of poverty, except in cases in which the mother married and had the benefit of two incomes for the family.

Promoting Physical Health and Decreasing Subsequent Pregnancy

Improving health outcomes for infants born to teenage mothers has been an important goal for several intervention programs. Intensive prenatal and postpartum programs have reported positive impacts such as reducing prematurity or low birth weight, limiting infant hospitalization, and increasing well-baby care and immunizations (Koniak-Griffin, Mathenge, Anderson, & Verzemnieks, 1999; Olds et al., 1999; O'Sullivan & Jacobsen, 1992).

Delaying subsequent births has also been a focus for many programs. Mothers who are more successful in delaying subsequent pregnancies are generally in a better position to complete school, obtain employment, leave welfare, and provide more positive child-rearing environments for their children. Reduction in subsequent pregnancy tends to be associated with long-term economic self-sufficiency for young mothers (Olds et al., 1997).

Programs aimed at increasing employment have shown little success in reducing repeated pregnancies or childbearing (Maynard, 1998; Quint et al., 1997). However, notable success in reducing subsequent childbearing among teen mothers was achieved by the Nurse Home Visiting programs in Elmira, New York, and Memphis, Tennessee. Young mothers who participated longer in a school-based comprehensive intervention program also were more likely to delay pregnancy for more than 5 years following the first birth (Seitz, Apfel, & Rosenbaum, 1991).

The nurse home visiting program also enhanced outcomes for children. Adolescent children of low-income unmarried mothers who were home visited reported less tobacco and alcohol use, fewer sex partners, and fewer arrests. Less child abuse and neglect were also found (Olds et al., 1999). The Parents as Teachers program also found that children benefited when teen mothers received comprehensive case management (Wagner & Clayton, 1999).

Evidence suggests that intervention programs have shown some success in improving the quality of prenatal care available to young mothers, improving life course outcomes related to income assistance, providing quality child care, and preventing subsequent pregnancies. Programs that work to build girls' health, school engagement, and career development before pregnancy may also be needed to reduce long-term negative consequences, and once a child is born to a teenager, more intensive and sustained home-based interventions appear to have success in promoting long-term positive developmental outcomes for the mothers and their children.

Building Parenting Skills

Some parent training programs have demonstrated positive effects on knowledge of child development and parenting skills (Field, Widmayer, Stringer, & Ignatoff, 1982), but others have not (Wagner & Clayton, 1999). Achieving substantial and lasting changes in parenting has proved to be challenging. Research also reveals that program characteristics may interact with personal variables to influence positive outcomes. For example, mothers who have little sense of control or mastery over the environment have higher rates of reported child maltreatment. Olds and his colleagues (1999) reported that the home visitation program moderated the risk associated with lower sense of personal control. As personal control and strength increased among program participants, reports of maltreatment decreased, providing further evidence in support of the strengths-based model.

Consistent with the strengths-based approach, programs that build on the mothers' own goals for themselves and their children tend to be more successful than programs that mandate goals and sanctions. On the other hand, strong management, authoritative nurses, and high expectations also seem to be ingredients of successful programs (Maynard, 1998). Timing also appears critical, as early intervention (beginning in the prenatal stage and continuing into the postnatal period) can produce the most lasting outcomes. Finally, comprehensive programs showed the more positive outcomes compared to programs that targeted single outcomes (like parenting skills).

RESEARCH NEEDS

The factors that select adolescents into early sexual activity, pregnancy, and parenthood would place them at higher risk even if they did not have a baby. Adding the social, emotional, and economic demands of early parenting increases the challenges to the optimal development of two generations. Nevertheless, teen mothers are not without strengths and resources. Research efforts need to explore the antecedents to positive outcomes. Studies that can simultaneously look at the influence of several factors are needed. What social, psychological, and economic foundations predict better outcomes for teenage mothers and their children? Do some antecedents predict better maternal outcomes, whereas others predict better development for the baby?

More research is also needed on the roles of the fathers of adolescent mothers and the fathers of their children. Given strong policy interest in encouraging paternity identification, research is needed that examines the circumstances that can support and sustain young couples' relationships. Similarly, research is needed on the timing of employment mandates for teen mothers and their partners. Should work and self-sufficiency be emphasized for these mothers at a time when their same-age peers are being encouraged to gain postsecondary training to prepare them for better paying jobs in the long term? Does providing sustained support services to delay repeat pregnancy and improve employment outcomes for young mothers have longer term yields in terms of the social capital they acquire by early adulthood?

Stronger evaluations of community-based interventions for early adolescents are also needed. Research indicates that youth engagement and school dropout prevention approaches prevent first pregnancies (Kirby, 2001; Philliber, Kaye, & Herrling, 2001). However, this research needs to be replicated and expanded to include high-risk girls. Early identification and treatment of aggression and depression in girls need to be instituted and evaluated.

Long-term positive outcomes are also likely to be affected by broad-based changes in social policy. There is clearly a need to systematically assess the effects of differences in the approaches states take to adolescent pregnancies and parenting and the effects of changes in policies that affect young couples and their children. The following section draws on the competence model to develop recommendations for the development of social policy to enhance outcomes for young couples and their children.

POLICY DIRECTIONS FOR SUPPORTING INDIVIDUAL, FAMILY, AND COMMUNITY RESOURCES

For several decades, policymakers have sought ways to reduce the incidence of adolescent pregnancy (Moore & Burt, 1982; Wertheimer, Jager, & Moore, 2000). However, no earlier efforts compare to the Personal Responsibility and Work Opportunity Reconcilation Act of 1996 in breadth and provision of resources. The law emphasizes the contribution of teenage and nonmarital childbearing to welfare and other societal problems and includes numerous provisions aimed at reducing sexual activity and increasing marriage. The four purposes of the bill are (a) to provide assistance to needy families; (b) to end the dependence of needy parents on government benefits by promoting job preparation, work, and marriage; (c) to prevent and reduce the incidence of out-of-wedlock pregnancies; and (d) to encourage the formation and maintenance of two-parent families (Sawhill, 2000).

A number of specific provisions focus on teens. Benefits to unmarried teen parents under age 18 are restricted if they do not live at home or in another supervised setting and remain in school. At the state level, $50 million is provided annually to the states for programs that promote abstinence until marriage. Bonuses are provided to the five states that have the largest reductions in nonmarital childbearing. States are required to outline goals and activities to reduce nonmarital pregnancies, and the Attorney General is required to study the link between teenage pregnancy and statutory rape (Wertheimer & Moore, 1998). Although the law is not predicated on a resilience or strengths-based framework, components of the Personal Responsibility and Work Opportunity Reconciliation Act of 1996 could be used to support the development of teen mothers and their children.

The law is quite broad in the kinds of activities that states can pursue to reduce teen pregnancy. Although the abstinence monies are specifically focused on promoting abstinence until marriage, other funds are available for contraception, and both youth development and sexuality education approaches are allowed. Moreover, while the economy was strong, states accumulated billions of dollars in unobligated funds because of declining welfare caseloads, which provided substantial resources available to focus on enhancing the lives of teen parents (Sawhill, 2000). For example, Second Chance Homes are being provided to teen mothers and their babies in Massachusetts (Sawhill, 2000). These homes help the mothers become self-sufficient, to be better mothers, and to enhance the prospects of their babies in a supervised residential setting. Such programs can address the residential, child care, and developmental needs of both the mother and child and deserve careful consideration.

It is important to consider the modest accomplishments of intervention programs that have attempted to assist teen parents when contemplating future initiatives. Teens who become pregnant and have a child, particularly those who become parents when 17 and younger, and especially those who are high school dropouts, face enormous obstacles to self-sufficiency and positive development and also lack many of the socioeconomic assets enjoyed by teens who are not parents. These very substantial obstacles may account for the limited impacts of programs designed to serve teen parents and suggest that programs targeting the prepregnancy resources of vulnerable teens should be considered. For example, results indicate short-term positive outcomes for the programs, but long-term positive improvements were difficult to sustain. It will be necessary to provide even more sustained and individualized programs to address the needs of young parents. In addition, because of the minimal success of most intervention approaches in reducing repeat pregnancy in teen parents, it will be necessary to concentrate resources on this problem.

Among approaches that have been evaluated, the nurse home visiting model has been one of the only successful approaches for teens (Olds et al.,

1999). This approach is particularly promising in view of the new contraceptive methods that became available in the early 1990s. Indeed, the decline in teen childbearing during the early years of the 1990s was driven by a reduction in repeat births, which in turn was fostered by the availability of new methods of contraception made available to teen mothers, specifically Depo Provera and to a lesser extent Norplant (Piccinino & Mosher, 1998). Because Depo Provera is a shot, it is well suited for use as part of a nurse home visiting program. Combining the nurse home visiting protocol with new and better methods of contraception should represent an important approach to assisting teen mothers.

Housing, marriage, and residential arrangements are another concern for teen mothers. Although marriage to—or even cohabitation with—a man with a steady income represents a route to economic self-sufficiency, marriage and cohabitation elevate the risk of repeat pregnancy and increase the risk of school dropout, while providing little certainty of long-term family stability. Identifying ways to strengthen the relationships between young parents seems critical. However, if it does not appear likely that a strong, economically viable and enduring relationship is likely, then other ways to support teen mothers and their babies need to be identified.

Schooling represents another crucial issue. Because the education of the young mother predicts both her own labor market successes and better child development, many programs have focused on getting teen parents into school or GED programs and parenting education. The minimal success achieved by these approaches suggests a need for a fresh look, especially for teen parents who are dropouts. Research has shown for decades that a substantial subgroup of teen mothers had dropped out before becoming pregnant (Upchurch & McCarthy, 1990), and this subgroup may require more intensive services such as tutoring and mentoring. Dropout prevention that targets early adolescent girls and their families is also needed (DeLeon, 1996).

A program approach that is predicated on a resilience model encompasses subtle but critical differences that enhance outcomes. Research indicates that even the most disadvantaged teen mothers have assets (Zaslow et al., 1999). Building on available supports in an individualized approach may be most effective. However, as indicated by the model described in this chapter, a wide variety of supports could be effective, including those that target girls' development in early adolescence and the resources of their families and communities. Following a pregnancy, assistance with the development of long-term self-sufficiency, delay in repeat pregnancies, child care, and enhanced school and work opportunities may be needed to maintain positive developmental trajectories. Long-term developmental approaches that begin during pregnancy and continue at least through the early adult years seem to be essential. Finally, supportive services need to recognize that although teen mothers do need help to get off welfare and be good parents, they also need developmentally appropriate support to meet the social and emotional challenges of adolescence and the transition to young adulthood.

REFERENCES

Barth, R. P., Schinke, S. P., & Maxwell, J. S. (1983). Psychological correlates of teenage motherhood. *Journal of Youth and Adolescence, 12,* 471–487.

Black, M. M., Dubowitz, H., & Starr, R. H. (1999). African American fathers in low income, urban families: Development, behavior, and home environment of their three-year-old children. *Child Development, 70,* 967–978.

Black, M. M., & Nitz, K. (1996). Grandmother co-residence, parenting, and child development among low income, urban teen mothers. *Journal of Adolescent Health, 18,* 218–226.

Camerena, P. M., Minor, K., Melmer, T., & Ferrie, C. (1998). The nature and support of adolescent mothers' life aspirations. *Family Relations, 47,* 129–137.

Chase-Lansdale, P. L., Brooks-Gunn, J., & Zamsky, E. S. (1994). Young African-American multigenerational families in poverty: Quality of mothering and grandmothering. *Child Development, 65,* 373–393.

Child Trends. (2001). *Facts at a glance.* Washington, DC: Author.

Coley, R., & Chase-Lansdale, P. (1998). Adolescent pregnancy and parenthood: Recent evidence and future directions. *American Psychologist, 53,* 152–166.

Cooley, M. L., & Unger, D. G. (1991). The role of family support in determining developmental outcomes in children of teen mothers. *Child Psychiatry and Human Development, 21,* 217–234.

Crnic, K. A., Greenberg, M. T., & Slough, N. (1986). Early stress and social support influences on mothers and high-risk functioning in late infancy. *Infant Mental Health Journal, 7,* 19–33.

Davis, A., & Rhodes, J. E. (1996). Pregnant and parenting, female African American adolescents' relationships with their mothers and fathers: Support, problems, and associations with depression. *Journal of Research on Adolescence, 7,* 331–348.

DeLeon, B. (1996). Career development of Hispanic adolescent girls. In B. J. Leadbeater & N. Way (Eds.), *Urban girls: Resisting stereotypes, creating identities* (pp. 380–398). New York: New York University Press.

Federal Interagency Forum on Child and Family Statistics. (1998). *Nurturing fatherhood: Improving data and research on male fertility, family foundation, and fatherhood.* Washington, DC: U.S. Government Printing Office.

Furstenberg, F. F., Brooks-Gunn, J., & Chase-Lansdale, L. (1989). Teenage pregnancy and childbearing. *American Psychologist, 44,* 313–320.

Furstenberg, F. F., Brooks-Gunn, J., & Morgan, S. P. (1987). *Adolescent mothers in later life.* Cambridge, England: Cambridge University Press.

Furstenberg, F. F., & Harris, K. M. (1993). When fathers matter, why fathers matter: The impact of paternal involvement on the offspring of adolescent mothers. In

A. Lawson & D. Rhodes (Eds), *The politics of pregnancy* (pp. 189–209). New Haven, CT: Yale University Press.

Gee, C. B., & Rhodes, J. E. (1999). Postpartum transitions in adolescent mothers' romantic and maternal relationships. *Merrill-Palmer Quarterly, 45,* 512–532.

Granger, R., & Cytron, R. (1999). Teenage parent programs: A synthesis of the long-term effects of the New Chance demonstration, Ohio's Learning, Earning and Parenting Program, and the Teenage Parent Demonstration. *Evaluation Review, 23*(2), 107–145.

Greene, A., & Moore, K. A. (2000). Nonresident father involvement and child well-being among young children in families on welfare. In H. E. Peters, G. Peterson, S. Steinmetz, & R. Day (Eds.), *Fatherhood: Research, interventions, and policies* (pp. 159–180). New York: Haworth Press.

Hair, E. C., McGroder, S. M., Zaslow, M. J., Ahluwalia, S. K., & Moore, K. A. (in press). How do maternal risk factors affect children on low-income families? Further evidence of two-generational implications. *Journal of Prevention and Intervention in the Community.*

Kirby, D. (2001). *Emerging answers: Research findings on programs to prevent teen pregnancy.* Washington, DC: National Campaign to Prevent Teen Pregnancy.

Koniak-Griffin, D., Mathenge, C., Anderson, N., & Verzemnieks, I. (1999). An early intervention program for adolescent mothers: A nursing demonstration project. *Journal of Obstetric, Gynecologic, and Neonatal Nursing, 28,* 51–59.

Leadbeater, B. J. (1996). School outcomes for minority group adolescent mothers at 28 to 36 months postpartum: A longitudinal follow-up. *Journal of Research on Adolescence, 6,* 629–648.

Leadbeater, B. J., & Bishop, S. (1994). Longitudinal predictors of behavior problems in preschool children of Black and Puerto Rican adolescent mothers. *Child Development, 65,* 638–648.

Leadbeater, B. J., Bishop, S., & Raver, C. (1996). Quality of mother-toddler interactions, maternal depressive symptoms, and behavior problems in preschoolers of adolescent mothers. *Developmental Psychology, 32,* 280–288.

Leadbeater, B. J. R., & Way, N. (2001). *Growing up fast: Transitions to early adulthood of inner-city adolescent mothers.* Mahwah, NJ: Erlbaum.

Leadbeater, B. J., Way, N., & Raden, A. (1996). Why not marry your baby's father? In B. J. Leadbeater & N. Way (Eds.), *Urban adolescent girls: Resisting stereotypes, creating identities* (pp. 193–212). New York: New York University Press.

Manlove, J., Mariner, C., & Papillo, A. R. (2000). Postponing second teen births in the 1990s: Longitudinal analyses of national data. *Journal of Marriage and the Family, 62,* 430–448.

Marsiglio, W. (1987). *Fatherhood: Contemporary theory, research, and social policy.* Thousand Oaks, CA: Sage.

Masten, A. S., & Coatsworth, J. D. (1998). The development of competence in favorable and unfavorable environments: Lessons from research on successful children. *American Psychologist, 53,* 205–220.

Maynard, R. (1998, May). *Research on teen parent programs: Program impacts on repeat pregnancies and births*. Presented at the American Enterprise Institute, Washington, DC.

Miller, B. C., Monson, B. H., & Norton, M. C. (1995). The effects of forced sexual intercourse on white female adolescents. *Child Abuse and Neglect, 19*, 1289–1301.

Miller-Johnson, S., Winn, D.-M., Coie, J., Maumary-Gremaud, A., Hyman, C., Terry, R., et al. (1999). Motherhood during the teen years: A developmental perspective on risk factors for children. *Development and Psychopathology, 11*, 85–100.

Moore, K. A., & Burt, M. R. (1982). *Private crisis, public cost: Policy perspectives on teenage parenting*. Washington, DC: The Urban Institute.

Moore, K. A., Miller, B. C., Glei, D. A., & Morrison, D. R. (1995). *Adolescent sex, contraception and childbearing: A review of recent research*. Washington, DC: Child Trends.

National Center for Health Statistics. (2000). *National vital statistics report, 50*, 104.

Olds, D. L., Eckenrode, J., Henderson, C. R., Jr., et al. (1997). Long-term effects of home visitation on maternal life course and child abuse and neglect: 15-year follow-up of a randomized trial. *Journal of the American Medical Association, 278*, 637–643.

Olds, D. L., Henderson, C., Jr., Kitzman, H., Eckenrode, J., Cole, R., & Tatelbaum, R. (1999). Prenatal and infancy home visitation by nurses: Recent findings. *Future of Children, 9*, 44–65.

O'Sullivan, A., & Jacobsen, B. (1992). A randomized trial of a health care program for first-time adolescent mothers and their infants. *Nursing Research, 41*, 210–215.

Personal Responsibility and Work Opportunity Reconciliation Act, H.R. §3734 (1996).

Philliber, S., Kaye, J., & Herrling, S. (2001). *The national evaluation of the children's aid society Carrera-Model Program to Prevent Teen Pregnancy*. Accord, NY: Philliber Research Associates.

Piccinino, L., & Mosher, W. (1998). Trends in contraceptive use in the United States: 1982–1995. *Family Planning Perspectives, 30*, 4–11.

Quint, J., Bos, J., & Polit, D. (1997). *New chance: Final report on a comprehensive program for young mothers in poverty and their children*. Washington, DC: Manpower Demonstration Research Corporation.

Rhodes, J. E. (in press). *Older and wiser: Mentoring relationships between adult volunteers and youth*. Cambridge, MA: Harvard University Press.

Sawhill, I. (2000). Welfare reform and reducing teen pregnancy. *The Public Interest, 138*, 40–51.

Seitz, V., Apfel, N. H., & Rosenbaum, L. K. (1991). Effects of an intervention program for pregnant adolescents: Educational outcomes at 2 years postpartum. *American Journal of Community Psychology, 19*, 911–930.

Singh, S., & Darroch, J. E. (2000). Adolescent pregnancy and childbearing: Levels and trends in developed countries. *Family Planning Perspectives, 32,* 14–23.

Spieker, S. J., & Bensley, L. (1994). Roles of living arrangements and grandmother social support in adolescent mothering and infant attachment. *Developmental Psychology, 30,* 102–111.

Sullivan, M. L. (1989). Absent fathers in the inner city. *Annals of the American Academy of Political and Social Science, 501,* 48–58.

Trent, K., & Harlan, S. L. (1994). Teenage mothers in nuclear and extended households: Differences by marital status and race/ethnicity. *Journal of Family Issues, 15,* 309–337.

Underwood, M. K., Kupersmidt, J. B., & Coie, J. D. (1996). Childhood peer sociometric status and aggression as predictors of adolescent childbearing. *Journal of Research on Adolescence, 6,* 201–223.

Unger, D., & Cooley, M. (1992). Partner and gradmother contact in Black and White teen parent families. *Journal of Adolescent Health, 13,* 546–552.

Upchurch, D., & McCarthy, J. (1990). The timing of a first birth and high school completion. *American Sociological Review, 55,* 224–234.

Wagner, M., & Clayton, S. (1999). The parents as teachers program: Results from two demonstrations. *Future of Children, 9,* 91–115.

Watson, B. J., Rowe, C. L., & Jones, D. J. (1989, Summer–Winter). Dispelling myths about teenage pregnancy and male responsibility: A research agenda. *Urban League Review,* pp. 119–127.

Way, N., & Leadbeater, B. J. (1999). Pathways toward educational achievement among African American and Puerto Rican adolescent mothers: Reexamining the role of social support from families. *Development and Psychopathology, 11,* 349–365.

Werner, E. E., & Smith, R. S. (1992). *Overcoming the odds: High risk children from birth to adulthood.* Ithaca, NY: Cornell University.

Wertheimer, R., Jager, J., & Moore, K. A. (2000). State policy initiatives for reducing teen and adult nonmarital childbearing: Family planning to family caps. In *Assessing the new federalism* (Series A, No. A-43). Washington, DC: The Urban Institute.

Wertheimer, R. F., & Moore, K. A. (1998). *Teenage sexual activity, pregnancy, and childbearing: An analysis using state-level data.* Washington, DC: Child Trends.

Whitman, T., Borkowski, J., Keogh, D., & Weed, K. (2001). *Interwoven lives: Adolescent mothers and their children.* Mahwah, NJ: Erlbaum.

Wilson, W. J. (1995). *Jobless ghettos: The disappearance of work and its effect on urban life.* New York: Knopf.

Zaslow, M., Dion, M. R., Morrison, D., Weifeld, N., Ogawa, J., & Tabors, P. (1999). Protective factors in development of preschool-age children of young mothers receiving welfare. In E. M. Hetherington (Ed.), *Coping with divorce, single parenting, and remarriage* (pp. 193–223). Mahwah, NJ: Erlbaum.

Zaslow, M., & Eldred, C. (Eds.). (1998). *Parenting behavior in a sample of young mothers in poverty: Results of the New Chance Observational Study*. New York: Manpower Demonstration Research Corporation.

8

FOSTERING RESILIENCE IN CHILDREN OF ALCOHOLIC PARENTS

LAURIE CHASSIN, ADAM C. CARLE, DENIS NISSIM-SABAT, AND KAROL L. KUMPFER

Parental alcoholism presents a significant adverse circumstance for children, increasing the chances that they will experience negative outcomes such as substance abuse, lower academic achievement, and conduct problems. However, there are also a number of protective factors that can act to increase the chances that these children will have positive outcomes. This chapter discusses risk and protective factors and describes strengths-based programs designed to prevent negative outcomes for children of alcoholic parents (COAs). Priorities are identified for research based on strengths-based models. The authors call for a shift to a public health model that emphasizes promoting mental health and make a number of policy recommendations to promote strengths-based research, interventions, organizations, and services in this arena.

* * *

Resilience has been defined as the achievement of competence or positive developmental outcomes under conditions that are adverse or that challenge adaptation (Masten & Coatsworth, 1998). Parental alcoholism not only presents such an adverse circumstance, it is a risk factor of great public health significance because it is highly prevalent. Recent estimates are that one in four U.S. children (19 million) under age 17 are exposed to parental alcoholism (Grant, 2000). Moreover, although this chapter focuses on parental alcoholism, similar adverse circumstances are present for children whose parents abuse illegal drugs (Luthar, Cushing, Merikangas, & Rounsaville, 1998). Thus, interventions to foster resilience among children of addicted parents have the potential to make an important contribution to reducing the risk of substance abuse and increasing positive life outcomes.

DIVERSITY OF OUTCOMES AMONG CHILDREN OF ALCOHOLICS

Reviews of the research (Sher, 1991; West & Prinz, 1987) attest to the negative impact of parental alcoholism on a wide range of child outcomes including conduct problems, psychological distress, lowered academic achievement, and alcohol and drug use. Before interpreting this literature, it is important to recognize some of its methodological limitations. Except for studies of prenatal exposure to alcohol, most studies have focused on paternal (rather than maternal) alcoholism, even though some data suggest that offspring of addicted mothers are at particular risk (Luthar et al., 1998). Moreover, until recently, studies have focused on clinically treated populations rather than community samples (Sher, 1991), and the extent of risk may differ in these samples. Finally, alcoholic parents often suffer from other psychiatric disorders, so that the extent to which children's outcomes are caused specifically by their parents' alcoholism is not well understood.

Despite these limitations, most studies find COAs to have elevated rates of symptoms. For example, COAs show heightened levels of conduct problems at preschool ages (Fitzgerald et al., 1993), elementary school ages (Carbonneau et al., 1998), and adolescence (Chassin, Rogosch, & Barrera, 1991), particularly if their parents also show antisocial behavior (Puttler, Zucker, Fitzgerald, & Bingham, 1998). COAs also show elevations in impulsivity and activity level (Fitzgerald et al., 1993; Tarter, Laird, & Moss, 1990), leading some researchers to view them as "behaviorally undercontrolled." Parental alcoholism has also been linked to anxiety and depression in children (Chassin et al., 1991; Roosa, Gensheimer, Ayers, & Shell, 1989); West and Prinz (1987) noted that COAs had higher levels of anxiety and depression than did controls in 10 of the 11 published studies they examined.

COAs show lower academic achievement than do non-COAs (McGrath, Watson, & Chassin, 1999), even in comparison to depressed children or children of divorce (Schuckit & Chiles, 1978), and they have poorer cognitive functioning than do non-COAs in the preschool years (Noll, Zucker, Fitzgerald, & Curtis, 1992). Sons of male alcoholics who have many alcoholic relatives across generations have been reported to show deficits in verbal and abstract reasoning and verbal learning (Harden & Pihl, 1995; Whipple, Parker, & Noble, 1988). For this subgroup, Pihl, Peterson, and Finn (1990) suggested that cognitive deficits may be caused by heritable dysfunctions of the prefrontal cortex and limbic systems. However, cognitive impairments may also stem from fetal alcohol exposure (Streissguth, Barr, Bookstein, Sampson, & Olson, 1999) or a lack of environmental stimulation or a chaotic home environment (Noll et al., 1992).

Perhaps the most widely studied outcomes among COAs are alcohol and drug use and abuse, for which parental alcoholism is a well-established risk factor. COAs show more adolescent substance use than do their non-COA peers (Chassin et al., 1991), they escalate their use more steeply during adolescence (Chassin, Curran, Hussong, & Colder, 1996), and they are more likely to be diagnosed with alcohol and drug abuse or dependence in young adulthood (Chassin, Pitts, & DeLucia, 1999; Sher, Walitzer, Wood, & Brent, 1991). For COAs, the risks of being diagnosed as alcoholic in adulthood are anywhere from 1.5 times to 9 times higher than those of their non-COA peers (Russell, 1990), depending on the density of the family history of alcoholism or type of alcoholism (Schuckit, 1998) and the extent of their parents' antisocial behavior and alcoholism severity.

These latter data serve to illustrate the great diversity of outcomes for COAs. That is, although having an alcoholic parent affects many aspects of a child's functioning, the magnitude of the effect is quite variable. In fact, the majority of COAs score in the normal range on measures of symptomatology and developmental functioning, and most COAs do not develop substance use disorders (Sher, 1991). The magnitude of the parent alcoholism effect varies with the severity and course of parental alcoholism. For example, children of parents who are actively alcoholic have higher levels of psychological distress than do those whose parents' alcoholism has gone into remission (Moos & Billings, 1982), particularly if the disorders were remitted before the child's sixth birthday (Moss, Clark, & Kirisci, 1997). Moreover, children are less affected if their alcoholic parents have no other associated disorders. For example, Jacob and Leonard (1986) found that among COAs whose alcoholic fathers had no other disorders and whose mothers had no psychiatric diagnoses, only 13% showed "clinical" levels of mental health symptoms, which is not substantially higher than the general population.

In summary, COAs show more conduct problems and emotional distress, lowered academic achievement, and more alcohol and drug use and abuse than do their non-COA peers. However, the magnitude of this effect varies greatly with the severity and course of parental alcoholism and with the extent of associated parental mental health problems, and the majority of COAs score within the normal range.

To date, research on COAs has focused almost exclusively on negative rather than positive outcomes. Furthermore, studies of protective factors have focused more on the absence of negative outcomes rather than the presence of positive outcomes. As a result, little is known about the positive mental health of COAs.

THE NATURE OF PARENT ALCOHOLISM
AS AN ADVERSE CIRCUMSTANCE

Parental alcoholism as an adverse circumstance presents considerable heterogeneity and complexity. It is best conceptualized as a chronic (versus acute) condition that influences child outcomes on multiple levels through multiple mechanisms (Sher, 1991). First, both adoptee and twin studies suggest that some risks are transmitted genetically (McGue, 1994). For example, it has been hypothesized that COAs are physiologically less sensitive to the negative effects of consuming alcohol or drugs (Schuckit, 1998) or more sensitive to its positive effects (Sher, 1991). Some COAs may inherit deficits in planning and organizational skills and under- or overreactivity to stimuli (Pihl et al., 1990). Second, maternal alcoholism carries unique risk through the mechanism of prenatal exposure to alcohol, which can have serious physical and cognitive consequences (Streissguth et al., 1999).

The postnatal environment of COAs is chaotic and unpredictable because an alcoholic parent may alternate not only between intoxication and sobriety within a single day, but also between more prolonged periods of relapse and remission, affecting marital satisfaction, parent–child interaction, and parenting behaviors (Moos & Billings, 1982). Disruptions of family routines, instability, and disorganization are common (Roosa et al., 1989; Sher, Gershuny, Peterson, & Raskin, 1997). COAs are also more likely to have to cope with parental loss and family breakups due to separation, divorce, and the death of a caregiver in childhood (Sher et al., 1997).

The less-than-optimal parenting and family environments that COAs experience extend beyond the relationship between the alcoholic parent and the child. Even in infancy, deficits in mother–infant attachment have been found in families with problem-drinking fathers (Eiden & Leonard, 1996). Moreover, parental alcoholism is associated with higher levels of parent–adolescent conflict (Barrera, Rogosch, & Chassin, 1993) and with higher levels of exposure to family conflict and violence (Miller, Maguin, & Downs, 1997; Sher et al., 1997), although parents are not necessarily the perpetrators of the violence (Miller et al., 1997).

Lastly, parental alcoholism is also associated with elevated levels of more general negative uncontrollable life events (Chassin et al., 1991; Roosa et al., 1989; Sher et al., 1997). In particular, because alcoholics are likely to have less education and lower income (Mullahy & Sindelar, 1994), COAs may have fewer economic resources available to them, and so may be more likely to be exposed to stressors associated with poverty (Fitzgerald & Zucker, 2000). Consistent with their lowered socioeconomic status, COAs are more likely to report that a parent was fired from a job and that their families suffered from financial problems (Sher et al., 1997). Although little is known about COAs' exposure to adverse neighborhoods or school environments, their lowered socioeconomic status raises the possibility that their broader social environments may also be less than ideal.

PATHWAYS TO RESILIENCE

The Resilience Framework (Kumpfer, 1999a) suggests that the development of resilience in high-risk children, such as COAs, is a complex transactional process between the child, his or her parents or caretakers, and their environment. Unfortunately, not enough research has yet been conducted to understand these resilience processes. In contrast to the substantial literature on the relationship between parental alcoholism and children's psychological problems, studies have generally failed to examine the development of resilience and competent performance or positive outcomes in COAs, although some relevant work has been done on the absence of negative outcomes. Generally, these studies have sought to specify factors that protect COAs from the negative outcomes associated with parental alcoholism. For example, Werner (1986) followed COAs from birth to age 18 and reported that those who did not develop serious problems had experienced fewer negative stress events, had more cuddly and affectionate infant temperaments, and had higher self-esteem and better communication skills.

Several studies have focused on positive family environment factors and have discovered a few protective factors or processes. Wolin, Bennett, Noonan, and Teitelbaum (1980) found that children in alcoholic families that maintained consistent rituals (e.g., vacations, birthday celebrations) were less likely to develop alcohol problems. Similarly, COAs whose families had higher levels of organization were less likely to initiate illegal drug use (Hussong & Chassin, 1997).

Higher levels of family cohesion and support have also been shown to enhance outcomes for COAs. Farrell, Barnes, and Banerjee (1995) found that COAs showed high levels of adolescent deviance and distress when family cohesion was low, but that these effects were reduced when family cohesion was higher. Similarly, Barrera and his colleagues (1993) found that COAs in low-conflict families resembled non-COAs, whereas COAs who experienced high levels of family conflict showed elevated levels of psychological distress. The notion that family cohesion and support are associated with better outcomes among COAs is consistent with Moos and Billings's (1982) finding that families in which paternal alcoholism had remitted after treatment had both higher levels of family cohesion and lower levels of psychological distress among their children. These data suggest that parental recovery may promote resilience for COAs, perhaps because the family environment also recovers. However, because these findings are from a sample of fathers who received alcohol treatment, they may not generalize to untreated families (DeLucia, Belz, & Chassin, 2001).

Research has also suggested that parental supervision is an important protective factor for COAs. Curran and Chassin (1996) found that consistent discipline and monitoring of their adolescents' behavior by mothers were associated with better outcomes among both COAs and non-COAs. However, consistency of discipline includes monitoring and positive reinforcement and should not be taken as synonymous with punishment, which has been associated with poorer outcomes among COAs (Vitaro, Dobkin, Carbonneau, & Tremblay, 1996).

Finally, some data point to the importance of extrafamilial influences. Ohannessian and Hesselbrock (1993) found that COAs with high levels of support from friends closely resembled non-COAs, whereas COAs with less peer support consumed more alcohol and had more alcohol-related problems. Moreover, Jordan and Chassin (1998) found that adolescent COAs who had greater involvement in positive activities outside the home were less likely to develop a substance use disorder in young adulthood. In the case of parental alcoholism, where adverse circumstances exist within the family environment, extrafamilial influences may be particularly important.

In summary, although research has not focused specifically on positive outcomes and competent performance among COAs, some work has been done to identify protective factors. These studies suggest that parental support and control and family environments that are characterized by stability, cohesion, organization, and preservation of routines and rituals are associated with better outcomes. These critical family protective processes (e.g., family attachment, parental supervision and monitoring, and organization and communication) were found to be the most important protective factors of later substance use in a major cross-site study of 8,500 high-risk youths funded by the Center for Substance Abuse Prevention (Springer et al., 2000). In addition, high levels of friend support and involvement in positive activities outside the home reduce negative outcomes for COAs. Finally, it has been suggested that parental recovery from alcoholism is itself protective.

RESEARCH NEEDS

Studies are needed that examine the prevalence and the predictors of positive outcomes (rather than simply the absence of negative outcomes) among COAs. Moreover, the limited body of existing knowledge on protective or resilience-promoting factors for COAs has focused largely on parenting and family factors. Little is known about the effects of extrafamilial supports (e.g., after-school programs, mentoring programs, tutoring programs, recreational programs). More research on extrafamilial influences is clearly warranted. More also needs to be known about the effect of parental recovery on children's outcomes. Finally, there is very little empirical evaluation of preventive interventions among COAs.

COA-SPECIFIC PREVENTION PROGRAMS

School-Based Primary Prevention Programs

Very few prevention programs have been developed specifically for COAs (Kumpfer, 1989; Williams, 1990). Most COA-specific programs are limited to school-based COA education programs that are relatively short in duration and are conducted with small groups of students who self-identify as children of alcohol or drug abusers (Price & Emshoff, 1997). Although there may be many such school-based COA programs, very few of them are described in the prevention literature, and even fewer have outcome evaluations (Price & Emshoff, 1997). Because of the positive research results for behavioral training models, COA programs are including more social competency skills training. In one of the few research-based models, Roosa and his colleagues (1989) found positive changes in knowledge, social support, and emotion-focused coping behavior in their 8-week, school-based COA program. Emshoff's (1990) STAR program teaches students social competency skills and provides accurate information about alcoholism and its effects on the family. Participants reported more friends and stronger social relations, increased sense of control, and improved self-concept with less depression.

Family-Focused Prevention Programs for Children of Alcoholics or Children of Substance Abusers

Several programs specific to COAs or children of substance abusers that include a family strengthening approach to increasing resilience through family skills training have been developed and tested in federally funded prevention research supported by the National Institute on Drug Abuse (NIDA), the Center for Substance Abuse Prevention (CSAP), and the National Institute of Mental Health, namely the Strengthening Families Program (Kumpfer, 1998; Kumpfer, Molgaard, & Spoth, 1996) and Focus on Families (Catalano, Haggerty, Gainey, & Hoppe, 1997). Positive results have been found for the Strengthening Families Program in improving social competencies and family relationships and in reducing later tobacco, alcohol, and drug use in children of addicted parents in treatment. Moreover, this program has been modified and evaluated for rural and urban African American, Latino, Asian and Pacific Islander, and American Indian families (Kumpfer, Alvarado, Smith, & Bellamy, 2002).

Community-Based COA Prevention Programs

There are very few community-based COA programs, but one popular one is Alateen. This self-help support program for COAs, which is implemented in the community through Alcoholics Anonymous, provides a safe environment in which children can share their feelings, experiences, and tips for surviving their parent's addictions and negative behaviors. The Cambridge and Somerville Program for Alcoholism Rehabilitation (CASPAR) program (Davis et al., 1994) offered junior high COAs or non-COAs a range of after-school services at schools or in community settings. DiCicco, Davis, Hogan, MacLean, and Orenstein (1984) found that mixing COAs and non-COAs in alcohol education groups compared to COA-specific groups resulted in reduced drinking and intentions to drink among COAs. Moreover, because of stigmatization issues, recruitment of COAs was easier for the basic education group than for the COA-specific group. These results suggest that nonspecific COA prevention programs may be a valuable option for recruiting and delivering services to children of addicted or abusing parents.

EFFECTIVE NON-COA-SPECIFIC PREVENTION PROGRAMS

Research-based prevention interventions developed for other high-risk youths can also be very effective for COAs if they address COAs' risk factors. In this section we summarize non-COA-specific prevention interventions that may be capable of strengthening resilience to later alcohol and drug use among COAs, organized by their targeted risk factors.

Programs That Increase Behavioral Control and Social Competency

A number of preventive interventions have been developed that are helpful for increasing social competencies, emotional management, and behavioral control, and these may be useful for children of alcoholics who manifest conduct disorders and aggression. When applied universally in classrooms (Botvin, 2000; Ialongo et al., 1999), these programs can reduce conduct problems and promote healthier friendships with prosocial children, and hence prevent substance abuse and violence. They are effective without the children having to be identified as children of alcoholics or drug abusers. Some of the indicated prevention programs, however, do require that the teacher refer children with aggressive tendencies and conduct disorders to a pull-out group. Because of possible negative contagion and labeling effects, it is best to also include socially skilled youths in the group.

Programs to Increase Emotional Resilience, Happiness, Self-Esteem, and Humor

Research on resilience in COAs (Werner, 1997; Wolin, 1995) suggests that hopefulness, happiness, and emotional management increase positive outcomes in COAs. Universal prevention programs that support improved mental health and resilience also help COAs. One middle school resilience program is the Strengthening Families Program for 10- to 14-year-olds (Kumpfer et al., 1996). This seven-session family intervention was found in a randomized control trial to significantly reduce alcohol, tobacco, and marijuana initiation (Spoth, Redmond, Trudeau, & Shin, 2002), with a $9.60 cost–benefit ratio (Spoth, Guyll, & Day, 2002). Because resilience studies with adult children of alcoholics (Kumpfer & Bluth, in press) have found that meaning or purpose in life is the most critical resilience factor in positive life adaptation, this new Strengthening Families Program focused the first sessions on parents supporting children in developing dreams and goals. Having children and their parents focus on hopefulness and positive dreams for the future has been found to reduce depression, and positive psychology suggests that feelings of well-being are more enhanced by doing kindness to others than by doing nice things for oneself. Thus, the program encourages youths to think about their talents and ways they can use these talents to help others through kind acts and a productive and successful career. Hence, parenting and family skills training programs that teach parents to negotiate chores, create chore charts, and monitor and reward completion of chores help to increase positive self-concept and increase happiness in COAs.

Because COAs have a higher likelihood of having alexithymia (i.e., an inability to identify feelings), some COA programs focus on feelings identification training and on training parents to label feelings the child appears to be having. This type of intervention may also help to promote stronger parent-child attachments (Eiden & Leonard, 1996).

Anxiety in COAs can be reduced by increasing the predictability of the family environment, as well as school and community environments, through family strengthening prevention programs that increase family organization and family management and foster increased supportiveness and feelings of love. COAs often do have realistic reasons to be worried about their parent's welfare, their own welfare, and the stability of the family, because child abuse and neglect (Kumpfer & Bayes, 1995), job loss and poverty, divorce, and parent deaths are more common in families with an alcoholic parent (Sher et al., 1997). Emotion-focused and problem-focused coping skills training within COA prevention programs (Nastasi & DeZolt, 1994) can help children to talk through feelings, reframe the negative aspects of situations, create emotional distance from their fears, and develop other emotionally supportive relationships with other adults. Mentoring and after-school programs can be very helpful to COAs in developing these needed supportive relationships with other caring adults. As found by Jordan and Chassin (1998), involvement in positive activities outside the home by young COAs tends to reduce the risk of substance use disorders in young adults.

Programs to Increase Cognitive Resilience Characteristics

Research with COAs (Johnson & Leff, 1999; Werner, 1997) has found that cognitive resilience characteristics include a conceptual understanding of the parent's disease and relationships and the capability to distance one-self from the alcoholic parent in terms of identification, humor, and academic skills and mastery. Both traditional COA educational programs and community media campaigns can be used to promote these resilience factors.

COA EDUCATIONAL INTERVENTIONS, SCREENING, AND REFERRAL

Like people affected by any "disease of lifestyle" (such as heart disease and diabetes), COAs and their parents need to know the results of the risk and resilience research on children of alcoholics. They need to know what signs and symptoms to watch for that might indicate that they or their children are high or low in resilience or in risk factors. Research has found that adolescent COAs who are aware of their family risk status drink significantly less than those who do not have this information (Kumpfer, 1989). Further research is needed to determine both the optimum age at which to inform COAs of their family history risk status and what kind of information is important to provide at different ages or stages of development. Unfortunately, despite years of research on COAs, the general public and even recovering alcoholics are woefully uninformed about the warning signs of a developmental trajectory likely to lead to alcohol or substance abuse disorders and how to intervene to increase resilience. Because of this, most COAs never receive any supportive services. Gatekeepers (i.e., physicians, teachers, youth workers, and parents) should be trained to identify COAs and their primary problems so appropriate referrals for intervention services can be made (Kumpfer, 2002).

Public media and education campaigns need to be developed that will disseminate this research and allow COAs to conduct risk and resilience assessments for themselves. They need to know that a high tolerance for alcohol and an ability "to drink others under the table" are not good signs. Public education campaigns are also needed to reduce stigma and provide additional legal, social, educational, and academic supports for COAs in a nonstigmatizing environment. Parents and youths should be informed that living with an alcoholic parent can, in fact, lead to increased cognitive, behavioral, and emotional management problems. Providing skills for coping with stress can improve COAs' ability to function in very stressful careers and in times of distress, thereby improving pride and self-confidence and reducing fear of a self-fulfilling prophecy. Prevention programs focusing on improving cognitive mastery, study skills, and reading and math skills all improve COAs' possible deficits in verbal and conceptual skills. Tutoring programs focusing on phonetic reading have been found to improve high-risk youths' grades and school behaviors.

POLICY RECOMMENDATIONS

> Aunt Sid wrote me and said I was resilient. I had to look the word up.
> . . . Resilient. I liked being resilient because it sounded like a jewel glittering in the sunlight. (Hamilton, 1998, pp. 91–92)

Resilience has been defined as the achievement of competence or positive developmental outcomes under conditions that are adverse or that challenge adaptation (Masten & Coatsworth, 1998); however, an operational definition of this term needs to be developed. The research on resilience of COAs points to the need to develop public policies that will result in a paradigm shift that comes closer to a public health model.

The Surgeon General's Report on Mental Health (U.S. Department of Health and Human Services, 1999) outlined the importance of studying mental health and substance abuse problems from a public health perspective. A public health model focuses on community-based and population-based methods of intervention, epidemiological surveillance, health promotion, disease prevention, and access to services (U.S. Department of Health and Human Services, 1999).

This chapter has identified the significant risk and protective factors faced by COAs and supports research that is based on a resilience model. However, inherent in the resilience model is the potential for misinterpretation by policymakers. Policymakers may claim that because some COAs survive with assistance from informal support systems within the school, family, and community, there is no need for government-supported intervention programs. The shift toward a resilience model rejects the position that children can lift themselves up by their bootstraps and get on with their lives. Rather, it maintains that a psychological model based solely on defects and deficits limits the potential for individual and social change.

A shift toward a public health model with COAs will shift the emphasis from diagnosis and treatment of the disorder toward promoting mental health. For example, one of the goals of the World Federation for Mental Health (1998) focuses on mental health promotion and the development of competencies, skills, and assets that lead to successful coping; these goals do not focus on the deficits associated with mental illness.

Successful interventions in the various domains, including individual, peer, family, school, community, and society, will be required to build resilience and competencies in COAs. Policymakers will need to consider this paradigm shift and the research supporting a resilience-based approach in developing policies affecting COAs. We make the following six recommendations for policy decisions regarding COAs:

1. Policymakers at the federal, state, and local levels should provide adequate funds for research, field tests, and wide-scale

dissemination of effective prevention approaches for children of alcohol and drug abusers.

2. National surveys should include information that assesses and evaluates resilience-based behaviors.

3. Legislation affecting agencies providing services to COAs should include language that specifically stipulates the importance of a resilience-based approach.

4. Future research should maintain the privacy and confidentiality of COAs enrolled in prevention, education, and intervention programs.

5. Results of interagency collaboration will be critical in shaping the public policy debate related to COAs.

6. A focus on resilience-based approaches should be significantly increased in the annual National Drug Control Strategy produced by the Office of National Drug Control Policy.

1. Provide Funding for Research and Dissemination

Primary prevention and intervention strategies that improve these children's developmental outcomes should be implemented and continuously evaluated to support improvements in the delivery of services. Improved research designs and methods should be used that include better definitions of resilience and ways to measure risks and outcomes of COAs (Kumpfer, 1999b). Research on resilience, as well as biological signs or markers of vulnerability in COAs, should be continued to allow for better predictive and assessment systems that balance both risk and protective factors.

2. Assess Resilience-Based Behaviors in National Surveys

If a paradigm shift is going to occur, additional data will need to be collected. The following surveys, among others, should all incorporate questions that assess strengths-based behaviors and resources in respondents:

- the National Household Survey on Drug Abuse administered by the Substance Abuse and Mental Health Services Administration (SAMHSA);
- the High School Senior Survey or the Monitoring the Future survey conducted by the University of Michigan under a grant from NIDA;
- the National Parents' Resource Institute for Drug Education (PRIDE);
- the Youth Risk Behavior Survey administered by the Centers for Disease Control and Prevention (CDC); and
- the National Longitudinal Study of Adolescent Health of the National Institute of Child Health and Human Development (NICHD).

These national surveys can provide researchers with valuable information on resilience-based behaviors that can lead to prudent public policies affecting COAs.

3. Stipulate Importance of Resilience-Based Approach for Agencies That Serve COAs

Future legislation should identify the importance of strengthening the environment of COAs by targeting interventions at both the family and community levels. In addition, future legislation should specifically highlight the protective factors that research has shown to be effective in building resilience in children of COAs.

Legislation should also include language that incorporates a resilience-based approach for educators, physicians, social workers, school nurses, criminal justice and juvenile justice professionals, psychologists, guidance counselors, child care specialists, and alcohol and drug counselors engaged in identifying, intervening, and treating COAs. Furthermore, support should be given to training these specialists to use interdisciplinary approaches to develop integrated models of intervention that provide services to both children and parents.

4. Maintain Privacy and Confidentiality of COAs

A crucial issue in addressing the needs of COAs is the difficulty in identifying them. Typically, psychological services are provided to COAs after their parents have entered a treatment program. Some groups, such as the National Association of Children of Alcoholics, support the position that children should be allowed to seek treatment without parental consent. This position may be defensible in certain circumstances, but it also raises a number of concerns.

Other alternatives include providing universal interventions that are provided or available to all youths in a setting (such as school-based programs that enhance competence) and providing services that are accessible by children and adolescents without barriers of cost, transportation, need for extensive parental involvement, or public labeling (such as services offered through school-based health clinics). We believe that labeling children as COAs can lead to stigmatization, and future research should determine the impact of such labeling (including whether it offsets the benefits of treatment). Providing services to children without parental consent will require extensive empirical research and public debate to define the circumstances under which this should occur. Attention should also be given to developing and using methodologies that maximize privacy and confidentiality protections for COAs, including the use of computer-based technologies.

5. Enhance Federal Interagency Collaboration

CSAP, NIDA, the National Institute on Alcoholism and Alcohol Abuse (NIAAA), NICHD, and the CDC must begin to work collaboratively on developing research programs that address the issues faced by COAs. By working collaboratively, they can pool financial resources and address one of the major issues involved in this field: How will COAs be identified, and what will be the most effective way of providing integrated services? Interagency collaboration will lead to blended funding in which research programs will be integrated and complement each other. The Drug and Underage Alcohol Research program sponsored by NIDA and NIAAA is just one example of such collaboration.

Emshoff and Anyan (1991) recommended the use of action research, a model that uses prevention interventions to study both the epidemiology and etiology of substance abuse over time. Action research can be used in studies of the most effective interventions for reducing substance abuse through a continuous cycle of testing basic theoretical hypotheses within applied research. This model stresses the dissemination of results and the field testing of effective research-based interventions and increases the relationship between research and practice. Agencies such as SAMHSA, CSAP, CDC, and NIDA should conduct field trials or effectiveness trials with modifications to make the interventions more acceptable and effective with diverse populations (e.g., different cultural groups, geographic locations, rural or urban environment).

6. Increase Focus on Resilience-Based Approaches in the National Drug Control Strategy

The Office of National Drug Control Policy was established in 1988 as part of the Anti-Drug Abuse Act of 1988. Each year, the office presents a National Drug Control Strategy (Office of National Drug Control Policy, 1998). The 1998 report identified five major goals; the first goal, "Educate and Enable America's Youth to Reject Illegal Drugs as Well as Alcohol and Tobacco," is the one goal whose purpose comes closest to the general area of prevention. However, it received only 11.8% of the FY 1999 budget for drug funding. It is imperative that future strategy reports incorporate a resilience approach as a goal and that the percentage of funding for this goal be increased significantly.

CONCLUSION

As this chapter demonstrates, parental alcoholism is a prevalent and significant risk factor for a broad range of negative outcomes among children, including conduct problems, mental health problems, alcohol and drug problems, cognitive deficits, impaired coping, and lowered academic achievement. However, the wide variation in outcomes among COAs offers encouraging opportunities both to study resilience and to design and implement programs to promote resilience for this high-risk group. Both programs that strengthen families as well as those that provide extra-familial supports should be implemented, particularly those that avoid the dangers of labeling and stigma for COAs. Incorporating insights from resilience models into legislation and ongoing national epidemiological studies will help to enhance our knowledge base. This stronger empirical knowledge base, along with added interagency collaboration, will enhance the provision of services for children of addicted parents.

REFERENCES

Anti-Drug Abuse Act of 1988. P.L. 100-690 §201.

Barrera, M., Jr., Rogosch, F., & Chassin, L. (1993). Social support and conflict among adolescent children of alcoholics. *Journal of Personality and Social Psychology, 64*, 602–613.

Botvin, G. (2000). Preventing adolescent drug abuse through life skills training: Theory, evidence of effectiveness, and implementation issues. In W. B. Hansen, S. M. Giles, & M. D. Fearnow-Kenney (Eds.), *Improving prevention effectiveness* (pp. 141–154). Greensboro, NC: Tanglewood Research.

Carbonneau, R., Tremblay, R., Vitaro, F., Dobkin, P., Saucier, J., & Pihl, R. (1998). Paternal alcoholism, paternal absence, and the development of problem behaviors in boys from six to twelve years. *Journal of Studies on Alcohol, 59*, 387–398.

Catalano, R. F., Haggerty, K. P., Gainey, R. R., & Hoppe, M. J. (1997). Reducing parental risk factors for children's substance misuse: Preliminary outcomes with opiate-addicted parents. *Substance Use & Misuse, 32*, 699–721.

Chassin, L., Curran, P., Hussong, A., & Colder, C. (1996). The relation of parent alcoholism to adolescent substance use: A longitudinal follow-up study. *Journal of Abnormal Psychology, 105*, 70–80.

Chassin, L., Pitts, S., & DeLucia, C. (1999). A longitudinal study of children of alcoholics: Predicting young adult substance use disorders, anxiety, and depression. *Journal of Abnormal Psychology, 108*, 106–119.

Chassin, L., Rogosch, F., & Barrera, M., Jr. (1991). Substance use and symptomatology among adolescent children of alcoholics. *Journal of Abnormal Psychology, 100*, 449–463.

Curran, P., & Chassin, L. (1996). A longitudinal study of parenting as a protective factor for children of alcoholic fathers. *Journal of Studies on Alcohol, 57*, 305–313.

Davis, R. B., Wolfe, J., Orenstein, A., Bergamo, P., Buetens, K., Fraster, B., et al. (1994). Intervening with high risk youth: A program model. *Adolescence, 29*, 763–774.

DeLucia, C., Belz, A., & Chassin, L. (2001). Do adolescent symptomatology and family environment vary over time with fluctuations in paternal alcohol impairment? *Developmental Psychology, 37,* 207–216.

DiCicco, L., Davis, R. B., Hogan, J., MacLean, A., & Orenstein, A. (1984). Group experiences for children of alcoholics. *Alcohol, Health and Research World, 8,* 20–24.

Eiden, R., & Leonard, K. (1996). Paternal alcohol use and the mother-infant relationship. *Development and Psychopathology, 8,* 307–323.

Emshoff, J. G. (1990). A preventive intervention with children of alcoholics. *Prevention in Human Services, 7,* 225–253.

Emshoff, J. G., & Anyan, L. L. (1991). From prevention to treatment: Issues for school-aged children of alcoholics. In M. Galanter (Ed.), *Recent developments in alcoholism* (Vol. 9, pp. 327–346). New York: Plenum Press.

Farrell, M., Barnes, G., & Banerjee, S. (1995). Family cohesion as a buffer against the effects of problem-drinking fathers on psychological distress, deviant behavior, and heavy drinking in adolescents. *Journal of Health and Social Behavior, 36,* 377–385.

Fitzgerald, H., Sullivan, L., Ham, H., Zucker, R., Bruckel, S., Schneider, A., et al. (1993). Predictors of behavior problems in three-year-old sons of alcoholics: Evidence for the onset of risk. *Child Development, 64,* 110–123.

Fitzgerald, H., & Zucker, R. (2000). The clinical and social ecology of childhood for children of alcoholics: Description of a study and implications for a differentiated social policy. In H. Fitzgerald & R. Zucker (Eds.), *Children of addiction* (pp. 109–141). New York: Routledge Falmer.

Grant, B. F. (2000). Estimates of U.S. children exposed to alcohol abuse and dependence in the family. *American Journal of Public Health, 90,* 112–115.

Hamilton, J. (1998). *The book of Ruth.* New York: Anchor.

Harden, P., & Pihl, R. (1995). Cognitive function, cardiovascular reactivity, and behavior in boys at high risk for alcoholism. *Journal of Abnormal Psychology, 104,* 94–103.

Hussong, A., & Chassin, L. (1997). Substance use initiation among adolescent children of alcoholics: Examining protective factors. *Journal of Studies on Alcohol, 58,* 272–279.

Ialongo, N. S., Werthamer, L., Kellam, S. G., Brown, C. H., Wang, S., & Lin, Y. (1999). Proximal impact of two first-grade preventive interventions on the early risk behaviors for later substance abuse, depression, and antisocial behavior. *American Journal of Community Psychology, 27,* 599–641.

Jacob, T., & Leonard, K. (1986). Psychological functioning in children of alcoholic fathers, depressed fathers, and control fathers. *Journal of Studies on Alcohol, 47,* 373–380.

Johnson, J., & Leff, M. (1999). Children of substance abusers: Overview of research findings. *Journal of the American Academy of Pediatrics, 103,* 1085–1099.

Jordan, L., & Chassin, L. (1998, August). *Protective factors for children of alcoholics: Parenting, family environment, child personality and contextual supports.* Presented at the 106th Annual Convention of the American Psychological Association, San Francisco.

Kumpfer, K. L. (1989). Promising prevention strategies for high-risk children of substance abusers. *OSAP High Risk Youth Update, 2*(1), 1–3.

Kumpfer, K. L. (1998). The Strengthening Families Program. In R. S. Ashery, E. Robertson, & K. L. Kumpfer (Eds.), *Drug abuse prevention through family interventions* (NIDA Research Monograph No. 177, NIH Publication No. 97-4135). Rockville, MD: National Institute on Drug Abuse.

Kumpfer, K. L. (1999a). Factors and processes contributing to resilience: The resilience framework. In M. D. Glantz & J. L. Johnson (Eds.), *Resilience and development: Positive life adaptions* (pp. 179–224). New York: Kluwer Academic/Plenum Publishers.

Kumpfer, K. L. (1999b). Outcome measures of interventions in the study of children of substance abusing parents. *Journal of the American Academy of Pediatrics, 103,* 1128–1144.

Kumpfer, K. L. (2002). Prevention of alcohol and drug use: What works? *Journal of Substance Abuse, 23* (Suppl. 3), 25–44.

Kumpfer, K. L., Alvarado, R., Smith, P., & Bellamy, N. (2002). Cultural sensitivity and adaptation in family-based prevention interventions. *Prevention Science, 3,* 241–246.

Kumpfer, K. L., & Bayes, J. (1995). Child abuse and alcohol, tobacco, and other drug abuse: Causality, coincidence, or controversy? In J. H. Jaffe (Ed.), *The encyclopedia of drugs and alcohol* (Vol. 1, pp. 217–222). New York: Simon & Schuster.

Kumpfer, K. L., & Bluth, B. (in press). Parent/child transactional processes predictive of substance abuse resilience or vulnerability. *Substance Use & Misuse.*

Kumpfer, K. L., Molgaard, V., & Spoth, R. (1996). The Strengthening Families Program for the prevention of delinquency and drug use. In R. D. Peters, & R. McMahon (Eds.), *Preventing childhood disorders, substance abuse, and delinquency* (pp. 241–267). Newbury Park, CA: Sage.

Luthar, S., Cushing, G., Merikangas, K., & Rounsaville, B. (1998). Multiple jeopardy: Risk and protective factors among addicted mothers' offspring. *Development and Psychopathology, 10,* 117–136.

Masten, A., & Coatsworth, D. (1998). The development of competence in favorable and unfavorable environments. *American Psychologist, 53,* 205–220.

McGrath, C., Watson, A., & Chassin, L. (1999). Academic achievement in adolescent children of alcoholics. *Journal of Studies on Alcohol, 60,* 18–26.

McGue, M. (1994). Genes, environment, and the etiology of alcoholism. In R. Zucker, G. Boyd, & J. Howard (Eds.), *The development of alcohol problems: Exploring the biopsychosocial matrix of risk* (NIAAA Research Monograph No. 26, NIH Publication No. 94-3495, pp. 1–40). Rockville, MD: Public Health Service, National Institute of Health and National Institute of Alcohol Abuse and Alcoholism.

Miller, B., Maguin, E., & Downs, W. (1997). Alcohol, drugs, and violence in children's lives. *Recent Developments in Alcoholism, 13,* 357–385.

Moos, R., & Billings, A. (1982). Children of alcoholics during the recovery process: Alcoholics and matched control families. *Addictive Behaviors, 7*, 155–163.

Moss, H., Clark, D., & Kirisci, L. (1997). Timing of paternal substance use disorder cessation and effects on problem behaviors in sons. *American Journal of Addiction, 6*, 30–37.

Mullahy, J., & Sindelar, J. (1994). Alcoholism and income: The role of indirect effects. *Milbank Quarterly, 72*, 359–375.

Nastasi, B. K., & DeZolt, D. M. (1994). *School interventions for children of alcoholics.* New York: Guilford Press.

Noll, R., Zucker, R., Fitzgerald, H., & Curtis, J. (1992). Cognitive and motoric functioning of sons of alcoholic fathers and controls: The early childhood years. *Child Development, 28*, 665–675.

Office of National Drug Control Policy. (1998). *The National Drug Control Policy, 1998.* Washington, DC: Author.

Ohannessian, C., & Hesselbrock, V. (1993). The influence of perceived social support on the relationship between family history of alcoholism and drinking behavior. *Addiction, 88*, 1651–1658.

Pihl, R., Peterson, J., & Finn, P. (1990). The inherited predisposition to alcoholism: Characteristics of sons of male alcoholics. *Journal of Abnormal Psychology, 99*, 291–301.

Price, A. W., & Emshoff, J. G. (1997). Breaking the cycle of addiction: Prevention and intervention with children of alcoholics. *Alcohol, Health and Research World, 21*, 241–246.

Puttler, L., Zucker, R., Fitzgerald, H., & Bingham, C. (1998). Behavioral outcomes among children of alcoholics during the early and middle childhood years: Familial subtype variations. *Alcoholism: Clinical and Experimental Research, 22*, 1962–1972.

Roosa, M., Gensheimer, L., Ayers, T., & Shell, R. A. (1989). Preventive intervention for children in alcoholic families: Results of a pilot study. *Family Relations, 38*, 295–300.

Russell, M. (1990). Prevalence of alcoholism among children of alcoholics. In M. Windle & J. Searles (Eds.), *Children of alcoholics: Critical perspectives* (pp. 9–38). New York: Guilford Press.

Schuckit, M. (1998). Biological, psychological, and environmental predictors of the alcoholism risk: A longitudinal study. *Journal of Studies on Alcohol, 59*, 558–565.

Schuckit, M. A., & Chiles, J. A. (1978). Family history as a diagnostic aid in two samples of adolescents. *Journal of Nervous and Mental Disease, 166*, 165–176.

Sher, K. (1991). *Children of alcoholics: A critical appraisal of theory and research.* Chicago: University of Chicago Press.

Sher, K., Gershuny, B., Peterson, L., & Raskin, G. (1997). The role of childhood stressors in the intergenerational transmission of alcohol use disorders. *Journal of Studies on Alcohol, 58*, 414–427.

Sher, K., Walitzer, K., Wood, P., & Brent, E. (1991). Characteristics of children of alcoholics: Putative risk factors, substance use and abuse, and psychopathology. *Journal of Abnormal Psychology, 100,* 427–448.

Spoth, R. L., Guyll, M., & Day, S. X. (2002). Universal family-focused interventions in alcohol-use disorder prevention: Cost-effectiveness and cost-benefit analyses of two interventions. *Journal of Studies on Alcohol, 63,* 219–228.

Spoth, R. L., Redmond, C., Trudeau, L., & Shin, C. (2002). Longitudinal substance initiation outcomes for a universal preventive intervention combining family and school programs. *Psychology of Addictive Behaviors, 16,* 129–134.

Springer, J. F., Sambrano, S., Sale, E., Nistler, M., Kisim, R., & Hermann, J. (2000). *The national cross-site evaluation of high-risk youth programs: Final report.* Rockville, MD: EMT Associates and ORC Macro, prepared for the Center for Substance Abuse Prevention.

Streissguth, A., Barr, H., Bookstein, F., Sampson, P., & Olson, H. (1999). The long-term neurocognitive consequences of prenatal alcohol exposure: A 14-year study. *Psychological Science, 10,* 186–190.

Tarter, R., Laird, S., & Moss, J. (1990). Neuropsychological and neurophysiological characteristics of children of alcoholics. In M. Windle & J. Searles (Eds.), *Children of alcoholics: Critical perspectives* (pp. 73–98). New York: Guilford Press.

U.S. Department of Health and Human Services. (1999). *Mental health: A report of the Surgeon General.* Rockville, MD: Author.

Vitaro, F., Dobkin, P., Carbonneau, R., & Tremblay, R. (1996). Personal and familial characteristics of resilient sons of male alcoholics. *Addiction, 91,* 1161–1177.

Werner, E. E. (1986). Resilient offspring of alcoholics: A longitudinal study from birth to age 18. *Journal of Studies on Alcohol, 47,* 34–40.

Werner, E. E. (1997). Vulnerable but invincible: High risk children from birth to adulthood. *Acta Pediatrica Supplement, 422,* 103–105.

West, M. O., & Prinz, R. (1987). Parental alcoholism and childhood psychopathology. *Psychological Bulletin, 102,* 204–218.

Whipple, S., Parker, E., & Noble, E. (1988). An atypical neurocognitive profile in alcoholic fathers and their sons. *Journal of Studies on Alcohol, 49,* 240–244.

Williams, C. N. (1990). Prevention and treatment approaches for children of alcoholics. In M. Windle & J. Searles (Eds.), *Children of alcoholics* (pp. 187–216). New York: Guilford Press.

Wolin, S. (1995). Resilience among youth growing up in substance-abusing families. *Pediatric Clinics of North America, 42,* 415–429.

Wolin, S., Bennett, L., Noonan, D., & Teitelbaum, M. (1980). Disrupted family rituals. *Journal of Studies on Alcohol, 41,* 199–214.

World Federation for Mental Health. (1998). *World Federation for Mental Health strategies vision statement.* Baltimore, MD: Author.

9

MENTAL HEALTH SERVICES: A FAMILY SYSTEMS APPROACH

WILLIAM BEARDSLEE AND JANE KNITZER

Using the example of families with depressive disorders, the authors argue that children's development can be enhanced by family-centered approaches to mental health care when a parent has a mental illness. Families respond as a system or unit to the stresses of parent mental illness. With support, most parents with mental illness can continue to be effective parents, and strengthening parenting roles can enhance child outcomes in these families. Effective family-centered approaches could minimize family disruptions, out-of-home child placements, and the intergenerational transfer of illnesses. This chapter recommends policies to increase families' early access to integrative mental health care through universal coverage.

* * *

Traditional mental health services provided through one-on-one relationships between health care providers and ill individuals may be inadequate when these individuals are also parents. Families respond as a unit to parent mental illness. These illnesses not only challenge parenting competence, but also expose children to many of the stresses that precede and are subsequent to the parent illness. In this chapter, we focus on families where a parent has a depressive disorder; however, challenges for families are similar whenever a parent experiences a serious mental health problem. We propose new treatment strategies for supporting families with chronic mental illnesses both

157

over time and during acute episodes. Family-level support is essential to halt the intergenerational transfer of risks for these disorders and to sustain and promote competence in both parents and children. All family members face these adversities together.

EPIDEMIOLOGY AND CLASSIFICATION OF DEPRESSION

There is little doubt that parent mental illnesses and their effects on children present a significant social and public health challenge. The Institute of Medicine (1994) indicates that as many as one third of American adults may experience a diagnosable mental disorder at some point in their life. In terms of depression, it has been estimated that 10%to 20% of adults will experience an episode of affective illness at some point during their lifetimes (Kessler et al., 1994; Robins & Regier, 1991). Because a significant portion of these adults are parents at any point in time, several million children are growing up in homes where parents have a severe mood disorder, and many more children are exposed to parental depression at some time during their childhood (Beardslee, Versage, & Gladstone, 1998).

Depression does not occur at random. Specific risk factors precede its onset. In adults, these factors have been grouped into two broad classes— those having to do with losses, bereavement, and other social adversities, and those having to do with a clustering of mental illness in families. The environment or the psychosocial surroundings of the individual contribute to the etiology of mental illness, and there may be familial or genetic factors. In particular, depression can result from severe psychosocial stressors (e.g., loss, acute and chronic stresses, exposure to violence), from a genetic cause, or from a combination of genetic vulnerabilities and environmental factors. In simplest terms, individuals with many relatives with major depressions are at higher risk, and those undergoing loss, social disadvantage, bereavement, and stress are at highest risk. In understanding the impact of parent mental illness on children, it is important to recognize that the children in these homes experience the same life events and losses and have the same ill relatives (e.g., grandparents) as the parents themselves.

There is increasing evidence that positive, close social relationships provide a buffer and support against a variety of risk factors, so that augmenting the effectiveness of these relationships may have widespread benefits (Eisenberg, 1979). On the other hand, disruptions or violence in these relationships are potent determinants of increased risk that can precipitate depressive episodes or sustain chronic depression and other mental health problems. A comprehensive approach to prevention of depression would require a substantial reduction in exposure to violence and in risk for child abuse and neglect (Beardslee, 2002); researchers have become increasingly aware of the enormous costs of these risk factors (Institute of Medicine, 1994). Adults who have had significant losses (particularly job loss, family disruptions, and bereavement) are vulnerable to depressive symptomatology and disorder. A number of programs (Lieberman & Videka-Sherman, 1986; Price, van Ryn, & Vinokur, 1992) have been developed to target these vulnerabilities, with positive results.

ADVANCES IN TREATMENT OF DEPRESSION

Over the last 3 decades, rapid advances in the treatment of mental illness have resulted in a much greater awareness of the difficulties that depressed individuals encounter and of what to do when they become ill. Reliance on evidenced-based treatments has significantly improved the prognosis for parents facing mental illness. Similarly, there has been rapid growth in the evidence base for the treatment of the major mental illnesses of childhood (Burns, Hoagwood, & Mrazek, 1999). Both talking therapies (in particular, cognitive behavioral therapy and interpersonal therapy) and medication (in particular, the selective seritonergic reuptake inhibitors) are effective in treating depression (Shea et al., 1992).

The typical course of depression, however, illustrates the problems with obtaining access to high-quality care that parents with many mental illnesses face. Although depression is eminently treatable, the majority of people with depression receive either inadequate treatment or none at all (Hirschfeld et al., 1997). Many depressed individuals blame their symptoms (e.g., fatigue, sadness, apathy, irritability, inability to make decisions, sleep and weight disturbances) on their own perceived inadequacies (e.g., laziness, not getting enough sleep, lack of self-control), and often those close to them fail to recognize their illness as treatable. The cyclical nature of depression also involves remissions that may encourage people to believe that they will get better, but episodes tend to recur if the depression is untreated. Moreover, those who do get treatment most often are treated not by professionals who are trained in mental health, but rather by family doctors, counselors, or even well-meaning friends and relatives (Regier, Goldberg, & Taube, 1978).

Making certain that adequate treatment is available to parents with depression or other mental illnesses is the first major requirement for addressing the needs of families. Treatment provides a necessary basis from which parents can improve how they deal with their children. Public education to increase understanding of the illness and counteract personal and social biases against seeking treatment for mental health problems must be a part of this effort.

CHILDREN IN FAMILIES WITH A DEPRESSED PARENT

Along with progress in understanding the major mental illnesses in general and depression in particular, there has been an equally significant increase in understanding of the difficulties that children encounter with depression and of the ways that they can overcome it. Youngsters in homes with depressed parents are two to four times more likely to experience depression themselves during adolescence compared to those whose parents do not have a mental illness (Beardslee et al., 1998; Cicchetti & Toth, 1995). They are also at risk for other disorders, general impairments in functioning in school, and problems in interpersonal relationships (Block & Gjerde, 1991; Hammen, 1991; Reinherz, Giaconia, Wasserman, Silverman, & Burton, 1999). Depression in adolescence has also been linked to additional problems such as work disruption, stressful life events, undergoing puberty, early pregnancy, and substance abuse (Kessler et al., 1997; Lewinsohn, Clarke, Seeley, & Rhode, 1994; Peterson, Compas, & Brooks-Gunn, 1992). Depression in mothers in the first 5 years of a child's life is also linked to multiple poor outcomes, including poor cognitive and emotional development, attachment and behavioral problems, and poor physical health (Radke-Yarrow, 1998; Sameroff, Bartko, Baldwin, Baldwin, & Seifer, 1998), particularly for children exposed to numerous stresses including poverty, social isolation, and teenage parents (Leadbeater & Bishop, 1994; McLoyd, 1998).

Misunderstanding and poor communication are associated with the transmission of affective illness from parent to child. Symptoms of depression, including fatigue, irritability, inability to make decisions, and lack of interest in day-to-day activities can severely interfere with the quality of interactions between parent and child (Field, 1992; Leadbeater, Bishop, & Raver, 1996). Correspondingly, families facing mental illness that experience fewer of these interferences with parenting and less problematic interactions do much better. In our own work on resilience of children and adolescents of depressed parents, we have identified the basis for the design of a preventive intervention program. Central to this program is the identification of the countervailing strengths of these families that can be enhanced and supported (Beardslee & Podorefsky, 1988).

A FAMILY SUPPORT PROGRAM FOR ENHANCEMENT OF RESILIENCE DURING CHILDHOOD AND ADOLESCENCE

This family support program was designed to increase family communication and understanding, provide information about treatments when needed, diminish discord, and, above all, enhance parenting. When the work began, no systematic preventive intervention approaches existed for children in families with affective disorders. The program incorporates a number of the features that characterize many good interventions for parents. In particular, it is focused on identifying what families want, listing their concerns, providing information about what depression is, discussing the risks to their children, evaluating what could be done to enhance their resilience, and committing to work with the families through crises should they recur. A system of evaluating the program used a rigorous empirical standard for preventive intervention research (Coie et al., 1993; Institute of Medicine, 1994).

The intervention framework provided parents with examples of resilient qualities (e.g., positive relationships, school engagement, sports involvement) that they could recognize, encourage, and reinforce in their children. Pursuits outside of the family were also encouraged for their children, including extracurricular activities that enhanced relations with peers and adults other than the parents and offered children opportunities to view themselves as separate individuals. Adolescents were also helped to find ways to be concerned for the depressed parent without assuming responsibility for the depression. Great care was taken to emphasize what the families were doing right, because negative criticism has been shown to reinforce depression (Hammen, 1991).

The intervention comprises two widely used formats for public health approaches with parents and children ages 8 to 15: a set of two lectures with opportunities for questions at the end, followed by a series of four to eight sessions involving a clinician and members of the affected families. Because we believed that many families would not initially identify themselves as needing prevention services and might not be treated by highly skilled mental health professionals, both formats are designed to be compatible with commonly available resources in managed care programs, private practices, community centers, and educational institutions.

In the lecture format, direct information is presented concerning the nature of depressive disorders, emphasizing the following issues:

- No one is to blame for affective illness;
- Affective illnesses have a biological basis;
- Effective treatment is available;
- It is important to get help when needed;
- It is possible to promote strengths and resilience in children; and
- Treatment should be prompt if children develop symptoms.

Information about treatment for depression is provided to both parents and children to help eliminate misunderstanding of the illness within the family and to give the family members a common vocabulary and knowledge base. The lecture components focus on children ages 8 to 15 on the premise that they are old enough to understand cognitive explanations. No attempt is made to link the information to specific individual family members beyond the question-and-answer period at the end of each lecture.

The clinician-facilitated intervention comprises initial sessions with the parents and individual ones with the children, a family meeting to which all children are invited, and a wrap-up session. The information presented is linked to the families' life experiences and to the individual lives of the family members. Efforts are made to initiate and support ongoing communications among family members, to decrease feelings of guilt and blame in children, to help the children develop relationships both within and outside the family, to facilitate the children's independent functioning in settings outside the home, and to help restore the natural equilibrium of the family.

Parents report that both the lectures and clinician-facilitated intervention were helpful in bringing about changes in illness-related behavior and attitudes but that the clinician-facilitated intervention had a greater impact. Continued study over the next 3 years found that the effects were sustained and that new, longer term changes emerged, again with greater and more sustained changes attributed to the clinician-facilitated intervention (Beardslee, Gladstone, Wright, Cooper, in press; Beardslee, Wright, Rothberg, Salt, & Versage, 1996).

This approach also focuses on providing adequate treatment if difficulties emerge and on creating and enhancing strengths within the family and within the child. The central point is that despite their having a mental illness, parents can be good parents when appropriate supports are offered. The provision of support for parenting can take place in many different ways—in work with mental health professionals, through classes in health centers, in work with pediatricians, and the like. The key, however, is to distinguish between having a mental illness and being a parent and to emphasize supporting the parents' actions as parents (Beardslee, 2002).

PROGRAMS FOR DEPRESSED PARENTS WITH INFANTS AND TODDLERS

Several specific programs for parents with depression who have younger children also show promising results. Compared to older children and adolescents, preschoolers need much greater support from caregivers to accomplish the key developmental challenges of their age group, including forming close attachments and learning to regulate their own strong emotions and behaviors. A great deal of research on effective programming has focused on strengthening attachment bonds and effective communicative interactions between depressed mothers and their infants (Cicchetti, 1993; Cicchetti & Toth, 1998; Field, Fox, Pickens, & Nawrocki, 1995; Field et al., 1991). In an evaluation of Cicchetti's Toddler-Parent Psychotherapy (TPP) program, cognitive problems in children of depressed mothers were less common for families who received the intervention than for those who did not (Cicchetti, Rogosch, & Toth, 2000). Field (1998) also found positive effects for interventions that improved the interactional quality between mother and infant. The findings from this work highlight the importance of high-quality interventions that promote positive verbal and nonverbal interactions and diminish the likelihood that illnesses will be perpetuated across generations.

For families facing multiple adversities, comprehensive and integrative services can enhance the youngsters' strengths at appropriate developmental stages. Programs for treating mental health problems in parents of young children must focus on providing the basic necessities for the children's adequate development. This frequently involves providing high-quality day care or nurse practitioners to assist mothers, as well as concrete support for mothers wrestling with multiple stresses that can engender or aggravate their depressive symptoms.

Many mothers in the inner city wrestle with depression, especially those who have suffered multiple adversities. Symptoms of depression (sadness, disinterest in everyday activities, fatigue, inability to work or make decisions) also can explain why depressed mothers may not take advantage of programs offered. Proactive intervention can help those who are depressed and those with other mental illnesses through two important mechanisms. First, adequate recognition and treatment can best be provided in the settings where parents present themselves (ranging from well-baby clinics and pediatrician offices to school and day care settings). Second, concrete supports that all at-risk mothers need should be provided to enhance their capacity to be a parent; these include, among others, adequate prenatal care, high-quality nurse home visitation, and high-quality day care. Unfortunately, all too often, opportunities to provide these early supports are missed, creating the need subsequently for more intensive, multilayered interventions for both parents and their children.

Research evidence supports the long-term and positive consequences of intensive early efforts to intervene with women at high risk and their preschoolers through nurse home visitations (Olds, Henderson, Tatelbaum, & Chamberlin, 1986; Olds, Henderson, Chamberlin, & Tatelbaum, 1986) and high-quality day care (Knitzer, 2000). Research evaluating the comprehensive strengths-building approach offered by Head Start programs and nurse home visitation shows that there are considerable advantages for high-risk mothers and children who receive these services compared to matched controls (Knitzer, 2000). These programs provide the necessary supports for parents that allow them to be good parents even when their children are in this vulnerable young age group. Again, the focus is on supporting parents to support their children's healthy development.

PROMOTING STRONG FAMILIES

Although several promising studies are being conducted, studies of the efficacy of early intervention with parents at risk for, or with symptoms of, mental illness are rare and piecemeal. Available research suggests that the most powerful effects in reducing long-term negative outcomes are found in programs that combine a strong focus on children with a strong family component (Yoshikawa, 1994). Several programs in early childhood mental health intervention offer models for effective practice. Keys to Caregiving is a visiting nurse program for new mothers for whom routine nursing services were ineffective. Nurses were asked to focus on relationship building between mother and child, decreasing the mother's social isolation, and increasing her sense of competence. Another program, the Partners Project, used group discussions that are based on videotapes of parent–child interactions in often troublesome situations and are led by trained family service workers and clinicians. The Parent Service Project aims to strengthen child care programs by reducing stress on low-income families with young children in child care settings. This is achieved through activities that bring parents together to create informal support networks among themselves (Center for Mental Health Services, 2000). Evaluations of these programs show decreased parental depression, increased parental competence, and increased involvement in the children's education (Knitzer, 2000).

Knitzer (2000) also cited examples of programs in Massachusetts and Hawaii, where mental health professionals were hired to supervise and train family service workers in mental health promotion programs to teach parents new ways to discipline and support their children and to create support groups for families involved in domestic violence (rather than the traditional approach of merely referring the families to child protection agencies). Results of the program included increased staff willingness to work with families suspected of abuse and neglect.

Another set of promising studies involve programs primarily concerned with helping adults that are ultimately helpful to children. These programs focus on the adult's role as a parent and aim to build and strengthen positive parenting strategies. Project Before in Kansas provides mentally ill or substance-abusing mothers with case managers trained in early child development, substance abuse, and mental illness. Evaluation results showed a dramatic increase in use of available health care services for both parent and child. The Relational Psychotherapy Mother's Group involves 6 months of group meetings in which substance-abusing mothers actively explore better parenting solutions through brainstorming and role playing. Evaluation results included decreases in maternal maltreatment, increased positive interactions with children, and increased satisfaction in the maternal role (Luthar & Suchman, 2000).

When considered together, the programs for young children and adolescents of families with a depressed parent reveal seven essential best practices. These programs

1. build on strengths that the parents already possess, as well as on the parents' knowledge of their own and their children's needs;

2. assume that helping parents is the most powerful and long-lasting way to help children;

3. avoid negative criticism and respond respectfully to the parents' current needs and wishes;
4. offer staff support and access to further training and knowledge in dealing with complex emotional and behavioral issues;
5. seek to help those with diagnosed disorders, those at risk of developing them, and those in any kind of crisis by strengthening parenting and addressing their specific difficulties;
6. use pull-out therapy (i.e., pulling children out of their family context) only as a last resort and for short periods of time; and
7. seek collaboration between different systems working with the same families to help make their strategies more cohesive.

Widespread implementation of strengths-based, family-focused programs would require a dynamic shift in thought for mental health practitioners, educators, and policymakers. A broad, integrated prevention program should address three principles. First, families need universal access to care for the treatment of parent mental illness, especially in the early stages of the disease before they might even meet diagnostic criteria. Programs mentioned in other areas of this volume, particularly around divorce, poverty, and race, could also be of benefit for children of depressed parents. Potent risk factors for depression in both adults and children include witnessing or being exposed to violence, being abused or neglected, undergoing loss or bereavement, or living in social isolation (Beardslee, 1998). The encouragement and development of adequate social support networks for those at risk for isolation should therefore help in both ameliorating depression and reducing risk of depression. Specific preventive interventions can effectively target factors for high-risk families (such as those with histories of mental illness), but developing national strategies to lessen the impacts of nonspecific risk factors could have a farther reaching effect in reducing multiple problems that affect families.

Second, families need to be considered as units, not as a collection of individuals. Social policies and intervention programs need to be directed beyond individuals toward supporting and strengthening families as a whole. Often, other caregivers, grandparents, aunts, uncles, or others are involved in the primary care of children, and these individuals also may need to be included. The lack of access to mental health care has a profound impact on those wrestling with depression (Beardslee, 2002) that is further complicated when one member of a family can get care from a provider or system but other members cannot.

Third, depression is among the most treatable of the major mental illnesses. Those who are most vulnerable—those who already have this mental illness and who also have other risk factors and are desperately in need of treatment—are least likely to receive care because they are more likely not to have health insurance. Providing both treatment for parents with depression and appropriate support for parenting could have a powerful positive impact on the prevention of illness in the next generation. The only way to ensure such treatment is to reframe the health care system to guarantee access to all, without barriers. This means national coverage, although the vehicle for achieving it may be a combination of different plans that are already in existence. From a scientific point of view, not treating those who are most vulnerable is both unacceptable and unwise. There is increasing evidence that the delivery of integrated services makes sense. The treatment of children in the same system that cares for their parents is needed, and coverage for mental health care must be available to all.

POLICIES TO ENHANCE FAMILY SUPPORT PROGRAMS

To build on research-based programming principles, policymakers must acknowledge the following:

- Adequate treatment of parents with mental illness is a priority that must be incorporated into approaches for high-risk parents;
- Strengths-based approaches must build parenting skills and resources within the family caregiving environment to support children in ways that are appropriate to their developmental level;
- Early intervention and prevention based on strengths-based approaches are preferable to waiting until children become ill; and
- There is a great deal of prejudice and misunderstanding that continues to surround mental illness that must be addressed through public education (Hinshaw & Cicchetti, 2000).

Building on these foundations, we make the following three specific policy recommendations:

1. A comprehensive, national, early childhood, family-centered mental health system is needed to provide parents, grandparents, and others with the emotional support and child-rearing knowledge needed to promote a nurturing relationship with children.
2. A life-span, developmental perspective is necessary to prevent difficulties in children of parents with mental disorders.
3. Policymakers and service providers need to work together to develop comprehensive, integrative, family-centered programs within which the various approaches for youngsters at risk are organized.

1. Develop a Comprehensive Mental Health System

It is absolutely essential that programs be integrative. Research on existing and future programs must be expanded to document their potential success. Funding issues and other obstacles should be viewed in light of the obvious and immediate benefit to the families, as well as the future consequences and public and private costs of leaving mental illness untreated, which include intergenerational transmission of illness, increased demands for special education, school dropout, delinquency, substance abuse, and reliance on welfare, to name a few.

2. Adopt a Life-Span, Developmental Perspective

Following the idea that mental disorders are markers of a constellation of risk factors, attention is required to how those risk factors come together and are sustained or ameliorated across the life span both for adults and their children. Nurse home visitation configured specifically for parents with mental illnesses and early, high-quality child care and day care have been promising components of effective programs. These programs would benefit all youngsters at risk, including but not limited to those affected by parent mental illness. As the youngsters mature, however, more specific programs that target the particular difficulties of the parents and their adolescents are warranted.

3. Develop Integrative Family-Centered Programs

Adequate services for mental health difficulties in parents, including substance abuse, posttraumatic stress disorder, depression, and personality disorder, are a part of an integrative approach to supporting families experiencing parent mental illness. But more importantly, such approaches need to be integrated into the comprehensive care of families, including schooling for children and job-seeking programs for parents.

Depression, although classified as a mental disorder, has a strong biological base. Treatment early in the course of this disorder makes a significant difference, and indeed there is some evidence that lack of treatment may actually change the structure of the brain and promote recurrence. Access to treatment without stigma or financial or availability barriers is essential, and yet such access is currently denied to large portions of the U.S. population, beginning with the 44 million individuals with no health insurance. Not having health insurance both denies adequate treatment when disorders develop and may lead to the development of more serious disorders. Health plans that place barriers in the way of quickly receiving treatment services (e.g., by requiring excessive paperwork) may also contribute to obstacles to care. Immediate and adequate treatment of parent depression is essential in preventing development of depression among other family members.

Emphasis on the specific programs that address particular risk factors (e.g., loss, stresses, genetic vulnerability) is important. However, it is also important to recognize that risk factors often occur together and are compounded by poverty and unemployment, being victimized, being different (e.g., of a different race or culture), lacking access to services, or living in neighborhoods that are not conducive to the development of social bonds and relationships. Hence, attention needs to be directed at reducing a variety of risk factors simultaneously. The developmental stages of young childhood and adolescence are particularly salient for lifelong health promotion, and programs need to combine developmentally appropriate strength enhancement with adequate treatment for all family members.

REFERENCES

Beardslee, W. R. (1998). Prevention and the clinical encounter. *American Journal of Orthopsychiatry, 68,* 521–533.

Beardslee, W. R. (2002). *Out of the darkened room: When a parent is depressed.* New York: Little, Brown, and Company.

Beardslee, W. R., Gladstone, T. R. G., Wright, E. J., & Cooper, A. B. (in press). A family-based approach to the prevention of depressive symptoms in children at risk: Evidence of parental and child change. *Pediatrics.*

Beardslee, W. R., & Podorefsky, D. (1988). Resilient adolescents whose parents have serious affective and other psychiatric disorders: The importance of self-understanding and relationships. *American Journal of Psychiatry, 145,* 63–69.

Beardslee, W. R., Versage, E. M., & Gladstone, T. R. G. (1998). Children of affectively ill parents: A review of the past ten years. *Journal of the American Academy of Child and Adolescent Psychiatry, 37,* 1134–1141.

Beardslee, W. R., Wright, E., Rothberg, P. C., Salt, P., & Versage, E. (1996). Response of families to two preventive intervention strategies: Long-term differences in behavior and attitude change. *Journal of the American Academy of Child and Adolescent Psychiatry, 35,* 774–782.

Block, J., & Gjerde, P. F. (1991). Depressive symptomatology in late adolescence: A longitudinal perspective on personality antecedents. In J. E. Rolf, A. Masten, D. Cicchetti, K. Nuechterlein, & S. Weintraub (Eds.), *Risk and protective factors in the development of psychopathology* (pp. 334–360). New York: Cambridge University Press.

Burns, B. J., Hoagwood, K., & Mrazek, P. J. (1999). Effective treatment for mental disorders in children and adolescents. *Clinical Child and Family Psychology Review, 2,* 199–254.

Center for Mental Health Services. (2000). *Children's programs in brief.* Rockville, MD: Author.

Cicchetti, D. (1993). Developmental psychopathology: Reactions, reflections, projections. *Developmental Review, 13*, 471–502.

Cicchetti, D., Rogosch, F. A., & Toth, S. L. (2000). The efficacy of toddler-parent psychotherapy for fostering cognitive development in offspring of depressed mothers. *Journal of Abnormal Child Psychology, 28*, 135–148.

Cicchetti, D., & Toth, S. L. (1995). Developmental psychopathology and disorders of affect. In D. Cicchetti & D. J. Cohen (Eds.), *Developmental psychopathology: Volume 2. Risk, disorder, and adaptation* (pp. 369–420).New York: Wiley.

Cicchetti, D., & Toth, S. L. (1998). The development of depression in children and adolescents. *American Psychologist, 53*, 221–241.

Coie, J. D., Watt, N. F., West, S. G., Hawkins, J. D., Asarnow, J. R., Markman, H. J., et al. (1993). The science of prevention: A conceptual framework and some directions for a national research program. *American Psychologist, 48*, 1013–1022.

Eisenberg, L. (1979). A friend, not an apple, a day will help keep the doctor away. *American Journal of Medicine, 66*, 551–553.

Field, T. (1992). Infants of depressed mothers. *Development and Psychopathology, 4*, 49–66.

Field, T. (1998). Maternal depression effects on infants and early interventions. *Preventive Medicine, 27*, 200–203.

Field, T., Fox, N., Pickens, J., & Nawrocki, T. (1995). Relative right frontal EEG activation in 3- to 6-month-old infants of "depressed" mothers. *Developmental Psychology, 31*, 358–363.

Field, T. M., Morrow, C. J., Healy, B. T., Foster, T., Adlestein, D., & Goldstein, S. (1991). Mothers with zero Beck depression scores act more "depressed" with their infants. *Development and Psychopathology, 3*, 253–262.

Hammen, C. (1991). *Depression runs in families.* New York: Springer-Verlag.

Hinshaw, S. P., & Cicchetti, D. (2000). Stigma and mental disorder: Conceptions of illness, public attitudes, personal disclosure, and social policy. *Development and Psychopathology, 12*, 555–598.

Hirschfeld, R. M., Keller, M. B., Panico, S., Arons, B. S., Barlow, D., Davidoff, F., et al. (1997). The National Depressive and Manic-Depressive Association consensus statement on the under treatment of depression. *Journal of the American Medical Association, 277*, 333–340.

Institute of Medicine. (1994). *Reducing risks for mental disorders: Frontiers for preventive intervention research.* Washington, DC: National Academy Press.

Kessler, R. C., Berglund, P. A., Foster, C. L., Saunders, W. B., Stang, P. E., & Walters, E. E. (1997). Social consequences of psychiatric disorders: II. Teenage parenthood. *American Journal of Psychiatry, 154*, 1405–1411.

Kessler, R. C., Mcgonagle, K. A., Zhao, S., Nelson, C. B., Hughes, M., Eshleman, S., et al. (1994). Lifetime and 12-month prevalence of DSM-III-R psychiatric disorders in the United States. *Archives of General Psychiatry, 51*, 8–19.

Knitzer, J. (2000). *Promoting resilience: Helping young children and parents affected by substance abuse, domestic violence, and depression in the context of welfare reform* (Issue Brief 8). New York: National Center for Children in Poverty.

Leadbeater, B. J., & Bishop, S. (1994). Predictors of behavioral problems in preschool children of inner-city Afro-American and Puerto Rican adolescent mothers. *Child Development, 65,* 638–648.

Leadbeater, B. J., Bishop, S., & Raver, C. C. (1996). Quality of mother-toddler interactions, maternal depressive symptoms, and behavior problems in preschoolers of adolescent mothers. *Developmental Psychology, 32,* 280–288.

Lewinsohn, P. M., Clarke, G. N., Seeley, J. R., & Rhode, P. (1994). Major depression in community adolescents: Age at onset, episode duration, and time to recurrence. *Journal of the American Academy of Child and Adolescent Psychiatry, 33,* 809–818.

Lieberman, M. A., & Videka-Sherman, L. (1986). The impact of self-help groups on the mental health of widows and widowers. *American Journal of Orthopsychiatry, 56,* 435–449.

Luthar, S. S., & Suchman, N. E. (2000). Relational psychotherapy mothers' group: A developmentally informed intervention for at-risk mothers. *Developmental Psychology, 12,* 235–253.

McLloyd, V. (1998). Socioeconomic disadvantage and child development. *American Psychologist, 53,* 185–204.

Olds, D. L., Henderson, C. R., Chamberlin, R. W., & Tatelbaum, R. (1986). Preventing child abuse and neglect: A randomized trial of nurse home visitation. *Pediatrics, 78,* 65–78.

Olds, D. L., Henderson, C. R., Tatelbaum, R., & Chamberlin, R. W. (1986). Improving the delivery of prenatal care and outcomes of pregnancy: A randomized trial of nurse home visitation. *Pediatrics, 77,* 16–28.

Peterson, A. C., Compas, B., & Brooks-Gunn, J. (1992). *Depression in adolescence: Current knowledge, research directions, and implications for programs and policy.* Unpublished manuscript.

Price, R. H., van Ryn, M., & Vinokur, A. (1992). Impact of a preventive job search intervention on the likelihood of depression among the unemployed. *Journal of Health and Social Behavior, 33,* 158–167.

Radke-Yarrow, M. (1998). *Children of depressed mothers.* New York: Cambridge University Press.

Regier, D. A., Goldberg, I. D., & Taube, C. A. (1978). The de facto U.S. mental health service system: A public health perspective. *Archives of General Psychiatry, 35,* 685–693.

Reinherz, H. Z., Giaconia, R. M., Wasserman, M. S., Silverman, A. B., & Burton, L. (1999). Coming of age in the 1990's: Influences of contemporary stressors on major depression in young adults. In P. Cohen, C. Slomkowski, & L. N. Robins (Eds.), *Historical and geographical influences on psychopathology* (pp. 141–161). Mahwah, NJ: Erlbaum.

Robins, L. N., & Regier, D. A. (1991). *Psychiatric disorders in America: The Epidemiologic Catchment Area Study.* New York: Free Press.

Sameroff, A. J., Bartko, W. T., Baldwin, A., Baldwin, C., & Seifer, R. (1998). Family and social influences on the development of child competence. In M. Lewis & C. Feiring (Eds.), *Families, risk, and competence* (pp. 161–185). Mahwah, NJ: Erlbaum.

Shea, M. T., Elkin, I., Imber, S. D., Sotsky, S. M., Watkins, J. T., Collins, J. F., et al. (1992). Course of depressive symptoms over follow-up: Findings from the National Institute of Mental Health Treatment of Depression Collaborative Research Program. *Archives of General Psychiatry, 49,* 782–787.

Yoshikawa, H. (1994). Prevention as a cumulative protection: Effects of early support and education on chronic delinquency and its risks. *Psychological Bulletin, 115,* 28–54.

10

CHILDREN AND FAMILIES COPING WITH PEDIATRIC CHRONIC ILLNESSES

CYNTHIA A. GERHARDT, NATALIE WALDERS, SUSAN L. ROSENTHAL, AND DENNIS D. DROTAR

Children with chronic illness and their families are at increased risk for social, emotional, and behavioral difficulties in addition to the sometimes substantial economic costs that they must manage. Much of the research to date has derived from deficits-based models focusing on maladjustment, to the neglect of data emphasizing adaptive processes such as hardiness, resilience, and enhanced functioning for these children. This chapter describes some of the stressors experienced by children with chronic illness and their families, along with individual, family, and community factors that help to promote positive outcomes. The authors identify several strategies for promoting health care systems that address the needs of families coping with childhood chronic illness and for improving the quality of research in this area.

* * *

An estimated 31% of U.S. children have a pediatric chronic illness that has the potential to disrupt their functioning and development (Newacheck & Taylor, 1992). Childhood chronic illnesses include more common conditions such as asthma, as well as rarer conditions such as cancer. Medical advances have extended the life expectancy of many children with chronic illnesses, as is the case with cystic fibrosis and leukemia, causing a shift from the short-term management of acute and frequently fatal

173

illnesses to the long-term management of potentially survivable chronic conditions.

Despite improvements in life expectancy, childhood chronic illnesses can impose a significant burden on children, families, and the community. For example, according to the Centers for Disease Control and Prevention (CDC), an estimated 4.8 million children have asthma, with a disproportionate number from poor, urban families (Centers for Disease Control [CDC], 2003. As the number one cause of absenteeism in the United States, asthma accounts for millions of lost school days each year and millions more lost work days for parents. Although clinical treatment is improving, asthma-related deaths, hospitalizations, and emergency room visits have risen dramatically; current treatment costs for children are estimated at $3.2 billion annually (CDC, 2003).

In addition to financial costs, children with a chronic illness and their families are at increased risk for psychosocial difficulties (Wallander & Varni, 1998). Challenges can vary in accordance with a range of child factors, including developmental status, temperament, and pre-existing emotional or behavioral problems. Although rarely the sole cause of adjustment problems, chronic illness can increase psychosocial risk in combination with other stressors. However, individuals can demonstrate substantial coping skills and personality strengths that lessen this risk. Factors that enhance illness management and psychosocial adjustment are often overlooked in research, yet they are critically important to clinical practice and policy. This chapter highlights the need for strengths-based approaches to research on childhood chronic illness and identifies aspects of resilience relevant to policy development. Research and policy recommendations are reviewed later in the chapter.

The need for a strengths-based approach to childhood chronic illness stems in part from the deficits-oriented tradition of psychological research and practice. Clinicians and researchers are often trained in deficits-based approaches that focus on psychopathology and that seek to identify and remedy maladaptive responses to stress. Insurance procedures, which require a diagnosis prior to payment, perpetuate this model. Early research in childhood chronic illness largely subscribed to the deficits-based model, overshadowing the importance of identifying and capitalizing on individual and family strengths. This approach has contributed to a neglect of data emphasizing adaptive outcomes and to the stigma that these children are weak and vulnerable to a host of problems. An alternative model is a strengths-based focus on human resilience and on the elements of successful functioning that are evident despite adversity.

DEVELOPMENTAL PATHWAYS

In the case of childhood chronic illness, the course of child and family adaptation varies (Frank et al., 1998; Lavigne & Faier-Routman, 1992).

Compas, Hinden, and Gerhardt (1995) provided a conceptual framework for understanding the pathways or trajectories that result in adaptive and maladaptive development (Figure 10.1). Child and family functioning are part of a continuum of adaptive and maladaptive outcomes that can remain static or change across time in response to risk and resistance factors. Risk factors decrease the likelihood of positive adaptation, whereas resistance factors increase its likelihood. Although "resilience" is often used as a broad term to denote adaptive functioning, it can also refer to one of three specific types of adaptive paths. These include hardiness, resilience, and enhanced functioning and occur when situations of adversity offer opportunities for children and families to hone coping skills and promote immunity to negative outcomes. *Hardiness* indicates that a child or family experience no negative or positive effects from a chronic illness and remain at a stable, functional level. *Resilience* suggests that the child or family experienced a temporary period of decreased functioning due to the illness, followed by a return to an adaptive level. *Enhancement* occurs when a child or family experience improved functioning or positive effects following an illness. The maladaptive trajectories, which were the primary foci of early studies, include *stable maladjustment* and *declining adjustment*.

A risk and resistance framework can help clarify factors that contribute to the variety of outcomes in response to a childhood chronic illness. Risk factors relevant to chronic illness include disease severity, major life events, and daily stressors. Parallel to research in the general population, resistance factors in chronic illness include individual characteristics (e.g., intelligence), family characteristics (e.g., cohesion), and community factors (e.g., support). However, chronic illnesses may present unique stressors that may foster or diminish resistance.

PROMOTING STRENGTHS

Child Factors

Cross-sectional studies indicate that children with chronic illness display all three adaptive pathways (i.e., resilience, hardiness, and enhancement); however, few longitudinal studies exist. Evidence of psychological hardiness or resilience has been found among children with cancer (Noll et al., 1999), juvenile rheumatoid arthritis (JRA; Noll et al., 2000), and sickle-cell diseases (Noll et al., 1996), with reports of functioning similar to healthy classmates. Enhanced functioning has been shown among children with JRA who reported more positive perceptions of their academic abilities (Noll et al., 2000) and among boys with sickle-cell disorders who exhibited fewer aggressive and disruptive behaviors (Noll et al., 1996). In addition, children with cancer have been found to receive higher sociability and leadership

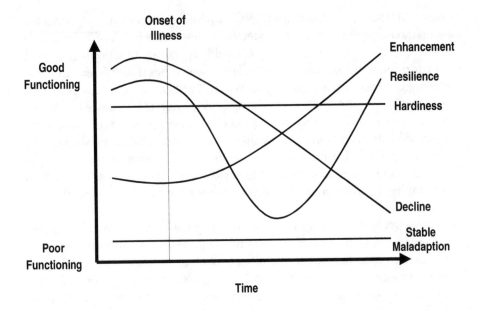

Figure 10.1. Five possible trajectories of functioning over time following the onset of a chronic illness.

ratings from teachers, to be rated by peers as less aggressive and disruptive, to be more socially accepted by peers, and to have lower rates of substance use than matched controls (Noll et al., 1999; Verrill, Schafer, Vannatta, & Noll, 2000).

Similar reports of enhanced functioning have been found in a multicenter study of adolescents with sickle-cell disease or cystic fibrosis (Britto et al., 1998). These youths reported significantly fewer risky behaviors and more injury-prevention behaviors than controls. It is suspected that disease or treatment factors (e.g., fatigue, hospitalization), paired with greater adult supervision, may disrupt or protect children from paths of decline and maladaption by limiting opportunities for negative peer influence and aggressive behavior (Noll et al., 1996; Verrill et al., 2000).

Some children with chronic illnesses appear to be at heightened risk for paths of decline or maladjustment, such as those undergoing bone marrow transplant or treatment for brain tumors (Vannatta, Gartstein, Short, & Noll, 1998; Vannatta, Zeller, Noll, & Koontz, 1998). Damage to the central nervous system, which is common among these children, may account for their problematic adjustment. In general, greater intelligence has been associated with better psychosocial adaptation, but children with chronic illnesses may have compromised cognitive functioning due to their illness or treatment (e.g., neurological changes after cranial radiation). Children with nonneurological conditions have been found to exhibit better adjustment than those with neurological conditions (Howe, Feinstein, Reiss, Molock, &

Berger, 1993). Illness characteristics (e.g., disease severity, type) also have been associated with parental resilience (Frank et al., 1998). However, rather than having a direct effect, illness characteristics often interact with individual and family variables (e.g., age, social support) to influence adjustment (Lavigne & Faier-Routman, 1993).

Physical and social development also may affect adjustment by changing the personal significance of an illness or its biological impact. Older children with cancer, as compared to younger children, have been found to be less susceptible to learning problems (Stehbens et al., 1991) and treatment-related distress (Kazak, 1998), but conflicting results regarding adjustment have been reported (Frank et al., 1998). An increase in cognitive ability and peer social contact can be a "catch-22." As children age, they gain a better understanding of their illness and treatment, and they may be less vulnerable to cognitive sequelae. At the same time, they can become more aware of the burdens and challenges associated with their illness. Relationships with peers can be supportive, but teens may be more affected by the barrier their illness imposes on social activities compared to younger children. Despite the lack of clarity in the role of physical and social development, children can demonstrate considerable variability in their adjustment, at both the individual and group levels and across a wide range of illnesses.

Family Factors

A child's adaptation to chronic illness is not an isolated process; family members, health care professionals, and the community have an influential impact. In particular, families play a pivotal role in the management of a child's illness. Many parents of children with chronic health conditions have described their family environment, marital satisfaction, and level of family conflict as similar to that of families of healthy children, indicating considerable hardiness or resilience (Noll et al., 1995; Quittner et al., 1998). Hardy or resilient functioning also has been shown among individual family members. For example, mothers of children with sickle-cell diseases have been reported to function as well as controls on a variety of indexes of emotional well-being (e.g., Noll et al., 1994). Although mothers of children with rheumatic diseases may experience greater psychological symptoms than fathers, both groups have been noted to fall in the normal range of functioning (Timko, Stovel, & Moos, 1992). Fathers of children with chronic illnesses consistently function as well as controls on multiple psychological indexes (e.g., Noll et al., 1994; Quittner et al., 1998), and compared to siblings of healthy children, siblings of children with chronic illnesses also fare well (Noll et al., 1995). Importantly, hardy or resilient paths of functioning in families can persist over the long term (e.g., Kupst et al., 1995). In addition, enhanced functioning has been noted among families who report more positive family attitudes and increased closeness following a child's illness (Sargent et al.,

1995). Siblings of children with a chronic illness have exhibited fewer behavior problems and a range of positive qualities, such as increased caring,
maturity, and helpfulness (Horowitz & Kazak, 1990; Sargent et al., 1995).

Risk for maladaptive or declining paths may be greater among mothers of children with chronic illness than fathers and siblings, presumably
because mothers often manage the day-to-day care of children. Some mothers have reported adjustment problems, such as anxiety and depression (Noll
et al., 1995; Wallander & Varni, 1998), but only a small subgroup experience severe emotional distress. Parental and child functioning also may
influence one another, such that decline in one part of the system (e.g., the
parents) may lead to less adaptive child functioning. However, dysfunction
is not universal across illnesses, and a broad range of outcomes has been
reported. It appears that a single family member, typically the mother, can
buffer the negative effects of a chronic illness and promote child adaptation through attentive caregiving (Drotar, 1997). However, additional support or respite may be needed to promote the adjustment of overburdened
mothers.

Family adaptability and cohesion are two additional factors linked to
adjustment. In general, greater adaptability (i.e., flexibility or ability to
change) and greater cohesion (i.e., emotional connection) are associated with
positive functioning in families. However, for families of children with chronic
illness, these relationships may not be consistent. For example, greater adaptability and cohesion have been found to be associated with fewer emotional
and behavior problems among siblings of children with cancer (Horowitz &
Kazak, 1990). Chaney and Peterson (1989) found that moderate levels of
adaptability and cohesion, as opposed to extreme levels, contributed to greater
medication adherence among children with JRA. Others have suggested that
less adaptability (i.e., greater rigidity) may be functional among these families, given the need for adherence to strict treatment regimens (Kazak, Reber,
& Snitzer, 1988).

Community Factors

An important source of resilience for families of children with a chronic
illness involves community-based supports (e.g., community agencies, schools,
and religious groups) that offer advocacy, education, and guidance. Community supports can provide individual assistance, offer broad-based resources,
and increase public awareness of health care issues. Schools, consumer advocacy organizations, and professional guilds (e.g., the American Medical Association) may be helpful to families. The American Academy of Pediatrics
has been particularly vocal in political advocacy efforts by promoting programs and policy for children with special medical needs.

Community programs, such as the School Intervention Program (SIP)
at Children's Hospital Medical Center in Cincinnati, can promote better

community integration for children with chronic illnesses. The SIP staff educate teachers, school nurses, and classmates about a child's chronic illness. They facilitate the child's return to school and help obtain special accommodations under the Individuals With Disabilities Education Act (IDEA, 1997). Participation in school activities can enhance a child's adjustment during a chronic illness, particularly after a long absence for surgery or hospitalization. A similar program showed positive effects on the adjustment of children with cancer (Katz, Rubinstein, Hubert, & Blew, 1988), but further data are needed to document the value of these community resources.

POLICY RECOMMENDATIONS AND FUTURE DIRECTIONS

Promoting Health Care Systems for Families of Children With Chronic Illness

In addition to community factors, aspects of the health care system play a critical role in promoting or undermining adaptive functioning (see Table 10.1). A number of factors may deplete rather than enhance the financial and psychological resources needed to manage the stressors associated with a chronic illness. Quality health care has the capacity to promote resilience and healthy outcomes in children and families. However, in the current era of cost containment and managed care, health care delivery is often inadequate for children with special needs. Research has shown that interdisciplinary health care models (e.g., involving medical, nursing, and mental health components) that are tailored to address a specific illness can result in greater patient and family satisfaction, fewer symptoms, and improved functioning (Evans et al., 1999; Greineder, Loane, & Parks, 1999). Although an emerging area of research, it appears that the following are key elements in laying the foundation for adaptive family functioning: unrestricted access to consistent pediatric primary care, access to medically indicated specialists for pediatric chronic illness, access to mental health care to address adjustment and illness management when needed, and access to insurance that offers both comprehensive coverage and parity for interdisciplinary illness management (American Academy of Pediatrics, 1999).

Access to quality health care specific to a chronic illness enables children and families to optimally manage symptoms and to successfully adhere to complex treatment regimens (Evans et al., 1999). Without appropriate health care, families are faced with added barriers to adaptive functioning. Consequences may include increased medical complications, financial burden, fragmented care, and family stress. A family's struggle to negotiate with insurance companies for reimbursement, specialist care, and coverage for preexisting medical conditions can consume valuable time, resources, and energy that could be better spent on coping and adaptation.

TABLE 10.1
Summary of Research and Policy Recommendations for Strengths-Based Approaches to Childhood Chronic Illness

Priorities	Recommendations
Policy	
Promote health care systems that address the needs of families coping with childhood chronic illness	Ensure consistent and comprehensive access to pediatric primary care services Promote access to specialists, mental health services, and ancillary health services when indicated Advocate for parity in reimbursements for health and mental health services
Address the potential consequences of public and private managed care systems for the management of childhood chronic illnesses	Expand the role of health care professionals as advocates for patients and families Provide families with knowledge to make informed and responsible decisions concerning health care Support innovative policies and legislation geared to meet the needs of families coping with childhood chronic illness
Increase communication and collaboration among researchers, clinicians, advocates, and policymakers	Fund policy-minded research that evaluates the appropriateness of existing programs for childhood chronic illness Promote innovative, empirically supported programs as models for widespread and large-scale programming Increase publication outlets and reciprocal dialogue between clinicians, researchers, advocates, and policymakers
Research	
Recognize the variability in adjustment to chronic illness	Evaluate different pathways of adjustment to childhood chronic illness within affected groups Recognize individual variability in adjustment over time Incorporate measures of strengths and competencies in addition to deficits and risks
Implement appropriate study designs	Perform comprehensive assessments at multiple points in prospective, longitudinal studies Use well-matched, appropriate comparison samples for controls Perform appropriate, advanced statistical procedures, such as growth curve or path analytic models
Conduct research that will inform and influence policy	Study the effects of shifts in health care on the quality and accessibility of services for children with chronic illness Examine the effectiveness of interdisciplinary services and programs for childhood chronic illness Conduct cost-effectiveness evaluations of prevention and intervention programs for childhood chronic illness

The Consequences of Health Care Delivery Systems and Employment Policies

The past decade has been marked by sweeping changes in health care service delivery (i.e., changes from fee-for-service to managed care models) and substantial reconstruction of the welfare system (i.e., shift from Aid to Families with Dependent Children [AFDC] to Temporary Aid to Needy Families [TANF]). Both changes have resulted in new advocacy priorities and challenges for promoting strengths and adaptation among those affected by childhood chronic illness. In contrast to traditional models of fee-for-service health care, an estimated 85% of employed families currently receive health care through a managed care plan, and more than 13 million Medicaid recipients obtain services through a Medicaid health maintenance organization (Deal, Shiono, & Behrman, 1998). Managed care plans are distinctive in their focus on cost containment, their use of primary care physicians as gatekeepers who monitor access to specialists, and their attempts to reduce health care utilization. Although managed care can increase access to well-child care, there are a variety of drawbacks, particularly for children with special health care needs (Fox, Wicks, & Newacheck, 1993; Horwitz & Stein, 1990).

To ensure that children's health care needs are met in managed care settings, providers and families should be familiar with new health care trends. For example, beyond providing direct clinical care, health care providers have an emerging role as advocates for patients and families, which includes educating families about insurance issues (e.g., pre-existing condition clauses, lifetime benefit caps). By assisting families with these issues during potentially confusing periods (e.g., diagnosis, transition in insurance or employment), health care providers can minimize gaps in coverage and treatment. Providers can also help families navigate the health care system in a proactive manner. Families with the resources to act as informed consumers should be encouraged to review the clauses of managed care programs before enrollment to ensure that they obtain the coverage necessary to handle the financial ramifications of a chronic illness.

The Family Opportunity Act of 2003 (S. 622) is an example of a creative option for addressing the financial demands of childhood chronic illness. This legislation was drafted to provide middle-income families of children with mental or physical disabilities the opportunity to "buy in" to the Medicaid program designed for poorer families. Medicaid provides access to special needs services that may pose an excessive financial burden for middle-income families traditionally ineligible for federal support. The Medicaid buy-in legislation (under committee review, Spring 2003) would provide access to a range of services (e.g., early intervention) and medical care typically not covered by private insurance. Another aspect of the legislation includes family-to-family health information centers. These centers, staffed by families with experience in managing health care issues for children with special needs, are intended to assist families in making informed decisions about health care and family management. This legislation is a public policy model grounded in a strengths-based perspective that supports and guides families through the challenging aspects of managing a childhood chronic illness.

A second shift has been the recent overhaul of the U.S. welfare system, which has resulted in widespread changes for families (Heymann & Earle, 1999). In 1996, the U.S. Congress dramatically reformed welfare and introduced a new system of time limits, work requirements, and the absence of guaranteed supports for families in poverty through the termination of AFDC and the introduction of TANF. Researchers have explored the effects of TANF on employment and poverty rates, and they are recognizing the impact of welfare-to-work policies on the ability of parents to care for ill children. From a strengths-based perspective, families must have the capacity to provide care and attention to children with chronic health conditions in order to maximize physical and emotional functioning. Heymann and Earle (1999) analyzed the caregiving demands and employment benefits of women who had made the transition from welfare to work. They found that former recipients of AFDC were more likely to be caring for at least one child with a chronic health condition, yet they were less likely to receive sick leave, paid leave, or flexible work schedules in comparison to mothers who had never received welfare. These findings, in conjunction with research indicating that a majority of working parents are often unable to care for their ill children due to restrictive employment policies (Heymann, Toomey, & Furstenberg, 1999), underscore the need for policymakers to examine the effects of welfare policies and employment practices on families of children with a chronic illness.

Another concern is the Family Medical Leave Act passed in 1993, which provides up to 12 weeks of unpaid leave to employees caring for an ill family member. Although the legislation took an important stance in recognizing family health as a priority, it is primarily tailored for long-term health care concerns and does not address the short-term problems that often accompany chronic illness (e.g., multiple health care appointments). Maximizing adaptive functioning requires the integral involvement of family members in all aspects of the management of their child's health, and legislation needs to reflect the complex demands placed on families caring for these children.

Increasing Collaboration Among Researchers, Clinicians, Advocates, and Policymakers

An additional priority is the translation and dissemination of research findings to policymakers and advocacy organizations in order to influence changes in policy. Traditionally, studies on childhood chronic illness have been published exclusively within the medical or pediatric psychology literature and may not be readily accessible or interpretable by policymakers. To maximize the impact of policy-minded research on program development and political decision making, researchers should consider other outlets for disseminating their findings (e.g., diverse journals on health care economics or health services research). Researchers should also communicate the benefits of strengths-based psychological interventions to a wider audience by working closely with child advocacy groups and delivering testimony at the local, state, and federal levels. Drafting and advocating for public policies that address the needs of families coping with childhood chronic illness require that policymakers have access to research findings, consumer and family perspectives, and the input and support of professionals involved in direct care. Establishing and maintaining open and reciprocal lines of communication will contribute to the development of appropriate policies and practices, providing children and families the opportunity to obtain a range of medical benefits and experience improved quality of life.

RESEARCH RECOMMENDATIONS AND FUTURE DIRECTIONS

A growing body of research has demonstrated the effectiveness of mental health interventions in facilitating positive outcomes for children and families. The traditional model of developing interventions has been to identify a problematic area of weakness (e.g., treatment nonadherence) and to design and implement a program to remedy the deficit (e.g., promote self-management skills). Although interventions from this framework have demonstrated improvements in outcomes for children with chronic illness, interventions from strengths-based perspectives also show promise. For example, psychological interventions that promote family adjustment through the delivery of family-centered services and parental support are valuable. In addition, interventions that promote the acquisition and enhancement of skills such as problem solving, relaxation, and social skills are important for building individual strengths. To more clearly understand the processes that promote adaptive functioning and to evaluate the efficacy of interventions, strengths-based research is needed. The following section includes recommendations for improving research methodology and design.

Assessing the Diversity of Pathways in Adjustment to Chronic Illness

To identify the various pathways of adjustment and the interplay of factors that affect these pathways, multiple assessments are needed and prospective data collection is recommended. In addition, it is important to consider how the timing and number of assessments affect the ability to accurately identify various developmental pathways. For example, assessments at diagnosis and 1 month postdiagnosis may lead to conclusions of declining functioning, whereas a 6-month assessment may indicate resilient functioning. Prospective assessments may also reveal factors that influence changes in adjustment.

To capture the full spectrum of adaptive and maladaptive pathways, researchers must move from the exclusive use of deficits-based measures, which assess psychopathology and negative outcomes, to the addition of positive outcome measures (e.g., achievement, competence). For example, measuring only functional ability or athleticism among children with JRA may lead to the impression that they are maladapted, whereas inclusion of measures of academic self-perception and achievement may indicate areas of enhanced functioning (e.g., Noll et al., 2000). Other important outcomes are quality of life and the attainment of developmental milestones. Quality of life applies to multiple dimensions of functioning, including perceptions of physical and psychological well-being. The assessment of developmental achievements includes indexes of normal developmental growth, such as graduating from school, obtaining employment, and dating.

Implementing Appropriate Study Designs

Discerning the true risk and resistance factors associated with pediatric chronic illness requires following large samples of children and families prior to and after a diagnosis, a process that is not always feasible due to the relatively small numbers of children who are diagnosed with a particular chronic illness and the substantial costs of such an endeavor. Larger samples can be obtained by accessing as many patients as possible from clinic rosters, collaborating across multiple sites, and using aggressive follow-up strategies to limit dropout. Other possibilities include studying multiple diseases simultaneously (Stein & Jessop, 1982) or evaluating large-scale epidemiological data sets.

When examining differences between those children who have a chronic condition and those who do not, it is important to choose appropriate comparisons. Studies often use siblings or volunteers as controls, despite the fact that both are often mismatched on age and other key factors. Sibling controls are especially problematic because they are exposed to a chronic illness in their family. Comparisons to normative scores on questionnaires are frequent, but these can introduce regional and cohort effects (Achenbach & Howell, 1993; Sandberg, Meyer-Bahlburg, & Yager, 1991). Well-controlled studies have been more likely to find children and families who display hardy, resilient, or enhanced pathways of functioning as opposed to noncontrolled studies (Lavigne & Faier-Routman, 1992). Thus, the use of healthy comparisons that are well matched across a range of factors is optimal.

Although it is important to understand how groups of children with chronic illnesses may differ from groups of healthy children, the identification of subgroups of individuals with a chronic illness who experience greater risk or resistance is especially important. The use of such within-group comparisons allows for the prediction of positive versus negative developmental trajectories and helps identify the factors and processes related to each trajectory. Such data are needed to inform intervention research and to identify subgroups of individuals who may benefit from alternative interventions.

Conducting Research That Will Inform and Influence Policy

Improving the well-being of children and families requires both the prevention of negative outcomes and the promotion of positive outcomes. Research can be viewed as a continuum from basic research findings that inform the design of interventions to outcome studies that influence public policy decision making. Research efforts at the individual, family, and community level are key, as well as research examining the effects of managed care on children with special health care needs.

A consumer organization for children with special needs, Family Voices has collected and distributed data on this issue through their two-phase Family Partners Project with Brandeis University (Family Voices, 1999). The first phase involves a national survey of the experiences of thousands of families who have children with special needs as they navigate the health care system on behalf of their children. The second phase includes a series of interviews with professionals from managed care organizations to assess how their systems serve children with special medical needs. Other large-scale evaluations of the effects of health care delivery systems on the management of chronic illnesses are needed. It is also important to recognize that the management of a chronic health condition is unique and should be examined apart from general pediatric care in order to formulate appropriate conclusions and recommendations for policy and practice.

Another important area for policy-related research is conducting cost-effectiveness evaluations of strengths-based interventions. Data demonstrating the cost-effectiveness of psychological interventions are critical in order to advocate successfully for the integration of mental health and general health care services for children with chronic health conditions. Research on the economic value of mental health and community services is particularly necessary in the current environment of cost containment and managed care.

A final set of recommendations involves the type of research that is necessary to inform policy making and the steps involved in translating research findings into succinct and meaningful recommendations that can shape public policy. From a strengths-based perspective, empirical evaluations of programs that maximize the adjustment and resources of children and families with pediatric chronic illness are recommended. There is a need for both intervention trials that ameliorate barriers or problems (e.g., nonadherence, misuse of health care) and for prevention programs that supply families with effective coping skills at diagnosis to minimize detrimental outcomes. Studies that demonstrate effectiveness in increasing resilience and reducing costs can inform policymakers about the type of programming that should be implemented and supported. However, the availability of federal funds and organizational support to offset the financial costs of conducting this research will ultimately dictate the extent to which these goals can be met.

REFERENCES

Achenbach, T. M., & Howell, C. T. (1993). Are America's children getting worse? A 13-year comparison. *Journal of the American Academy of Child and Adolescent Psychiatry, 32*, 1145–1154.

American Academy of Pediatrics. (1999). *Medical home program for children with special needs* [Brochure]. Elk Grove Village, IL: Author.

Britto, M. T., Garrett, J. M., Dugliss, M. A. J., Daeschner, C. W., Jr., Johnson, C. A., Leigh, M. W., et al. (1998). Risky behavior in teens with cystic fibrosis or sickle cell disease: A multicenter study. *Pediatrics, 101*, 250–256.

Centers for Disease Control and Prevention. (2003). *Asthma control programs related to children and adolescents*. Retrieved June 12, 2003, from http://www.cdc.gov/nceh/airpollution/asthma/children.htm

Chaney, J. M., & Peterson, L. (1989). Family variables and disease management in juvenile rheumatoid arthritis. *Journal of Pediatric Psychology, 14*, 389–403.

Compas, B. E., Hinden, B. R., & Gerhardt, C. A. (1995). Adolescent development: Pathways and processes of risk and resilience. *Annual Review of Psychology, 46*, 265–293.

Deal, L. W., Shiono, P. H., & Behrman, R. E. (1998). Children and managed health care: Analysis and recommendations. *Future of Children, 8*, 4–24.

Drotar, D. (1997). Relating parent and family functioning to the psychological adjustment of children with chronic health conditions: What have we learned? What do we need to know? *Journal of Pediatric Psychology, 22*, 149–165.

Evans, R., Gergen, P. J., Mitchell, H., Kattan, M., Kercsmar, C., Crain, E., et al. (1999). A randomized clinical trial to reduce asthma morbidity among inner-city children: Results of the National Cooperative Inner-City Asthma Study. *Journal of Pediatrics, 135*, 332–338.

Evans, R., LeBailly, S., Gordon, K. K., Sawyer, A., Christoffel, K. K., & Pearce, B. (1999). Restructuring asthma care in a hospital setting to improve outcomes. *Chest, 116*, 210S–216S.

Family and Medical Leave Act of 1993. Pub. L. No. 103-3 (1993).

Family Opportunity Act of 2003. HR 1811, § 622 (2003).

Family Voices. (1999). *Family Voices and Brandeis University Family Partners Project* [Brochure]. Algodones, NM: Author.

Fox, H. B., Wicks, L. B., & Newacheck, P. W. (1993). Health maintenance organizations and children with special health needs: A suitable match? *American Journal of Diseases in Childhood, 147*, 546–552.

Frank, R. G., Thayer, J. F., Hagglund, C. J., Vieth, A. Z., Schopp, L. H., Beck, N. C., et al. (1998). Trajectories of adaptation in pediatric chronic illness: The importance of the individual. *Journal of Consulting and Clinical Psychology, 66*, 521–532.

Greineder, D. K., Loane, K. C., & Parks, P. (1999). A randomized controlled trial of a pediatric asthma outreach program. *Journal of Allergy and Clinical Immunology, 103*, 436–440.

Heymann, S. J., & Earle, A. (1999). The impact of welfare reform on parents' ability to care for their children's health. *American Journal of Public Health, 89*, 502–505.

Heymann, S. J., Toomey, S., & Furstenberg, F. (1999). Working parents: What factors are involved in their ability to take time off from work when their children are sick? *Archives of Pediatrics and Adolescent Medicine, 153*, 870–874.

Horowitz, W. A., & Kazak, A. E. (1990). Family adaptation to childhood cancer: Sibling and family systems variables. *Journal of Clinical Child Psychology, 19*, 221–228.

Horwitz, S. M., & Stein, R. E. K. (1990). Health maintenance organizations vs. indemnity insurance for children with chronic illness: Trading gaps in coverage. *American Journal of Diseases of Children, 144*, 581–586.

Howe, G. W., Feinstein, C., Reiss, D., Molock, S., & Berger, K. (1993). Adolescent adjustment to chronic physical disorders: I. Comparing neurological and non-neurological conditions. *Journal of Child Psychology and Psychiatry, 34*, 1153–1171.

Individuals With Disabilities Education Act Ammendments of 1997. Pub. L. No. 105-17 (1997).

Katz, E. R., Rubinstein, C. L., Hubert, N. C., & Blew, A. (1988). School and social reintegration of children with cancer. *Journal of Psychosocial Oncology, 6*, 123–140.

Kazak, A. E. (1998). Posttraumatic distress in childhood cancer survivors and their parents. *Medical and Pediatric Oncology*, Suppl. 1, 60–68.

Kazak, A. E., Reber, M., & Snitzer, L. (1988). Childhood chronic disease and family functioning: A study of phenylketonuria. *Pediatrics, 81*, 224–230.

Kupst, M. J., Natta, M. B., Richardson, C. C., Schulman, J. L., Lavigne, J. V., & Das, L. (1995). *Journal of Pediatric Psychology, 20*, 601–617.

Lavigne, J. V., & Faier-Routman, J. (1992). Psychological adjustment to pediatric physical disorders: A meta-analytic review. *Journal of Pediatric Psychology, 17*, 133–157.

Lavigne, J. V., & Faier-Routman, J. (1993). Correlates of psychological adjustment to pediatric physical disorders: A meta-analytic review and comparison with existing models. *Developmental and Behavioral Pediatrics, 14*, 117–123.

Newacheck, P. W., & Taylor, W. R. (1992). Childhood chronic illness: Prevalence, severity, and impact. *American Journal of Public Health, 82*, 364–371.

Noll, R. B., Gartstein, M. A., Vannatta, K., Correll, J., Bukowski, W. M., & Davies, W. H. (1999). Social, emotional, and behavioral functioning of children with cancer. *Pediatrics, 103*, 71–78.

Noll, R. B., Kozlowski, K., Gerhardt, C. A., Vannatta, K., Passo, M., & Taylor, J. (2000). The social, emotional, and behavioral functioning of children with juvenile rheumatoid arthritis. *Arthritis and Rheumatism, 43*, 1387–1396.

Noll, R. B., Swiecki, E., Garstein, M., Vannatta, K., Kalinyak, K. A., Davies, W. H., et al. (1994). Parental distress, family conflict, and role of social support for caregivers with or without a child with sickle cell disease. *Family Systems Medicine, 12*, 281–294.

Noll, R. B., Vannatta, K., Koontz, K., Kalinyak, K. A., Bukowski, W. M., & Davies, W. H. (1996). Peer relationships and emotional well-being of children with sickle cell disease. *Child Development, 67*, 423–436.

Noll, R. B., Yoshua, L. A., Vannatta, K., Kalinyak, K., Bukowski, W. M., & Davies, W. H. (1995). Social competence of siblings of children with sickle cell anemia. *Journal of Pediatric Psychology, 20*, 165–172.

Quittner, A. L., Opipari, L. C., Espelage, D. L., Carter, B., Eid, N., & Eigen, H. (1998). Role strain in couples with and without a child with a chronic illness: Associations with marital satisfaction, intimacy, and daily mood. *Health Psychology, 17*, 112–124.

Sandberg, D. E., Meyer-Bahlburg, H. F. L., & Yager, T. J. (1991). The Child Behavior Checklist nonclinical standardization samples: Should they be used as norms? *Journal of the American Academy of Child and Adolescent Psychiatry, 30*, 124–134.

Sargent, J. R., Sahler, O. J., Roghmann, K. J., Mulhern, R. K., Barbarin, O. A., Carpenter, P. J., et al. (1995). Sibling adaptation to childhood cancer collaborative study: Siblings' perceptions of the cancer experience. *Journal of Pediatric Psychology, 20*, 151–164.

Stehbens, J. A., Kaleita, T. A., Noll, R. B., MacLean, W. E., Jr., O'Brien, R. T., Waskerwitz, M. J., et al. (1991). CNS prophylaxis of childhood leukemia: What are the long-term neurological, neuropsychological, and behavioral effects? *Neuropsychology Review, 2*, 147–177.

Stein, R. E. K., & Jessop, D. J. (1982). A noncategorical approach to chronic childhood illness. *Public Health Reports, 97*, 354–362.

Timko, C., Stovel, K. W., & Moos, R. H. (1992). Functioning among mothers and fathers of children with juvenile rheumatic disease: A longitudinal study. *Journal of Pediatric Psychology, 6*, 705–724.

Vannatta, K., Gartstein, M. A., Short, A., & Noll, R. B. (1998). A controlled study of peer relationships of children surviving brain tumors. *Journal of Pediatric Psychology, 23*, 279–287.

Vannatta, K., Zeller, M., Noll, R. B., & Koontz, K. (1998). Social functioning of children surviving bone marrow transplantation. *Journal of Pediatric Psychology, 23*, 169–178.

Verrill, J. R., Schafer, J., Vannatta, K., & Noll, R. B. (2000). Aggression, antisocial behavior, and substance use in survivors of pediatric cancer: Possible protective effects of cancer and its treatment. *Journal of Pediatric Psychology, 25*, 493–502.

Wallander, J. L., & Varni, J. W. (1998). Effects of pediatric chronic physical disorders on child and family adjustment. *Journal of Child Psychology and Psychiatry, 39*, 29–46.

III

OVERCOMING ADVERSE CIRCUMSTANCES IN THE COMMUNITY AND SOCIETY

11

BUILDING PROTECTION, SUPPORT, AND OPPORTUNITY FOR INNER-CITY CHILDREN AND YOUTH AND THEIR FAMILIES

PATRICK H. TOLAN, LONNIE R. SHERROD, DEBORAH GORMAN-SMITH, AND DAVID B. HENRY

Children and families living in inner-city environments face formidable challenges to healthy development. And yet, most children who grow up in inner cities become productive and contributing members of society. This chapter describes some of the threats to healthy development for those living in the inner city, as well as the individual, family, and community factors that act to buffer the negative effects of those threats. The authors suggest that positive youth development approaches are particularly promising strengths-based approaches for promoting healthy development for youths. Public policies should help ensure that inner-city youths and families have access to the same protections, opportunities, and supports enjoyed by families not subject to these challenging conditions.

* * *

The conditions in the inner city create formidable impediments to healthy development, effective adaptation, and individual well-being. Inner-city neighborhoods are characterized by concentrated poverty, high crime rates, low owner occupancy, and elevated rates of health and social problems (Wilson, 1987). As a setting for children's development, the inner city involves scarce and unreliable resources and frequent threats that come in multiple forms and may be beyond a child's or family's control. Many sources cause levels of stress that would strain the coping skills of almost anyone; this multiplicity and frequency of threats can seriously harm children and families. The cumulative effect is to make healthy and safe development difficult to achieve. Responses that are adaptive and effective elsewhere may be ineffective in the inner city, and those that are adaptive in this setting—such as providing immediate safety and status—may, in the longer term, seriously limit life opportunities and social competence. For example, whereas involvement in antisocial groups marginalizes children in most communities, in the inner city gang membership may provide protection and status that are very hard to ensure otherwise.

In this chapter, we use what has been called a *developmental–ecological perspective* to explore the complex sources of stress that come with growing up in the inner city and the means of coping effectively with that stress. We identify four major types of stress that inner-city youths must manage in order to attain effective and successful development. The focus is on how to provide the support, protection, and opportunities that address the stresses that these children face. The four types of stress must be understood within a social and economic structure (the inner city) that is vastly different from most other U.S. communities. This structure of extreme poverty, economic inequity, racism, and oppression affect all inner-city residents but especially families rearing children. These conditions can act as "background conditions," or chronic environmental stressors, that impede development and require strong support, protection, and opportunity if inner-city children are to have their due opportunity for healthy development (Anderson, 1991).

KEY SOCIAL PROBLEMS RELATED TO INNER-CITY RISK

In the late 1980s, U.S. inner cities faced an increasing concentration of social problems accompanying the loss of an economic base and the exit of middle-class residents. Increased gang activity, diminished community-sanctioned social control of behavior (e.g., loss of respect for public property), high rates of teenage pregnancy and single parenting, and the rising prominence of drug sales as a major part of the economy engendered an ecology of isolation, despair, and danger (Wilson, 1987). The increasing alienation of inner cities from the rest of society prompted a fading attraction to and belief in conventional accomplishments and conventional avenues to success. Of particular concern are the highly elevated rates of violence to which children and youths in inner cities are exposed that frequently result in injury and death. Pervasive yet unpredictable violence can promote an emotional numbness, a preoccupying vigilance against potential harm from others, or aggressive tendencies that are characteristic of posttraumatic stress disorder (Garbarino, Kostelny, & Dubrow, 1991).

These social conditions present a bleak portrayal of life fraught with ever-present potential harm, impediments, and limited resources for successful development. However, despite these conditions and the level of threat, most inner-city youths do *not* fail in school, become parents too soon, show serious psychopathology, or engage in delinquency and violence. Most develop into productive and contributing members of society. Despite grave inequities in the quality of health care and schools, they succeed. Despite social and economic disconnection, families protect, nurture, and support their children toward conventional success and integration into the larger society.

Emerging evidence also suggests that inner-city families may not have lesser skills or fewer of the qualities that aid child development than do families living elsewhere (Gorman-Smith, Tolan, & Henry, 1998). What constitutes effective parenting may, in fact, depend much on the setting. Careful, controlling parenting that limits exposure to peers and to a violent neighborhood may elsewhere stifle social involvement (Mason, Cauce, Gonzales, Hiraga, & Grove, 1994), but in the inner city, obedience is as important, or more so, than autonomy. Fostering strong family loyalty and linking of behavior and self to heritage may play a more importrant role than has been previously assumed (Garcia Coll, Meyer, & Brillon, 1995). What defines good parenting may depend on the context, including how inner-city parents manage exposure to potentially harmful influences (Harwood, Schoelmerich, Ventura-Cook, Schulze, & Wilson, 1996; Mason et al., 1994).

DEVELOPMENTAL THREATS AS STRESS

We have identified four types of stress that merit consideration in understanding risk for inner-city children and youths: (a) chronic environmental stress, (b) life events, (c) daily hassles, and (d) role strain (Tolan & Gorman-Smith, 1997). This organization differentiates stress by its specific impact and required coping tasks. A major feature of the organization is that it considers how conditions of chronic environmental stress relate to increased levels of the other types of stressors in this setting and how it complicates coping.

Chronic environmental stress is defined as a constant background level of threat based in the environmental physical and social structure (Anderson, 1991). It includes racism and economic inequity, but also heightened danger and the intrusion of social problems into everyday life. Chronic environmental stress impinges on optimism, sense of control, and goal-directed behavior—cognitive features that can propel a child to be industrious and engaged with the world (Anderson, 1991). Similarly, these pervasive and routine conditions may seriously constrain the positive effects that more action-oriented coping can have. This form of stress may lead to coping responses that focus only on short-term benefits (i.e., keeping oneself safe), often at the expense of positive long-term outcomes (Garbarino et al., 1991).

Life events are defined as the stressful events and life transitions that, by their occurrence, cause distress to the person experiencing them (e.g., temporary economic disruptions, death of a family member, property loss; Tolan, Miller, & Thomas, 1988). Life events are distinguished from the minor irritations of daily hassles by their relative brevity and the disruption they cause to ongoing conditions. Although all children may experience life events stress (Compas, Worsham, & Ey, 1992), inner-city children are likely to experience more of these events than other children. For example, nearly half of the poor, urban, elementary school children surveyed in one study reported a loss of a friend or family member, significant health problems in the family, or witnessing violence in the preceding year (Attar, Guerra, & Tolan, 1994). The overall rate was four to six times higher than that reported by suburban children (Dubow, Tisak, Causey, Hryshko, & Reid, 1991). Also, children from the most economically distressed and violent neighborhoods experienced rates twice those of youths in less distressed but still poor urban communities. It may be not only that life events are more frequent in their lives, but also that they a have greater impact (Neff, 1985). This increased impact may be due to the fewer resources available to facilitate coping, the rapidity and constancy of stressful events, or the reduced impact of individual coping on outcomes (Anderson, 1991; McLoyd, 1990), as well as these youths' status as being both poor and minority (Ulbrich, Warheit, & Zimmerman, 1989).

Daily hassles are minor stressors that are part of day-to-day life (Tolan et al., 1988). Daily hassles are considered harmful because they can detract from well-being and interfere with productive activities. In the face of chronic environmental stress, high levels of stressful life events, and limited resources and support, it becomes more difficult to manage daily hassles. Two common complications for inner-city residents are the exacerbation of daily hassles due to racism (for ethnic minority residents) and the compounding effect community characteristics can have on hassles. For children of the inner city, racism may be experienced in many forms. It can be an insult or personal humiliation, disruption of a simple interaction or completion of a daily task, or blocked access to opportunities and resources needed for daily functioning. For example, approaching a teacher about schoolwork or a dispute about a grade—a daily hassle for most children in most communities—can be overwhelming if the teacher has shown prejudice.

Role strain is defined as stress due to one's inability to fulfill socially ascribed roles (Pearlin, 1983). For inner-city children and youths, role strain can result from many factors—inadequate schools, limited access to mentoring about conventional social roles, limited knowledge about entry to and training for esteemed social roles, or rejection and teasing for being "snobbish" or self-important if one is perceived to be pursuing conventional achievement too earnestly (McLoyd, 1990; Wilson, 1987). Members of ethnic minority groups can experience role strain because of conflict between the values of their culture and those of mainstream society (Anderson, 1991; Ogbu, 1985). For example, the value of family loyalty in Mexican culture can conflict with the mainstream culture's emphasis on autonomy, thereby increasing risk (Florsheim, Tolan, & Gorman-Smith, 1996). Further, an inner-city child who focuses on "moving up" may do so at the cost of losing close affiliation to family and group attachment (Laosa, 1979; Spencer, Dobbs, & Swanson, 1988). Such individual-oriented action may be seen as forsaking culturally valued loyalty to others before self. The consequences of individual achievement may be disaffection with family members as well as a literal move away to a higher socioeconomic neighborhood (Anderson, 1991). What elsewhere is a positive outcome and a sanctioned developmental process can be an emotionally charged dilemma for inner-city ethnic minority children and their families.

These multiple forms of stress and their social–economic setting create a tough challenge for families and children of the inner city and for the institutions and agencies attempting to support and aid them. Responses must incorporate multiple levels of support to manage child and family well-being. It is imperative that the programs and policies embed normal parenting concerns within networks of family and friends (Tolan & Gorman-Smith, 1997). Too often, families of the inner city are isolated from neighbors and the support they may offer. This support encompasses both social and psychological support as well as material aid and help with day-to-day tasks. The myriad threats require that this connection to networks be strong, perhaps stronger than elsewhere.

Economic incentives to reintegrate inner cities into the larger political economy of the city, region, and nation are critical for addressing this array of stress and the coping it requires. Also critical are opportunities for conventional success, for adult supervision and structured activities in free time, and for participation in the formal and informal social processes that teach youths about planning for the future. The structural features can provide a basis for realizing family hopes for children, for diminishing the conflict between adaptive and effective coping, and for permitting families to protect their children and manage the normal demands of rearing children.

WHAT WORKS, WHAT DOESN'T, WHAT'S NEEDED

There is a long history of interventions meant to support inner-city families, youths, and schools. Unfortunately, few of these have focused on linking families, schools, and other institutions and functions. In addition, most have not focused on supporting the family (versus the individual) or on working to build normal levels of protection, support, and opportunity. Also, many of the empirically tested interventions have not been based in the inner city. Although there are important exceptions and attention to these factors is increasing, the overall pattern of research has been to focus on deficits in the family or the individual that account for academic, behavioral, and social inadequacies (Luthar, 1999).

The limitations imposed by inner city conditions can be overcome if interventions focus on supporting normative family functioning, engage social networks to support parenting, and emphasize issues that are relevant in that context. It may be that the best approaches are those that direct efforts at supporting families in managing developmental and environmental challenges as well as those that promote youth supports and capitalize on youth strengths. These factors are described in more detail in the following sections.

Family as Buffer

Important family characteristics that mitigate the stress of inner-city life for children are family resourcefulness, adaptability, and organization (McAdoo, 1982); the development of reliable and effective social ties (McAdoo, 1982); and protective parenting styles (Ogbu, 1985). Staples (1978) noted that, historically, African American families have provided their members with a sanctuary that buttresses against pervasive oppression and racism (Mason et al., 1994). Another commonly cited form of buffering is the extended family and informal kin networks (Massey, Scott, & Dornbusch, 1975). Compas and his colleagues (1992) suggested that a well-functioning family may protect an inner-city child from the deleterious effects of stress, although they noted that this has not been adequately evaluated.

Parenting practices have been linked to the impact of stress on youth, although there have been few specific studies of buffering effects among inner-city children. Research has shown that responsive, accepting, and stimulating parental care can promote resilience among low birth weight, premature children living in poverty (Bradley et al., 1994). It has also been demonstrated (Gorman-Smith, Tolan, & Henry, 1998, 2000) that families that have good parenting skills, adequate problem-solving skills, and emotional cohesion have a protective effect in inner-city communities. However, that protective effect depends on the extent of the family's sense of community involvement and ownership, including a social support network for parents. These results suggest that focusing on skills and within-family relationships alone may be inadequate. Instead, focusing on supporting or promoting parenting functions that are embedded in the community is critical for promoting the positive effect that good family functioning can have on development.

Family Coping

In addition to the buffering and refuge from harm that families can provide, inner-city families may enhance the coping of children by teaching them strategies for survival and methods of mutual support and by fighting negative myths of society (Massey et al., 1975). The effectiveness of a child's coping also depends on family functioning, and the best approaches are those that are sanctioned by the family, modeled by others, and consistent with family beliefs and expectations (Tolan & Gorman-Smith, 1997). For example, Peters (1976) found that most African American parents expected their children to encounter racism by age 6 but were uncertain how to prepare them or how to help them cope with it. Although it was clear that parents saw racism as an inevitable stressor, they also worried that preparing for it would have undue influence, making the child overly self-conscious about race and racism. Their primary strategy was to delay the encounter as long as possible. Thus, the effectiveness of coping can be compromised when the stress cannot be prevented or adequately prepared for. Coping is directed toward minimizing actual and potential harm. As increasing evidence surfaces on the effectiveness for inner-city youths of incorporating a sociopolitical understanding of racism and economic inequities, more programs are needed that aid parents in determining how to navigate these and other difficult issues (Zimmerman, Ramirez-Valles, & Maton, 1999).

A very promising avenue for helping to lower risk among inner-city youths is to support families in managing the challenging environment and in connecting to health care institutions and schools and to neighbors and extended family. There are options for promoting these supports and opportunities, even if the needed structural changes that isolate the inner city economically and socially do not occur. Another avenue of great promise is to develop resources and opportunities that assist youths directly in their developmental needs. This approach focuses not only on aiding youths by protecting them and maintaining high levels of involvement with invested adults, but also providing opportunities for involvement in meaningful activities and useful roles within their communities. This approach has shown some success in reducing risk among high-risk youths, suggesting promise for youths living in risky environments (Tolan & Guerra, 1994).

Promoting Positive Youth Development

Unlike an approach that focuses on which children have "what it takes" to overcome even the most arduous odds, the most promising strengths-based approaches for inner-city youths are those that assume that individuals have different inherent protective factors, skills, and opportunities. One indicator of resilience is the ability of young people to take advantage of naturally occurring resources. However, a more important index of resilience is the level of resources available to youths to meet their developmental needs, regardless of their individual ability to use those resources. Few of urban youths' needs are met naturally; therefore, they require more socially constructed interventions than other youths. An important aspect of a strengths-based intervention approach is a focus on encouraging the positive development of youth rather than on fixing problems or eliminating defects. For several decades, research and policy have been devoted to identifying and correcting problems of youth: high-risk sexual behavior, teen pregnancy, school failure and dropout, substance use and abuse, and violence and crime, to name a few. It was because of this focus that the emphasis on risk factors became prominent. Because not all youths succumb equally to risks, the concept of resilience emerged, and prevention efforts were developed. Although these efforts have enjoyed some success in reducing risks and health-compromising behaviors, their achievement is constrained by inadequate funding and by the limited evidence of sustained behavior change after the program has ended (Leffert et al., 1998).

A focus on promoting the positive development of youths rather than on fixing problems leads to the development-promoting qualities of families and communities and to policies that make up for the shortfalls of the environments. If society provides the supports that youths need, all have the potential to beat the odds. This positive youth development approach is based on working groups such as the Search Institute (Leffert et al., 1998), the International Youth Foundation (Cahill, 1997), and the Youth Policy Forum.

Both external and internal assets of youths have been identified and correlated with environmental and individual resilience factors. Internal factors include commitment to learning, positive values, social competencies, and positive identity. Broad categories of external factors include family and community supports, empowerment, boundaries and expectations, and constructive use of time. The presence of risk behaviors is inversely correlated with assets. These assets, of course, interact in complex ways and vary substantially by community (Leffert et al., 1998). However, the positive youth development approach demonstrates how providing the means to meet youths' multiple developmental needs by ensuring protection, support, and opportunities across these important contexts is a preferred focus for intervention.

The interest in positive youth development has focused primarily on adolescents. However, there are many examples of programs that focus on building the strengths of young mothers (e.g., Olds' visiting nurse program; Olds, Henderson, & Kitzman, 1994), of families with school-age children (e.g., the SAFE Children program of Tolan, Gorman-Smith, & Henry, 2002), and of preadolescents (e.g., Lochman's coping power program; Lochman & Wells, 1996). Each of these programs focuses on helping participants meet normative developmental challenges as well as the extraordinary challenges that urban poor communities can impose. For example, in the SAFE Children program, families with 1st-graders attending schools in high-crime, high-poverty neighborhoods participate in family group meetings to help with normal parenting issues, the transition to 1st grade, establishing and using support from other parents, and managing school relations. Children are also tutored to help them maintain national levels of reading achievement. Parents in the program were found to have maintained the initial level of enthusiasm for school involvement through 2nd grade, whereas the levels of involvement among parents in the comparison group dropped off quickly. Similarly, children in the program kept pace with national norms, whereas the comparison group fell steadily behind over time.

The National Research Council (NRC) and Institute of Medicine (IOM) Committee on Community-Level Programs for Youth (NRC & IOM, 2000) recently outlined a set of 10 key ingredients in strengths-based programs that promote effective development and support family coping:

1. Programs have clear goals and intended outcomes.
2. The content and focus are age appropriate but challenging.
3. The involvement is based on active learning processes.
4. The program provides a positive and safe environment.
5. There are adequate materials and facilities to conduct the program.
6. The staff is well prepared and supported and stable.
7. The staff is culturally competent and conducts outreach to diverse groups.
8. The program or approach works with parents and existing community groups and organizations.
9. The program elicits, supports, and promotes parental involvement and integrates youth needs with those of the family and parents.
10. The program or approach is conducted within a "learning organization," meaning that the organization is willing to adapt, improve, and develop as the setting, youth needs, and opportunities shift.

These are ideal hypothetical qualities of programs that both meet the needs of developing adolescents and attempt to promote strengths rather than correct deficiencies; that is, they are intended to convey the elements of a promising youth development program. There are now several good examples of positive youth development programs that focus on inner-city youths. All aim to provide youths with protection, support, and opportunities through relationships and constructive experiences that build on developmentally appropriate internal assets, such as social competencies, optimism, future orientation, and positive self-concept.

Although these programs are promising, for the most part their effectiveness has not yet been empirically proved, and the degree to which they display the qualities listed in the NRC and IOM (2000) report has not been assessed. Although several sources point to the effectiveness of such programs, there are far too few systematic, rigorous evaluations (Roth, Brooks-Gunn, Murray, & Foster, 1998). As with other types of programs, including risk-oriented programs, there is a need to demonstrate the public health benefits of such programs and to test the theorized process by which effects occur. Additionally, few programs have sufficient resources to allow them to develop management information systems (MIS) that would enable them to track easily the numbers and demographic characteristics of participants. Hence, such data typically only become available as part of a funded evaluation. Because of the paucity of evaluations and the lack of good MIS data sets, there are few programs with demonstrated effectiveness and fewer still that have available data needed for cost–benefit analyses. The exceptions are the larger and older national or citywide programs, of which we describe three.

Youth Build (www.youthbuild.org) is a training and leadership program that employs out-of-school youths ages 16 to 21 to rehabilitate housing in low-income areas. Participants come from diverse backgrounds, but most (73%) are from low-income families. Since the program started in 1993, more than 7,000 units of low-income housing have been built by youths involved in 180 Youth Build programs across the country. Nationwide, 89% of the students who enter the program get their high school diplomas, and 86% go on to college or jobs paying an average of $7.61 per hour. The success of Youth Build is based on several qualities. For example, youths are connected to meaningful experiences, do something to help communities, develop relationships with building supervisors and peers, and learn practical as well as social skills. Participants also have a strong commitment and connection to the program—many of the youths become so attached that they move into management-level positions with the program after completing the initial experience. The average cost per participant is $20,000 per year, including stipends, which is less than the cost of training in military, prisons, boot camps, job corps, or most colleges.

The largest municipally funded youth initiative in the country, the New York City Beacons, involves school-based community centers that seek to comprehensively address unmet needs of inner-city youth through a range of services and activities to participants before and after school as well as on weekends (www.aed.org/news/beacons.html). The programs, which are funded by the city's Department of Youth and Community Development, are based on school, community, and family partnerships. Initiated in 1991 with $5 million in funding, by 1998 the program had expanded to a budget of $40 million, serving more than 76,000 youths up to the age of 21 in 40 centers. By 1999, there were 76 Beacon centers, each receiving a base grant of $450,000. An evaluation by the Academy for Educational Development, in which 7,406 Beacons participants were surveyed over a 2-day period, found that Beacons attracts participants of all ages. About a quarter of the participants were under 12 years old, 49% were between 12 and 18, and 27% were age 19 or older (Warren, Brown, & Freudenberg, 1999). About a third of the participants (30%) reported that they visited the centers five to eight times per week, and nearly half (45%) visited more than eight times. Over a third had been involved for at least 3 years and about one fourth for 4 or more years. These centers work well because they are based in the community and use the resources of schools; as a result, youths come to them.

4-H, the U.S. Department of Agriculture and Cooperative Extension System's nationwide program for young people in kindergarten through grade 12, is the largest youth development program in the country (www.national4-hheadquarters.gov). It is also one of its most long-standing and celebrated its centennial in 2002. 4-H was created for the educational development of youths and to tap their creativity and energy. Its mission is to empower youths to meet their full potential, working and learning in partnership with caring adults. Although the program originally focused on farm-related activities, it more recently redirected its attention to urban youths, and by 1960 more than half of 4-H participants were nonfarm youths. Today, 45% of participants are from rural areas (populations up to 10,000) and 55% are from urban areas. In 2001, 6.7 million young people in kindergarten through grade 12 participated in 4-H, 30% of whom were minority youths. Current programs focus on such varied themes as citizenship, communications and expressive arts, personal development and leadership, environmental education, plants and animals, and consumer science.

The three programs described above are large national programs, including a large urban program. But there are also hundreds of local programs that may meet many of the qualities described in the NRC and IOM (2000) report that do not have Web sites or other direct sources of information about them available. For example, the Valued Youth Partnership Program in San Antonio (NRC & IOM, 2000) paired adolescents who had below-grade-level reading skills and poor school attendance with children in the first years of school. The adolescents' basic reading skills were sufficient for tutoring and mentoring the new readers. An evaluation demonstrated that the program lowered the school dropout rate of the mentors from 45% to 2% and showed similar magnitude in increases in self-esteem and school behavior. These small programs may be particularly important in furthering the development of local youths in their communities, but because there is so little research on such efforts, their effectiveness cannot be demonstrated, nor can one learn what works, for whom, under what conditions. One of the great research needs in the field is for applied research that not only evaluates such programs and details their use and value, but also explores them as contexts for positive youth development (Sherrod, 1997).

The notion of promoting youth development has become popular. A positive youth development approach has been embraced by programs serving youth (a computer search for positive youth development programs turned up 872,812 entries) and federal agencies such as the U.S. Department of Health and Human Services and the Department of Education. The National Youth Development Information Center (www.nydic.org) provides information on numerous positive youth development programs and evaluations. The final accomplishment is to design policies based on this approach.

POLICY SOLUTIONS

A strengths-based approach to urban children and youths necessitates some fundamental shifts in current policy approaches. Most fundamentally, most youth policies limit involvement to only those found at risk for the target problem, even though it is clear many youth problems co-occur and that in many youths at risk for one social or psychological problem are also at risk for others (Dryfoos, 1990). This results in categorical funding of programs that divide and disconnect programs' administration and resource distribution from other resources and in coordination in working with a given youth. Program providers focus on very specific programs, even though families and youths may face multiple strains. Integrated service provision is needed. However, given that financial survival and agency recognition depend on garnering as much funding and prominence as possible, usually through concentration on one particular problem, such integration is unlikely. Rather than building infrastructure that permits adaptive and reflexive responses to strengths and needs, and organizes services around meeting youths' complex needs, current policies tend to impose a view of youths and families as "cases" with a problem to be addressed independently of the many other issues in their lives.

Funding strengths-based programs rather than fix-it programs for specific deficits invests in infrastructure—which can further enhance capabilities—and moves away from a focus on services that depend on continuous funding. Another critical shift in policy required for a strengths-based approach is to change the circumstances under which services are accessible. Currently, youths and families have access to resources only if they demonstrate some failure, and they can gain access only to resources for that specific failure. When resources are thin, as they usually are in categorical funding, the effect is to delay support until the most dire circumstances and needs are demonstrated. Also, with problem-oriented categorical programming, even those with severe problems in one area of life may not have access to aid in other areas. Strengths-based approaches, in contrast, rest on integrating services and supports based on youths' and families' capabilities and needs—not the areas of specific failure, or even failure per se. Thus, to address the needs of urban poor families, policies must move from categorical and problem-focused approaches, with access restricted (based on need), to those that integrate resources and permit access as needs are identified. More open access and greater integration are likely to lead to more service use at points of less serious failure, thus lowering the costs of the programs and resources per family compared with the superficially frugal current approach of requiring a specific need and a specific level of failure to obtain support.

What would such shifts entail? Broadly speaking, the new approach would define policies as those that create support and opportunity that permit inner-city families to meet the normal developmental challenges their children face. These approaches would help ensure adequate progress in school, adequate nutrition and health from infancy through adolescence, and less disparity in the educational, recreational, and social settings in which these children develop (Carnegie Corporation of New York, 1989). Such policies would remove impediments to meeting the developmental challenges at each stage of childhood, promote competence in multiple domains, permit continued reliance on existing competencies, and recognize the interdependence of the well-being of inner-city children and families with those in other segments of society (National Commission on Children, 1991). Rather than aiming to stem harm or limit failure, these policies would aim to promote for youths a strong sense of their role in their family, the community, and the world. They would help reconnect young children to older persons and help youths understand the responsibilities they will and should have (Carnegie Corporation of New York, 1989).

Such an approach must affect many levels of influences on the inner-city community. Policies must be reoriented toward integrating the inner city economically and socially with the broader society. Changes in the social and economic base of communities are important for providing inner-city youths the protection, support, and opportunities that all children need and deserve. From an individual development perspective, both research and policy attention should focus on mentoring and other ties to adults, civic engagement among youths, the impact of new technologies on development and class inequities in access, the increasing diversity of the population, the impact of culture on youth development, and intergroup relationships. Finally, we must recognize that the transition to adulthood has changed profoundly in recent decades and that we must design policies to aid youths accordingly (Sherrod, 1997).

We recognize that these policy suggestions are often difficult to realize. Efforts can fail because they offer ineffective content and activities, because the service format and delivery constrain effectiveness, or because there is no sustainable organization of service delivery and personnel responsible for services (Tolan, 2000). These same issues also apply to strengths-based approaches and to efforts aimed at inner-city families and other segments of the population. Thus, for these strength-based approaches and specific policy shifts to be useful, there are several features of program development and organization of their funding and delivery that should be considered.

One such feature is to move from the exemplars listed in this chapter to strong empirical demonstrations of effects from community-based implementations. In some cases, it may be that exemplars need dissemination in pure form to be effective. It may also be that these exemplars can serve as a database of valuable approaches from which communities could incorporate the most useful and promising approaches for their particular locale. Second, careful attention should be paid to the funding basis and to the sustainability of support for programs. Staffing issues must be considered as well, including the importance of adequate support for attracting quality employees and of offering stimulating career paths that permit talented contributors to remain involved as they advance. Finally, there is a need for evaluation that informs modifications and further development and that assesses the effectiveness of promising approaches. The goal should be to modify or abandon ineffective approaches and move ahead with those that are most effective (Tolan & Guerra, 1998). Finally, for policies to succeed, they must be implemented with a focus on the family or on the child or adolescent as part of a family (Dryfoos, 1990).

It perhaps goes without saying that basing policy decisions in research is critical and that too frequently this does not occur. Research-based policy is more objective, and it endures and transcends highly charged political environments; therefore, it is more effective in the long term. It promotes investment in youth capital, addresses core causes rather than treating symptoms, promotes a long-term perspective, and acknowledges that it is never too late to invest in children (Sherrod, 1997). Second, research-based policy that is strengths-based clearly charts avenues for success in the surroundings in which youths grow up, rather than attempting to rehabilitate or remedy personal characteristics. Finally, it orients research and policy to "kids at promise," to use one program director's substitute for the phrase "youths at risk."

In moving to a strengths-based approach, based on the empirical literature reviewed in this chapter and the growing evidence from strengths-based programs, we can identify four areas of policy review and initiative that are clearly needed:

1. Inner-city families should be accorded the same protections, opportunities, and supports that families not subjected to these environmental conditions enjoy.
2. Programs should work to improve and support family and youth coping skills rather than to remedy perceived deficits.
3. Program approaches should have a "local fit," meaning that they should be designed to work within existing social structures, to incorporate the issues that are central to families in the community, and to incorporate or reflect culturally appropriate values.
4. Programs established to address the needs of people in the inner city should be based on sound research and evaluation.

1. Accord Inner-City Families the Same Protections, Opportunities, and Supports

Improving the adequacy of health care facilities and access, educational institutions, family support services, and safety in inner cities can have a substantial impact on risk levels among inner-city youths and should reduce the prevalence rates of school failure and dropout, early pregnancy, serious drug and alcohol abuse, and involvement in gangs and other criminal activity.

2. Support Coping Rather Than Remedy Deficits

Inner-city families and children and youths have many strengths. In many areas, most families living in these very challenging conditions are functioning at levels comparable to families and children elsewhere. However, they face less adequate health and educational systems, fewer life opportunities, less support for normal challenges to family and individual skills, and some extraordinary challenges and threats to health and life that call on extraordinary coping skills. Programs and policies that strengthen family capability, youth attachment to schools and communities, and access to day care, employment opportunities, and youth recreation and social programs are more likely to improve social problems than those that are focused on remedying or stemming the rate of a specific problem.

3. Design Programs to Fit Local Settings

Program approaches must be context sensitive—that is, they must consider that coping skills may have different effects in different settings, and they may need to change as developmental stages of family and youth change.

4. Base Programs on Sound Research

Policies and funding that encourage more collaboration among researchers, evaluators, and community-based programs is important, as is better integration of social safety net programs.

CONCLUSION

With each of these recommended approaches, program design or initiative development must involve inner-city communities. For example, strengths must be defined from within the community as well as from the outside. Subtle variations, not only by ethnicity and class, but also by region and history, are important influences on the viability, effectiveness, and sustainability of efforts that are strengths based.

It is easy to summarize what we need to do for youth. Hugh Price, president and chief executive officer of the National Urban League, put it most succinctly: "Youth development is what you'd do for your own kid on a good day. We don't need a fancy definition to know what to do." We must reconnect what we would do for all our children with what we would do for inner-city youths; policy must reconfirm that they are all our children (Edelman, 1989).

REFERENCES

Anderson, L. P. (1991). Acculturative stress: A theory of relevance to Black Americans. *Clinical Psychology Review, 11*, 685–702.

Attar, B. K., Guerra, N., & Tolan, P. H. (1994). Neighborhood disadvantage, stressful life events, and adjustment in urban elementary-school children. *Journal of Clinical Child Psychology, 23*, 391–400.

Bradley, R. H., Whiteside, L., Mundfrom, D. J., Casey, P. H., Kelleher, K., & Pope, K. (1994). Contribution of early intervention and early caregiving experiences to resilience in low-birthweight, premature children living in poverty. *Journal of Clinical Child Psychology, 23*, 425–434.

Cahill, M. (1997, April). *Youth development and community development: Promises and challenges of convergence* (Paper No. 2). New York: Youth Development Institute Fund for the City of New York, Ford Foundation, and International Youth Foundation.

Carnegie Corporation of New York. (1989). *Turning points: Preparing American youth for the 21st century. A report of the Task Force on Education of Young Adolescents.* New York: Carnegie Council on Adolescent Development.

Compas, B. E., Worsham, N. L., & Ey, S. (1992). Conceptual and developmental issues in children's coping with stress. In A. M. LaGreca, L. J. Siegel, J. L. Wallander, & C. E. Walker (Eds.), *Stress and coping in child health* (pp. 7–24). New York: Guilford Press.

Dryfoos, J. G. (1990). *Adolescents at risk: Prevalence and prevention.* New York: Oxford University Press.

Dubow, E. F., Tisak, J., Causey, D., Hryshko, A., & Reid, G. (1991). A two-year longitudinal study of stressful life events, social support, and social problem-solving skills: Contributions to children's behavioral and academic adjustment. *Child Development, 62*, 583–599.

Edelman, M. W. (1989). Black children in America. In J. Dewart (Ed.), *The state of Black America* (pp. 63–75). New York: National Urban League.

Florsheim, P., Tolan, P. H., & Gorman-Smith, D. (1996). Family processes and risk for externalizing behavior problems among African-American and Hispanic boys. *Journal of Consulting and Clinical Psychology, 64*, 1222–1230.

Garbarino, J., Kostelny, K., & Dubrow, N. (1991). What children can tell us about living in danger. *American Psychologist, 46*, 376–383.

Garcia Coll, C. T., Meyer, E. C., & Brillon, L. (1995). Ethnic and minority parenting. In M. H. Bornstein (Ed.), *Handbook of parenting* (Vol. 2, pp. 189–210). Mahwah, NJ: Erlbaum.

Gorman-Smith, D., Tolan, P. H., & Henry, D. (1998). The role of exposure to community violence and developmental problems among inner-city youth. *Development and Psychopathology, 10,* 101–116.

Gorman-Smith, D., Tolan, P. H., & Henry, D. B. (2000). A developmental-ecological model of the relation of family functioning to patterns of delinquency. *Journal of Quantitative Criminology, 16,* 169–198.

Harwood, R. L., Schoelmerich, A., Ventura-Cook, E., Schulze, P. A., & Wilson, S. P. (1996). Culture and class influences on Anglo and Puerto Rican mothers' beliefs regarding long-term socialization goals and child behavior. *Child Development, 67,* 2446–2461.

Laosa, L. (1979). Psychological stress, coping, and development of Hispanic immigrant children. In F. C. Serafica, A. I., Schwebel, & R. K. Russsell (Eds.), *Mental health of ethnic minorities.* New York: Praeger.

Leffert, N., Benson, P. L., Scales, P. C., Sharma, A. R., Drake, D. R., & Blyth, D. A. (1998). Developmental assets: Measurement and prediction of risk behaviors among adolescents. *Applied Developmental Science, 2,* 209–230.

Lochman, J. E., & Wells, K. C. (1996). A social-cognitive intervention with aggressive children: Prevention effects and contextual implementation issues. In R. D. Peters & R. J. McMahon (Eds.), *Preventing childhood disorders, substance abuse, and delinquency: Banff international behavorial science series* (pp. 111–143). Thousand Oaks, CA: Sage.

Luthar, S. S. (1999). *Poverty and children's adjustment* (Vol. 41, Developmental Clinical Psychology and Psychiatry). Thousand Oaks, CA: Sage.

Mason, C., Cauce, A., Gonzales, N., Hiraga, Y., & Grove, K. (1994). An ecological model of externalizing behaviors in African-American adolescents: No family is an island. *Journal of Research on Adolescence, 4,* 639–655.

Massey, G. C., Scott, M., & Dornbusch, S. M. (1975). Racism without racists: Institutional racism in urban schools. *Black Scholar, 7,* 3.

McAdoo, H. P. (1982). Stress absorbing systems in Black families. *Family Relations, 31,* 479–488.

McLoyd, V. C. (1990). The impact of economic hardship on Black families and children: Psychological distress, parenting, and socioemotional development. *Child Development, 61,* 311–346.

National Commission on Children. (1991). *Beyond rhetoric.* Washington, DC: National Commission on Children.

National Research Council, & Institute of Medicine. (2000). *After-school programs to promote child and adolescent development: Summary of a workshop.* Washington, DC: National Academy Press.

Neff, J. A. (1985). Race and vulnerability to stress: An examination of differential vulnerability. *Journal of Personality and Social Psychology, 49,* 481–491.

Ogbu, J. U. (1985). A cultural ecology of competence among inner-city blacks. In M. B. Spencer & G. K. Brookins (Eds.), *Beginnings: The social and affective development of Black children* (pp. 45–66). Hillsdale, NJ: Erlbaum.

Olds, D. L., Henderson, C. R., Jr., & Kitzman, H. (1994). Does prenatal and infancy nurse home visitation have enduring effects on qualities of parental caregiving and child health at 25 to 50 months of life? *Pediatrics, 93,* 89–98.

Pearlin, L. I. (1983). Role strain and personal stress. In H. Kaplan (Ed.), *Psychosocial stress* (pp. 189–205). New York: Academic Press.

Peters, M. F. (1976). *Nine Black families: A study of household management and childrearing in Black families with working mothers.* Ann Arbor, MI: University Microfilms.

Roth, J., Brooks-Gunn, J., Murray, L., & Foster, W. (1998). Promoting healthy adolescents: Synthesis of youth development program evaluations. *Journal of Research on Adolescence, 8,* 423–459.

Sherrod, L. R. (1997). Promoting youth development through reseach-based policies. *Applied Developmental Science, 1,* 17–27.

Spencer, M. B., Dobbs, B., & Swanson, D. P. (1988). African American adolescents: Adaptational processes and socio-economic diversity in behavioral outcomes. *Journal of Adolescence, 11,* 117–137.

Staples, R. (1978). *The Black family: Essays and studies.* Belmont, CA: Wadsworth.

Tolan, P. H. (2000, February 7–11). *The inner-city of the United States and risk for substance use among youth.* Monograph prepared for the World Health Organization Meeting on Urbanization, Youth and Risk Factors for Substance Use, Kobe, Japan.

Tolan, P. H., & Gorman-Smith, D. (1997). Families and the development of urban children. In O. Reyes, H. Walberg, & R. Weissberg (Eds.), *Interdisciplinary perspectives on children and youth* (pp. 67–91). Newbuy Park, CA: Sage.

Tolan, P. H., Gorman-Smith, D., & Henry, D. (2002). *Supporting families in a high risk setting: Proximal effects of the SAFE Children prevention program.* Manuscript submitted for publication.

Tolan, P. H., & Guerra, N. G. (1994). *What works in reducing adolescent violence: An empirical review of the field* (Monograph prepared for the Center for the Study and Prevention of Youth Violence). Boulder, CO: University of Colorado.

Tolan, P. H., & Guerra, N. (1998). Societal causes of violence towards children. In P. K. Trickett & C. Schellenbach (Eds.), *Violence against children in the family and the community* (pp. 195–210). Washington, DC: American Psychological Association.

Tolan, P. H., Miller, L., & Thomas, P. (1988). Perception and experience of types of social stress and self-image among adolescents. *Journal of Youth and Adolescence, 17,* 147–163.

Ulbrich, P. M., Warheit, G. J., & Zimmerman, R. S. (1989). Race, socioeconomic status, and psychological distress: An examination of differential vulnerability. *Journal of Health and Social Behavior, 30*(1), 131–146.

Warren, C., Brown, P., & Freudenberg, N. (1999). *Evaluation of the New York City Beacons: Summary of phase I findings*. Unpublished report, Chapin Hall for Children, University of Chicago. Retrieved December 12, 1999, from http://www.aed.org/beacons.html

Wilson, W. J. (1987). *The truly disadvantaged: The inner-city, the underclass, and public policy*. Chicago: University of Chicago Press.

Zimmerman, M. A., Ramirez-Valles, J., & Maton, K. I. (1999). Resilience among urban African American male adolescents: A study of the protective effects of sociopolitical control on their mental health. *American Journal of Community Psychology, 27*, 733–751.

12

OPPORTUNITIES FOR SCHOOLS TO PROMOTE RESILIENCE IN CHILDREN AND YOUTH

EMILIE PHILLIPS SMITH, GLORIA SWINDLER BOUTTE,
EDWARD ZIGLER, AND MATIA FINN-STEVENSON

This chapter emphasizes the potential of schools to contribute positively to the academic and psychological development of at-risk children. To achieve this potential, the authors propose changes in multiple domains of schooling, including teacher attitudes and relationships with students, instructional approaches, classroom behavioral environments, curricula, and school climate. In particular, the authors advocate the development of home–school–community partnerships and the integrated and comprehensive provision of family services. Deficits-based approaches emphasize the remediation of academic problems and the treatment of psychological problems affecting problematic students and families. In contrast, a whole-school approach emphasizes the importance of strengthening the school environment and mission and promotes a process of change that builds on existing strengths of students, teachers, families, and communities.

* * *

Schools, along with families and communities, are important influences that can contribute to the development of healthy and successful young people, even those thought to be at risk. Schools can serve as a negative influence, to perpetuate the status quo, or use the opportunity to serve as a positive trans-

213

forming influence in the lives of children and youth. This chapter focuses on the ways in which schools can help to promote resilience in children, with attention to some of the implications for public policy.

Resilience is the ability to survive, and even to thrive, in the face of adversity (Haggerty, Sherrod, Garmezy, & Rutter, 1996; Werner, 1994). Resilient children are those who have been exposed to various risk factors but have been able to surmount these risks and challenges to their development and emerge relatively well adjusted. The research identifying the importance of schools in the lives of children indicates that it is worthwhile to focus time and attention on school reform and policy specifically aimed at the school setting. These efforts recognize that to help children, they must be focused not only on individual children, but also on the important influences in children's lives, including the school, that either unknowingly perpetuate risk or help to ameliorate it.

This chapter explores the ways that schools can contribute to the academic and psychosocial development of children and promote resilience, especially for those who are most in need. First, the school is explored as one of a number of important ecological settings influencing children's social and behavioral development. Second, the relationship between school achievement and children's psychosocial outcomes is explored. Next, the research examining the role of the school setting in children's academic and behavioral outcomes (e.g., violence, delinquency, substance abuse) is summarized. Lastly and importantly, building on the summary of research on schools, policy directions are proposed that build strengths in the school setting with demonstrated effectiveness in enhancing children's resilience and success.

AN ECOLOGICAL VIEW OF THE SETTINGS
IN CHILDREN'S LIVES

An ecological perspective of children's development views families, schools, and communities as settings where young people interact with others who influence their values, perceptions, and behavior (Bronfenbrenner, 1986). These relationships are reciprocal—families, schools, and communities influence children just as children influence the tone of the family, school, and community. These interactions are also developmental—they change and mature.

Substantial research supports the role of the family as the most primary and proximal influence on children's lives (see, e.g., Baumrind, 1985; Brody, Stoneman, & Flor, 1995; Hirschi, 1969; Patterson, 1982). The family setting is the first one in which children grow, learn, and interact. Yet for many American children, the family setting changes over time, and nearly half of them spend time living apart from one or both of their biological parents by the time they reach age 18 (Bianchi, 1995). The dynamic nature of families in the United States does not negate the influence of family, but instead draws more attention to the need to understand and help strengthen families for their critical role in children's lives.

In addition to the family, school is an important setting for developing young people. In the United States, school-age children spend many of their waking hours in school, ranging from 3 to 7 hours daily, 5 days a week, at least 9 months of the year. Additionally, a number of schools are expanding to year-round programs. For children in early childhood settings or after-school care, the amount of time spent in school-based settings may be higher, possibly reaching 10 to 12 hours daily in these settings. These long hours may be especially common for children in dual career and single-parent working families, which constitute increasing proportions of the children served by schools (Bianchi, 1995). For more and more children, schooling begins at the age of 3 or 4 years, when they enter a prekindergarten program or child care setting (Finn-Stevenson & Zigler, 1999).

However, though children spend a great deal of their time in school and school-based settings, the influence of the school is also dynamic. Children typically change teachers at least every year, and in the course of their education, they change schools two to three times as they move from elementary to high school. Twenty to thirty percent of children change schools in the course of a residential move, and approximately 13% of children change schools within a given school year (Nelson, Simoni, & Adelman, 2000). Nevertheless, school remains one of a number of important influences in children's lives. Epstein (1990) aptly describes the dual influence of home and school in her observation, "All the years that children attend school, they also attend home" (p. 99).

Schools are influential on children, for better or for worse. Schools lacking standards and rigor, with strained relationships between students and school staff, with irrelevant and uninteresting curriculum, and with policies and practices that are insensitive to current demands on family life are not likely to be successful in helping children and families avoid the risks to their positive development. On the other hand, caring staff, visionary principals, high behavioral and academic standards and supports, supportive community partners, and insightful policies and practices that support children and families are all important aspects of the school environment in promoting resilience in children and youth.

An ecological perspective acknowledges that families and schools exist in a larger ecological context; both are part of a community. Communities marked by a combination of lower socioeconomic status, pervasive dropout and/or school failure, dilapidated settings, and high levels of crime, violence, and substance abuse expose children to higher levels of community risk (Attar, Guerra, & Tolan, 1994; Williams, Stiffman, & O'Neal, 1998). On the other hand, communities can also be sources of support and resources to families, providing services to families and sources of advice, support, and accountability for schools (Adelman & Taylor, 2000; Dryfoos, 1994). Families, schools, and communities are all settings that can act and interact to influence children's academic, social, and behavioral success.

SCHOOL ACHIEVEMENT AND CHILDREN'S LIFE OUTCOMES

Academic achievement is very important in a society in which career and professional opportunities increasingly involve higher levels of training and education. Underachievement costs society in lost human potential. Additionally, underachievement costs society in remediating and supporting those who have not been successful academically. Students who fail to complete high school earn less, are more likely to be unemployed, and are more likely to receive public assistance than those who graduate (Dryfoos, 1990). Academic achievement and interest in school are critical factors related to young people being less likely to be involved in violence, delinquency, substance abuse, and teenage parenthood (Dishion, Patterson, Stoolmiller, & Skinner, 1991; Dryfoos, 1990; O'Donnell, Hawkins, Catalano, Abbott, & Day, 1995). Academic achievement contributes to higher levels of occupational attainment and the avoidance of negative life courses.

Gains have been made in academic attainment in the United States. Between 1971 and 1998, the high school graduation rate increased from 75% to 87% (U.S. Department of Education, 1999). These gains have also been evident among ethnic minority groups. For example, whereas the rate of high school completion for African Americans was 72% of the rate for European Americans in 1971, in 1998 it was 94%. The good news is that it is possible to make gains in schooling even for children of disenfranchised racial and ethnic groups. However, the school experiences of U.S. children still vary immensely. For example, in the first grade, African American and European American students are more similar on standardized test scores, but by fourth grade only 31% of African American students evidence reading proficiency, as compared to 71% of European American students (Frederick D. Patterson Research Institute, 1997). Disparities in attainment and an increasingly widening gap on standardized tests as children age call for attention to the educational settings entrusted with helping children to learn, especially those most in need.

THE ROLE OF THE SCHOOL IN ACADEMIC AND
PSYCHOSOCIAL OUTCOMES

School settings can potentially serve as either risk or protective influences, or both, in children's lives (Haggerty et al., 1996; Werner, 1994). In research on children and families, proportionately more of the research has sought to identify risk-related issues rather than to identify strengths and pathways toward children's resilience. A search of PsycINFO, a database of scholarship in the social sciences, revealed that for the last two decades, the references available on risk factors number more than three times those that could be located on protective factors or mechanisms. Rutter (1990) highlights the need to extend knowledge about "protective factors" into an understanding of "protective processes," or the sequence of events whereby children with a number of risk factors in their lives additionally have a number of experiences that work together to promote resilience, even in the face of adversity. The following sections explore the ways in which school-related factors can positively influence children's academic and psychosocial outcomes.

Teacher Attitudes and Relationships With Students

The relationship between young people and their teachers is an important factor in children's academic engagement and attainment. Children who feel labeled by teachers and believe that teachers have negative expectations of them do not achieve or behave at the same levels as students who have more positive relationships with their teachers (Kingery, Biafora, & Zimmerman, 1996; Kingery, Coggeshall, & Alford, 1998). In the nearly 4 decades of research in this area, the role of teacher expectancies has been hotly debated. However, reviews of the more than 300 studies in teacher expectancies show no advantage to negative expectancies on the part of teachers (Raudenbush, 1984; Rist, 2000). Observations of teachers have shown that teacher expectancies are related to the way teachers interact with students. A teacher with high expectations of a particular student gives that student opportunities to think and problem solve and correct initially incorrect responses, opportunities teachers do not give to students about whom they have pessimistic attitudes (Brophy & Good, 1986; Good & Brophy, 1987). Being optimistic about student achievement and communicating those expectancies through healthy instructional opportunities positively influence achievement. Perceived teacher support is a protective factor contributing to students' feeling competent and understood, especially when other areas of support are less available for students (Bowen, Richman, Brewster, & Bowen, 1998; Hughes, Cavell, & Jackson, 1999). To students "growing up in poor, urban neighborhoods that are filled with danger, hopelessness, and despair," the feeling that teachers support and care about them may be more influential on student feelings than how much danger they perceive in the environment (Bowen et al., 1998, p. 282). Caring teachers who have high expectations and supportive relationships with their students and who provide all young people opportunities to think critically are important in helping young people to feel competent and to learn more.

Interactive Instructional Approaches

The instructional approach teachers use in classrooms can be a tool that not only promotes learning but also engages students (Brophy & Good, 1986; Slavin, 1991). Teaching strategies that are interactive and cooperative, particularly when combined with effective classroom management strategies, have been found to result in more positive attitudes toward school, more interest and engagement in learning activities, more bonding to school overall, and fewer suspensions and expulsions, particularly among lower achieving students (Abbott et al., 1998; Hawkins, Doueck, & Lishner, 1988). The use of interactive teaching strategies results in more interest in learning, greater attachment to and interest in school, and less problem behavior.

Classroom Behavioral Environments

An area of struggle for many teachers concerns their efforts to promote positive classroom learning environments. To teach their subject matter, teachers have to manage classroom behavior effectively. A number of research studies demonstrate that teachers who consistently attend to and reward the students who are on task and behaving well and teachers who are consistent and fair in setting and enforcing clear academic and behavioral standards for the classroom are those whose students behave better and achieve more academically (Abbott et al., 1998; Kellam, Ling, Merisca, Brown, & Ialongo, 1998). In fact, a number of programs and curricula have been developed to help teachers establish clear systems that monitor and reward good behavior in their classrooms (e.g., the "Good Behavior Game" and "Catch Them Being Good"). These programs help teachers create classroom environments in which the children know the rules and are encouraged to observe them. A number of these programs include regular communication between school and families, a pattern of interactions that begins with teachers sharing the children's successes with families and keeping families informed about children's progress and attainment (Abbott et al., 1998; Dumas, Prinz, Smith, & Laughlin, 1999; Kellam, Mayer, Rebok, & Hawkins, 1998). In turn, families reward and encourage children at home to reinforce what is being learned at school. Classroom management strategies that establish standards of behavior, reward and encourage good behavior while sanctioning unacceptable behavior help to promote achievement and positive psychosocial outcomes. Partnering with the home to monitor and reward behavior is important in communicating to children that their home and school are united in encouraging their positive behavior and achievement.

Cultural Relevance of the Curriculum and Instruction

Schools that foster resilience often include sensitivity to student diversity and an ability to bridge the cultures of home and school (Wright &

Smith, 1998). Heath's (1983) classic decade-long study that examined language learning in an African American community demonstrated that reducing sociolinguistic discontinuity between home and school positively influenced the students' participation in school lessons. Teachers learned to use students' "home language" as a transition to "school language." As a result, the students' overall achievement improved.

School curricula and instruction also play an important role. When the curriculum is interesting and relevant to the students, they are more attentive and involved than when the curriculum has little relevance to them. For example, recent efforts to develop standardized tests acknowledge the role of culturally relevant content on student interest and performance, and the procedures for test development include review processes for balanced presentation across gender and racial–ethnic groups (Johnson, 1998; Kubota & Connell, 1991). Furthermore, the negative stereotypes and images that poverty and racism impose on the lives of poor and ethnic minority children can be loosened by using curricula that include examples of empowerment and success among typically disenfranchised ethnic minority groups (Boutte, 1999; Ladson-Billings, 1994).

From an instructional perspective, the Kamehameha Elementary Education Program (KEEP) in Hawaii is a particularly striking example of effective use of culturally relevant pedagogy (Vogt, Jordan, & Tharp, 1993). Educational strategies that proved to be successful in reducing the students' chronic academic underachievement included changing from a phonics approach to one emphasizing comprehension using "talk-story," a familiar linguistic characteristic in Hawaiian culture; showing preference for cooperative work and group accomplishment (Slavin & Madden, 2001); and changing from individual praise to more culturally appropriate indirect and group praise. The KEEP culturally compatible kindergarten through grade 3 language arts program has demonstrated significant gains in reading achievement.

Although not explicitly focused on cultural competence per se, the whole-school reform approaches of the Comer School Development Program can be cited as an example of an approach that provides professional development designed to alter teacher and school practices and attitudes in urban schools (Comer & Haynes, 1991; Haynes & Comer, 1996). The goal is to enhance respectful staff interactions with families and positive expectancies toward ethnic minority children. Curricula and instruction that transcend negative stereotypes, portray positive examples of success from students' own racial–ethnic group, and use culturally compatible approaches can help children achieve at higher academic levels, an important factor related to positive behavioral outcomes.

School Environment and Climate

Schools do not always serve as the equalizing institutions that they are purported to be, as alluded to in the earlier discussion of high school completion rates. Kozol (1991) aptly and graphically demonstrated that for many students of color and poor children, schools are grossly substandard in terms of physical facilities and resources. Because funding for most public schools is based in part on local property taxes, "inner city" schools are typically grossly underfunded for their facilities in comparison to suburban schools. Poor children face the worst effects of poor-quality schools (Connell, 1994). For both male and female students, the quality of the school environment is related to exposure to, involvement in, and victimization by violence (Williams et al., 1998). Research on bullying and victimization shows that by making improvements to the school's recreational facilities, children can be engaged in more positive and interesting activities and fewer coercive ones (Olweus, 1993). Poor physical facilities are factors contributing to the risky, more violent circumstances in which some children attend school. Enhancing the physical recreational properties creates more opportunities for interesting positive social interaction and less reliance on aggressive, coercive interactions.

Schoolwide policies and programming designed to improve the environment has shown promise in international research on schools in reducing bullying and victimization. The components of programming include

1. clear rules and sanctions for bullying behavior;
2. openness and encouragement of the reporting of bullying;
3. positive opportunities and activities for children to talk, interact, and develop social skills, because many victims benefit from opportunities to develop confidence;
4. more staffing and supervision of recess and less-structured school settings; and
5. schoolwide coordination of plans and activities to reduce bullying and victimization (Olweus, 1993).

Schoolwide efforts to address bullying have been found to show results on the school grounds and on the number of instances of bullying and victimization occurring en route to and from school.

The climate of the school can also influence the job and instructional tasks that have to be undertaken. There is a voluminous body of research on various school climate factors that help to promote positive behavior and achievement. To summarize, work on school climate reveals that schools that are organized with strong, clear leadership, high academic and behavioral standards, a belief and expectation that all children can learn, concrete strategies to improve academic achievement, methods for assessing if the goals have been achieved, and involvement of families and communities in positive ways are more supportive and are more likely to achieve their mission (Epstein, 1990; Lezotte, 1989).

Home–School–Community Partnerships

The most valuable feature of an ecological perspective is that it recognizes that the child's home, school, and community are all important settings helping or hindering positive development. When children perceive that their parents and teachers are united in encouraging their achievement and good behavior, they feel better about their teachers, their school, and their performance. Parents and teachers also report more feelings of personal efficacy and positive perceptions of each other (Epstein, 1990). Effective partnerships between home and school are established when schools reach out to parents to celebrate children's successes and not just to report problems. Good communication results when mechanisms are established for regular parental information and involvement in children's learning experiences (Abbott et al., 1998; Epstein, 1990; Kellam et al., 1998; Smith et al., 1997). Parental involvement in their children's education spans a range of activities, including meeting the basic obligations of having their children at school on time, ready and prepared to learn (e.g., with books, pens, pencils, paper, completed homework); communicating regularly with their children regarding school and their expectations for their achievement; engaging in school-based activities such as volunteering at school; and serving in leadership roles at the school in parent–teacher–student organizations and on local school advisory boards (Epstein, 1990; Smith et al., 1997).

Among the most promising examples of home–school–community partnerships is the Comer School Development Program. This model includes an emphasis on building teams of school staff, parents, and students who plan, implement, and evaluate systemic reform and school improvement. This model has been found to result in increased student achievement, improved behavior, and better overall adjustment (Comer & Haynes, 1991; Haynes & Comer, 1996). More recently, the Comer School Development Program has been linked to Edward Zigler's School of the 21st Century to create "COZI schools," a partnership that includes parents, teachers, and community partners in an increasing number of schools across the country (Comer & Haynes, 1991; Zigler, Kagan, & Hall, 1996).

COMPREHENSIVE AND INTEGRATED SCHOOL APPROACHES

Many families experience circumstances and stresses that impede their ability to be involved in their children's education both at school and at home (Norman & Smith, 1997). These stresses also may have an adverse influence on the family in general, on children's development, and on their ability to do well in school. Families today are managing the demands of work and home, helping their children meet the obligations of school and valuable extracurricular activities, and more often than not living far away from grandparents and other family members. There are many pressures that affect all families. However, stressful living conditions may be more intense among low-income families, who disproportionately have female heads of households shouldering the responsibility of parenting, and all that entails in addition to often working multiple jobs to make ends meet. The provision of family support by the school may mitigate against the negative influences of parental stress (Gore, 1980).

Research evidence suggests that action is best taken early in children's lives to promote healthy development. Children's capacity to learn depends on a number of attributes (e.g., curiosity, motivation, and ability to seek help from adults) that develop during infancy and the preschool years and are influenced by circumstances in family life as well as by the quality of the environments in which the children spend time (Boyer, 1992; Carnegie Corporation of New York, 1996). Increasingly, young children spend their days in child care facilities. Some facilities are of good or fair quality (National Institute of Child Health and Human Development, 1999), but many are not. National studies have found that the quality of care in some child care centers and family child care homes is so poor that it undermines children's social, emotional, and cognitive development (Cost, Quality, and Child Outcomes Study Team, 1995; Galinsky, Howe, Kontos, & Shinn, 1994).

Although children's ability to succeed academically may be enhanced by good-quality child care during the preschool years (Shore, 1997), it is also important to provide quality care during the school-age years. Children's experiences during out-of-school time largely determine whether they will engage in crime, substance abuse, or sexual relations (Richardson et al., 1989). Additionally, supervision before and after school—or lack thereof—correlates directly with school attendance rates, literacy and reading comprehension, grade point average, office referrals, suspensions, and academic achievement scores (U.S. Department of Education, 1997, 1998).

Although child care programs and other support services are traditionally provided by community-based organizations, an increasing number of schools are expanding their role to provide a range of early care and family support services. Whole-school reform efforts involve parents, teachers, and community partners in building strong, effective schools. Examples of such schools are those that have implemented a program known as the School of the 21st Century (21C). The 21C program is designed to help all children realize their developmental and educational potential through schools' provision of the following:

- high-quality and developmentally appropriate education and child care services for preschool-age children;
- diverse, supervised before- and after-school activities and vacation care for school-age children;

- home visits and education for parents of children ages 0 to 3 so that they become their children's first teachers;
- information and referral sources for community services;
- outreach and training for all child care and family child care homes; and
- health and nutrition services.

Schools implementing the 21C program expand their traditional mission as well as their hours of operation, providing services from 6 a.m. until 6 p.m., 12 months a year (Finn-Stevenson & Zigler, 1999). The program is consistent with the first U.S. National Educational Goal that all children will start school ready to learn.

The School of the 21st Century has been successfully implemented in more than 600 schools in 17 states, operating with a combination of parent fees for the school-based child care programs, donations from the local community, and grant funding, often from the state or local level. The school district provides in-kind support by donating space for child care programs, family outreach events, and staff time. Evaluations of 21C programs in rural, urban, and suburban areas, as well as in affluent, middle-class, and poor communities, indicate that children participating in 21C programs are more likely than those who do not to begin formal schooling ready to learn, to perform better academically, to have parents who are more involved in their children's education, and with reduced behavioral problems and need for special services (Finn-Stevenson, Desimone, & Chung, 1998).

Recognizing the potential of the school to serve as the "center of the community" in that it provides a physical facility and a normal point of linkage to children and families, models of service provision have been developed at the school site. School-based initiatives are operated within the school by establishing partnerships with local collaborators, some from the university research community. A number of these programs are preventive and seek to enhance children's behavior. Programs include PATHS (Promoting Alternative Thinking Strategies), developed to help children better manage and express their emotions (Greenberg, Kusche, Cook, & Quamma, 1995); the Social-Competence Promotion Program (Weissberg et al., 1981), and ICPS (Interpersonal Cognitive Problem-Solving, or I Can Problem Solve), programs developed to help children better resolve everyday problems and ultimately prevent longer term problems, including violence, substance abuse, and teen pregnancy (Spivack & Shure, 1974). Rones and Hoagwood (2000) found in their extensive review of school-based prevention efforts for students that there are programs that impact a number of behavioral outcomes resulting in less aggression, fewer behavioral problems, better approaches to resolving problems and conflicts nonviolently, and more prosocial behavior. A major issue concerns the ability to sustain these efforts demonstrated to be effective by researchers within the school environment.

The whole-school reform and full service school approaches recognize the need to coordinate important school-based student prevention efforts with school reform and improvement and to provide important health and mental health services on the school site. These efforts are based on promoting strengths and a focus on enhancing protective factors. A holistic approach to school reform would include plans for increasing parental involvement and positive teaching strategies. The provision of school-based services could involve a range of services from prevention aimed at child and youth problems to a system of identification and intervention for youths who are already experiencing problems (e.g., emotional problems, substance abuse, teen pregnancy, serious delinquency and aggression; Adelman & Taylor, 2000). Additionally, early identification and intervention with youths experiencing serious social and psychological issues is a critically needed function in schools where rarer but still unacceptable incidences of school violence are occurring.

In summary, efforts that bridge home, school, and community seek to provide access to quality prekindergarten settings that give children an early start in learning; provide access to quality before- and after-school care settings that monitor children's activities and support homework completion; help parents be more involved in their children's education; help teachers to interact effectively and respectfully with parents; coordinate school reform efforts and school-based health and mental health efforts; and use the school to help children and families connect to needed community resources.

POLICY IMPLICATIONS

This emerging work on school protective factors and resilience points to the influential role of schools in partnership with families and communities in promoting positive behavior, interest in school, and academic achievement. Efforts targeted solely to the child will not be the most effective without consideration of the everyday influences on children. We should attend to the ways in which schools can help promote engagement, high achievement and positive behavioral outcomes. Examinations of schools should be ecological in nature and consider many levels of influence (e.g., students, educators, homes, communities) and the interactions among them. Some of the critical school-related factors with policy implications are as follows:

- Teachers with high expectations and supportive relationships with students help students to feel better about school, to perform better academically, and to exhibit less problem behavior. Professional development and in-service training should be provided that help all teachers develop good relationships with their students.

- Research on prevention programs indicates that classroom management methods can be used that reward and encourage good behavior, establish early links with parents by informing them about children's successes and progress, and communicate intolerance of aggressive behavior. Continued identification, evaluation, and dissemination of programs are needed to help train and support teachers in effective strategies. Public policy should provide both funding and incentives for schools that provide these important supports to teachers.

- Instructional approaches exist that increase student interest in learning both by involving students more actively and by representing their own experiences and background. Professional development and in-service training should be available for teachers in implementing innovative instructional practices that are well researched and have been shown to increase learning and positive behavior in the classroom. These efforts should also include curriculum efforts to include positive examples dispelling stereotypes for children of diverse racial–ethnic backgrounds. Funding and incentives are needed for schools implementing well-documented effective curriculum and instructional practice.

- The foundation for school success begins early in life and is dependent on experiences that help children acquire fundamental skills. Children with access to quality prekindergarten experiences enter school better prepared for learning and often with more supports for doing so. Support and access to quality prekindergarten experiences ensures that all children have the opportunity to profit from instruction. Although some schools can implement programs of this sort with current resources, public funding is essential to enabling more schools to provide quality early educational experiences to all children.

- Our society is changing, as are the needs of children and families. Educators need to assess the needs of the children and families they serve and implement activities to address these needs. Some programs, such as before- and after-school and vacation care can be paid for by instituting fees that parents pay on a sliding scale basis according to their income level. Yet schools depend on some start-up funds to initiate these important family support services. Schools contribute to the operation of the programs by making available space and the administrative structure within which to operate these support services. Most important, however, is a change in attitude toward the traditional mission of the school and the recognition that for children to succeed academically, they need a variety of child care and other support services. Schools with a mission that includes assessing child and family needs and providing family supportive services such as before- and after-school and vacation care are needed for parents with less flexible work schedules. These types of services may also provide access to positive activities in the after-school hours when more violence, delinquency, substance abuse, and teen pregnancy usually occur. Public funding, in addition to sliding fee scales, is needed to implement these important family supports.

- Having the home, school, and community join together to promote success can enhance resilience in children. Schools reaching out to homes, removing barriers to parental involvement, and facilitating connections to community resources and support, as well as families encouraging children's behavior and achievement through actions at home and at school, together help schools accomplish their mission of supporting families and involving communities in the important role of educating children.

- Providing for children's and families' needs should move beyond linking children to outside sources of support that may or may not ever reach families. Increasingly, schools represent the most likely site to identify children and families in need of further services. Early identification and intervention could be crucial to the safety and well-being of the entire staff and student body of the school. Comprehensive, integrated school reform efforts involve planning, implementation, and evaluation with the provision of a range of supportive services for preventing, identifying, and addressing social, health, and mental health issues. These schools bring the community into the school and also bring community resources to the children and families.

One of the largest challenges facing schools and school reform is that of fragmentation of programs and strategies intended to foster resilience. The school reform process must include attention to various players (e.g., students, families, teachers, business partners, community agents) and be mapped on a multicomponent reform process that includes student and family assistance, home involvement, classroom-focused instructional and management efforts, crisis prevention and intervention, and community involvement (Adelman & Taylor, 2000). Policy initiatives can help schools face the inevitable challenges that will arise by providing needed resources, staff, space, and infrastructures for coordination of efforts.

Finally, any efforts to help students become more resilient should build on the strengths of the students, families, schools, and communities, identifying and enhancing protective processes that already exist in children and their school settings. Schools can be important protective influences in children's lives, helping them to overcome risk and adversity and emerge successful and resilient.

REFERENCES

Abbott, R. D., O'Donnell, J., Hawkins, J. D., Hill, K. G., Kosterman, R., & Catalano, R. F. (1998). Changing teaching practices to promote achievement and bonding to school. *American Journal of Orthopsychiatry, 68,* 542–552.

Adelman, H. S., & Taylor, L. (2000). Moving prevention from the fringes into the fabric of school improvement. *Journal of Educational and Psychological Consultation, 11,* 7–36.

Attar, B. K., Guerra, N. G., & Tolan, P. H. (1994). Neighborhood disadvantage, stressful life events, and adjustment in urban elementary-school children. *Journal of Clinical Child Psychology, 23,* 391–400.

Baumrind, D. (1985). The influence of parenting style on adolescent competence and substance use. *Journal of Early Adolescence, 11,* 56–95.

Bianchi, S. M. (1995). The changing demographic and socieconomic characteristics of single-parent families. *Marriage and Family Review, 20,* 71–97.

Boutte, G. (1999). *Multicultural education: Raising consciousness.* Atlanta, GA: Wadsworth.

Bowen, G. L., Richman, J. M., Brewster, A., & Bowen, N. (1998). Sense of school coherence, perceptions of danger at school, and teacher support among youth at risk of school failure. *Child and Adolescent Social Work Journal, 15,* 273–286.

Boyer, E. (1992). Foreword. In National Center for Clinical Infant Programs, *Head Start: The emotional foundations of school readiness.* Arlington, VA: Author.

Brody, G., Stoneman, Z., & Flor, D. (1995). Linking family processes and academic competence among rural African American youths. *Journal of Marriage and Family, 57,* 567–579.

Bronfenbrenner, U. (1986). Ecology of the family as a context for human development: Research perspectives. *Developmental Psychology, 22,* 723–742.

Brophy, J., & Good, T. L. (1986). Teacher behavior and achievement. In M. C. Wittrock (Ed.), *Handbook of research on teaching* (pp. 328–375). New York: Macmillan.

Carnegie Corporation of New York. (1996). *Years of promise.* New York: Author.

Comer, J. P., & Haynes, N. M. (1991). Parent involvement in school: An ecological approach. *Elementary School Journal, 91,* 271–277.

Comer, J. P., Haynes, N. M., Joyner, E. T., & Ben-Avie, M. (Eds.). (1996). *Rallying the whole village: The Comer process for reforming education.* New York: Teachers College Press.

Connell, R. W. (1994). Poverty and education. *Harvard Educational Review, 64,* 125–149.

Cost, Quality, and Child Outcomes Study Team. (1995). *Cost quality and child outcomes in child care centers*. Denver, CO: Department of Economics, University of Colorado at Denver.

Dishion, T. J., Patterson, G. R., Stoolmiller, M., & Skinner, M. L. (1991). Family, school, and behavioral antecedents to early adolescent involvement with antisocial peers. *Developmental Psychology, 27*, 172–180.

Dryfoos, J. G. (1990). *Adolescents at risk: Prevalence and prevention*. New York: Oxford University Press.

Dryfoos, J. G. (1994). *Full-service schools: A revolution in health and social services for children, youth, and families*. San Francisco: Jossey-Bass.

Dumas, J. E., Prinz, R. J., Smith, E., & Laughlin, J. (1999). The Early Alliance prevention trial: An integrated set of interventions to promote competence and reduce risk for conduct disorder, substance abuse, and school failure. *Clinical Child and Family Psychology Review, 2*, 37–53.

Epstein, J. L. (1990). School and family connections: Theory, research and implications for integrating sociologies of education and family. In D. G. Unger & M. B. Sussman (Eds.), *Families in community settings: Interdisciplinary perspectives* (pp. 99–126). New York: Haworth.

Finn-Stevenson, M., Desimone, L., & Chung, A. (1998). Linking child care and support services with the school: Pilot evaluation of the School of the 21st Century. *Children and Youth Services Review, 20*, 177–205.

Finn-Stevenson, M., & Zigler, E. (1999). *Linking child care and education: The school of the 21st century*. Boulder, CO: Westview.

Frederick D. Patterson Research Institute. (1997). *The African American education data book* (Vol. 2). Alexandria, VA: United Negro College Fund.

Galinsky, E., Howe, C., Kontos, S., & Shinn, M. B. (1994). *The study of children in family child care and relative care*. New York: Family and Work Institute.

Good, T. L., & Brophy, J. E. (1987). *Looking in classrooms*. New York: Harper & Row.

Gore, S. (1980). Stress buffering functions of social supports: An appraisal and clarification of research models. In B. S. Dohrenwend & B. P. Dohrenwend (Eds.), *Stressful life events: Their nature and effects* (pp. 65–80). New York: Wiley.

Greenberg, M. T., Kusche, C. C. A., Cook, E. T., & Quamma, J. P. (1995). Promoting emotional competence in school-aged children: The effects of the PATHS curriculum. *Development and Psychopathology, 7*, 117–136.

Haggerty, R. J., Sherrod, L. R., Garmezy, N., & Rutter, M. (1996). *Stress, risk, and resilience in children and adolescents*. Cambridge, England: Cambridge University Press.

Hawkins, J. D., Doueck, H. J., & Lishner, D. M. (1988). Changing teaching practices in mainstream classrooms to reduce discipline problems among low achievers. *American Educational Research Journal, 25*, 31–50.

Haynes, N. M., & Comer, J. P. (1996). Integrating schools, families, and communities through successful school reform: The School Development Program. *School Psychology Review, 25*, 501–506.

Heath, S. (1983). *Way with words: Language, life, and work in communities and classrooms*. New York: Cambridge University Press.

Hirschi, T. (1969). *Causes of delinquency*. Berkeley, CA: University of California Press.

Hughes, J. N., Cavell, T. A., & Jackson, T. (1999). Influence of the teacher-student relationship on childhood conduct problems: A prospective study. *Journal of Clinical Child Psychology, 28*, 173–184.

Johnson, S. T. (1998). The importance of culture for improving assessment and pedagogy. *Journal of Negro Education, 67*, 181–183.

Kellam, S. G., Ling, X., Merisca, R., Brown, H. C., & Ialongo, N. (1998). The effect of the level of aggression in the first grade classroom on the course and malleability of aggressive behavior into middle school. *Development and Psychopathology, 10*, 165–185.

Kellam, S. G., Mayer, L. S., Rebok, G. W., & Hawkins, W. E. (1998). Effects of improving achievement on aggressive behavior and of improving aggressive behavior on achievement through two preventive interventions: An investigation of causal paths. In B. P. Dohrenwend (Ed.), *Adversity, stress, and psychopathology* (pp. 486–505). New York: Oxford University Press.

Kingery, P. M., Biafora, F. A., & Zimmerman, R. S. (1996). Risk factors for violent behaviors among ethnically diverse urban adolescents. *School Psychology International, 17*, 171–188.

Kingery, P. M., Coggeshall, M. B., & Alford, A. A. (1998). Violence at school: Recent evidence from four national surveys. *Psychology in the Schools, 35*, 247–258.

Kozol, J. (1991). *Savage inequalities*. New York: Crown Publishers.

Kubota, M. N., & Connell, A. (1991). On diversity, and the SAT. *College Board Review, 162*, 6–17.

Ladson-Billings, G. (1994). *Dreamkeepers: Successful teachers of African American children*. San Francisco: Jossey-Bass.

Lezotte, L. W. (1989). School improvement based on the effective schools research. In D. Lipsky & A. Gartner (Eds.), *Beyond separate education: Quality education for all* (pp. 25–37). Baltimore: Paul H. Brookes.

National Institute of Child Health and Human Development. (1999, January). *Higher quality child care related to less problem behavior*. Presented at the American Association for the Advancement of Science, Anaheim, CA.

Nelson, P. S., Simoni, J. M., & Adelman, H. S. (2000). Mobility and school functioning in early grades. *Journal of Educational Research, 89*, 365–369.

Norman, J. M., & Smith, E. P. (1997). Families and school, islands unto themselves: Opportunities to construct bridges. *Family Futures, 1*, 5–7.

O'Donnell, J., Hawkins, J. D., Catalano, R. F., Abbott, R. D., & Day, L. E. (1995). Preventing school failure, drug use, and delinquency among low-income children: Long-term intervention in elementary schools. *American Journal of Orthopsychiatry, 65*, 87–100.

Olweus, D. (1993). *Bullying at school: What we know and what we can do*. Cambridge, MA: Blackwell.

Patterson, G. R. (1982). *Coercive family process: A social learning approach* (Vol. 3). Eugene, OR: Castalia.

Raudenbush, S. W. (1984). Magnitude of teacher expectancy effects on pupil IQ as a function of the credibility of expectancy induction: A synthesis of findings of 18 experiments. *Journal of Educational Psychology, 76*, 85–97.

Richardson, J. L., Dwyer, K., McQuigan, K., Hansen, W. B., Dent, C., Johnson, C. A., et al. (1989). Substance use among eighth grade students who take care of themselves after school. *Pediatrics, 84*, 556–560.

Rist, R. C. (2000). Student social class and teacher expectations: The self-fulfilling prophecy in ghetto education. *Harvard Educational Review, 70*, 266–301.

Rones, M., & Hoagwood, K. (2000). School-based mental health services: A research review. *Clinical Child and Family Psychology Review, 3*, 223–241.

Shore, R. (1997). *Rethinking the brain: New insights in child development*. New York: Families and Work Institute.

Slavin, R. E. (1991). Synthesis of research on cooperative learning. *Educational Leadership, 48*, 71–82.

Slavin, R. E., & Madden, N. A. (2001). *One million children: Success for all*. Thousand Oaks, CA: Corwin Press.

Smith, E. P., Connell, C. M., Wright, G., Sizer, M., Norman, J. M., Hurley, A., & Walker, S. N. (1997). An ecological model of home, school, and community partnership: Implications for research and practice. *Journal of Educational and Psychological Consultation, 8*, 339–360.

Spivack, G., & Shure, M. B. (1974). *Social adjustment of young children: A cognitive approach to solving real life problems*. San Francisco: Jossey-Bass.

U.S. Department of Education. (1997). *Keeping schools open as community learning centers: Extending learning in a safe and drug free environment before and after school*. Washington, DC: U.S. Government Printing Office.

U.S. Department of Education. (1998). *Safe and smart: Making after school hours work for kids*. Washington, DC: U.S. Government Printing Office.

U.S. Department of Education. (1999). *Digest of education statistics*. Washington, DC: U.S. Government Printing Office.

Vogt, L. A., Jordan, C., & Tharp, R. G. (1993). Explaining school failure, producing school success: Two cases. In E. Jacob & C. Jordan (Eds.), *Minority education: Anthropological perspectives*. Norwood, NJ: Ablex.

Weissberg, R. P., Gesten, E. L., Carnilce, C. L., Toro, P. A., Rapkin, B. D., Davidson, E., et al. (1981). Social problem-solving skills training: A competence building intervention with 2nd–4th grade children. *American Journal of Community Psychology, 9*, 411–424.

Werner, E. E. (1994). Overcoming the odds. *Developmental and Behavioral Pediatrics, 15*, 131–136.

Williams, J. H., Stiffman, A. R., & O'Neal, J. L. (1998). Violence among urban African American youths: An analysis of environmental and behavioral risk factors. *Social Work Research, 22,* 3–13.

Wright, G., & Smith, E. P. (1998). Home, school, and community partnerships: Integrating issues of race, culture, and social class. *Clinical Child and Family Psychology Review, 1*(3), 145–162.

Zigler, E., Kagan, S., & Hall, N. (1996). *Children, families, and government: Preparing for the 21st century.* New York: Cambridge Press.

13

THE ORGANIZATION OF SCHOOLING AND ADOLESCENT DEVELOPMENT

EDWARD SEIDMAN, J. LAWRENCE ABER, AND SABINE E. FRENCH

The transition to a secondary school can take a significant human and social toll on early adolescents, leading to a decline in academic performance and psychological well-being. Rather than simply allowing youths to cope as best they can, the authors envision changes in the organization of schooling as the optimal means to address the school transition dilemma. Specifically, a case is made for the creation (and maintenance) of kindergarten through grade 8 (K–8) schools and, where this is not feasible, for restructuring middle or junior high schools into small learning communities ("schools within schools"). These strengths-based approaches to school transitions underscore the critical importance of matching the school environment with the developmental needs of early adolescents.

*   *   *

Are the academic, behavioral, and social problems that occur during adolescence, and those that continue into adulthood, triggered in part by the normative school transition to either middle or junior or senior high school? If so, how do these transitions trigger these problems? What can be done about the nature of school transitions to reduce these problems and launch

The authors express their appreciation to Mariano Santo Domingo, Peggy Clements, Barton Hirsch, Kenneth Maton, and Hirokazu Yoshikawa for their constructive feedback on a prior draft of this manuscript.

larger proportions of youth onto positive trajectories? What is the optimal timing and locus of intervention? This chapter reviews the knowledge base bearing on each of these questions and its implications for policy and action.

Within a year or two after adolescents enter senior high school, the human and social toll on these youths include the following:

- precipitous declines in academic achievement and attendance and an exponential rise in the rates of school dropout,
- a peak in serious delinquent offenses,
- peaks in reports of alcohol and marijuana use,
- dramatic increases in teenage pregnancy, and
- the occurrences of first episodes of depressive disorders and peaks in reports of suicidal ideation.

The costs in lost human capital and increased social services are astounding. For example, the income and taxes lost over the course of a lifetime for each year's class of dropouts was estimated at $260 billion over a decade ago (Catterall, 1987). As is well known, the rates of educational failure are disproportionately higher among adolescents growing up in economically impoverished urban communities and among Latino and African American youth.

These diminished opportunities and life chances stem from a pattern of disengagement from the educational enterprise or a lack of both academic and social integration. At the disengagement pole are not only dropout, but school failure and disaffection as well. Disengagement is associated with the greater amount of time youths spend "on the streets" in the company of peers who are disengaged from normalizing social systems. The process of progressive disengagement of youths from the educational enterprise has been linked to long-term human and social costs borne by society from unemployment and low productivity to teenage parenting and illegal activities.

Many continue to believe that the blame for, and solutions to, the problems of adolescence lie within the youths themselves or with their families. The factors that produce these outcomes are often attributed to an individual's genes, temperament, or ability to read social cues, and their families are often viewed as lacking in child-rearing skills or the "appropriate" values. Among educational reformers, the disjunction between the developmental needs of adolescents and the organization of schooling is infrequently looked to as either a source of the problem or a critical part of the solution. Strengthening academic environments so that they are educationally and developmentally attuned to the needs of adolescents can both prevent youths from beginning this process of disengagement and enhance the likelihood that others will continue or increase their engagement with the educational enterprise.

Does the normative (i.e., planned and expected) transition into senior high school, which occurs around the time when the rates of educational failure, school dropout, and antisocial behavior peak, initiate this process of disengagement, or is this process triggered at an earlier time and place? Recent evidence suggests that the earlier, normative transition to middle or junior high school may set this process into motion by initiating a trajectory of disengagement from the educational enterprise (Alspaugh, 1998; Roderick, 1995; Seidman & French, 1997). This school transition may represent a key turning point or "risky" transition in the long-term developmental trajectories of adolescents (Price, 1980). If so, this transition into middle or junior high school represents a more opportune time and locus for preventive and policy intervention, when negative pathways can be redirected to more adaptive trajectories, than does the transition into high school.

This chapter reviews the evidentiary basis for the mutual influence between adolescent development and the organization of schooling prior to and after the transition to both middle or junior high school and senior high school. We then examine the variability and efficacy of educational reforms targeted to youths and schools following each of these normative school transitions. Based on this analysis, we recommend a set of policy reforms to maintain adolescents' engagement in the educational enterprise and their normative developmental trajectories, as well as to reduce the number of human casualties and the long-range costs to society.

IMPACT OF NORMATIVE SCHOOL TRANSITIONS

We will be discussing three different patterns of grade-level organization of schools that have evolved over the course of the 20th century. Before the turn of the last century, students often attended an elementary school from 1st grade (or kindergarten) through 8th grade and, perhaps, then entered high school (9th to 12th grades), where physical resources were greater and teachers were specialists in particular disciplines. Although this pattern of grade-level and school organization continues to this day, it has been eliminated from most school systems. Junior high schools (7th to 8th or 9th grades) were developed around the turn of the 20th century for a variety of different motives (Cuban, 1992). Nevertheless, these schools came to represent "junior" versions of high schools in that they too were characterized by students constantly changing classrooms with different classmates and teachers who specialized in particular disciplines.

In the last 40 years, middle school pedagogy was developed to better suit the needs of the early adolescent. Ideally, a small number of teachers collaboratively teach students a more integrated curriculum, get to know the strengths and weaknesses of each student, and are equally concerned with students' social and emotional learning as with their academic learning. Students also spend more time in classes with the same cohort of peers. Most often, middle school begins in 6th as opposed to 7th grade and ends in 8th as opposed to 9th grade, though in some districts middle school begins in 5th grade; there are also less-common variations on the theme. Unfortunately, far too often, middle schools simply represent a change in the grade-level organization of the school, or in the grade at which a new school is entered, without successfully implementing true middle school pedagogy. Thus, in practice many middle schools often function more like junior high schools, even though they are organized by different grade levels (Cuban, 1992). This is particularly true in large public school districts.

Transition Into Middle or Junior High School

When children make the transition from elementary school to a middle or junior high school, they often encounter an entirely new system of social connections, rules, and routines. In the local neighborhood elementary school, children spend the bulk of their day with one teacher in one classroom. When changing classrooms for a special class, assembly, or lunch, teachers line up students and guide them to their destination. Elementary school teachers tend to be protective and supportive of their students. Fifth graders, as the oldest students in the elementary school, have high social status. Upon entry into junior high school, these students face the following:

> Every 50 minutes, perhaps, 6 or 7 times each day, assemble with 30 or so of your peers, each time in a different group, sit silently in a chair in neat, frozen rows, and try to catch hold of knowledge as it whizzes by you in words of an adult you met only at the beginning of this school year. (Carnegie Council of Adolescent Development, 1989, p. 37)

Ability tracking begins or becomes more stratified in a climate where competition and ability relative to others is emphasized.

The teachers and classroom environments of middle or junior high schools are more constraining of adolescent development than elementary school classrooms. Junior high school classrooms emphasize teacher control and discipline, provide fewer opportunities for student choice and decision making, and are more competitive and use higher standards of comparison (Eccles et al., 1993). Junior high school math teachers, even when they are math specialists, have been found to have less confidence in their teaching ability than elementary school teachers. In addition, students exposed to these teachers, and in particular low-achieving students, decline in confidence in their ability to master math (Midgley, Feldlaufer, & Eccles, 1989). It is not surprising that in these classroom environments students experience less-personal and fewer positive teacher–student relationships than in elementary schools.

Early adolescence (10 to 14 years of age) is a time of considerable developmental change—biological, emotional, cognitive, and interpersonal. The timing of the onset of puberty is related to some negative outcomes. For example, early-maturing girls are pressured to begin dating by older boys because their bodies appear mature, even though their psychological maturity does not match their physical development. Early adolescents begin to think and feel in new ways—for example, they are more self-conscious, think more abstractly, and see things in relative terms. Not surprisingly, they question more as they strive for autonomy and the opportunity to make their own decisions and search for their own identity. Interpersonally, although they desire more independence and decision making in family matters, they also need to maintain the security that the family provides. The struggle to negotiate this balance with their parents is frequently a difficult one. At the same time, they are becoming more peer oriented. Individually and collectively, these developmental changes that early adolescents experience lead, on a daily basis, to different patterns of social transactions with the adults and peers in youths' life spaces. Thus, early adolescents present teachers with a considerable challenge.

After the transition to middle or junior high school, studies uniformly report decrements in academic performance. Entry into middle or junior high school consistently corresponds with a drop in academic performance (Chung, Elias, & Schneider, 1998; Eccles et al., 1993; Seidman, Allen, Aber, Mitchell, & Feinman, 1994; Simmons & Blyth, 1987). Using data from the National Educational Longitudinal Study, Eccles, Lord, and Midgley (1991) found that students in K–8 schools were more prepared for class, attended classes more regularly, were less truant, and were more engaged than those making a middle or junior high school transition. In primarily rural and small-town school districts of Missouri, Alspaugh (1998) found that youths who attended K–8, then 9th- to 12th-grade schools, who therefore did not make a normative school transition during early adolescence, experienced an increase in academic achievement at 6th grade. On the other hand, students making a middle school transition into 6th grade (i.e., in a K–5, 6th–8th, 9th–12th grade-level organization) declined precipitously in academic achievement.

Decrements in academic performance precipitated by the transition to middle or junior high school are associated with continuing academic difficulties and eventual disengagement from the educational enterprise. In Missouri, Alspaugh (1998) found a higher average dropout rate in high schools whose students had already made a transition at 6th grade than those whose students had come from K–8 schools. Similarly, in a cohort of urban Massachusetts youths, Roderick (1995) demonstrated that the drop in grades after the transition to middle school increased the probability of later school leaving, independent of students' later school performance. Alspaugh (1998) suggested that students who make two normative school transitions during the adolescent years may be placed in double jeopardy, in accordance with Seidman et al.'s (1994) speculation.

Quite often, but not always, declines in self-esteem and other dimensions of psychological distress are associated with this early adolescent normative school transition. In middle or junior high schools, declines in self-esteem have been consistent across studies of urban and large heterogeneous suburban school districts (for a review, see Ruble & Seidman, 1996). Declines in self-esteem have been less universal in studies conducted among primarily White, suburban, middle-class communities or small cities (Chung et al., 1998; Crockett, Petersen, Graber, Schulenberg, & Ebata, 1989; Fenzel & Blyth, 1986; Hirsch & Rapkin, 1987; Jones & Thornburg, 1985; Nottlemann, 1987). Despite the failure to detect declines in self-esteem in the latter group of studies, several studies did uncover appreciable increases in psychological distress or depression across the transition in smaller communities (Chung et al., 1998; Hirsch & Rapkin, 1987). In the instances where declines in self-esteem and increases in psychological distress were not found, these studies were usually carried out in middle or junior high schools where "true" middle school pedagogy appeared to be practiced (Ruble & Seidman, 1996).

In terms of subgroup differences, few differences have been found between boys and girls. One noteworthy exception found girls to be more adversely affected, particularly when the transition coincided with the early onset of menses and another major life event (Simmons, Burgerson, Carton-Ford, & Blyth, 1987). Few studies have explicitly examined race or ethnicity differences. In a reanalysis of data collected in the mid-1970s in Milwaukee, Wisconsin, the decline in grade point average (GPA) over the transition was greater for African American than for White students (Simmons, Black, & Zhou, 1991). However, in a report comparing poor Black, White, and Latino public school students in northeastern cities, no differential effects by race and ethnicity were evident (Seidman et al., 1994).

Decrements in feelings about the self after the transition to middle or junior high school seem to be an important marker of future difficulties. In school districts in southeastern Michigan, Eccles, Lord, Roeser, Barber, and Jozefowicz (1997) found that students who experienced a decline in self-esteem across the transition to junior high were most likely to report the lowest self-esteem and highest depression when assessed in 10th and 12th grades. Decline in self-esteem also predicted lower GPA in 12th grade among boys and a trend toward failing to graduate on time. Similarly, in the classic Milwaukee study, youths whose self-esteem and GPA declined between the 6th- and 7th-grade transition were more likely to experience further declines by the time they reached 10th grade (Simmons et al., 1991).

In addition, a few studies report differential patterns of self-esteem or distress over time in response to the transition to middle or junior high school (Chung et al., 1998; Hirsch & DuBois, 1991; Seidman et al., 2003). Not surprisingly, some trajectories of self-esteem remain stable (high or low) across the transition, whereas others show fluctuation, including "continual decline" and "bounce back" patterns. One study demonstrated that the continual decline pattern differed from all other trajectories of students who had scored high in self-esteem prior to the transition. These youths lived in the most underresourced neighborhoods and families, where it may be more difficult to mobilize support to aid them through this risky school transition (Seidman et al., 2003).

The developmental mismatch between the adolescent's needs and the timing of the change in school structure and organization is greater than at any other time during adolescence (Eccles et al., 1993). Critical declines in academic performance and psychological functioning commonly coincide with the transition to middle or junior high school, but not for children who remain in K–8 structures. The transition and accompanying changes represent a disruption in adolescents' relationships with school-affiliated adults and peers (Ruble & Seidman, 1996). Early adolescents' evolving need and motivation for autonomy and challenge are disrupted by the organization of school after the transition to middle or junior high school. In addition, the transition occurs at a time when they are beginning to explore their own identities, and the new environment often restricts the "possible selves" youths can explore, in terms of their possible academic and psychological identies (Clements & Seidman, 2001). This set of circumstances heightens the likelihood that a process of disengagement from the educational enterprise is initiated.

Transition Into Senior High School

When children make the transition to a new senior high school, the routines and social regularities that they encounter are somewhat similar to those that they already experienced in middle or junior high school. The transition is not as drastic a change in terms of the organizational structure. Students follow a similar pattern of changing teachers and classmates every 45 minutes.

The pressures to succeed academically intensify. From the day of entry into high school, students are bombarded by the fact that their high school grades will determine their future, and simultaneously ability tracking becomes more rigid. Once enrolled in a track, students virtually never change tracks. The chances of students in the lower tracks of gaining college admission or high-quality employment in the future are severely limited.

Studies uniformly report decrements in academic performance after this transition as well. Academic achievement and attendance declines are associated with the transition to high school (Gillock & Reyes, 1996; Roderick, 1995). School dropout becomes more prevalent (Rumberger, 1987).

Many dysfunctional behavioral, psychological, and social outcomes peak within a year or two of the transition to high school. However, these outcomes have not been linked empirically to the transition itself. Less attention has been paid to the impact of the transition to high school on self-esteem. When it has been assessed, no impact on self-esteem has been observed (Gillock & Reyes, 1996; Seidman, Aber, Allen, & French, 1996).

Students continue to disengage from the educational enterprise with the transition to senior high school. Student reports of the quality of their relationships and social support from school staff continue to decline (Reyes, Gillock, & Kobus, 1994; Seidman et al., 1996). The disengagement with the educational enterprise that began developing in junior high school expands in scope and intensity.

The mismatch between the evolving developmental needs of middle adolescents (15 to 18 years old) and the structure and organization of the new senior high school they enter is not as dramatic as during the previous school transition. Although stressful for many students, the transition to high school does not represent as dramatic a disjuncture with junior high school as did the transition from elementary to middle or junior high school. Moreover, middle adolescents are less likely to be in the midst of their first experience with major hormonal changes, new-found emotional and motivational needs, and cognitive abilities. For those who do not make an early transition and continue in a K–8 school, the transition into high school confronts them with a new organizational structure, though at a less vulnerable time in their development.

Summary of Research Findings

Typically, remaining in a K–8 school appears to have fewer deleterious academic and psychological consequences than making a transition into middle or junior high school. The social organization of elementary school classrooms seems to be more attuned to the developmental needs of the early adolescent. Furthermore, a transition into middle or junior high school appears to represent an even riskier and more dramatic turning point in the daily routines and social relationships of adolescents than does the transition into senior high school. Some, but by no means all, adolescents who make an early school transition are launched on a trajectory of disengagement that may result in a wide variety of negative developmental outcomes. These negative outcomes appear to fall disproportionately on youths living under the most disadvantaged circumstances.

INTERVENTION AND POLICY RESPONSES TO SCHOOL TRANSITIONS

Historically, the most common responses of educators and interventionists to academic, emotional, and behavioral difficulties experienced by adolescents has been to develop either secondary prevention programs (i.e., early detection and intervention) that inoculate the most vulnerable children or programs to strengthen the resources and competencies of all children. In secondary prevention programs, individual children are singled out for some form of early intervention, often in a group format. They are viewed as deficient in some way and as both the source of the problem and the locus of change. Less frequently, interventions and policies to restructure the organization of schooling have been developed. In the section that follows, we focus on inoculation programs and restructuring efforts because they represent the more common policy (as opposed to clinical, deficits-based) responses to the stress of normative, but risky, school transitions. After describing the essential differences between inoculation programs and school restructuring, we examine the nature and efficacy of restructuring experiments and policy changes surrounding the transitions first to high school and second to middle or junior high school.

Contemporary inoculation methods have the virtue of providing intervention to all youths that may be at risk, and not simply those identified as manifesting early signs of difficulty, as in secondary prevention. The goal of inoculation programs is to enable youths to become more resourceful and competent in resolving future dilemmas and conflicts, such as when they are confronted with peer pressure to use drugs or when they feel lonely and lack social relationships. Thus, before or shortly after students make a risky school transition, all youths in a grade or classroom are provided with a series of classes and exercises in decision making and problem solving (Weissberg & Greenberg, 1998). Although the whole group or population, not an identified individual, is the target of intervention, inoculation programs primarily target social cognitive processes within youths themselves as the proximal locus of change (Seidman & French, 1997). Finally, a major advantage of inoculation methods is the ease with which they can be incorporated into the curriculum as another set of "lessons" delivered as part of the normal classroom routine.

However, the increased rates of poorer academic performance and psychological functioning following normative school transitions have led other educators and interventionists to focus on restructuring the physical and social organization of classrooms and schools; these interventions are often referred to as the creation of "schools within schools" or "houses" (Oxley, 2000). Both the target of intervention and the proximal locus of change are the social regularities of the classroom and school as a social system, and not the population of students as in inoculation programs.

Policies to restructure schools are emphasized because they are more consistent with the data reviewed in this chapter that suggest that the normative transition into middle or junior high school is both risky and the locus of a developmental mismatch between the changing needs of the adolescent and the organization of schooling. By restructuring the physical, social, and learning arrangements, both students' and teachers' engagement in the educational enterprise is strengthened. In this way, both those students already at risk on psychological, social, or economic grounds and those placed in jeopardy as a function of the hazardous ecological transition per se can benefit.

For educators, policymakers, and the public at large, academic failure, school dropout, delinquency, and drug use are dramatic and poignant events. Because the rates of these outcomes peak shortly after entry into high school, particularly among poor ethnic minorities in urban public school systems, the social and physical organization of high schools has become a focal point of concern. Accordingly, the need to reorganize high schools has received not only considerable attention from the media, corporate America, government, foundations, and the public, but also resources for innovations and, in particular, for creating smaller urban high schools.

Interventions at the Transition Into High School

The goal of interventions following the transition to high school is to strengthen engagement, empowerment, and a sense of ownership of both students and staff with the educational enterprise. Beyond the reduction in school size, smaller working units of students and teachers (or ancillary personnel) are created, and these integral units are housed in a particular wing or floor or adjacent spaces of a building (Oxley, 2000). With smaller units, fewer teachers can get to know and teach fewer children more intensively and in a more holistic and integrated fashion. Smaller units allow teachers to become more aware of students and the fuller context of their lives. It also encourages pedagogical innovations. At the same time, students "live and learn" with a common set of classmates throughout most of the day and week, except for elective subjects. Thus, these programs not only alter the physical and social context of secondary education, they also fundamentally change the day-to-day experiences among all the school's inhabitants.

Restructuring high schools along the lines of the schools-within-schools model has been shown to maintain youths on positive educational and behavioral trajectories. A few qualitative research investigations provide support for the idea (e.g., Fine, 1994; Oxley, 2000). As an illustration, Fine described the Philadelphia School Collaborative:

> Two to four hundred students constitute a charter, with ten to twelve core teachers who work together from 9th (or 10th grades) through to graduation. The charter faculty enjoy a common preparation period daily, share responsibility for a cohort of students, and invent curriculum, pedagogies and assessment strategies that reflect a commitment to a common intellectual project. Students travel together to classes, and across their four years in high school. With teachers, counselors and parents they constitute a semi-autonomous community within a building of charters. (p. 5)

She continued,

The point of restructuring . . . [is] full school transformation. That is, all teachers, staff and students, as well as parents, it was felt, needed to feel attached to and be engaged with academic communities from 9th grade through 12th. (p. 5)

The most rigorous, quantitative evaluations of schools-within-schools experiments have been implemented exclusively at the critical juncture year of entry into high school. The success of such programs suggests that restructuring schools during the transition year may be sufficient to substantially reduce the rates of school disengagement and other negative behavioral outcomes. The School Transitional Environment Project (STEP) is one illustration of a school-within-school intervention program that was quantitatively evaluated (Felner, Brand, Adan, & Mulhall, 1993). The major goal of STEP was to reduce the disruption in students' relationships with teachers and peers making the transition to an inner-city New Haven high school. Youths were randomly assigned to either a small, intimate learning environment for 9th grade or to the usual high school routine. STEP students were placed in one physical section of the school; moved through all their primary classes (e.g., English, math) as a single unit; and assigned to a single adult who served as their advisor, counselor, and link to their family. During the transition year, randomly assigned control students declined in their academic, emotional, and behavioral adjustment and viewed the school environment as negative, in contrast to the STEP students, whose adjustment and perceptions of the school environment remained stable. The long-term findings were even more impressive: Only 24% of STEP youths dropped out of high school by 12th grade, in contrast to 43% of the controls. Thus, STEP students were more likely to have remained engaged in high school.

A similar but teacher-designed school restructuring intervention targeted to students entering a Chicago high school failed to yield positive results (Reyes & Jason, 1991). There were, however, several critical differences between the teacher-designed and STEP intervention programs. In light of the data reviewed in this section, two differences stand out as most critical. First, not housing students in the same physical area of the school severely compromises the school-within-school or house concept. Second, because these students entered high school directly from K–8 schools and did not experience a normative school transition during early adolescence, they missed the double jeopardy of a second normative school transition during adolescence.

Transition Into Middle or Junior High School

Nearly 15 years ago, the Carnegie Corporation published its seminal report *Turning Points* calling for the reform of middle-grades schools (Carnegie Council on Adolescent Development, 1989). At its core, the foundation of the report was the developmental mismatch notion, and as a result, the central recommendation of *Turning Points* was to

> create small communities for learning where stable, close, mutually respectful relationships with adults and peers are considered fundamental for intellectual development and personal growth. The key elements of these communities are schools-within-schools or houses, students and teachers grouped together as teams, and small group advisories that ensure that every student is known well by at least one adult. (p. 9)

In response, the Carnegie Corporation developed and supported a national initiative to encourage experimentation in middle-grades schools reform, known as the Middle Grade School State Policy Initiative. Twenty-seven states received planning grants, and 15 were initially awarded matching grants to encourage local schools to adopt promising practices. The most intensive experimentation has been conducted under the aegis of the Illinois Middle Grades Network (IMGN). In a vein similar to the Carnegie Corporation, the Lilly Endowment supported the Middle Grades Improvement Program in Indiana and the W. K. Kellogg Foundation the Middle Start Initiative in Michigan (Lipsitz, Jackson, & Austin, 1997). Most of these initiatives had an emphasis on supporting the implementation of reforms in middle schools with high concentrations of academically underperforming students. The greater the degree of implementation of interventions to restructure the ecology of middle or junior high schools, the more engaged in the educational enterprise students remained. Positive academic and behavioral outcomes were promoted, with the greatest gains occurring for higher risk youths.

The IMGN was based largely on the STEP model that was originally designed for the transition year of high school and replicated in the transition year of middle or junior high school. In the latter replication study, four STEP schools and four control schools were compared. Students in the STEP schools performed better academically and maintained more positive self-concepts than students in the comparison schools (Felner et al., 1993).

Formally, IMGN reforms began in 11 adopting schools in 1991 and increased to 31 schools in 1992 and to 97 schools in 1997. All schools had to demonstrate a serious commitment to implementing the reforms before they could become a participating member of the network. A central question of the evaluation was the extent to which the degree of implementation in schools related to changes in student academic, emotional, and behavioral performance (Felner et al., 1997). On the basis of the number of weekly team teacher planning meetings (4 or 5), the number of students for whom a team was responsible (not more than 120), the teacher–student ratio (1:20 to 1:25), and the number and ratio of weekly student–teacher advisory meetings (4 to 5 per week with a ratio of 1 teacher per 22 students or fewer), an implementation index was created. Using data from the schools that began their participation early, schools were classified into categories that represented the degree of implementation. The amount of school-level implementation and change in level of implementation over a 2-year period were positively associated with aggregate student outcomes in terms of academic achievement, standardized reading and math scores, and emotional and behavioral adjustment. Finally, the degree of implementation was even more strongly associated with the gain in achievement and adjustment scores for higher risk students.

Summary of Intervention Results

Conceptually, a strategy aimed at restructuring secondary schools along the lines of the schools-within-schools model is appealing. The strength of restructuring strategies of intervention resides in their ability to directly improve the processes of engagement with the educational enterprise. If successful, the creation of a more stable and constructive environment enables educators and students to collaboratively use the most creative, engaging, and effective educational techniques available. They do not target or stigmatize individual students. As such, these strategies can promote positive well-being and reduce the negative academic and behavioral sequelae of school transitions. Moreover, restructuring secondary schools has the greatest long-term impact on youths' life trajectories when it is implemented at the risky juncture between elementary and middle or junior high school. Here too, the ultimate success of these interventions is a function of how faithfully the policy is implemented at the level of the participating school.

RECOMMENDATIONS FOR POLICY AND INTERVENTION

The evidence base is not definitive. Unfortunately, according to Murphy (1993) and others, "There is a notable paucity of empirical studies and research on school restructuring" (p. 4). This remains true to this day. More policy-relevant research on the effectiveness of school restructuring experiments, mechanisms of change, and implementation processes would help educators and policymakers make the tough decisions required. But based on the evidence to date, policymakers can act to improve conditions for, and the trajectories of, adolescents over key school transitions.

Because education is a state and local responsibility in the United States, the recommendations that follow are aimed at educational policymakers and administrators at the state, district, and school levels. Nevertheless, the federal government and the U.S. Department of Education, in particular, need to play a critical role in financially supporting experiments in school restructuring as well as other educational policy initiatives. Only with continued support for experimentation and research will we be able to identify successes and failures and, even more importantly, the specific mechanisms and practices responsible for success. In this way, the success of future endeavors will be enhanced. Equally important, the federal government must take a leadership role in the dissemination of these and other innovations. We recommend the following policy priorities:

1. Educational policymakers at the state and district levels should maintain or create K–8 schools and avoid the perpetuation or creation of middle or junior high school grade-level organizations.
2. When a middle or junior high school organization is an unalterable reality, educators at state, district, and school levels should restructure these organizations along the lines of the schools-within-schools or houses model.
3. Support for full and faithful implementation of such interventions is critical to their success.
4. Other pedagogical and inoculation programs deemed necessary and useful should be implemented in a schools-within-schools model.
5. Implementation of houses or schools within schools in high schools is warranted to maintain the educational engagement of more students.

1. Avoid Creation of Middle or Junior High Schools

Underlying the recommendation to avoid the perpetuation or creation of middle or junior high school grade-level organizations is the finding that gains or stability in academic performance and psychological well-being characterize youths who do *not* make a normative school transition during early adolescence and who remain in K–8 schools as compared to those who do make this school transition. The social arrangements of a typical elementary school classroom seem more developmentally attuned to the needs of the typical early adolescent than the junior high school classroom.

2. Restructure Middle or Junior High Schools

When middle or junior high school grade-level organization is an unalterable reality, educators at state, district, and school levels should restructure these organizations along the lines of the schools-within-schools or houses model to maximize the likelihood of positive developmental trajectories by minimizing the disruptions in the lives of these adolescents at a critical time in their development. The key element is to divide schools into smaller communities of learning that permit a more personalized experience for the children. There are several requirements. First, small numbers of students and teachers need to be located in the same physical area of the school throughout most of the day. Second, students need to move together as an integral unit through the classrooms of their primary subjects. Third, students need to be taught their primary subjects by a small core of teachers who work closely together. Fourth, teachers need to get to know the strengths and liabilities of each student through, for example, advisory groups.

With these changes in the physical structure and social organization of middle or junior high schools, the nature and quality of the pattern of daily transactions among students and teachers can become more personal and facilitative of all parties' functioning and well-being. Student and teacher engagement in the educational enterprise is maintained. Early adolescents are less likely to begin to disengage from the educational enterprise at this critical juncture in their lives. The likelihood that students' academic, behavioral, and socioemotional development will not decline is greatly enhanced. Early adolescents may then be better able to explore a wider range of positive possible selves, enhancing the likelihood that they will be launched on trajectories of productive and prosocial development. Optimally, the new school structure should be maintained throughout the middle or junior high school years.

3. Provide Full Support for Implementation

Successful implementation requires that teachers and administrators be enabled to "own" the changes and make key pedagogical, organizational, and management decisions. It also requires special training for teachers in understanding, teaching, and motivating early adolescents. Connections with families and communities to support schools' commitments to their students are important as well.

4. Make Available Other Pedagogical and Inoculation Programs

Other pedagogical and inoculation programs may be required to help children adjust to the school environment. Innovations of any kind are difficult to implement in the chaotic environment of many junior high schools. Team teaching or cooperative learning innovations would be difficult to implement in such a setting. The same holds true for various socioemotional and life skills training programs.

5. Implement Schools Within Schools or Houses in High Schools

Even though the transition into high school is not the point at which a trajectory of educational disengagement is initiated, implementation of schools within schools or houses is still warranted to maintain the educational engagement of more students. Educational policymakers and administrators should seek the full implementation of these interventions in the transition year and beyond.

REFERENCES

Alspaugh, J. W. (1998). Achievement loss associated with the transition to middle school and high school. *Journal of Educational Research, 92,* 20–25.

Carnegie Council of Adolescent Development. (1989). *Turning points: Preparing American youth for the 21st century.* Washington, DC: Author.

Catterall, J. S. (1987). On the social costs of dropping out of school. *High School Journal, 71,* 19–30.

Chung, H., Elias, M., & Schneider, K. (1998). Patterns of individual adjustment changes during middle school transition. *Journal of School Psychology, 36,* 83–101.

Clements, M., & Seidman, E. (2001). The ecology of middle grades schools and possible selves: Theory, research, and action. In T. M. Brinthaupt & R. P. Lipka (Eds.), *Understanding the self of the early adolescent* (pp. 133–164). Albany, NY: State University of New York Press.

Crockett, L. J., Petersen, A. C., Graber, J. A., Schulenberg, J. E., & Ebata, A. (1989). School transitions and adjustment during early adolescence. *Journal of Early Adolescence, 9,* 181–210.

Cuban, L. (1992). What happens to reforms that last? The case of the junior high school. *American Educational Research Journal, 29,* 227–251.

Eccles, J. S., Lord, S., & Midgley, C. (1991). What are we doing to early adolescents? The impact of educational contexts on early adolescents. *American Journal of Education, 99,* 521–542.

Eccles, J. S., Lord, S. E., Roeser, R. W., Barber, B. L., & Jozefowicz, D. M. H. (1997). The association of school transition in early adolescence with developmental trajectories through high school. In J. Schulenberg, J. L. Maggs, & K. Hurrelmann (Eds.), *Health risks and developmental transitions during adolescence* (pp. 283–320). New York: Cambridge University Press.

Eccles, J. S., Midgley, C., Wigfield, A., Buchanan, C. M., Reuman, D., Flanagan, C., et al. (1993). Development during adolescence: The impact of stage-environment fit on young adolescents' experiences in schools and families. *American Psychologist, 48,* 90–101.

Felner, R. D., Brand, S., Adan, A. M., & Mulhall, P. F. (1993). Restructuring the ecology of the school as an approach to prevention during school transitions: Longitudinal follow-ups and extensions of the School Transitional Environment Project (STEP). *Prevention in Human Services, 10,* 103–136.

Felner, R. D., Jackson, A. W., Kasak, D., Mulhall, P., Brand, S., & Flowers, N. (1997). The impact of school reform for the middle years: Longitudinal study of a network engaged in *Turning Points*-based comprehensive school transformation. *Phi Delta Kappan, 78,* 528–532, 541–550.

Fenzel, L. M., & Blyth, D. A. (1986). Individual adjustment to school transitions: An exploration of the role of supportive peer relations. *Journal of Early Adolescence, 9*, 315–329.

Fine, M. (1994). *Chartering urban reform*. New York: Teachers College Press.

Gillock, K. L., & Reyes, O. (1996). High school transition-related change in urban minority students' academic performance and perception of self and school environment. *Journal of Community Psychology, 24*, 245–261.

Hirsch, B. J., & DuBois, D. L. (1991). Self-esteem in early adolescence: The identification and prediction of contrasting longitudinal trajectories. *Journal of Youth and Adolescence, 20*, 53–72.

Hirsch, B. J., & Rapkin, B. D. (1987). The transition to junior high school: A longitudinal study of self-esteem, psychological symptomatology, school life, and social support. *Child Development, 58*, 1235–1243.

Jones, R. M., & Thornburg, H. D. (1985). The experience of school-transfer: Does previous location facilitate the transition from elementary- to middle-level educational environments? *Journal of Early Adolescence, 5*, 229–237.

Lipsitz, J., Jackson, A. W., & Austin, L. M. (1997). What works in middle-grades school reform. *Phi Delta Kappan, 78*, 517–519.

Midgley, C., Feldlaufer, H., & Eccles, J. S. (1989). Student/teacher relations and attitudes toward mathematics before and after the transition to junior high school. *Child Development, 60*, 981–992.

Murphy, J. (1993). Restructuring: In search of a movement. In J. Murphy & P. Hallinger (Eds.), *Restructuring schooling: Learning from ongoing efforts* (pp. 1–31). Newbury Park, CA: Corwin Press.

Nottelmann, E. D. (1987). Competence and self-esteem during the transition from childhood to adolescence. *Developmental Psychology, 23*, 441–450.

Oxley, D. (2000). The school reform movement: Opportunities for community psychology. In J. Rappaport & E. Seidman (Eds.), *Handbook of community psychology* (pp. 565–590). New York: Kluwer/Plenum.

Price, R. H. (1980). Risky situations. In D. Magnusson (Ed.), *Toward a psychology of situations: An international perspective* (pp. 103–112). Hillsdale, NJ: Erlbaum.

Reyes, O., Gillock, K., & Kobus, K. (1994). A longitudinal study of school adjustment in urban, minority adolescents: Effects of a high school transition program. *American Journal of Community Psychology, 22*, 341–369.

Reyes, O., & Jason, L. (1991). An evaluation of a high school dropout prevention program. *Journal of Community Psychology, 19*, 221–230.

Roderick, M. (1995). School transitions and school dropout. In K. Wong (Ed.), *Advances in educational policy*. Greenwich, CT: JAI Press.

Ruble, D. N., & Seidman, E. (1996). Social transition: Windows into social psychological processes. In E. T. Higgins & A. W. Kruglanski (Eds.), *Social psychology: Handbook of basic principles* (pp. 830–856). New York: Guilford Press.

Rumberger, R. W. (1987). High school dropouts: A review of issues and evidence. *Review of Educational Research, 57*, 101–121.

Seidman, E., Aber, J. L., Allen, L., & French, S. E. (1996). The impact of the transition to high school on the self-system and perceived social context of poor urban youth. *American Journal of Community Psychology, 24,* 489–515.

Seidman, E., Allen, L., Aber, J. L., Mitchell, C., & Feinman, J. (1994). The impact of school transitions in early adolescence on the self-system and perceived social context of poor urban youth. *Child Development, 65,* 507–522.

Seidman, E., & French, S. E. (1997). Normative school transitions among urban adolescents: When, where, and how to intervene. In H. J. Walberg, O. Reyes, & R. P. Weissberg (Eds.), *Children and youth: Interdisciplinary perspectives* (Vol. 7, pp. 166–189). Thousand Oaks, CA: Sage.

Seidman, E., French, S. E., Younes, M., Aber, L. J., Allen, L., & Hsueh, J. (2003). *Trajectories of self-esteem across the transition to junior high school.* Unpublished manuscript, New York University.

Simmons, R. G., Black, A., & Zhou, Y. (1991). African-American versus White children and the transition to junior high school. *American Journal of Education, 99,* 481–520.

Simmons, R. G., & Blyth, D. A. (1987). *Moving into adolescence: The impact of pubertal change and school context.* Hawthorn, NY: Aldine de Gruyter.

Simmons, R. G., Burgerson, R., Carton-Ford, S., & Blyth, D. A. (1987). The impact of cumulative change in early adolescence. *Child Development, 58,* 1220–1234.

Weissberg, R. P., & Greenberg, M. T. (1998). School and community competence-enhancement and prevention programs. In I. E. Sigel & A. Renninger (Eds.), *Handbook of child psychology: Volume 4. Child psychology in practice* (5th ed., pp. 955–998). New York: John Wiley.

14

RESILIENCE IN CHILDREN EXPOSED TO NEGATIVE PEER INFLUENCES

JANIS B. KUPERSMIDT, JOHN D. COIE, AND JAMES C. HOWELL

This chapter draws attention to the rejection by and progressive isolation from conventional peers that is often experienced by aggressive children. Aggressive children make friends with other rejected youngsters, from whom they often learn deviant behavior, and sometimes also join antisocial youth gangs. Efforts to manage, discipline, or treat aggressive children using isolation techniques (e.g., school suspensions, classroom segregation, group therapies focused only on deviant youths, detention) can further remove them from their socializing apprenticeships with conventional peers. Capitalizing on strategies that strengthen the social environments of aggressive youths, the authors review strengths-based programs that could prevent this spiraling of negative peer influences by promoting and maintaining contacts between children and youths who are at risk for deviance and rejection by their more conventional peers.

* * *

Basic research findings indicate that aggressive and antisocial youths affiliate with one another beginning in childhood (Kupersmidt, DeRosier, & Patterson, 1995) and that this pattern of aggressive friendships continues

The authors thank Mary Ellen Voegler, Laura Kate Hennis, and Jamie Roberson for their assistance in preparing this chapter. Portions of this chapter were presented at the 7th Biennial Conference on Community Research and Action, June 1999, in New Haven, CT.

through adolescence (Cairns & Cairns, 1994). In fact, aggressive elementary school-age children tend to play with other aggressive schoolmates at home and at school and are rarely chosen by nonaggressive peers as playmates or friends (Kupersmidt et al., 1995). Cairns, Cairns, Neckerman, Gest, and Gariepy (1988) also reported that aggressive children and aggressive young adolescents tend to associate with each other in cliques and are often central members of these cliques. Given that these types of friendships are consistently reported across a wide age range, it raises the question of whether problems are associated with friendships among aggressive youths.

Unfortunately, the answer to this question is yes. Antisocial youths report that their antisocial friends negatively influence them and even teach them how to do things that get them into trouble. In contrast, they report that their conventional friends are less likely to encourage existing deviant behavior (Sigda, Kupersmidt, & Martin, 1996). Notably, Berndt (1979) reported that peer conformity to antisocial behavior peaks in 9th grade, as teenagers are naturally acquiring increased independence from their parents.

This pattern of self-reported findings has been corroborated by an elegant set of observational studies of aggressive youths and their friends. Aggressive friends were observed to reward the rule-breaking talk (Dishion, Andrews, & Crosby, 1995) and rule-breaking behavior (Bagwell & Coie, 1999) of each other in a way that can be described as "deviancy training." With adolescents, this training sometimes took place through laughter at the recounting of aggressive or antisocial activities. With younger children it involved talk of rule breaking that was accompanied by one child urging the other to "go ahead and do it." These findings mean that if aggressive children mention taking a "forbidden" candy bar in a lab setting, they are more likely to do so if their aggressive friends encourage or support this behavior. Observations of youths within institutional settings indicate that peers provide a much higher rate of reinforcement than adult staff members. This peer support for deviance undermines the positive socializing impact of adult rules and norms (Buehler, Patterson, & Furniss, 1966).

In fact, exposure to deviant peers precedes delinquent behavior (Kennan, Loeber, Zhaang, Stouthamer-Loeber, & Van Kammen, 1995), particularly for more serious forms of offending (Elliott & Menard, 1996). Also, deviant peers influence the onset or escalation of offending behavior among preadolescents who already are exhibiting disruptive behavior problems (Vitaro, Tremblay, Kerr, Pagani, & Bukowski, 1997). A small group of persistent offenders recruit less experienced co-offenders (Reiss & Farrington, 1994). Even after antisocial behavior patterns are established, antisocial youths continue to commit crimes and use drugs with peers rather than alone (Coie & Miller-Johnson, 2001). The negative long-term consequences of deviancy training have recently been reported and include increased initiation of substance use and increased reports of antisocial behavior (Dishion, McCord, & Poulin,

1999). Thus, deviant friends reinforce and shape each other's antisocial behavior in both direct and indirect ways.

These findings demonstrate the negative impact that deviance-prone youths have on each other, as well as on the initiation to offending of those who have not yet committed delinquent acts. The findings also point to the role of social reinforcement and group acceptance in this process. Social acceptance and appreciation are prized commodities for all youths and serve as powerful motivators of children's behavior (Kupersmidt, Buchele, Voegler, & Sedikides, 1996). There is some evidence that antisocial youths are finding this acceptance and support wherever they can. Some antisocial adolescents indicated that they had more antisocial friends and fewer conventional friends than they would like to have (Kupersmidt, Sigda, & Martin, 1995), whereas antisocial adolescents who self-identified as gang members reported being satisfied with their friendships and not being interested in having more conventional friends. Nonincarcerated high school students, however, reported that they were not interested in friendships with antisocial peers.

Why is it important to consider the youth gang context of adolescent violence? The proliferation of gang activity in the United States reflects the tendency of antisocial youths to affiliate and reinforce each other's antisocial behaviors. The estimated number of gang members rose from nearly 100,000 in 1980 (Miller, 1992) to approximately 840,500 in 1999 (Egley, 2000). Every state and all of the nation's large cities reported gang problems in 1999. Although the gang problem is more entrenched in large cities and adjacent suburban counties, it affects communities of all sizes. Furthermore, surveys indicate that up to 30% of adolescents in urban inner-city areas join gangs at some point in their lives (Howell, 1998). Gang membership increases in midadolescence at ages 14 to 16 (Coie & Miller-Johnson, 2001), and violence increases in the adolescent period (Howell & Hawkins, 1998).

This increase in gang activity is disturbing for several reasons. First, self-report studies of adolescent samples in large cities show that a very large proportion of all adolescent violence is committed by gang members (Thornberry, 1998), with estimates ranging from 68% to 89% of all adolescent violent offenses. Gang membership is one of the strongest predictors of self-reported violence during adolescence (Hawkins et al., 1998). In addition, the influence of the gang on levels of violent offending has been shown to be greater than the influence of other delinquent peers (Battin, Hill, Abbott, Catalano, & Hawkins, 1998). Moreover, while they are in gangs youths commit offenses at higher rates than before joining or after leaving (Thornberry, Krohn, Lizotte, & Chard-Wierschem, 1993).

Second, studies of urban adolescents showed that risk factors for gang membership span the community, family, peer group, school, and individual attribute domains (Hill, Howell, Hawkins, & Battin, 1999). Associating with delinquent friends was found to be a potent combination for predicting gang membership, whereas having a strong attachment to conventional peers decreased the probability of joining gangs (Hill et al., 1999). In addition, youths on a trajectory of worsening antisocial behavior who had aggressive friends were found most likely to join gangs (Lahey, Gordon, Loeber, Stouthamer-Loeber, & Farrington, 1999). However, with the recent emergence of gangs in less populated areas (National Youth Gang Center, 1999), many lower risk youths are also joining gangs. This suggests the increasingly pervasive nature of gangs across demographic groups.

Third, much of the gang violence in adolescence occurs in and around schools on school days (Wiebe, Meeker, & Vila, 1999). Violent gang crimes begin to escalate sharply early in the school day and peak early in the afternoon and again long after the school day ends (Wiebe et al., 1999)—unlike overall juvenile violence, which tends to peak immediately after the end of the school day (Snyder & Sickmund, 1999b). In 1995, 37% of students surveyed nationally reported the presence of gangs in their schools (Howell & Lynch, 2000). The percentage of students reporting gangs in schools more than doubled from 1989 to 1995, and the presence of gangs more than doubles the likelihood of violent victimization at school (Chandler, Chapman, Rand, & Taylor, 1998).

CHALLENGES TO INTERVENTION

Three sets of findings describe a very complex situation in which to intervene if the goal is to wean antisocial youths off of their deviant friendships and into more conventional friendships. First, it is important to reach at-risk youths before they become committed to the social identity of gang membership. Second, it will not suffice to simply put them in contact with more conventional youths without addressing the barriers that will arise to potential friendships. A range of self-reported barriers to the development of cross-behavior-type friendships have been examined for both antisocial and conventional adolescents (Kupersmidt et al., 1996). These include peer pressure from a conventional peer group to avoid antisocial peers, lack of trust in antisocial peers, parental disapproval of affiliating with antisocial peers, and lack of common interests. In fact, even after intervention efforts with aggressive youths result in an increase in prosocial behavior and a decrease in aggressive behavior, these youths remain disliked by their conventional peers, and the objectively observed reductions in their aggressive behavior are not reported by peers (see Bierman, 1990, for review). Thus, a further barrier to overcome in establishing friendships between antisocial and conventional youths is the persistence of a negative reputation.

Third, there is evidence that some aggressive children do not know how to establish friendships of the quality they might like. Despite the fact that they rate their deviant friendships highly on many relationship qualities, unbiased observers rate their friendships significantly lower on these qualities than the friendships of nonaggressive children (Bagwell & Coie, 1999). Friendships of antisocial youths have been characterized by more conflict and less stability than conventional adolescent friendships (Dishion et al., 1995). All of this suggests that even if the barriers to friendship were erased, many antisocial youths would need help in learning to maintain stable, high-quality friendships.

There is a further point to be made about peer influences, one that has bearing on intervention planning. Evidence for the iatrogenic effects of grouping antisocial youths in interventions has emerged in several studies. Low-achieving high school students who received intensive group counseling reported increases in school alienation after counseling as compared to a control group (Catterall, 1987). Further, children placed in group homes had more deviant peer contacts and fewer reductions in delinquency than children placed in treatment foster care homes (Chamberlain & Reid, 1998). High-risk adolescents who participated in group therapy with similar peers had more tobacco use and delinquent behavior than a control group following treatment, and these iatrogenic effects persisted through a 3-year follow-up period (Dishion et al., 1999). These findings led Dishion et al. to conclude that interventions that place antisocial youths together in groups inadvertently promote friendships and alliances that undermine the goals of the group intervention.

The dilemma that these findings create for intervention planning is that antisocial youths may need training in social skills and self-regulation techniques before they can effectively develop more positive prosocial friendships, yet training them in homogeneous groups can have deleterious effects. Furthermore, the barriers of negative reputation that keep conventional youths from wanting friendships with antisocial youths must be addressed. A solution to this dilemma may be found in the St. Louis experiment (Feldman, 1992). Antisocial youths were randomly assigned to groups of homogeneously antisocial youths, conventional youths only, or a mix of antisocial and conventional youths for positive skill-enhancing activities. Antisocial youths improved most in the mixed groups, with surprisingly negligible adverse effects to the conventional youths. This suggests that an intervention combination of skilled leaders in a well-structured group context that includes a substantial proportion of conventional youths can have a positive effect on the antisocial youths without risking the well-being of the conventional youths. This strategy might also build more constructive friendships between antisocial and prosocial youths, because it provides the antisocial youths with a way to overcome their negative reputations.

These findings have important implications. Some of the best prevention efforts result in the creation of deviant peer groups through activities such as social skills training groups for aggressive children or parent training groups for parents of aggressive children. Special attention needs to be paid to the group dynamics that develop during participation in therapeutic and recreational group activities that do not include a mix of conventional and antisocial youths.

PUBLIC POLICY IMPLICATIONS OF THE RESEARCH FINDINGS

The most prevalent reaction to youth crime is to isolate antisocial youths from mainstream society into prisons, detention centers, psychiatric hospitals, wilderness camps, and training or alternative schools. The fear among parents and school administrators of having a potentially violent youth in the classroom or in the community has resulted in an increase in legislative and administrative initiatives at the state and local levels to isolate these youths. None of these strategies helps high-risk children get to the point where they will not have to be isolated, nor do they prevent the deviancy training described in this chapter.

The normalizing socialization influences of observing and interacting with conventional peers are absent from these isolation procedures, and affiliation and identification with a deviant peer group are intensified. Consistent with the deviancy training findings, incarcerated youths often become more antisocial after incarceration than prior to it. At best, these efforts delay their inevitable reintegration into society, often without any accompanying graduated and structured exposure to conventional peers and society.

HOW DO WE PREVENT UNSUPERVISED EXPOSURE OF CONVENTIONAL YOUTHS TO NEGATIVE PEER INFLUENCES?

Develop and Disseminate Parent Education Programs

One extreme method that inner-city parents often use to protect their children from exposure to gangs and negative peer influences is to lock their children inside the house when school is not in session. Although this method may reduce exposure to potentially dangerous situations and deviant peers, it also prevents children from experiencing positive unstructured and semistructured activities with peers.

A more strengths-based approach could involve educating parents about the importance of play and relationships with conventional peers, helping parents find or provide supervised activities for their children, and developing their capacity to monitor their children's activities near home. These approaches can be accomplished through parent training sessions on strategies for monitoring and supervising their child's behavior, friends, and activities. (We recognize that some parents forbid their children to leave home when they cannot be present to supervise them. Low-income, single parents have a particularly difficult problem in this respect, and this problem calls for a community response, in addition to parent training.)

Efforts directed at developing high-quality parent–child relationships can also have positive long-term benefits. For example, parenting qualities such as increasing warmth in the mother–child relationship and involvement of fathers can reduce delinquent behavior through lowering contact with deviant peers (Mason, Cauce, Gonzales, & Hiraga, 1994).

Create Accessible Prosocial and Adult-Structured Activities for Aggressive Youths

Another strengths-based approach is for communities to increase opportunities for supervised activities for aggressive youths to participate in with prosocial peers, while simultaneously promoting skill development in both groups. Lack of adult supervision has been found to make children more vulnerable to pressure from peers to engage in antisocial behavior (Steinberg, 1986). With many youths living in homes with working parents, there is a great need for structured after-school activities such as school-based programs, midnight basketball leagues, and Boys' and Girls' clubs. Low-income youths who attended formal after-school activities had better grades and peer relations and fewer behavioral and emotional problems than children engaged in unstructured activities (Posner & Vandell, 1994). Many of these structured activities cost money and involve transportation, so they may not be readily accessible to low-income families. A policy approach to this problem would be to provide block grants, training and technical assistance, and incentives to schools to develop high-quality after-school programs. In this way, these kinds of enrichment programs can be accessible to children from all income levels. These approaches have in common the goals of reducing unsupervised time and activities as well as increasing exposure to positive role models and enhancing skills and abilities.

HOW DO WE PREVENT EXTENSIVE EXPOSURE TO NEGATIVE PEER INFLUENCES FOR ANTISOCIAL YOUTHS?

The prevention of exposure to negative peer influences for already aggressive youths is a difficult problem to solve. First, the research reviewed in this chapter consistently suggests that these youths tend to affiliate with one another and that there are substantial barriers to conventional friendships. In addition, antisocial youths usually realize that they will continue to be in trouble if they hang out with their antisocial friends but often passively accept it. This suggests that the drive to have a friend, even an unsatisfactory friend, is stronger than the drive to avoid trouble. Nonetheless, no empirically validated treatment programs could be located that specifically address how to help antisocial youths make and keep conventional friends.

Develop and Disseminate Social Skills Training to Aggressive and Antisocial Youths

Generic social skills training programs can provide guidance for the clinician and policymaker in establishing programs for antisocial youths (Asher, Parker, & Walker, 1998). By building social skills and social cognitive skills, particularly in conflict management, and increasing prosocial behavior, the friendship-making skills of aggressive youths are also likely to be positively affected. Consistent with this hypothesis, Vitaro et al. (1997) reported that an early social skills intervention with 1st and 2nd graders reduced delinquency at age 13 and reduced interaction with deviant peers.

The Fast Track project (Conduct Problems Prevention Research Group, 1999) has demonstrated success in improving social skills and promoting friendships with conventional youths. Aggressive, disruptive 1st graders were trained weekly in positive social skills and anger control, and their parents participated in sessions on behavior management and promoting positive behavior. In addition, classrooms received comparable training, and the high-risk children were coached in one-on-one play with classmates. Peer status improved significantly by the end of 1 year compared to control high-risk children. The long-term goal of Fast Track is to reduce deviant peer influence and chronic antisocial behavior.

Create Programs for Volunteers to Mentor Aggressive and Antisocial Youths

Another approach to increasing exposure to conventional peers is to provide volunteer mentors for at-risk youths. Initial evaluation reports on the effectiveness of the Big Brother/Big Sister program suggest many positive effects of having a positive, ongoing relationship with a conventional adult, including a decrease in the initiation of substance use and improvements in school achievement and attendance (Grossman & Tierney, 1998). Volunteer mentors can also provide prosocial extracurricular experiences with conventional adults and peers. Mentoring programs may need some modification, including additional training and supervision for volunteers who develop a relationship with an aggressive or antisocial youth.

Re-Entry or Aftercare Programs for Incarcerated Youths

In addition, specific intervention efforts may need to be developed for incarcerated youths, particularly as they are about to make the transition to re-enter society. Re-entry or aftercare programs have been the focus of many intervention efforts for incarcerated adults and need to be further developed for adolescents. One therapeutic approach often used in preparation for this transition is the creation of a relapse prevention contract. Optimally, these contracts contain detailed, prospective diaries of daily activities and companions and are composed with the help of a trained counselor prior to release from a juvenile facility. In these diaries, it would be important to identify when each person anticipates that he or she will be monitored and supervised by conventional adults and which peers will participate with him or her in each activity. It is equally important for counselors to encourage participation in activities that will provide opportunities for supervised interactions with conventional peers. One program for high-risk juveniles has been shown to produce very positive short-term effects (Josi & Sechrest, 1999). The Lifeskills '95 program, in San Bernadino and Riverside County, California, is an aftercare program for youthful offenders released from the California Youth Authority. In addition to other impressive results, the program reduced frequent gang affiliations, with only 8% of the program youths having frequent gang affiliations as compared to 27% of the control group.

Create and Disseminate Coping Skills Curricula for Antisocial Youths

Another strengths-based approach to help prevent relapse or involvement with deviant peers is to provide skills-based training in coping with stress. This is particularly salient for incarcerated youths, who become easily disappointed postrelease and have difficulty making the transition to less structure. Helping them anticipate stressful life experiences and cope with everyday and major life stressors without turning to drugs, crime, or antisocial peers is critical.

HOW DO WE PREVENT THE FORMATION OF DEVIANT PEER GROUPS?

Reduce Classroom Size and Train Teachers in Cooperative Learning Methods

Another important question concerns what can be done to prevent the formation of deviant peer groups. Small classroom research studies may provide ideas about the importance of each child feeling valued and appreciated in the school context so that cliques of rejected and aggressive children do not begin to form. Methods for involving all students in school activities and reducing school alienation are needed. For example, cooperative learning activities are designed to encourage the social mixing of students with various characteristics and abilities, which has been found to enhance social relationships among diverse classmates (Slavin, 1996).

Create and Disseminate School Principal Training Programs

Another approach is for school principals to assess the level of aggressive behavior of each student at the conclusion of a school year. Then, when forming new classes, each principal can attempt to keep groups of aggressive children out of the same classrooms by splitting them up across classes in a grade. Reducing the aggregation of aggressive or antisocial children or adolescents in a classroom could be a powerful prevention strategy.

Create and Disseminate Teacher Training Programs

Teachers often do not notice which children are aggressive (Leff, Kupersmidt, Patterson, & Power, in press). Thus, a third approach might be to train teachers to observe and monitor group affiliations during free play, lunchroom, and playground activities (Leff, Costigan, Manz, & Power, 1999), because bullying commonly occurs during unstructured activities (Craig & Pepler, 1997). Teachers can then organize games and activities that include heightened structure and supervision, systematic reinforcement procedures, and cooperative activities to use with a mix of aggressive and conventional students (Nabors, Willoughby, Leff, & McMenamin, in press).

These primary prevention strategies focus on structuring the classroom and school environments to be optimally conducive to prosocial behavior and friendships among diverse groups of students. As communities begin to expand after-school programs, adult supervision of these programs will need to use strategies similar to those described for school staff.

HOW DO WE CONSTRUCT A POSITIVE PEER CULTURE FOR ANTISOCIAL YOUTHS?

Despite many efforts to protect society from exposure to violent and deviant youths, these efforts to isolate antisocial youths have been time limited, at best, and short sighted. A complementary approach is to accept that violence and deviant children and adolescents are a predictable part of the fabric of conventional society, so that intervention efforts might be better oriented at changing the behavior of deviant individuals while simultaneously regulating exposure to them. Strategies for accomplishing this may have to vary according to the age group being addressed because of the shifting impact of adult and peer influence across development.

Research on the effects of developing a positive peer culture may provide guidance in these efforts. Deviant youths often set the norms for the peer group, particularly in middle school. Active efforts by adults to set prosocial norms to counteract this negative influence have been successful with younger children. For example, the Good Behavior game, which attempts to create a positive peer culture through group contingencies for good behavior, has been successful with aggressive children in the elementary school setting (Werthamer-Larsson, Kellam, & Wheeler, 1991). Group-based interventions in the school setting also have been successful when they include a mix of conventional and aggressive youths (Tremblay, Pagani-Kurtz, Masse, Vitaro, & Pihl, 1995). Structured and repeated social interactions among aggressive and conventional children may be a critical mechanism for change. If the interactions among group members are rewarding, then these therapeutic group experiences may also serve the function of providing positive experiences with a peer who typically is experienced as an aversive social partner. This may, in turn, enhance the social standing and likeability of the antisocial peer while simultaneously increasing prosocial behaviors.

An additional approach to middle school peer culture identified leaders of social networks and enlisted them in advocating for non-risk-taking, nonviolent behaviors (Coie & Jacobs, 1993). By using the authority that the leaders of deviant groups possess to influence their peers in a positive way, the goal was to develop a nonviolent value system with prosocial alternatives. These values would be fostered and maintained by giving group leaders opportunities to spend time with appealing prosocial role models, to experience success with conventional others, to have access to community resources such as jobs and skills training, and to have access to therapeutic resources for deviant peers. In a similar vein, media leaders could be encouraged to create adolescent role models that promote prosocial goals and behaviors. The mass media could also provide examples within a fictional format about ways youths can be socially accepted, if not popular, and still solve complex social problems in a prosocial way.

Classroom behavior management plans might also address the antisocial peer behavior discussed in this chapter. These plans can include reinforcement of prosocial peer talk and behavior and response costs for antisocial peer talk and behavior. This type of systematic approach to the shaping of prosocial behavior is critically needed in institutional settings, where bragging about aggressive prowess is often shared by peers and accompanied by laughter and attention.

The North Carolina Willie M. Program provides a successful model of how a carefully planned system of mental health care can be developed for the treatment of extremely violent youths. This program was created as a result of an out-of-court settlement of a federal class action lawsuit (i.e., *Willie M. et al. v. Governor James B. Hunt, Jr., State of North Carolina, et al.*) guaranteeing the right to treatment for assaultive and violent children who suffered from emotional, mental, or neurological handicaps, for whom the state had not provided appropriate treatment and educational programs. This innovative program provided treatment within the least restrictive setting with the goal of keeping Willie M. clients in their community rather than institutionalized in residential care or juvenile justice facilities (Soler & Warboys,

1990). This program was accomplished, in part, through the adoption of a no eject–no reject policy and the identification and enhancement of modifiable protective factors. In addition to traditional mental health services, creative approaches were developed such as extensive use of both professional and paraprofessional mentors and individualized classroom crisis aides (less expensive per school year than incarceration), parent training and family respite services, therapeutic foster care, and structured prosocial after-school and weekend activities. These strategies aimed at increasing protective factors underscore the viability of reducing the social isolation of even the most violent children in U.S. society.

Treatment efforts with already antisocial youths require concentrated efforts that include both school- and community-based approaches as well as individualized interventions to be optimally successful. They also reflect the need for maintaining the safety of the community while providing the least restrictive setting for the child with behavior problems.

HOW CAN WE INTERVENE SPECIFICALLY IN THE REDUCTION OF GANG PEER INFLUENCE?

Interventions to prevent and reduce negative gang peer influence are needed at several levels. First, preventing the onset of delinquency is an indirect method of preventing gang involvement, because gangs recruit youngsters who already are delinquent (see Thornberry, 1998, for a review). Indeed, an evaluation of the Montreal Preventive Treatment Program (Tremblay, Masse, Pagani, & Vitaro, 1996), in a follow-up at age 15, showed that significantly fewer boys in the treatment group than in the control group had joined a gang.

Create and Disseminate Social Skills Programs for Gang Members

Second, discouraging children and adolescents from joining gangs is important because gangs are perceived as providing excitement, enhancing prestige or status among friends, and helping members deal with the challenges of adolescence (Howell, 1998). One approach to preventing the joining of gangs is to build resilience through promoting positive social skill development and providing alternatives to gang life. This approach is particularly important in inner-city areas, where gangs are more prevalent, dangerous, and difficult for youths to resist (Howell, 1998, 1999).

Create and Disseminate Programs With Community-Based Organizations

A key component of such successful gang-reduction programs appears to be the active involvement of community-based organizations. These programs provide outreach to high-risk youths in a number of ways. Some programs, such as the Gang Prevention Through Targeted Outreach (Howell, 2000), use a referral network that links local clubs with courts, police departments, schools, social service agencies, and other agencies to recruit at-risk youths into programs in a nonstigmatizing way. Another promising model program establishes Violence-Free Zones in gang-involved neighborhoods, including public housing projects (National Center for Neighborhood Enterprise, 1999). Indigenous community leaders help effect truces among gangs and discourage gang violence. The Violence-Free Zone model includes family-like supports and mentoring for youths at risk for joining gangs and for gang-involved youths. Job training and work opportunities are provided to help youths make a transition from gang life and criminality to violence-free lives and productive citizenry. Successful youths also are given the opportunity to collaborate with youths in other communities and cities to expand the project.

Develop and Disseminate Gang Prevention Curricula

Third, preventing and reducing adolescent delinquency in the school context should be a priority, given the prevalence of gang activity during the school day (Wiebe et al., 1999). A universal school-based Gang Resistance Education and Training (G.R.E.A.T.) curriculum has proved to be effective in preventing gang affiliation (Esbensen, 2000). This 9-week curriculum, primarily for 7th graders, introduces students to conflict resolution skills, cultural sensitivity, and the negative aspects of gang life. The strategy is a cognitive approach that seeks to produce a change in attitude and behavior through instruction, discussion, and role playing. An evaluation of the program (Esbensen & Osgood, 1999) compared students who had completed the program with a comparable group of students who did not participate. G.R.E.A.T. students self-reported less delinquency and had lower levels of gang affiliation, higher levels of school commitment, and greater commitment to prosocial peers, among other positive outcomes.

A national study of school-based gang prevention and intervention programs is in progress that should provide guidance with respect to other promising and effective school-based gang programs. The study makes use of a nationally representative sample of 1,287 schools, two thirds of which provided information on gang prevention and intervention programs and characteristics (e.g., prevention curriculum, mentoring, tutoring; Gottfredson & Gottfredson, 1999). Current school programs will be compared with "best practices."

These programs suggest that engagement in conventional relationships and activities is fundamental to avoiding gang membership. To provide youths with social and behavioral alternatives, substantial community-level support is needed in gang-prevention programming.

HOW DO WE USE A STRENGTHS-BASED APPROACH TO BUILD RESILIENCE IN CHILDREN EXPOSED TO NEGATIVE PEER INFLUENCES?

Taken together, the approaches described in this chapter use a range of strengths-based methods to reduce the exposure to and impact of negative peers. These methods include emphasizing the development of hobbies, skills, and interests; providing training in interpersonal problem-solving skills; constructing experiences aimed at developing bonds with conventional youths and mainstream norms; developing methods to increase feelings of inclusion in conventional peer groups; keeping children busy and enhancing their skills with nonacademic and academic activities; and enhancing adult supervision and monitoring of children and adolescent activities within the home, school, and neighborhood settings.

This review highlighted the need for additional basic and applied research efforts to address the problem of negative peer influences. There are relatively few studies on the friendship-making and -keeping skills of antisocial youths. There are even fewer studies that explore the social cognitive functioning of antisocial youths and, specifically, their cognitions about their friendships and the friendships of others. Clearly, basic research on these developmental processes has provided many productive ideas for prevention and treatment studies. There is also a continued need for empirically validated prevention programs that are aimed at the reduction of antisocial behavior in individuals and in groups using a strengths-based perspective. Treatment outcome studies on how antisocial youths can develop and keep conventional friendships in a way that is safe for all concerned parties (including parents, the community, and the children involved) are also lacking. Thus, the integration of a strengths-based approach suggests important directions for future research and intervention efforts.

REFERENCES

Asher, S., Parker, J., & Walker, D. (1998). Distinguishing friendship from acceptance: Implications for intervention and assessment. In W. M. Bukowski, A. F. Newcomb, & W. W. Hartup (Eds.), *The company they keep: Friendship in childhood and adolescence* (pp. 366–405). New York: Cambridge University Press.

Bagwell, C. L., & Coie, J. D. (1999, April). *Social influence in the friendship relations of aggressive boys.* Paper presented at the meeting of the Society for Research in Child Development, Albuquerque, New Mexico.

Battin, S. R., Hill, K. G., Abbott, R. D., Catalano, R. F., & Hawkins, J. D. (1998). The contribution of gang membership to delinquency beyond delinquent friends. *Criminology, 36,* 93–115.

Berndt, T. (1979). Developmental changes in conformity to peers and parents. *Developmental Psychology, 15,* 608–616.

Bierman, K. (1990). Improving the peer relations of rejected children. In B. B. Lahey & A. E. Kazdin (Eds.), *Advances in clinical child psychology* (pp. 131–149). New York: Plenum Press.

Buehler, R. E., Patterson, G. R., & Furniss, J. M. (1966). The reinforcement of behavior in institutional settings. *Behavior Research and Therapy, 4,* 157–167.

Cairns, R. B., & Cairns, B. D. (1994). *Lifelines and risks: Pathways of youth in our time.* Cambridge, England: Cambridge University Press.

Cairns, R. B., Cairns, B. D., Neckerman, H. J., Gest, S. D., & Gariepy, J. L. (1988). Social networks and aggressive behavior: Peer support or peer rejection. *Developmental Psychology, 24,* 815–823.

Catterall, J. S. (1987). An intensive group counseling drop-out prevention intervention: Some cautions on isolating at-risk adolescents within high schools. *American Educational Research Journal, 24,* 521–540.

Chamberlain, P., & Reid, J. B. (1998). Comparison of two community alternatives to incarceration for chronic juvenile offenders. *Journal of Consulting and Clinical Psychology, 6,* 624–633.

Chandler, K. A., Chapman, C. D., Rand, M. R., & Taylor, B. M. (1998). *Students' reports of school crime: 1989 and 1995.* Washington, DC: U.S. Department of Education & U.S. Department of Justice.

Coie, J. D., & Jacobs, M. R. (1993). The role of social context in the prevention of conduct disorder. *Development and Psychopathology, 5,* 263–275.

Coie, J. D., & Miller-Johnson, S. (2001). Family risk factors and interventions. In R. Loeber & D. P. Farrington (Eds.), *Child delinquents: Development, interventions, and service needs* (pp. 191–209). Thousand Oaks, CA: Sage.

Conduct Problems Prevention Research Group. (1999). Initial impact of the Fast Track prevention trial for conduct problems: I. The high-risk sample. *Journal of Consulting and Clinical Psychology, 67,* 631–647.

Craig, W., & Pepler, D. J. (1997). Observations of bullying and victimization in the school yard. *Canadian Journal of School Psychology, 13*(2), 41–59.

Dishion, T. J., Andrews, D. W., & Crosby, L. (1995). Antisocial boys and their friends in early adolescence: Relationship characteristics, quality, and interactional process. *Child Development, 66,* 139–151.

Dishion, T. J., McCord, J., & Poulin, F. (1999). When interventions harm: Peer groups and problem behavior. *American Psychologist, 54,* 755–764.

Egley, A., Jr. (2000). *Highlights of the 1999 National Youth Gang Survey* (Fact Sheet No. 2000–20). Washington, DC: U.S. Department of Justice, Office of Juvenile Justice and Delinquency Prevention.

Elliott, D. S., & Menard, S. (1996). Delinquent friends and delinquent behavior: Temporal and developmental patterns. In J. D. Hawkins (Ed.), *Delinquency and crime: Current theories* (pp. 28–67). New York: Cambridge University Press.

Esbensen, F. (2000). Preventing adolescent gang involvement: Risk factors and prevention strategies. In *Juvenile Justice Bulletin* (Youth Gang Series). Retrieved July 29, 2003, from http://www.ncjrs.org/pdffiles1/ojjdp/182210.pdf

Esbensen, F., & Osgood, D. W. (1999). Gang Resistance Education and Training (GREAT): Results from the national evaluation. *Journal of Research in Crime and Delinquency, 36*, 194–225.

Feldman, R. A. (1992). The St. Louis experiment: Effective treatment of antisocial youths in prosocial peer groups. In J. McCord & R. E. Tremblay (Eds.), *Preventing antisocial behavior: Intervention from birth through adolescence* (pp. 233–252). New York: Guilford Press.

Gottfredson, G. D., & Gottfredson, D. C. (1999, July 29). *Survey of school-based gang prevention and intervention programs: Preliminary findings.* Paper presented at the National Youth Gang Symposium, Las Vegas, NV.

Grossman, J. B., & Tierney, J. P. (1998). Does mentoring work? An impact study of the Big Brothers Big Sisters program. *Evaluation Review, 22*, 403–426.

Hawkins, J. D., Herrenkohl, T., Farrington, D. P., Brewer, D., Catalano, R. F., & Harachi, T. W. (1998). A review of predictors of youth violence. In R. Loeber & D. P. Farrington (Eds.), *Serious and violent juvenile offenders: Risk factors and successful interventions* (pp. 106–146). Thousand Oaks, CA: Sage.

Hill, K. G., Howell, J. C., Hawkins, J. D., & Battin, S. R. (1999). Childhood risk factors for adolescent gang membership: Results from the Seattle Social Development Project. *Journal of Research in Crime and Delinquency, 36*, 300–322.

Howell, J. C. (1998). Youth gangs: An overview. In *Juvenile Justice Bulletin* (Youth Gang Series). Retrieved July 29, 2003, from http://www.ncjrs.org/pdffiles/167249.pdf

Howell, J. C. (1999). Youth gang homicides: A literature review. *Crime and Delinquency, 45*, 208–241.

Howell, J. C. (2000). *Youth gang programs and strategies.* Washington, DC: U.S. Department of Justice, Office of Justice Programs, Office of Juvenile Justice and Delinquency Prevention.

Howell, J. C., & Hawkins, J. D. (1998). Prevention of youth violence. In M. Tonry & M. Moore (Eds.), *Crime and justice: A review of research: Volume 24. Youth violence* (pp. 263–315). Chicago: University of Chicago.

Howell, J. C., & Lynch, J. P. (2000). Youth gangs in schools. In *Juvenile Justice Bulletin* (Youth Gang Series). Retrieved July 29, 2003, from http://www.ncjrs.org/pdffiles1/ojjdp/183015.pdf

Josi, D., & Sechrest, D. K. (1999). A pragmatic approach to parole aftercare: Evaluation of a community reintegration program for high-risk youthful offenders. *Justice Quarterly, 16*(1), 51–80.

Kennan, K., Loeber, R., Zhaang, Q., Stouthamer-Loeber, M., & Van Kammen, W. B. (1995). The influence of deviant peers on the development of boys' disruptive and delinquent behavior: A temporal analysis. *Development and Psychopathology, 7*, 715–726.

Kupersmidt, J. B., Buchele, K. S., Voegler, M. E., & Sedikides, C. (1996). Social self-discrepancy: A theory relating peer relations problems and school maladjustment. In K. R. Wentzel & J. Juvonen (Eds.), *Social motivation: Understanding children's school adjustment* (pp. 66–97). New York: Cambridge University Press.

Kupersmidt, J. B., DeRosier, M. E., & Patterson, C. J. (1995). Similarity as the basis for companionship among children: The roles of sociometric status, aggressive and withdrawn behavior, academic achievement, and demographic characteristics. *Journal of Social and Personal Relationships, 12*, 439–452.

Kupersmidt, J. B., Sigda, K. B., & Martin, S. L. (1995, November). Attitudes about friendships with prosocial peers among incarcerated adolescents. In J. B. Kupersmidt (Chair), *Friendships of antisocial youths*. Paper presented at the annual meeting of the American Society of Criminology, Boston.

Lahey, B. J., Gordon, R. A., Loeber, R., Stouthamer-Loeber, M., & Farrington, D. P. (1999). Boys who join gangs: A prospective study of predictors of first gang entry. *Journal of Abnormal Child Psychology, 27*, 261–276.

Leff, S. S., Costigan, T. E., Manz, P., & Power, T. J. (1999, April). *The development of a needs assessment questionnaire for playground and lunchroom violence prevention programming*. Poster presented at the meeting of the Society for Research in Child Development, Washington, DC.

Leff, S. S., Kupersmidt, J. B., Patterson, C. J., & Power, T. J. (1999). Factors influencing teacher identification of peer bullies and victims. *School Psychology Review, 28*, 505–517.

Mason, C. A., Cauce, A. M., Gonzales, N., & Hiraga, Y. (1994). Adolescent problem behavior: The effect of peers and the moderating role of father absence and the mother/child relationship. *American Journal of Community Psychology, 22*, 723–743.

Miller, W. B. (1992). *Crime by youth gangs and groups in the United States*. Washington, DC: U.S. Department of Justice, Office of Juvenile Justice and Delinquency Prevention.

Nabors, L., Willoughby, J., Leff, S. S., & McMenamin, S. (2001). Promoting inclusion for young children with special needs on playgrounds. *Journal of Developmental and Physical Disabilities, 13*, 179–190.

National Center for Neighborhood Enterprise. (1999). *Violence-free zone initiatives*. Washington, DC: National Center for Neighborhood Enterprise.

National Youth Gang Center. (1999). *1996 national youth gang survey*. Washington, DC: U.S. Department of Justice, Office of Juvenile Justice and Delinquency Prevention.

Posner, J. K., & Vandell, D. L. (1994). Low-income children's after-school care: Are there beneficial effects of after-school programs? *Child Development, 65*, 440–456.

Reiss, A. J., & Farrington, D. P. (1994). Advancing knowledge about co-offending: Results from a prospective longitudinal survey of London males. In D. P. Farrington (Ed.), *Psychological explanations of crime: The international library of criminology, criminal justice & penology* (pp. 315–350). Aldershot, England: Dartmouth Publishing.

Sigda, K. B., Kupersmidt, J. B., & Martin, S. L. (1996, March). Attitudes about prosocial and antisocial peers among incarcerated adolescents. In W. Bukowski (Chair), *Friendship and aggression*. Paper presented at the meeting of the Society for Research on Adolescence, Boston.

Slavin, R. E. (1996). Research on cooperative learning and achievement: What we know, what we need to know. *Contemporary Educational Psychology, 21*, 43–69.

Snyder, H. N., & Sickmund, M. (1999). Violence after school. In *Juvenile Justice Bulletin* (1999 National Report Series). Retrieved July 29, 2003, from http://www.ncjrs.org/pdffiles1/ojjdp/178992.pdf

Soler, M., & Warboys, L. (1990). Services for violent and severely disturbed children: The Willie M. litigation. In S. Dicker (Ed.), *Stepping stones: Successful advocacy for children* (pp. 61–112). New York: Foundation for Child Development.

Steinberg, L. (1986). Latchkey children and susceptibility to peer pressure: An ecological analysis. *Developmental Psychology, 22*, 433–439.

Thornberry, T. P. (1998). Membership in youth gangs and involvement in serious and violent offending. In R. Loeber & D. P. Farrington (Eds.), *Serious and violent juvenile offenders: Risk factors and successful interventions* (pp. 147–166). Thousand Oaks, CA: Sage.

Thornberry, T. P., Krohn, M. D., Lizotte, A. J., & Chard-Wierschem, D. (1993). The role of juvenile gangs in facilitating delinquent behavior. *Journal of Research in Crime and Delinquency, 30*, 55–87.

Tremblay, R. E., Masse, L., Pagani, L., & Vitaro, F. (1996). From childhood physical aggression to adolescent maladjustment: The Montreal Prevention Experiment. In R. D. Peters & R. J. McMahon (Eds.), *Preventing childhood disorders, substance abuse, and delinquency* (pp. 268–298). Thousand Oaks, CA: Sage.

Tremblay, R. E., Pagani-Kurtz, L., Masse, L. C., Vitaro, F., & Pihl, R. O. (1995). Disruptiveness, friends' characteristics, and delinquency in early adolescence: A test of two competing models of development. *Child Development, 68*, 676–689.

Vitaro, F., Tremblay, R. E., Kerr, M., Pagani, L., & Bukowski, W. M. (1997). Disruptiveness, friends' characteristics, and delinquency in early adolescence: A test of two competing models of development. *Child Development 68*, 676–689.

Werthamer-Larsson, L., Kellam, S. G., & Wheeler, L. (1991). Effect of first grade classroom environment on shy behavior, aggressive behavior, and concentration problems. *American Journal of Community Psychology, 19*, 585–602.

Wiebe, D. J., Meeker, J. W., & Vila, B. (1999). *Hourly trends of gang crime incidents, 1995–1998* (Fact Sheet). Irvine, CA: University of California, Focused Research Group on Gangs.

15

RACIAL AND ETHNIC STATUS: RISK AND PROTECTIVE PROCESSES AMONG AFRICAN AMERICAN FAMILIES

ALGEA O. HARRISON-HALE, VONNIE C. MCLOYD, AND BRIAN SMEDLEY

Researchers suggest that racism and racial disparities in economic resources are pathways to adverse outcomes for people of color. In this chapter, the authors explore the literature on factors that facilitate positive outcomes among children, youths, families, and communities of color. The functioning of protective factors such as support from extended families, racial and ethnic socialization practices, and religiosity are reviewed. Finally, the authors recommend several policies designed to improve resilient outcomes among individuals in ethnic minority communities. These include policies that enhance personal skills through existing community institutions, strengthen family supports, and build the social capital of communities.

* * *

It is incontrovertible that their racial and ethnic status poses unique threats to the healthy functioning of children, youth, families, and commu-

The authors express their appreciation to Autumn Kelly and Sheba Shakir for their diligent bibliographic and secretarial assistance.

nities of color. These threats derive from historical and contemporary acts of commission and omission that together have resulted in a system of disadvantage for people of color. Yet people of color have developed strengths and coping strategies to facilitate positive and adaptive outcomes when facing these unfair social systems. In this chapter, we discuss two pervasive and inextricably linked circumstances that render racial and ethnic status a risk factor at both the individual and group level: racism and racial disparities in economic resources. Throughout our discussion of economic resources, we highlight racial and ethnic disparities in both poverty and wealth. Attention is given to factors that buffer the adverse effects of the two stressors and generally contribute to strengths in children, youth, families, and communities of color. We conclude with a discussion of the policy implications of our analyses.

Research on African Americans and Hispanics, especially mainland Puerto Ricans, is used to exemplify risk and protective processes relative to racial and ethnic status. These two groups are selected because they are the largest among people of color in the United States and the foci of most psychological research on risk and resilience factors. In addition, of all racial or ethnic groups, African Americans and Puerto Ricans generally occupy the most unfavorable positions on indexes of development (e.g., infant mortality) and social well-being (e.g., school dropout), perhaps with the exception of certain Native American groups (see Garcia Coll et al., 1996, for a detailed discussion). It is notable from a historical perspective that both African Americans and Puerto Ricans are "caste-like" people of color in that they were incorporated into American society involuntarily and permanently through slavery, conquest, and colonization (Ogbu, 1981).

ECONOMIC RESOURCES

Racial and ethnic disparity in economic well-being is among the most significant and stubborn legacies of institutionalized racism in American society. Through diverse pathways, long-standing racial discrimination in education, employment, and housing has translated into both glaring (e.g., poverty) and concealed (e.g., financial assets) economic disadvantage among African Americans and certain groups of Hispanics (Oliver & Shapiro, 1995). The poverty rate in 1997 among African American families (23.6%), like that of Hispanic families (24.7%), was about three times that of White American families (8.4%). Data for 1997 indicate that the percentage of families of householders who worked year-round and full time but were still poor was markedly higher among African Americans and Hispanics than White Americans (6.3%, 11.2%, and 2.9%, respectively; U.S. Bureau of the Census, 1999).

The most concealed yet profound legacy of racial and ethnic discrimination is racial disparity in net financial assets and net worth. *Net financial assets* consist of readily liquid sources of wealth that can be used for a family's immediate needs and desires (e.g., saving accounts, stocks, bonds, mutual funds, business equity) and differ from *net worth* in that the latter includes, whereas the former excludes, equity in vehicles and homes (both exclude debts). Net financial assets are the best indicator of the current generation's command over future resources, whereas net worth provides a more accurate estimate of the wealth likely to be inherited by the next generation (Oliver & Shapiro, 1995). Because of our keen interest in the consequences of economic resources for the current generation, we focus here on net financial assets.

Data from the 1987 Panel of the National Survey of Income and Program Participation (SIPP) administered by the Bureau of the Census indicate substantial racial disparities in the median net financial assets of households (Oliver & Shapiro, 1995). During that year, the average African American household had $0 median net financial assets, as compared to $7,000 for White households. Poverty-level White Americans had mean net financial assets almost equal to those of the highest earning African Americans ($26,683 and $28,310, respectively). Race differences in assets were also evident within households at similar income levels. Among middle-income households ($25,000 to $50,000), African Americans had only 3% of the median net financial assets of their White American counterparts ($138 vs. $5,500). Even among high-income households (over $50,000), African Americans possessed only 23 cents of median net financial assets for every dollar of assets held by White Americans ($7,200 vs. $31,706).

Race and ethnic differences in poverty and economic well-being are fundamentally rooted in structural forces that have produced layers of accumulated economic disadvantage. Systemic forces operating to the detriment of people of color through macrolevel policies—some explicitly race conscious and others not—also partially account for racial disparities in wealth accumulation. Oliver and Shapiro (1995) meticulously detailed the systemic exclusion of African Americans from more than a century of asset-building policies in the United States, including the Homestead Act of 1862 and the mortgage system of both the Federal Housing Authority (FHA) and the Veterans Administration. Established in 1934, the FHA recommended use of restrictive covenants based on race and social class (rescinded in 1950, this policy was motivated ostensibly by a desire to retain neighborhood stability). These policies effectively fueled the movement of White Americans to the suburbs during the 1940s and 1950s and deepened the isolation of African Americans in inner cities.

Likewise, the mortgage policies of the Veterans Administration, intended to help World War II veterans buy low-cost homes in emerging suburban areas, favored White Americans and promoted racial segregation through both overt and subtle means. These policies effectively locked African Americans out of the "greatest mass-based opportunity for wealth accumulation in American history and had a lasting and adverse impact on the wealth portfolios of African Americans" (Oliver & Shapiro, 1995, p. 18). The race differences in wealth White Americans created have translated into staggering race differences in inheritance to this day and are compounded by current racial disparities in access to mortgage and housing markets and by welfare state policies that create racial disparities in their implementation.

Because home ownership is the major source of wealth (i.e., net worth) held by the average American, racial valuing of neighborhoods on the basis of segregated markets is also a core contributor to race differences in wealth accumulation. Whereas segregated housing has attenuated African Americans' net worth on the one hand, it has increased the price they pay for goods and services (e.g., new cars, automobile insurance, home mortgages, food) on the other. The higher price that African Americans pay for essentials means that they have less money to save, invest, spend on child-related activities and services, and use for other goods and services than their White American counterparts with the same level of family income (see McLoyd & Ceballo, 1998, for a more detailed discussion).

Poverty and low income at the family level are associated with a range of problems, including depressed moods in parents, strained marital relations, conflictual parent–child relations, and among children, lower cognitive functioning, school achievement, and socioemotional well-being (McLoyd, 1990, 1998). Recent investigations also have found that, controlling for family-level income, negative neighborhood conditions such as scarce social and educational resources and high rates of neighborhood-level poverty, joblessness, crime, and other forms of social disorder, are linked to lower academic performance and higher rates of pregnancy, childbearing, delinquency and psychosocial problems among adolescents (for a review of these studies, see McLoyd, 1998; McLoyd & Ceballo, 1998).

RACISM

Racism is a complex belief system marked by the belief that racial characteristics are biologically based, the belief that one's race is superior to others', and endorsement and enactment of behavior intended to maintain the superior position of one's race over others' (Jones, 1997). Others have defined racism in both individual and systemic terms, arguing that it is not only personal ideology based on negative racial prejudice, but also a "system of advantage based on race" (Tatum, 1997, p. 7). This two-prong system, which is sustained by cultural messages and institutional policies and practices as well as beliefs and actions of individuals, operates to the advantage of White Americans and to the disadvantage of people of color.

Recent years have witnessed a burgeoning of conceptual and empirical work concerning the impact of perceived racism and discrimination on psychological and physiological functioning. Whereas early research focused on the beliefs, stereotypes, and behavior of the purveyors of racism, this new generation of work shifts the focus to the targets of racism and the factors that both moderate and mediate the biopsychosocial effects of perceived racism (Clark, Anderson, Clark, & Williams, 1999; Harrell, 2000; Jackson et al., 1996). Clark et al. (1999) conceptualized racism as both a chronic and acute stressor, the perception of which can result in psychological (anger, paranoia, anxiety, helplessness–hopelessness, frustration, resentment, fear) and physiological (e.g., cardiovascular and neuroendocrine) stress symptoms. These symptoms are moderated by a complex organization of constitutional, sociodemographic, psychological, and behavioral factors and coping responses. Drawing on a rich body of research in the general stress literature documenting links between stress and health status, theorists postulate that perceived racism adversely affects the individual by precipitating physiological and psychological stress symptoms (Clark et al., 1999; Harrell, 2000). Evidence also exists that lifetime estimates of unfair treatment (e.g., being treated with less courtesy than others, receiving poorer service than others in restaurants or stores, being treated as if one is not smart) attributed to racial or ethnic discrimination predict greater psychological distress, lower well-being, poorer self-reported health, and a greater number of bed days among African Americans (Williams, Yu, Jackson, & Anderson, 1997).

Substantial proportions of White Americans still hold negative racial and ethnic stereotypes. Bobo (2000) reported that White Americans in the 1990 national General Social Survey rated African Americans as less intelligent (54%), lazier (62%), more prone to violence (56%), and preferring to live off of welfare (78%), as compared to Whites. In view of these data, it is hardly surprising that African Americans are much more likely than White Americans to report discriminatory events, both over their lifetimes and in the past year (e.g., unfairly fired or denied a promotion; not hired for a job; harassed by police; received poorer service than others in restaurants or stores), most of which occur in semipublic and public settings (Forman, Williams, & Jackson, 1997). Notably, most studies of African Americans find no relation between income and reports of discrimination (e.g., Gary, 1995).

The experimental research of Steele and Aronson (1995) suggests that the widespread stereotype of African Americans as intellectually inferior—a major belief undergirding racism—can undermine intellectual functioning. In a series of laboratory experiments, Steele and Aronson found that, controlling for verbal and quantitative scores on the Scholastic Aptitude Test, African American college students at a prestigious private university underperformed in relation to White Americans when tests (items taken from the Graduate Record Examination study guides) were presented as diagnostic of intellectual ability. However, they matched the performance of White Americans when the same tests were described simply as laboratory problem-solving tasks that were not diagnostic of ability.

Smedley and colleagues (Smedley, Myers, & Harrell, 1993) also documented the impact of race- and ethnic-related stressors among students attending a large, public, and highly competitive university (e.g., perceptions by White American peers and professors that they were there because of affirmative action, questions about their ability to succeed academically, experiences of racism). These stressors contributed to social adjustment problems over and above generic stressors normally experienced by students during their first year of college (e.g., academic demands).

SOURCES OF STRENGTH AND BUFFERS OF RACE- AND ETHNIC-RELATED STRESSORS

Although there is wide diversity within individuals and groups of color, religiosity, extended families, and social support networks are prevalent and unifying characteristics that strengthen their individual and group-level functioning.

Religiosity

Scholars studying communities of people of color have conceptualized religion as an adaptive coping mechanism maintained and reinforced by cultural traditions and worldviews (Cone, 1984; Ellison, 1993; Lincoln & Mamiya, 1990). These coping mechanisms enable people of color to transcend the limitations and harshness of their social realities, to adjust to their environments, and to give meaning and direction to their individual and collective existence. The coastal areas of West Africa were a major source of slaves, and scholars attest to the highly developed political and legal systems, art and cultural forms, and arrangements of interpersonal and family relations present in these societies when the slave trade began (Day, Jennings, Beckett, & Leashore, 1995). A large number of leaders of religious groups were among the Africans brought to America as slaves. These leaders provided religious explanations, rituals, and ceremonies that fostered coping strategies based on African worldviews, practices, and group cohesiveness among enslaved Africans (Houston, 1990).

At the beginning of the 1990s, 70% of African Americans reported themselves to be members of religious organizations (Billingsley & Caldwell, 1991). When polled in the late 1990s as to what religion they practiced, the responses of African Americans were 75% Protestant, 10% Roman Catholic, 8% other, and 7% none. Empirical investigations based on national data affirm the role of organized religion in the family life of African Americans (Lincoln & Mamiya, 1990). Religious organizations afford a range of benefits to African Americans. They provide informal support (e.g., companionship, advice and comfort, help during illness, financial assistance), formal services (e.g., meals on wheels, transportation, group vacations, housing for elderly, ministerial counseling), and an infrastructure for organizing political participation (Taylor, 1993; Taylor & Thornton, 1993). African American churches established the Free African Society in 1787, a benevolent organization that provided charitable services within the slave community and higher education programs for emancipated slaves (Lincoln & Mamyia, 1990). The organizational context of religion increases political participation among its members (Taylor & Thornton, 1993).

Religious organizations are a defining element of individual attitudes and belief systems. They are perceived by their members as key sources of moral guidance for personal conduct (Taylor, 1993). They also provide a unique structure and context for African Americans' reflected appraisals about the self. Because these organizations afford an interpersonal context in which one is evaluated by other believers, members come to evaluate themselves on criteria different from those of mainstream society. Within the belief system of African American organizations of faith, criteria for self-evaluation are one's inherent uniqueness as an individual, one's sociability and service to others, and one's spiritual qualities, such as wisdom and morality (Ellison, 1992, 1993). Members evaluate and respect others in terms of their social performance (e.g., friendliness, amicability, sociability, service to others) and their spiritual resources (e.g., morality, insight, wisdom; Ellison, 1992, 1993).

Prayers are constructed to meet the demands of particular situations (Scarlett & Periello, 1991) and are the very essence of the African American religious experience (Cone, 1970). In the process of developing an intimate relationship with God through prayer, the divine other becomes analogous to a significant social other (Ellison, 1993). Thus, the looking-glass self-appraisal becomes, "How does God see me?" African American theology teaches that God sees each individual as both special—he or she is created by God—and a sinner—but God hates the sin, not the sinner. Embedded in these teachings is the idea that God has unconditional regard for his creations and loves them all regardless of race because all are created in his image (Cone, 1970; Ellison, 1993; Lincoln & Mamiya, 1990).

Self-esteem is enhanced by the perception that one is held in high regard by an omnipotent divine other who makes his or her presence felt in one's life (Ellison, 1992). National surveys of African Americans repeatedly indicate that public and private religiosity is positively associated with high self-esteem (Ellison, 1993). Research with older African Americans reveals that although stressors tend to erode feelings of mastery and self-esteem, these negative effects are offset or counterbalanced by religious involvement (Krause & Tran, 1989). It is notable that having a mother who seeks spiritual support is one of several factors that distinguish African American children who are stress resilient from those who are stress impaired (Myers & Taylor, 1998).

Extended Families

Extensive kinship bonds existed among Africans before their arrival in America. These bonds were maintained during slavery and have been sustained since slavery as a means of adaptation, survival, and community cohesiveness (Harrison, Wilson, Pine, Chan, & Buriel, 1990). Extended families are close kin relations within and across generations whose members are intensely involved in the reciprocal exchange of goods, services, and emotional support (McAdoo, 1978). As such, they are problem-solving and stress-coping systems.

African American respondents in national surveys repeatedly report substantial receipt of informal and formal assistance from extended family members (Benin & Keith, 1995; Taylor, Chatters, & Jackson, 1993). The type of assistance given and received varies with the age of the recipient, socioeconomic status, and marital status, among other factors. Elderly family members are more likely than younger members to receive companionship, goods and services, transportation, help when sick, and total support (Perry & Johnson, 1994). Child care assistance, care for sick and out-of-school children, and help with transportation typically are the types of assistance granted to parents, especially single mothers. Among contemporary African American families in rural and urban areas, child rearing is often shared by several kin and may not be performed primarily by biological parents (Draper, 1989). Middle-class family members are more likely than less economically advantaged family members to contribute financially to extended family networks (Allen, 1978). Assistance also varies by marital status, with poor, single-parent families having a greater likelihood of involvement with extended family than two-parent families. Typically, this involvement is beneficial to young children and adolescents. For example, adolescents whose single parent was involved in extended family activities reported fewer problem behaviors (Taylor, Casten, & Flickinger, 1993). Single mothers who are active participants in an extended family system also have more opportunities for self-improvement, employment, and contact with peers.

Social Support Networks

A social support network entails a functional collective of persons providing or making available to individual members opportunities for security, recognition, affirmation, instrumental assistance, emotional comfort, personal growth, and social control (Wilson & Tolson, 1990). Social support is a quality of interaction within the collective that leads the individual to believe he or she is cared for and about and can anticipate assistance from members of the network (Dressler, 1991).

African American adolescents living in extended families give high rankings to members of their networks as sources of reliable affection, self-enhancing assistance, intimacy, and companionship (Harrison, Stewart, Myambo, & Teveraishe, 1995). Social support also is an important ingredient in the parenting experiences of persons of color. African American and Hispanic adolescent mothers who reported higher levels of grandmother support had fewer psychological problems, more positive interactions with their babies, and higher levels of educational attainment. It is important to note, however, that the impact of grandmother involvement, especially when mother and grandmother are coresiding or co-parenting, is not uniformly positive. We do not yet have a good understanding of what aspects are detrimental or inert (McLoyd, Cauce, Takeuchi, & Wilson, 2000). In general, though, parents' support networks lessen the tendency toward punitive, coercive, and inconsistent parenting and, in turn, foster socioemotional development in children (McLoyd, 1990).

DESIGNING STRENGTHS-BASED POLICIES FOR PEOPLE OF COLOR

The preceding discussion illustrates that racism and racial disparities in economic resources exert broad negative effects on the health and well-being of persons of color. As we have argued, the experiences of racism and devalued status have their roots in historical, social, political, and economic forces operative in the United States. In response to these conditions, people of color have developed a variety of protective processes that address both direct experiences of racism as well as the effects of poverty and economic deprivation. Because risk factors associated with race and ethnic status among people of color are systemic and external, these factors may be directly addressed by policy strategies that seek to reduce economic disparities and disadvantage caused by discrimination and systemic racism. Similarly, public policies may enhance sources of strength and resilience among people of color. This section discusses theoretical and empirical evidence for strengths-based policies, as well as policies that may reduce race-based disadvantage.

In addition to the mortgage policies of the FHA and Veterans Administration, U.S. history is replete with social policies guided by a race-conscious framework that assumed the fundamental inferiority of African American, Native American, and other persons of non-European descent. These policies have reinforced the inferior status of racial and ethnic groups, whether expressed in overt forms of state-sanctioned discrimination (e.g., legalized slavery, Jim Crow segregation) or in less explicit but no less harmful policies that fail to address social inequities (e.g., poorer educational opportunities for children of color). It is crucial that policymakers are mindful that past policies have often had harmful and negative consequences for racial and ethnic peoples of color.

These dynamics must be fully understood to craft policies that strengthen racial and ethnic communities of people of color and reduce disadvantage. This is especially significant given the current debate over social policies such as affirmative action. Opponents of such policies argue that policy must be "color-blind," whereas proponents argue that race and ethnicity are significantly linked to social advantages and disadvantages and therefore must be explicitly considered when allocating resources. We support the latter perspective, given the considerable salience of race in policy, social, and economic life over the course of much of U.S. history.

"Color-conscious" policies, however, generate little public support (Jackson, 2000). Americans explicitly reject racial "spoils." Murrell, Dietz-Uhler, Dovidio, and Gaertner (1994), for example, found that White undergraduates were more strongly opposed to affirmative action when policies specify African Americans as the targeted beneficiary group rather than other common affirmative action target groups, such as elderly or the handicapped people. Policies benefiting African Americans were more strongly opposed when presented without justification. Thus, from a political standpoint, policies that enhance the strengths of ethnic minority communities are more likely to receive support if they are perceived by the public as equitable and fair for all (Jackson, 2000). Several policy options emerge that address this political reality by providing resources and strategies to improve resilience among individuals in ethnic minority communities. These options include policies that enhance personal skills through existing community institutions, that enhance family supports, and that enhance the social capital of communities.

Enhancing Personal Skills and Knowledge Through Community Institutions

Many institutions in ethnic minority communities—most notably, African American churches—are substantial sources of individual and community support. African American churches not only provide a ready mechanism for social and spiritual support, but also are an important vehicle for shaping social attitudes and belief systems. Some public and private institutions have attempted to capitalize on the influence of churches and other houses of worship by working with religious leaders and congregations to provide needed services and to enhance the knowledge and personal skills of parishioners. For example, several researchers funded through the National Institutes of Health are working with clergy to inform congregations about research protocols and clinical research trials that increase access to disease therapies or preventive techniques (Brown, 1997). These outreach efforts have significantly increased the numbers of ethnic minority individuals enrolled in clinical research trials, which provides the twofold benefit of increasing community access to high-quality care and enhancing scientists' knowledge of the effects of therapeutic interventions among ethnic minority individuals. Others, including grantees of state and local health departments, as well as the federal Centers for Disease Control and Prevention, provide parishioners with health screening, health promotion and disease prevention information, and access to health care professionals (Brown, 1997). Churches can also serve as a mechanism for the dissemination of scientific information and planning of community-based research projects, creating two-way communication between scientists and community members and increasing community participation in research.

Enhancing Family Supports

Familial and kinship ties are a significant source of resilience and coping mechanisms among many in ethnic minority communities. Economic, historical, and sociopolitical factors contribute to variations in family structures across U.S. racial and ethnic groups (e.g., extended family networks among African Americans), but these structures nonetheless can be strengthened to enhance resilience, especially among youths. Policies that increase access to programs such as high-quality center-based child care, home visitation from trained professionals, and parent training can bolster the capacity of families to address socioeconomic disadvantage. Although research support is positive yet inconsistent in studies of the effectiveness of home visitation programs and parent training, evidence of the effectiveness of center-based child care is less equivocal. In a review of policy options to address the needs of children from low socioeconomic backgrounds, Fuligni and Brooks-Gunn (2000), for example, found extensive evidence of the impact of center-based child care quality on child outcomes, including early educational achievement, as well as on parental caregiving. The authors also reviewed evidence suggesting that federally supported Head Start programs are generally of higher quality than other center-based child care programs, including school-based, nonprofit, for-profit, and preschool centers. Home visitation programs offering parents a curriculum focused on improving parental functioning and child health and development (e.g., Nurse Home Visitation Program) have been found to improve some early educational and health outcomes among children, although the findings have not been entirely consistent (Olds et al., 1999). These data suggest that federal- and state-supported programs that disproportionately serve children of color, such as Head Start and Healthy Start programs, should be expanded to serve more eligible children and families (Fuligni & Brooks-Gunn, 2000).

Enhancing Social Capital

A host of formal and informal social support networks in ethnic minority communities may provide instrumental assistance, social control, and material and emotional support. As with support from family structures, religious institutions, and other community groups, these social supports have evolved to serve the needs of individuals in ethnic minority communities and have been shaped by historical, cultural, and political forces. At a broader, community level, social supports are an element of social capital. *Social capital* is a resource realized through the kinds and quality of social relationships in a community. Such resources are characterized by shared norms and mutual trust, which facilitate cooperation toward shared goals (Sampson & Morenoff, 2000).

A growing body of research relates social capital to both community-level indicators, such as levels of crime and environmental degradation, and individual-level health and social outcomes, such as infant mortality, child maltreatment, and levels of disease. Unfortunately, many communities of color characterized by high levels of poverty also possess low levels of social cohesion and social capital. The percentage of individuals of color living in communities of concentrated poverty is increasing (Gephart, 1997). Policies must reverse these trends by

- addressing material and infrastructure needs of poor communities, such as by providing low- and no-interest loans for upgrading housing, transportation systems, school, and child care facilities, and addressing other structural deficits that disrupt economic development (Jackson, 2000);
- strengthening community institutions such as grassroots and community service organizations; and
- encouraging efforts to promote income diversity within neighborhoods and reduce concentrated poverty.

Broader policy strategies are ultimately needed to address race-based socioeconomic disadvantage and institutionalized racism that limit the life circumstances and health, economic, and educational status of individuals of color. Until such time, the policy options outlined in this chapter offer promise to increase individual and community supports and enhance existing sources of strength and resilience in communities of color. These strategies offer broad-based benefits that may improve individual and community resources across all racial and ethnic groups but that may be particularly beneficial for people of color, given existing sources of strength and resilience in these communities. Importantly, social science research and theory are important tools to guide policy development and must play a central role in the policy process.

REFERENCES

Allen, W. (1978). Black family research in the United States: A review, assessment and extension. *Journal of Comparative Family Studies, 9,* 167–189.

Benin, M., & Keith, V. M. (1995). The social support of employed African American and Anglo mothers. *Journal of Family Issues, 16*, 275–297.

Billingsley, A., & Caldwell, C. H. (1991). The church, the family, and the school in the African American community. *Journal of Negro Education, 60*, 427–440.

Bobo, L. D. (2000). Racial attitudes and relations at the close of the twentieth century. In N. Smelser, W. J. Wilson, & F. Mitchell (Eds.), *America becoming: Racial trends and their consequences* (pp. 264–301). Washington, DC: National Academy Press.

Brown, K. S. (1997, February 17). Scientists, African American clergy join forces for trial recruitment. *Scientist*, 1–10.

Clark, R., Anderson, N. B., Clark, V. R., & Williams, D. R. (1999). Racism as a stressor for African Americans. *American Psychologist, 54*, 805–816.

Cone, J. (1970). *A Black theology of liberation*. Philadelphia: Lippincott.

Cone, J. (1984). *For my people: Black theology and the black church*. Maryknoll, NY: Orbis.

Day, A., Jennings, J., Beckett, J. O., & Leashore, B. R. (1995). Effective coping strategies of African Americans. *Social Work, 40*, 240–248.

Draper, P. (1989). African marriage systems: Perspectives from evolutionary ecology. *Ethnology and Sociobiology, 10*, 145–169.

Dressler, W. W. (1991). Social support, lifestyle incongruity, and arterial blood pressure in a southern Black community. *Psychosomatic Medicine, 53*, 608–620.

Ellison, C. G. (1992). Are religious people nice people? Evidence from the National Survey of Black Americans. *Social Forces, 71*, 411–430.

Ellison, C. G. (1993). Religious involvement and self-perceptions among Black Americans. *Social Forces, 71*, 1027–1055.

Forman, T. A., Williams, D. R., & Jackson, J. S. (1997). Race, place, and discrimination. *Perspectives on Social Problems, 9*, 231–261.

Fuligni A. S., & Brooks-Gunn, J. (2000). The healthy development of young children: SES disparities, prevention strategies, and policy opportunities. In B. D. Smedley & S. L. Syme (Eds.), *Promoting health: Intervention strategies from social and behavioral research* (pp.170–216). Washington, DC: National Academy Press.

Garcia Coll, C., Lamberty, G., Jenkins, R., McAdoo, H. P., Crnic, K., Wasik, B. H., et al. (1996). An integrative model for the study of developmental competencies in minority children. *Child Development, 67*, 1891–1914.

Gary, L. (1995). African American men's perceptions of racial discrimination: A sociocultural analysis. *Social Work Research, 19*, 207–217.

Gephart, M. (1997). Neighborhoods and community as context for development. In J. Brooks-Gunn, G. J. Duncan, & J. Lawrence (Eds.), *Neighborhood poverty: Context and consequences for children* (Vol. 1, pp. 1–43). New York: Russel Sale.

Harrell, S. P. (2000). A multidimensional conceptualization of racism-related stress: Implications for the well-being of people of color. *American Journal of Orthopsychiatry, 70*, 42–57.

Harrison, A. O., Stewart, R. B., Myambo, K., & Teveraishe, C. (1995). Perception of social networks among adolescents from Zimbabwe and United States. *Journal of Black Psychology, 21,* 382–407.

Harrison, A. O., Wilson, M. N., Pine, C. J., Chan, S. Q., & Buriel, R. (1990). Family ecologies of ethnic minority children. *Child Development, 61,* 347–362.

Houston, L. N. (1990). *Psychological principles and the Black experience.* New York: University Press of America.

Jackson, J. S. (2000). African American prospects in the 21st century: A framework for strategies and policies. In J. S. Jackson (Ed.), *New directions: African Americans in a diversifying nation* (pp. 276–290). Washington, DC: National Policy Association.

Jackson, J. S., Brown, T. N., Williams, D. R., Torres, M., Sellers, S. L., & Brown, K. (1996). Racism and the physical and mental health of African Americans: A thirteen year national panel study. *Ethnicity & Disease, 6,* 132–147.

Jones, J. M. (1997). *Prejudice and racism* (2nd ed.). New York: McGraw-Hill.

Krause, N., & Tran, T. (1989). Stress and religious involvement among older Blacks. *Journal of Gerontology: Social Sciences, 44,* S4–S13.

Lincoln, C. E., & Mamiya, L. H. (1990). *The Black church in the American experience.* Durham, NC: Duke University Press.

McAdoo, H. P. (1978). Factors related to stability in upwardly mobile Black families. *Journal of Marriage and the Family, 40,* 761–776.

McLoyd, V. C. (1990). The impact of economic hardship on Black families and children: Psychological distress, parenting, and socioemotional development. *Child Development, 61,* 311–346.

McLoyd, V. C. (1998). Socioeconomic disadvantage and child development. *American Psychologist, 53,* 185–204.

McLoyd, V. C., Cauce, A. M., Takeuchi, D., & Wilson, L. (2000). Marital processes and parental socialization in families of color: A decade review of research. *Journal of Marriage and the Family, 62,* 1070–1093.

McLoyd, V. C., & Ceballo, R. (1998). Conceptualizing and assessing economic context: Issues in the study of race and child development. In V. C. McLoyd & L. Steinberg (Eds.), *Studying minority adolescents: Conceptual, methodological, and theoretical issues* (pp. 251–278). Mahwah, NJ: Erlbaum.

Murrell, A. J., Dietz-Uhler, B. L., Dovidio, J. F., & Gaertner, S. L. (1994). Aversive racism and resistance to affirmative action: Perception of justice is not necessarily color blind. *Basic and Applied Social Psychology, 15*(1–2), 71–86.

Myers, H. F., & Taylor, S. (1998). Family contributions to risk and resilience in African American children. *Journal of Comparative Family Studies, 29,* 215–229.

Ogbu, J. U. (1981). Origins of human competence: A cultural-ecological perspective. *Child Development, 52,* 413–429.

Olds, D. L., Henderson, C. R., Kitzman, H. J., Eckenrode, J. J., Cole, R. E., & Tatelbaum, R. C. (1999). Prenatal and infancy home visitation by nurses: Recent findings. *Future of Children, 9,* 44–65.

Oliver, M., & Shapiro, T. (1995). *Black wealth/White wealth: A new perspective on racial inequality*. New York: Routledge.

Perry, C. M., & Johnson, C. L. (1994). Families and support networks among African American oldest-old. *International Journal of Aging and Human Development, 38*, 41–50.

Sampson, R. J., & Morenoff, J. D. (2000). Public health and safety in context: Lessons from community-level theory on social capital. In B. D. Smedley & S. L. Syme (Eds.), *Promoting health: Intervention strategies from social and behavioral research*. Washington, DC: National Academy Press.

Scarlett, W. G., & Periello, L. (1991). The development of prayer in adolescence. In F. Oser & W. G.Scarlett (Eds.), *Religious development in childhood and adolescence* (pp. 63–77). San Francisco: Jossey-Bass.

Smedley, B. D., Myers, H. F., & Harrell, S. P. (1993). Minority-status stresses and the college adjustment of ethnic minority freshman. *Journal of Higher Education, 64*, 435–451.

Steele, C., & Aronson, J. (1995). Stereotype threat and the intellectual test performance of African Americans. *Journal of Personality and Social Psychology, 69*, 797–811.

Tatum, B. D. (1997). *"Why are all the Black kids sitting together in the cafeteria?" And other conversations about race*. New York: Basic Books.

Taylor, R. J. (1993). Religion and religious observances. In J. S. Jackson, L. M. Chatters, & R. J. Taylor (Eds.), *Aging in Black America* (pp. 101–123). Newbury Park, CA: Sage.

Taylor, R. D., Casten, R., & Flickinger, S. (1993). The influence of kinship social support on parenting experiences and psychosocial adjustment of African American adolescents. *Developmental Psychology, 29*, 382–388.

Taylor, R. J., Chatters, L. M., & Jackson, J. S. (1993). A profile of familial relations among three-generation black families. *Family Relations, 42*, 332–341.

Taylor, R. J., & Thornton, M. C. (1993). Demographic and religious correlates of voting behavior. In J. S. Jackson, L. M. Chatters, & R. J. Taylor (Eds.), *Aging in Black America* (pp. 233–249). Newbury Park, CA: Sage.

U.S. Bureau of the Census. (1999). *Statistical abstract of the United States: 1999*. Washington, DC: Author.

Williams, D. R., Yu, Y., Jackson, J. S., & Anderson, N. B. (1997). Racial differences in physical and mental health: Socioeconomic status, stress and discrimination. *Journal of Health Psychology, 23*, 335–351.

Wilson, M. N., & Tolson, T. F. J. (1990). Familial support in Black community. *Journal of Clinical Child Psychology, 19*, 347–355.

16

ACCULTURATION AND ENCULTURATION AMONG LATINO YOUTH

NANCY A. GONZALES, GEORGE P. KNIGHT, DINA BIRMAN,
AND AMALIA A. SIROLLI

The ethnic culture of immigrant families is traditionally viewed as a deficit and as an impediment to adjustment to the new society. In contrast, in this chapter the authors present evidence of the psychological and behavioral importance, in this case for Latino youth, of learning the ways both of the U.S. culture and of their own ethnic culture. Applying this viewpoint to the critical issue of school adaptation and success in schooling, the authors emphasize the importance of increasing Latino parents' access to schools, supporting teachers in working effectively with cultural minority groups, respecting ethnic culture, and promoting biculturalism. These approaches embody the strengths-based principles of building new strengths, such as cultural competence among school personnel, and building on existing strengths, such as the ethnic culture of immigrant families.

* * *

Many ethnic minority youths in the United States live in relatively impoverished environments. The potential risks these environments create

The authors thank Charles Barone and Daniel S. Strouse for their assistance with background information for this chapter.

for these youths is well documented. However, these youths often also face additional challenges associated with being a member of a minority group and adapting to life in a host culture with different rules and values, often a different language, and sometimes a loss of familiar support systems. The pressure to simultaneously adapt to two cultures can be quite powerful in the lives of minority youths, even for those whose families have lived in the United States for generations.

Consider, for example, what a recently immigrated child is confronted with on a daily basis. Though many families immigrate to the United States specifically to provide their children with access to educational and financial opportunities, their children often attend schools that are not prepared to teach them in their native tongue. They may find themselves immersed in English-only classes or in English as a second language (ESL) classes that are underfunded and unable to provide an appropriately challenging level of intellectual stimulation. Their teachers and classmates may not understand or appreciate their values and customs, and the immigrant children may fail to establish meaningful social ties. When they struggle in school, they may not be able to ask parents for help with homework, and their parents may not be able to intervene on their behalf because they are unfamiliar with the organization and expectations of U.S. schools.

Immigrant families often respect the authority of schools by not interfering with the school program. As a result, teachers may view parents as apathetic or unsupportive of their child's achievement, and they may be less inclined to invest themselves in their students' progress. Because immigrant children typically learn English more rapidly than their parents, the children may be placed in the position of cultural broker, translating and interpreting for family members as they link their parents to the dominant culture. The parent's ability to maintain authority may, in turn, be compromised. The children are encouraged to succeed in the United States, yet at the same time they face resentments from family members. Educational opportunities may therefore come at considerable cost.

Though the majority of second- and third-generation youths speak English, they may still confront discrimination in the larger community, and they may be more vulnerable to the damaging negative stereotypes often directed at Latinos. At the same time, later-generation youths are typically more acculturated along other dimensions, including values and behavioral norms, which may make them more susceptible to other acculturative strains such as conflicts with parents and the influence of delinquent peer groups (Fridrich & Flannery, 1995; Samaniego & Gonzales, 1999).

Several authors have suggested that these challenges represent a substantial risk for some ethnic minority youths and may well lead to increased psychological and social problems (e.g., Gonzales & Kim, 1997; Marin, 1989; Phinney, 1990; Szapocznik & Kurtines, 1980). Although the extent of this risk is difficult to quantify, research has documented a link between global indicators of acculturation and poor psychological functioning. For example, Vega and colleagues (1998) reported differential rates of negative mental health outcomes in successive generations of Mexican Americans; first-generation immigrants and Mexicans in Mexico City had similar rates of mental health problems, but Mexican Americans born in the United States were nearly twice as likely to have such problems. Similar generational trends have been reported for other Latino groups. Research with Cubans, Puerto Ricans, and Mexican Americans has shown higher rates of antisocial behavior problems, substance use, and school dropout across generations and for youths who had been in the United States for longer periods of time. Poor birth outcomes, including low birth weight and preterm delivery, also increase linearly as a function of acculturation (Brattan-Wolf & Portis, 1996). Research also has shown higher rates of delinquency, symptoms of depression, and suicidal ideation in youths who report greater exposure to acculturative stress (Hovery & King, 1996; Katragadda & Tidwell, 1998; Rasmussen, Negy, Carlson, & Burns, 1997).

And yet, despite these findings, there are clearly substantial numbers of acculturating youths who adapt quite successfully, succeed in school, and suffer no negative mental health outcomes. Moreover, some authors (e.g., Bernal, 1996; Phinney & Chavira, 1995; Zimmerman, Ramirez, Washienko, Walt, & Dyer, 1998) have suggested that the dual processes of acculturation and enculturation may each have some salutary effects on psychosocial development and, together, may contribute to unique adaptive resources for some youths. For example, M. E. Bernal (personal communication, December 1, 1996) suggested that

> an immigrant from a poor country may readily and willingly take on the dominant group's cultural characteristics in exchange for alleviation of severe economic deprivation. This immigrant may experience renewed physical and mental health, as well as economic well-being, and these effects may counteract some of the negative effects of adopting a new country.

A RESILIENCE AGENDA FOR ACCULTURATION RESEARCH AND POLICY

We believe there are several problems with the existing literature and ongoing policy debates relevant to acculturation of minority youths that limit our understanding of how many of these youths are quite resilient and able to make the most of these cultural challenges. First, most current research and policy discussions are focused on *acculturation*, the process by which individuals acquire knowledge, behavioral expectations, attitudes, and values associated with the host or mainstream culture, without also considering *enculturation*, the process of acquiring knowledge, behavioral expectations, attitudes, and values associated with their ethnic culture. Acculturation is largely the result of contact with the host culture in the form of interactions with majority members at school and in the community, including experiences with the mainstream media. Enculturation is largely the result of the socialization experiences of the youths within the family and ethnic community and leads to the formation of the youths' ethnic social identity. It is our contention that *both* are important processes that operate together to help determine the nature of the risks and protective resources to which minority youths are exposed. We also believe that both processes should be considered in public policy discussions about how to optimize developmental trajectories for minority youths.

Second, much of the extant literature has focused almost exclusively on the perils of acculturation without consideration of how acculturation and enculturation processes, and the need to simultaneously integrate the experiences and influences of two cultures, can lead to beneficial outcomes (e.g., Bernal, 1996; Phinney & Chavira, 1995; Zimmerman et al., 1998). In contrast, proponents of a strengths-based perspective argue that a focus on environmental and personal protective factors, many of which may be characteristic of the ethnic culture, may ultimately represent the best opportunities for prevention and intervention efforts (e.g., Hernandez & Lucero, 1996; Jessor, 1993).

Finally, the research that examines acculturation processes and their psychosocial effects has been limited by methodological problems stemming from difficulties in measuring the complexity of the changes associated with acculturation, a nearly complete absence of longitudinal research that can more rigorously examine the underlying processes of culture change, and a relatively small research base (see Gonzales, Knight, Morgan-Lopez, Saenz, & Sirolli, 2002). Given these limitations, our interpretation of the literature as described in this chapter, and its application to policy, must be considered tentative.

In our attempt to apply a strengths-based perspective, this chapter will first discuss theory and empirical evidence regarding the psychosocial effects of acculturation and enculturation and how they may operate together to shape risk and protective processes for Latino youths. We focus on Latinos, an extremely diverse group that includes individuals whose families originated in Mexico, Puerto Rico, Cuba, or one of the many South or Central American countries. We do so because they are the largest and fastest growing segment of the ethnic minority population of the United States and because enculturation and acculturation processes have been investigated for Latinos more than for any other ethnic subgroup. In addition, because the diversity of their experience is potentially illustrative in understanding both the immigration and ethnic minority experiences, the issues and processes described herein are likely relevant to other ethnic minority populations, even though the specific behavioral outcomes of dual cultural adaptation may be somewhat different for other ethnic groups.

A wide range of policies can have an impact on the adjustment and adaptation of immigrant and ethnic children by encouraging or discouraging acculturation to the U.S. culture and by supporting or discouraging mainte- nance of their native culture. Immigration and antidiscrimination laws, poli- cies concerning immigrant access to welfare, and many other policies have an impact on the lives of immigrant families and youths. The schools, how- ever, occupy a central place in the lives of children and youths. Historically, schools in the United States have taken on the role of "acculturating" new arrivals as transmitters of culture, language, and civic knowledge. Thus, with respect to policies, this chapter will focus on ways in which schools, more broadly, and policies concerning language of instruction (e.g., bilingual edu- cation), specifically, might apply a strengths-based approach to reduce risk and enhance the psychological and social adaptation of Latino youth.

Research and Theory on Acculturation and Enculturation

Acculturation theory suggests that the joint processes of acculturation and enculturation may place ethnic minority youths at risk for negative mental health and academic outcomes, depending on the degree to which these two different processes encourage behaviors, values, and attitudes that are in- compatible (Bernal, Saenz, & Knight, 1991; Berry, 1988). For example, a traditional collectivistic Latino family may try to foster a sense of respect for authority and cooperative orientation in their children that is quite incom- patible with the individualistic demands of the schools that encourage inde- pendent and competitive behaviors. These incompatible values may lead to internal conflict for youths, who must make decisions about how to behave across contexts and how to cope with a variety of potentially ambiguous situ- ations. For example, whereas many highly enculturated Latino youths act deferentially toward adults in the family, they may experience confusion about whether to conform to the behavior of peers who are more assertive with authority figures outside the home. Discriminatory and prejudicial experi- ences, in particular, may create ambivalence regarding the appropriateness of specific behaviors in specific contexts and may result in internal conflict. This internal conflict, in turn, may have negative consequences for children's self-concept, identity formation, and mental health (Ethier & Deaux, 1994). Research has shown that when youths are exposed to discrimination in their schools and communities, they are more likely to hold separatist attitudes, engage in interethnic conflicts, and become involved in delinquent activi- ties (Rotheram-Borus, 1990; Vega, Khoury, Zimmerman, Gil, & Warheit, 1995).

Cultural incompatibilities also might lead to negative outcomes when an individual's shifting cultural values and expectations lead that individual to behave in a manner that is unacceptable to significant others, such as family members or peers (Baptiste, 1993). For example, based on her experiences with mainstream peers, a young Latina may have expectations about the appropriate nature of social relationships with opposite-sex peers, expecting to begin dating or participating in mixed-sex gatherings at an earlier age than her parents will allow. These experiences may lead her to engage in activities that provoke conflict with parents and other family members, who may view her behavior as a moral transgression and a symbol of her move away from her culture.

Such intergenerational differences in values and expectations are expected to occur frequently in acculturating families because parents and children are differentially exposed to ethnic versus mainstream cultural values. Almost without exception, parents maintain stronger ties with the ethnic culture, whereas their children face pressures to adopt their host society's customs. As they become Americanized and move away from their roots, youngsters may reject their parents and their culture of origin, giving rise to intrapersonal identity conflicts and family conflicts. These culture-based conflicts can disrupt the structure of the Latino family and exacerbate the typical struggles that occur between adolescents and their parents. In its most extreme form, this often leads to the adolescents' loss of emotional and social support from their family and to parent–child alienation (Szapocznik & Kurtines, 1993; Szapocznik, Scopetta, & King, 1978).

Cultural incompatibilities also can lead to a lack of important linkages among the primary social contexts of Latino youth. For example, a lack of connection between the family and peer group may occur when parents are culturally and linguistically dissimilar from their child's peers. Parental monitoring of their children's whereabouts and activities may be compromised as a result, contributing to an increased risk for problem behavior. A lack of parental involvement in school stemming from cultural incompatibilities between the home and school context also has a negative impact on school success for Latino youth (Suarez-Orozco & Suarez-Orozco, 1995). Faced with linguistic difficulties, lack of knowledge of how public schools operate, and a cultural background where parental involvement in schools was not normative, immigrant parents face a number of barriers in contacting the school (Delgado-Gaitan, 1992). Because of their own low levels of education, many Latino parents also are unable to provide positive educational role models or active guidance on schoolwork (Haveman & Wolfe, 1994). And because they are themselves struggling with professional, economic, and social adjustment to the new country, they may have little time to devote to such activities. Teachers also may fail to initiate communication with parents because they cannot speak Spanish, do not understand the expectations of Latino parents, and view parents as part of the problem in educating children, rather than as a resource (Delgado-Gaitan, 1992; Epstein, 1986). As a result, the gap between parents and children becomes even wider.

Benefits of Maintaining Positive Aspects of Ethnic Culture

Relatively little attention has been focused on the potential for positive outcomes associated with either acculturation or enculturation. However, several authors have suggested that enculturation and a strong ethnic identity serve as protective factors for ethnic minority individuals (Parra & Guarnaccia, 1998; Phinney & Chavira, 1995; Zimmerman et al., 1998). Ethnic minority individuals who feel pride in their heritage and have a strong cultural identification may have greater self-esteem, improved psychological well-being, and greater resilience against stressful life circumstances because of the social support and sense of belonging provided by their extended family and ethnic community and, for some, by their religious involvement. Indeed, there is some empirical evidence consistent with this theorizing. For example, Phinney and Chavira found that more ethnically identified Latino and Asian American adolescents had higher self-esteem than did less ethnically identified adolescents. Zimmerman et al. observed this pattern of higher self-esteem among more ethnically identified Native American youths. There also is evidence that a strong ethnic identity moderates drug-related risk factors and lessens drug use among Latino adolescents (Brook, Whiteman, Balka, Win, & Gursen, 1998).

Traditional family values also may serve a protective function for Latino youths. *Familism,* one of the most important culture-specific values of Latinos, is the term for a strong identification with and attachment of individuals to their families (nuclear and extended) and strong feelings of loyalty and solidarity among family members (e.g., Sabogal et al., 1987). Although Latino families become more involved with social systems outside the family as they acculturate, many families maintain their internal patterns of relationships and familistic values from generation to generation (Rueschenberg & Buriel, 1989; Sabogal et al., 1987). Research has shown that when familistic values and behaviors are maintained, they function to promote healthy family interactions and decrease susceptibility to acculturative strains and other negative influences outside the family. For example, Vega and colleagues (Gil, Vega, & Dimas, 1994; Vega, Gil, Warheit, Zimmerman, & Apospori, 1993) found that family pride and loyalty, two important aspects of familism, buffered Latino adolescents from the negative effects of acculturation strain in predicting self-esteem and problem behavior.

Biculturalism and Positive Adaptation for Latino Youth

Several scholars have suggested that biculturalism may be the most adaptive form of acculturation for Latinos and other visible minorities (e.g., Birman,

1994; Cortes, Rogler, & Malgady, 1994; LaFromboise, Coleman, & Gerton, 1993; Szapocznik & Kurtines, 1980). Bicultural individuals benefit from knowing and participating in the host culture while retaining the positive, protective factors of their traditional culture. In addition, biculturalism is advantageous because it allows personal flexibility to draw on different sets of skills depending on the specific cultural demands of different situations. Consistent with this theorizing and with a strengths-based perspective, biculturalism has been related to greater self-esteem, ability to socialize in diverse settings, leadership abilities, peer competence, and psychological well-being for Latino youth (Birman, 1998; Szapocznik, Kurtines, & Fernandez, 1980).

Educational Policies Concerning Acculturation and Language of Instruction

Schools are in a unique and extremely powerful position to shape the enculturation and acculturation experiences of their students because they send powerful messages to children and families about which paths of acculturation students should take. Historically, the U.S. public education system has conveyed assimilationist goals for immigrants and ethnic minorities through its educational policies. Public education was seen in the early 20th century as a means toward Americanizing the large waves of immigrants resettling in the United States. At that time, assimilation proved to be a rewarding strategy for European immigrants, as later generations were able to make the transition into the White middle class and essentially attain the American dream. However, as visible ethnic minorities, Latinos occupy a different niche than the immigrants of 100 years ago. For new immigrants, acculturation to the American culture carries some positive benefits (i.e., instrumental knowledge of how to survive). However, discrimination precludes the possibility of assimilation for visible minorities. For them, pressure to assimilate in the face of limited life chances may produce results opposite to those intended by assimilationist policies—for example, *reactive identification* (Portes & Zhou, 1993), or insistence on preserving the ethnic identification and resistance to assimilation. Thus, policies of assimilation can be harmful for ethnic minority youths, particularly if they pressure these youths to accept a culture that may reject them.

The current debate around whether assimilationist policies should be implemented in U.S. public schools has almost exclusively focused on language of instruction or bilingual education. For this reason, and because few other policies have as much potential to influence acculturation and enculturation processes for Latino youths in the United States, the following section presents a brief history of this specific policy arena. Then, rather than focusing on the academic merits of bilingual education policies and strategies, we discuss the potential impact of such policies on children's mental health. We then conclude by urging researchers and policymakers to engage a strengths-based perspective and consider children's psychological well-being more broadly when discussing future research and policy and when developing interventions to meet the unique needs of immigrants and other cultural minority groups.

The ongoing debate about bilingual education has had a long history in U.S. public schools (Crawford, 1992, 1995). Many of the non-English speaking European immigrant communities in the 18th and 19th centuries had native-language schooling for their children. However, such educational opportunities were not afforded to American Indians, because English-language learning was seen as a mechanism of Americanization, providing a "civilizing influence" (Crawford, 1995). Early in the 20th century, bilingual education was all but abolished across the board. As new waves of immigrants began to enter the country, attempts to Americanize the newcomers were instituted in settlement houses and public schools. Further, the entry of the United States into World War I created negative sentiment about German bilingual education, which was discontinued nationwide. With respect to Latinos, English-only legislation in California and Texas was introduced in the early 20th and mid-19th centuries, respectively. In New Mexico, however, Spanish-language instruction continued well into the 20th century, because the majority of that population continued to be predominantly Spanish speaking.

The renaissance of bilingual education occurred in the 1960s, with Cuban refugees in Miami, in an attempt to create true bilingualism among the children of the exiles (Crawford, 1995). In the context of the civil rights movement, concern with the poor academic performance of minority children also led to the passage of the 1968 Bilingual Education Act (1968, §701). In particular, the concern was that learning in the assimilationist school context resulted in their home language and culture being devalued. This was seen as potentially leading to "bicultural ambivalence," or feelings of shame about his or her language that could lead to hostility toward the dominant culture or to damaging shifts in family alliances. Though still focused primarily on alleviating the damaging effects of assimilation, these movements considered the importance and value of ethnic culture more fully than had previously been considered.

Since passage of the Bilingual Education Act, schools across the country have adopted a broad range of strategies to educate the steady growth of children with limited English proficiency (LEP) in the United States. The foreign-born population increased from 9.6 million in 1970 to 28.4 million in 2000 and currently constitutes 10.4% of the total U.S. population. More than half (51%) of all foreign-born residents are Latinos (U.S. Census Bureau, 2002). Conceptually, at one end of the continuum, schools can adopt a policy of assimilation and make no special programmatic efforts to adapt their practices to reach these students or their parents. At the other extreme, schools could emphasize native language maintenance to the extent that they develop completely separate programs for LEP students in their first language, thus isolating these students and giving them few opportunities to transition or interact with English-speaking mainstream students. In practice, schools and school systems struggle with finding a reasonable accommodation along this continuum. Many school systems have ESL programs that represent a compromise position; they do not use the students' native language for instruction but rather teach English at various levels appropriate for students learning it as a second language, for a full day or for a portion of the school day. Some school systems designate particular schools to house all ESL students or ESL students from a particular ethnic group, transitioning individual students into their local neighborhood school only when the students are ready. In other cases, each school within a school system has an ESL program. In some school systems ESL instruction includes content instruction (e.g., social studies) taught specifically and separately to ESL students, whereas other ESL classes teach language only, and students are expected to attend regular content classes with mainstream students the rest of the day.

In recent years, dissatisfaction with bilingual education has been on the rise in the United States. Most notably, California's Proposition 227 (1998), also known as the Unz initiative, was passed in 1998 with 61% of California voters supporting the measure. This proposition was designed to curtail an extensive state bilingual education program by limiting the length of time LEP children could spend in special language instruction to 1 full year. It further insisted that the focus of such classes be "sheltered English immersion," or immersion in English to the extent possible, sheltered from input beyond their comprehension. Similar legislation was passed by a voter initiative in Arizona in 2000 and is currently being promoted by the originators of the California and Arizona initiatives in several other states throughout the country.

POLICY RECOMMENDATIONS FOR PROMOTING RESILIENCE

Although debates about the impact of bilingual education reforms on academic achievement of LEP students will undoubtedly continue, it is important for policymakers to consider that in addition to having educational and achievement implications, education policies also have important implications for children's mental health. Careful consideration of how policies will affect acculturating children and families more broadly (e.g., beyond language acquisition), either by increasing the associated risks or facilitating protective resources, should be used as guidelines for implementation of existing bilingual education policies and for future reforms. For example, assimilationist policies that require linguistic minority children to transition quickly into English may widen the cultural gap between the home and school environments. Further, an exclusively English-language curriculum taught by nonbilingual teachers can make access to the schools more difficult for Latino parents and make it more difficult for them to be an educational resource for their children. These types of policies can increase acculturative stress and undermine parental authority and ultimately may lead to poor psychological adjustment for Latino youths. At the other extreme, continued teaching of students in their native language without serious progress toward English proficiency prohibits children from becoming integrated into and taking advantage of opportunities in the dominant culture. Poorly funded bilingual education programs also place ESL students at an educational disadvantage because they provide unchallenging and limited course offerings.

Regardless of how educational policies may fit onto the bilingual–full mainstream education continuum, policymakers need to consider whether the level of funding and structure of these programs will lead to a high-quality educational experience and whether they address the socioemotional needs of Latino youths and their families. Such programs need to be suited to the ecology of the community and the school and the culture and context of the local community (see also Trickett & Birman, 1989). Specifically, these programs should meet the needs of immigrant parents, students, and teachers and provide resources to reduce cultural gaps among these constituencies. For example, schools without bilingual education teachers may need other resources to maintain contact with Spanish-speaking parents.

Developing ways to enhance ethnic culture and biculturalism also should become a major goal for intervention and policy, whether or not they are specifically focused on language of instruction. Politicians often focus too narrowly on how to best integrate minority youth into the mainstream without considering ties to protective aspects of their ethnic culture. More recently, there have been efforts in schools across the country to institute policies and practices that incorporate cultural diversity in school activities and curriculum and that reach out to parents of immigrants and other cultural minorities. Unfortunately, because there is a lack of research on the effects of these programs on children's psychological and social adjustment, it is impossible to identify proven methods to promote the resilience of acculturating youths. Nevertheless, the literature reviewed in this chapter supports a number of strengths-based goals to be used as guidelines for policy and intervention planning. In the following sections we highlight three guiding principles or goals—to increase parents' access to schools, to support teachers in working effectively with cultural minority groups, and to respect ethnic culture and promote biculturalism—that are consistent with theory and research on acculturation and enculturation of Latino youth, along with examples of strategies that have been used (though not tested) to meet these goals. There is a pressing need for such interventions and for research to determine which strategies are most effective.

Increasing Parents' Access to Schools

For local schools to meet the needs and understand the cultures of immigrant and other ethnic minority students, they need to involve the parents of these students in the schools and work to eliminate the linguistic and cultural barriers that prevent them from doing so. This goal is critical, regardless of the school's specific stance on bilingual education, particularly in schools that have eliminated bilingual education entirely. Even if all Spanish-dominant students were able to successfully transition into mainstream classes in these schools, many of their parents would still be unable to speak English. Thus, schools need to make special efforts to include immigrant parents in school activities and provide additional resources to help them connect to the school. When parents and schools are in contact and in agreement about the educational and behavioral expectations, they can support each other's authority and influence over the child, strengthening the effectiveness of the "mesosystem" (Bronfenbrenner, 1979) in providing guidance and supervision. This can help re-establish the lines of authority in the household and take the burden off children who feel they must serve as translators or culture brokers between their parents and schools. Bridging the cultural gap between parents and schools also creates greater sociocultural congruency between home and school settings (Delgado-Gaitan, 1991; see also Hao & Bonstead-Burns, 1998) and can help families address many of the cultural conflicts and problems described in this chapter. Specific strategies include the following:

- invite parents to participate in and assist school personnel as contributors to school events and assemblies and to be advisors to various school committees on how to address issues involving their children;
- invite parents to participate in policy decisions at the school building and school system level involving programs for LEP and mainstream Latino children;
- hire qualified bilingual staff or train bicultural or bilingual community members as school–parent liaisons who are knowledgeable about school policies, practices, and expectations and able to accompany parents to school meetings and serve as advocates;
- provide parents with information about school structure and policies, their children's rights, school activities and services, and standard school practices regarding such matters as grading, tracking, and disciplinary procedures in a format that is accessible, even to parents with low literacy skills;
- make special efforts to meet with parents who face structural barriers to parental involvement, such as nonregular work hours,

and interpersonal barriers, such as discomfort with the school setting;

- provide opportunities for parents to regularly interact with other parents in the schools to facilitate social support and community building; and
- develop clear rules and policies restricting the involvement of students as interpreters for parents regarding discipline and academic concerns. Policies must place responsibility on school personnel, not on children, for effective communication with parents.

Supporting Teachers in Working Effectively With Cultural Minority Groups

The burden of bridging cultural gaps, with both students in the classroom and with parents, often rests exclusively with teachers who have limited resources, minimal incentives, and, in many cases, limited training to do so. For example, it is often impossible for mainstream teachers to attend to the needs of LEP students in a classroom of 30 or more students. Additional resources are therefore needed to enable teachers to reach out to parents when necessary, particularly those who do not speak English. Teachers' school policies also must address the issue of whether ESL or bilingual and mainstream teachers are sufficiently rewarded and not unwittingly penalized for working with LEP students (see also Trickett & Birman, 1989). Specific recommendations include the following:

- provide teachers with bilingual or bicultural aides, such as parents, to help identify the specific needs of their students and help facilitate ongoing communication with parents;
- provide specialized services such as a mental health consultant, when necessary, to help teachers plan classroomwide or individual strategies to deal with particular problems such as those of refugee youths who have been traumatized;
- offer workshops for teachers and other school staff to address community concerns, provide education regarding the cultural beliefs and practices of immigrant and other minority groups, and provide training to interact effectively with these groups. Cultural competence training opportunities should not reinforce cultural stereotypes but instead enable teachers to challenge their biases about ethnic minority groups;
- ensure that policies provide incentives or rewards for ESL and mainstream teachers who are effective at working with LEP students and that they do not penalize teachers for having LEP students in their classrooms. For example, when teacher evalu-

ations are based on standardized test scores, teachers may be penalized for having LEP students in their classroom because their test scores are often lower; and

- ensure that the structure of the school, including its physical layout and location of classrooms and offices, and norms around teacher communication do not make ESL or bilingual education teachers feel excluded from the daily life of the school.

Respecting Ethnic Culture and Promoting Biculturalism

With respect to students, schools should welcome and respect cultural differences, regardless of the type of ESL or bilingual education structure it has, so that all students feel understood and valued in the school. A strengths-based approach would suggest that Latino and other ethnic minority students are a great educational resource to a school, being able to offer mainstream students the opportunity to learn firsthand about other cultures. Thus, rather than simply labeling minority groups as a high-risk category in need of intervention, the entire school community can be the target of an intervention to increase multicultural competence and appreciation. To be most effective, such policies must be genuinely embraced by schools and districts and allowed to influence decisions at all levels of school governance. Specific strategies for promoting biculturalism include the following:

- incorporate content related to students' backgrounds (culture, language, art, literature, history) into the school curriculum for all students. Culturally diverse content should be a regular feature throughout the curriculum and not just for special events.
- hold school assemblies, field trips, or other events to celebrate the diversity of students. Parents and students can be invited to participate in these events and to contribute to the educational content of the school.
- facilitate opportunities for all staff, regardless of ethnic background, to increase their own bicultural competence.

CONCLUSION

This chapter has reviewed the acculturation and adjustment literature for Latino youths and has focused on policy issues around the schooling of cultural minorities, with a particular emphasis on the education of limited English proficiency students. We have argued that although acculturation to the U.S. culture may put Latino immigrant children at risk, enculturation can serve a protective function. School policies must address educational issues, but they can also serve the important function of helping bridge the cultural worlds of the home and school environments. Schools can do this by supporting maintenance of their native culture (enculturation) of Latino youth, as well as by reaching out to parents of these children. In this way schools can enhance the resilience of Latino youth and strengthen parents' abilities to guide their children to succeed in the dominant culture and be better prepared for an increasingly global society.

REFERENCES

Baptiste, D. A. (1993). Immigrant families, adolescents and acculturation: Insight for the therapists. *Marriage and Family Review, 19,* 341–363.

Bernal, M. E. (1996). How did you do it? *Counseling Psychologist, 24,* 269–272.

Bernal, M. E., Saenz, D. S., & Knight, G. P. (1991). Ethnic identity and adaptation of Mexican American youths in school settings. *Hispanic Journal of Behavioral Sciences, 13,* 135–154.

Berry, J. W. (1993). Ethnic identity in plural societies. In M. E. Bernal & G. P. Knight (Eds.), *Ethnic identity: Formation and transmission among Hispanics and other minorities* (pp. 271–296). Albany, NY: State University of New York Press.

Bilingual Education Act (1968). Pub. L. No. 90-2247, 81 Stat. 816.

Birman, D. (1994). Acculturation and human diversity in a multicultural society. In E. J. Trickett, R. J. Watts, & D. Birman (Eds.), *Human diversity: Perspectives on people in context* (pp. 261–284). San Francisco: Jossey-Bass.

Birman, D. (1998). Biculturalism and perceived competence of Latino immigrant adolescents. *American Journal of Community Psychology, 26,* 335–354.

Brattan-Wolf, C., & Portis, M. (1996). Smoking, acculturation and pregnancy outcome among Mexican Americans. *Health Care for Women International, 17,* 563–574.

Bronfenbrenner, U. (1979). *The ecology of human development: Experiments by nature and design.* Cambridge, MA: Harvard University Press.

Brook, J. S., Whiteman, M., Balka, E. B., Win, P. T., & Gursen, M. D. (1998). Drug use among Puerto Ricans: Ethnic identity as a protective factor. *Hispanic Journal of Behavioral Sciences, 20,* 241–254.

Cortes, D. E., Rogler, L. H., & Malgady, R. G. (1994). Biculturality among Puerto Rican adults in the United States. *American Journal of Community Psychology, 22,* 707–721.

Crawford, J. (1992). *Hold your tongue: Bilingualism and the politics of English-only.* Reading, MA: Addison-Wesley.

Crawford, J. (1995). *Bilingual education: History, politics, theory, and practice* (3rd ed.). Los Angeles: Bilingual Educational Services.

Delgado-Gaitan, C. (1991). Involving parents in the schools: A process of empowerment. *American Journal of Education, 100,* 20–46.

Delgado-Gaitan, C. (1992). School matters in the Mexican-American home: Socializing children to education. *American Educational Research Journal, 29*, 495–513.

Epstein, J. L. (1986). Parents' reactions to teachers' practices of parent involvement. *Elementary School Journal, 86*, 277–294.

Ethier, K. A., & Deaux, K. (1994). Change: Maintaining identification and responding to threat. *Journal of Personality and Social Psychology, 67*, 243–251.

Fridrich, A. H., & Flannery, D. J. (1995). The effects of ethnicity and acculturation on early adolescent delinquency. *Journal of Child and Family Studies, 4*, 69–87.

Gil, A. G., Vega, W. A., & Dimas, J. M. (1994). Acculturative stress and personal adjustment among Hispanic adolescent boys. *Journal of Community Psychology, 22*, 43–54.

Gonzales, N. A., & Kim, L. S. (1997). Stress and coping in an ethnic minority context: Children's cultural ecologies. In S. A. Wolchik & I. N. Sandler (Eds.), *Handbook of children's coping: Linking theory and intervention. Issues in clinical child psychology* (pp. 481–511). New York: Plenum Press.

Gonzales, N. A., Knight, G. P., Morgan-Lopez, A., Saenz, D., & Sirolli, A. (2002). Acculturation and the mental health of Latino youths: An integration and critique of the literature. In J. M. Contreras, K. A. Kerns, & A. M. Neal-Barnett (Eds.), *Latino children and families in the United States* (pp. 45–74). Westport, CT: Greenwood.

Hao, L., & Bonstead-Burns, M. (1998). Parent-child differences in educational expectations and the academic achievement of immigrant and native students. *Sociology of Education, 71*, 175–198.

Haveman, R., & Wolfe, B. (1994). *Succeeding generations: On the effect of investing in children.* New York: Russell Sage.

Hernandez, L., & Lucero, E. (1996). DAYS La Familia community drug and alcohol prevention program: Family centered model for working with inner-city Hispanic families. *Journal of Primary Prevention, 16*, 255–271.

Hovery, J. D., & King, C. A. (1996). Acculturative stress, depression, and suicidal ideation among immigrant and second-generation Latino adolescents. *Journal of the American Academy of Child and Adolescent Psychiatry, 35*, 1183–1192.

Jessor, R. (1993). Successful adolescent development among youth in high-risk settings. *American Psychologist, 48*, 117–126.

Katragadda, C. P., & Tidwell, R. (1998). Rural Hispanic adolescents at risk for depressive symptoms. *Journal of Applied Social Psychology, 28*, 1916–1930.

LaFromboise, T., Coleman, H. L., & Gerton, J. (1993). Psychological impact of biculturalism: Evidence and theory. *Psychological Bulletin, 114*, 395–412.

Marin, G. (1989). AIDS prevention among Hispanics: Needs, risk behaviors, and cultural values. *Public Health Reports, 104*, 411–415.

Parra, P. A., & Guarnaccia, P. (1998). Ethnicity, culture, and resiliency in caregivers of a seriously mentally ill family member. In H. I. McCubbin & E. A. Thompson (Eds.), *Resiliency in Native American and immigrant families* (Vol. 2, Resiliency in Families series, pp. 431–450). Thousand Oaks, CA: Sage.

Phinney, J. S. (1990). Ethnic identity in adolescents and adults: Review of research. *Psychological Bulletin, 108,* 499–514.

Phinney, J. S., & Chavira, V. (1995). Parental ethnic socialization and adolescent coping with problems related to ethnicity. *Journal of Research on Adolescence, 5,* 31–53.

Proposition 227 (1998). *English language in public schools: Initiative statute.* Retrieved July 28, 2003, from http://primary98.ss.ca.gov/VoterGuide/Propositions/227text.htm

Portes, A., & Zhou, M. (1993). The new second generation: Segmented assimilation and its variants. *Annals of the American Academy of Political and Social Science, 530,* 74–96.

Rasmussen, K. M., Negy, C., Carlson, R., & Burns, J. M. (1997). Suicide ideation and acculturation among low socioeconomic status Mexican American adolescents. *Journal of Early Adolescence, 17,* 390–407.

Rotheram-Borus, M. J. (1990). Adolescents' reference-group choices, self esteem, and adjustment. *Journal of Personality and Social Psychology, 59,* 1075–1081.

Rueschenberg, E., & Buriel, R. (1989). Mexican-American family functioning and acculturation: A family systems perspective. *Hispanic Journal of Behavioral Sciences, 11,* 232–244.

Sabogal, F., Marin, G., Otero Sabogal, R., Marin, B. V., & Perez-Stable, E. J. (1987). Hispanic familism and acculturation: What changes and what doesn't? *Hispanic Journal of Behavioral Sciences, 9,* 397–412.

Samaniego, R. Y., & Gonzales, N. A. (1999). Multiple mediators of the effects of acculturation status on delinquency for Mexican American adolescents. *American Journal of Community Psychology, 27,* 189–210.

Suarez-Orozco, C., & Suarez-Orozco, M. (1995). *Transformations: Immigration, family life, and achievement motivation among Latino adolescents.* Stanford, CA: Stanford University Press.

Szapocznik, J., & Kurtines, W. M. (1980). Acculturation, biculturalism and adjustment among Cuban Americans. In A. M. Padilla (Ed.), *Acculturation: Theory, models, and some new findings* (pp. 139–159). Boulder, CO: Westview Press.

Szapocznik, J., & Kurtines, W. M. (1993). Family psychology and cultural diversity: Opportunities for theory, research and application. *American Psychologist, 48,* 400–407.

Szapocznik, J., Kurtines, W. M., & Fernandez, T. (1980). Bicultural involvement and adjustment in Hispanic-American youths. *International Journal of Intercultural Relations, 4,* 353–365.

Szapocznik, J., Scopetta, M. A., & King, O. E. (1978). Theory and practice in matching treatment to the special characteristics and problems of Cuban immigrants. *Journal of Community Psychology, 6,* 112–122.

Trickett, E. J., & Birman, D. (1989). Taking ecology seriously: A community development approach to individually based preventive intervention in schools. In B. Compas & L. Bond (Eds.), *Primary prevention in the schools* (pp. 361–390). Newbury Park, CA: Sage.

U.S. Census Bureau. (2002). Profile of the foreign-born population in the United States. Retrieved July 29, 2003, from http://census.gov/population/estimates/nation/intfile3-1.txt

Vega, W. A., Gil, A. G., Warheit, G. J., Zimmerman, R. S., & Apospori, E. (1993). Acculturation and delinquent behavior among Cuban American adolescents: Toward an empirical model. *American Journal of Community Psychology, 21*, 113–125.

Vega, W. A., Khoury, E. L., Zimmerman, R. S., Gil, A. G., & Warheit, G. J. (1995). Cultural conflicts and problem behaviors of Latino adolescents in home and school environments. *Journal of Community Psychology, 23*, 167–179.

Vega, W. A., Kolody, B., Aguilar-Gaxiola, S., Alderete, E., Catalano, R., & Caraveo Anduaga, J. (1998). Lifetime prevalence of DSM-III-R psychiatric disorders among urban and rural Mexican Americans in California. *Archives of General Psychiatry, 55*, 771–778.

Zimmerman, M. A., Ramirez, J., Washienko, K. M., Walt, B., & Dyer, S. (1998). Enculturation hypothesis: Exploring direct and protective effects among Native American youth. In H. I. McCubbin & E. A. Thompson (Eds.), *Resiliency in Native American and immigrant families* (Vol. 2, Resiliency in Families series, pp. 199–220). Thousand Oaks, CA: Sage.

17

COMMUNITY VIOLENCE AND CHILDREN: PREVENTING EXPOSURE AND REDUCING HARM

JAMES GARBARINO, W. RODNEY HAMMOND,
JAMES MERCY, AND BETTY R. YUNG

This chapter draws attention to the parallels between international and urban war zones in their negative impact on children's development. Not only do the multiple risks of community violence (risks related to poverty and family disruption) compound chances for negative outcomes for children in the most vulnerable populations, they can also permanently distort children's beliefs about what they need to do to ensure their personal safety and about the spiritual meaning of their lives. If they do not believe that adults can keep them safe and if they lack a belief in a meaningful life, children can be lured into gang membership, gun cultures, and ongoing violence. Public policies are recommended that would support parents' capacities to move out of areas of violence and to protect their children, that would improve access to early treatment for traumatized children, and that would empower communities to create safe havens for children (particularly after school) and to reduce violence.

* * *

This chapter is based, in part, on "An Ecological Perspective on the Effects of Violence on Children," by James Garbarino, 2001, *Journal of Community Psychology, 29,* 189–193. Adapted with permission.

303

This chapter describes the impact of community violence from the unique perspective of research based on extensive interviews with children and families who live in violent urban neighborhoods (Garbarino, 1995, 1999a, 2001; Garbarino, Kostelny, & Dubrow, 1991). This research has used the concept of the urban war zone to provide a framework for understanding the similarities in the developmental issues that are faced by children exposed to international war zones and to chronic urban violence. Urban violence results in an accumulation of risk factors and increases children's exposure to trauma experiences. These problems can overwhelm resilience; lead to the development of negative expectations about the future in children and youth; and create serious challenges to their social, emotional, and spiritual development. Policy directives are outlined that are consistent with the need to reduce the impact of urban violence on children through individual, family, and community initiatives and through improved access to treatment for children exposed to traumatic experiences. These directives have value in setting priorities for a policy-research agenda directed at reducing the harm caused by community violence.

Children have been involved directly in wars in increasing numbers throughout the 20th century. UNICEF has estimated that in 1900 the ratio of civilian to military casualties was about 1:9. In recent decades, this pattern has reversed and now stands at approximately 8:1. An understanding of the impact of war on children and youths is important not only to countries that have overt war within their borders, but also to those that accept refugees coming directly from foreign war zones (see also Garbarino et al., 1991). In some countries, including the United States, chronic community violence creates an "urban war zone" that affects the development of children and youths (Garbarino, Dubrow, Kostelny, & Pardo, 1992).

This chapter starts with a brief overview of the socioeconomic and demographic contexts of community violence in urban war zones. We then discuss the developmental consequences, many of which are permanent, of children's exposure to violence. This analysis addresses the following:

- how and when children suffer the most adverse consequences of exposure to community violence and how and when these adversities exceed the limits of their resilience;
- how children's "social maps" or expectations of the social world are affected by their experiences of violence; and
- how chronic trauma acts as a philosophical wound that can undermine the very meaningfulness of life for children.

The family and community risks and supports that determine the effects of violence on children's development warrant policy attention. There is, however, a lack of empirical evidence to support programs and policies that could reduce the effects of community violence on children. The chapter concludes with recommendations for policy research.

SOCIOECONOMICS AND DEMOGRAPHICS OF
VIOLENCE IN THE URBAN WAR ZONE

Homicide rates provide an imprecise indicator of the overall problem of violence in the lives of American children and youth, for behind each murder stand many nonlethal assaults. The ratio between assault and death varies as a function of both medical trauma technology (which prevents assaults from becoming homicides) and weapons technology (which can affect the lethality of assaults). Chicago homicide rates in 1973 and 1993 were approximately the same. Reflecting improvements in medical treatment of trauma, however, the ratio of assaults to homicides increased substantially, from 100:1 in 1973 to 400:1 in 1993 (Garbarino, 2001).

Class, race, and gender exert important influences on exposure to community violence. The odds of being a homicide victim range from 1:21 for young Black men to 1:369 for young White women, with young White men at 1:131 and young Black women at 1:104 (Bell & Jenkins, 1991). Being an American itself is a risk factor; the U.S. homicide rate far exceeds that of all other modern industrialized nations. At 11.2 per 100,000, it is more than twice the rate in Scotland, the second-place country, of 5.0 per 100,000 (Richters & Martinez, 1993).

Children growing up in the United States have particularly high levels of exposure to community violence when they live in neighborhoods that simulate urban war zones. A survey of 6th to 10th graders in New Haven, Connecticut, revealed that 40% had witnessed at least one incident of violent crime within the previous 12 months (Marans & Cohen, 1993). In three inner-city, poor neighborhoods in Chicago, 17% of the elementary school-age children had witnessed domestic violence, 31% had seen someone shot, and 84% had seen someone "beat up" (Bell & Jenkins, 1991). Richters and Martinez (1993) found that 43% of 5th and 6th graders had witnessed a mugging in a moderately violent neighborhood in Washington, DC. These figures are much more like the experience of children in actual war zones in other countries (Garbarino et al., 1991) than like what we should expect for American children—living in peace.

Drugs, guns, and gangs together create dangerous environments for children and youths in urban neighborhoods—and, increasingly, elsewhere in U.S. society. A few narrative examples illuminate the effects of the spread of community violence on the experience of childhood. In Detroit, a young boy whose idolized teenage brother was killed in a gang-related attack was asked, "If you could have anything in the whole world, what would it be?" He answered, "A gun, so I could blow away the person that killed my brother" (Marin, 1988). In California, when a 9-year-old boy who lived in a neighborhood characterized by declining security was asked, "What would it take to make you feel safer here?" he replied simply, "If I had a gun of my own" (Garbarino, 1995). In a middle-class suburb of Chicago, a classroom of 8-

year-olds was asked, "If you needed a gun, could you get one?" A third of the children were able to describe in detail how to obtain a gun. In a prison in North Carolina, when three incarcerated teenagers were asked why they had done the shooting that had landed them in prison, all three replied, "What else was I supposed to do?" (Garbarino, 1995).

A final example comes from a study in which youths incarcerated for homicide or other crimes of severe violence were interviewed intensively over a period of months (Garbarino & Bedard, 1997). Allan's story reveals the interplay of traumatic experience and guns in his experience of the urban war zone. He told about the transition in his thinking about his own safety when his life was threatened at age 12 by an older acquaintance, who accused him of stealing his gun. Allen remembered,

> I was like, "Why he threaten me like that?" Why would I take his gun when I'm cool with him, you know what I mean. I see him as my peoples. And then that made me disconnect from him, because it was like, if he felt that I took his gun, he would think many other things of me. . . . I never had that heart. But, when that man put the gun on me, when he pointed that gun at me and told me that he was gonna kill me and told me that I better protect myself and do the killing before somebody else kill me. From then, I was in the way of being cannibalistic. (Garbarino, 2001, p. 362).

Of course, most children and youths who are drawn to guns, who know how to get guns, and who say that having a gun would make them feel safer will not actually end up using a gun. This parallels adult gun ownership; even most armed police are likely to go through an entire career without actually firing their weapon in the line of duty. Whether or not a child's integration into the gun culture results in actually shooting someone depends on the particular circumstances of that child. Children who experience an accumulation of social and psychological risk factors in the absence of compensatory factors or opportunities are the most vulnerable.

ACCUMULATION OF RISK MODEL

As negative (pathogenic) influences or risks increase, the child's capacity for resilience can be exceeded. Conversely, as positive or protective (salutary) influences or opportunities increase, the probability of recovery and enhanced development increases (Garbarino, 2001; see also chaps. 3 and 11, this volume). Sameroff, Seifer, Barocas, Zax, and Greenspan (1987) considered eight risk factors that included indicators of maternal dysfunction (e.g., mental illness, substance abuse, low educational attainment), family structure (e.g., absent father, large number of siblings), and social status (e.g., low income). They found that one or two major risk factors, alone, had little effect on children's development (i.e., IQ scores remained within, or even above, the normal range). However, the addition of a third and fourth risk factor exponentially increased the risk for developmental problems (i.e., IQ scores dropped significantly below average).

Perry, Pollard, Blakley, Baker, and Vigilante (1995) also documented the impact of early trauma (particularly neglect and abuse) on brain development. Trauma can produce deficient development of the brain's cortex (the site of higher faculties such as abstract reasoning, moral development, and impulse control). The processes involved in the link between war and brain development appear to be both direct (by stimulating cortisol, a stress-related hormone that impedes brain growth) and indirect (by disrupting normal caregiving environments).

Simultaneous assessment of both risk and opportunity is essential to understanding the long-term effects of early developmental experience. Resources and assets in the social environment of family, school, neighborhood, and community can compensate for risks. Dunst and Trivette (1992) augmented Sameroff et al.'s (1987) approach by including measures of protective factors or opportunities (e.g., a present and highly involved father may offset the risk factor of absent father, and a flexible and highly supportive parent may offset the presence of a "rigid and punitive" parent).

This developmental model is particularly relevant to understanding the impact of war and community violence on children. Children and youths who are most at risk for the negative consequences associated with community violence are those who already live in the context of accumulated risk. They often are poor, live in father-absent families, contend with parental incapacity due to depression or substance abuse, are raised by parents with little education or employment prospects, and are exposed to domestic violence (Garbarino et al., 1991). In contrast, children who experience actual or urban war zones from a position of relative strength—that is, with the salutary resources of social support, intact and functional families, and parents who model social competence—can deal with the resulting risk factors more positively in the long run, even if they show short term disturbances (Garbarino & Kostelny, 1996).

Research on resilience (e.g., Garmezy & Masten, 1986; Losel & Bliesener, 1990) suggests that even under adverse circumstances, children may "bounce back" from developmental challenges (particularly if they have had adequate care during their first 2 years of life). However, under conditions of extreme risk accumulation, resilience may be diminished drastically. The magnitude of risk accumulation as a pathogenic influence and the corresponding limits of resilience were illustrated in research conducted by Tolan and his colleagues (e.g., Tolan, 1996; see also chap. 11, this volume). In some environments, virtually all youths demonstrate negative effects of highly stressful and threatening environments. Indeed, one of the worst features of living in an urban war zone may be the dismantling of the compensatory resources of the affected families, schools, and communities.

SOCIAL MAPS OF CHILDREN IN URBAN WAR ZONES

One of the most important features of child development is the child's emerging capacity to form and maintain "social maps," or expectations about their social environment that guide behavior (Garbarino, 1995, 1999a, 2001; Rutter, 1989). These representations reflect children's cognitive competence, as well as their moral and affective development. They are not only based on past experiences, but also anticipate children's views of the future. These pathways or maps are crucial in mediating the experience of risk and later developmental outcomes.

For children facing community violence, we are concerned with the beliefs about the world that are contained in their social maps. Will they believe that "adults are powerless and unreliable" or that "adults are to be trusted because they know what they are doing"? Will they learn that "you can never be too careful in dealing with people" or that "people will generally treat you well and meet your needs"? Will their experience be that "the only safe place is at home" or that "school is a safe place"? Interviews confirm the reality of these alternative maps among children and youths exposed to community violence and war (Garbarino, 1995, 1999a; Garbarino & Bedard, 2001; Garbarino et al., 1991, 1992).

Security is vitally important for children's well-being. When children feel safe, they relax and start to explore their environments. When a parent or other familiar person is around, a child treats the adult as a secure base from which to explore the nearby space. If frightened, young children will quickly retreat to the familiar person. Children who do not use their parents this way are thought to have a less than adequate attachment relationship. They are "insecure" or "ambivalent" or "avoidant" (Ainsworth & Bowlby, 1991). As children get older and their social worlds expand, their security needs are transformed and their social maps change accordingly, but security remains a constant theme for them: "Am I safe here? Will I be safe if I go there? Would I be safe then?" One important process that translates war directly into pathogenic experiences for children is the social disruption of families that often accompanies it (e.g., Garbarino, 1999a).

Many children do not feel safe. A national survey conducted by *Newsweek* and the Children's Defense Fund in 1993 found that only a minority of children nationwide said they felt "very safe" once they walked out the door, most said they only felt "somewhat safe," and about 12% said they felt "unsafe" ("Growing Up Fast," 1992). Other surveys report similar results. For example, a Harris Poll (1994) of 6th to 12th graders revealed that 35% worried they would not live to old age because they would be shot.

Children act like anthropologists as they watch and listen to what goes on around them. What are they learning from the news, from their favorite television programs, from the latest action movie, from cartoons, from current events lessons at school, from watching and listening to their parents and aunts and uncles and grandparents? Bombarded with messages of threat via the news and more informal sources (such as worried parents and other well-meaning adults), children draw the logical conclusion, "If the adults are so scared, I should be too." More and more they are learning that the world is a very dangerous place. But for some children, the level of their fright exceeds the actual dangers they face. For others, the fact of the matter is that they *are* surrounded by violence. The world *is* a dangerous place.

Community violence and its consequences can make children prime candidates for involvement in social groups that augment or replace families and offer a sense of affiliation and security (and perhaps revenge). In many urban war zones, this means gangs (see chap. 14, this volume). These peer alliances offer some sense of security in a hostile world. If these children do not develop a sense of confidence that adults are able and committed to providing a safe zone for their development, children's willingness and ability to explore and take advantage of opportunities (for education, job training, social relationships) that could enhance their healthy development are diminished. On the other hand, their willingness to participate in risky or illegal activities in exchange for involvement in activities and relationships that they perceive to offer greater security is increased.

A few examples illustrate the parallels in the experiences of youths and families in refugee camps and in public housing projects of urban war zones (Garbarino, 2001). In refugee camps, there is a proliferation of violence, sometimes a kind of "arms race," that exacerbates the effects of conflict. It is common for young people, particularly young men, to be heavily involved in this violence and to be engaged in armed attacks and reprisals. Moreover, representatives of mainstream society have only partial control over what happens. International relief workers leave the camps at the end of the working day. In public housing projects, violence is endemic, gun possession by youths is also extraordinarily high, and violent crime rates are typically many times the average for the rest of the city. Projects are frequently under the control of the local gangs at night (Gabarino, Dubrow, Kostelny, & Pardo, 1992).

In refugee camps, many women (particularly mothers) are under enormous stress; they are targets of domestic violence, and they have few economic or educational resources and prospects. Studies have reported that 50% of the women in these settings are seriously depressed. Men often play a marginal role in the enduring life of families, having lost access to economically productive roles and being absent for reasons that include participating in the fighting, fleeing to escape enemies, or having been injured or killed. In public housing projects, survey research confirms similarly difficult conditions for mothers, including depression at rates comparable to the refugee camps (Osofsky, 1995). Fathers are similarly marginalized by high rates of unemployment, incarceration, and injuries in urban war zones. Maternal depression, in turn, is related to problems with early attachment relationships between mothers and children and child neglect (see chap. 9, this volume).

THE CONCEPT OF TRAUMA AS A PSYCHOLOGICAL WOUND

Trauma has two principal components: overwhelming arousal and overwhelming negative cognition. Trauma involves an inability to handle effectively the physiological responses of stress in situations of threat. This is especially relevant to young children who have not developed fully functioning systems to modulate arousal (e.g., brain stem maturation is not complete until age 8). One study of nonwar trauma reported that those exposed to psychological or physical trauma before age 10 were three times more likely to exhibit posttraumatic stress disorders (PTSD) than those exposed after age 12 (Davidson & Smith, 1990). The second component of trauma, overwhelming negative cognition, is captured in Herman's (1992) formulation that to experience trauma is to come face to face with both one's own vulnerability and the capacity for evil in human nature.

Chronic traumatic danger rewrites children's past, redraws their social map, and redirects their behavior. This is particularly true when that danger comes from the violent overthrow of day-to-day social reality—when communities are altered substantially, when people are displaced, or when children experience the death of an important family member. Fifty percent of children exposed to the chronic horrors of Pol Pot's Khmer Rouge regime in Cambodia in the 1970s exhibited persistent symptoms of PTSD 8 years after exposure (Kinzie, Sack, Angell, Manson, & Rath, 1986).

Trauma represents an enormous challenge to any individual's understanding of the meaning and purpose of life—its spiritual dimensions (Garbarino & Bedard, 1996). The spiritual dissonance engendered by confronting the problem of evil is itself a fundamental religious issue. Spirituality and religion rely on an intrinsic belief in a higher, all-benevolent power, and trauma can temporarily or permanently shatter this belief.

Young children must contend with dangers that derive not only from their physical immaturity, but also from their capacity for magical thinking. Magical thinking forms the basis for fantasy play, which itself is an important resource for children in developing and working through alternative scenarios as solutions for day-to-day issues and problems in their lives. When trauma overwhelms the child's play and constricts it in repetitive unproductive patterns, that play may be said to be "captured" (Garbarino & Manley, 1996). Children seek unsuccessfully to find a meaningful solution to the crisis of meaning imposed by the shattered assumptions they experience in the wake of trauma. Trauma inflicted on others may also trigger this kind of questioning. For example, our interviews with teenagers involved in acts of severe violence (e.g., shooting) suggest the possible traumatic dimensions of committing assault (Garbarino, 1995, 1999a).

Again, adults are crucial resources for children attempting to cope with the chronic danger and stress of living in a war zone. Generations of studies focusing on the experience of children living in war zones testify to the importance of adult responses to danger as mediators of psychological responses in children exposed to war (Garbarino, 1999b). So long as adults can take charge of themselves and present children with a role model of calm, positive determination, most children can cope with a great deal of acute, war-related violence (Apfel & Simon, 1996; Garbarino, 1999b, 2001).

One major risk resulting from childhood trauma is an extreme loss of future orientation. This "terminal thinking" grows out of chronically traumatic situations in which youngsters come to believe that violent death is an inevitable fact of their lives and respond with fatalistic violence, depression, and antisocial behavior (Garbarino, 1995). Children in urban war zones need teaching that matches their developmental phase and experience to move beyond the "default option" of terminal thinking and revenge-oriented morality. Families can do much to provide the emotional context for the necessary processing to make positive moral sense of danger (Garbarino & Bedard, 2001; Garbarino & Kostelny, 1996) but it also takes help from outside the home.

If schoolteachers and other adult representatives of the community are unwilling or unable to demonstrate and teach moral reasoning, or if they are intimidated when they try to do so, then the moral truncation that is "natural" to situations of violent conflict will proceed unimpeded. In Northern Ireland, for example, both Protestant and Catholic teachers in some communities learned that if they tried to engage their students in dialogue that could promote debates that underline principled, moral reasoning, they would be silenced by extremist elements (Conroy, 1987). This is a common situation under conditions of war, in which narrow concepts of loyalty and the exigencies of the immediate tactical situation lead to the suppression of teaching dialogue. Although this danger is greatest in societies that were totalitarian prior to war, it may be an issue even in otherwise democratic societies.

One focus of international initiatives (such as the United Nations Convention on the Rights of the Child) is to create "zones of peace" for children and generally to encourage combatants to institute and respect protected areas for children. International action does bring change for children living in actual war zones. For example, the signing of a peace accord has meant that the Khmer can be repatriated, and these people are returning to Cambodia to take up a more genuine community life. However, without efforts to achieve reconciliation, social justice, and a major peacekeeping force in highly conflicted areas, many of the children in urban war zones will get stuck there psychologically (Garbarino, 1999b).

RESEARCH-BASED PRINCIPLES TO INCREASE STRENGTHS FOR CHILDREN IN URBAN WAR ZONES

Respond to Trauma in Early Childhood

Efforts to respond to trauma in early childhood should help train and support early childhood educators and primary health care providers in recognizing traumatic experiences in the lives of young children in their care and symptoms of depression in their parents. Professionals who have daily contact with children may be particularly important as a focal point for initiating mental health services targeting these children and their parents. Even more than physical health care, mental health services to children and their families who live in violent communities are typically underfunded and hard to obtain.

Programmatic efforts must alter the "legitimization of aggression" among children and youths. These efforts should include school-based programs that start early to stimulate nonviolent responses to conflict, anger, frustration, injustice, and threat.

Mobilize Prosocial Adult and Youth Members of the Community to Take Charge

The greatest threat to young children comes when positive adults are defeated by the antisocial forces of community violence. Efforts to mobilize adults and prosocial youths to have a visible presence can convey a clear message of strength and responsibility that is crucial for redrawing the social maps of children living in violent communities.

Support and Rehabilitate the Spiritual and Moral Development of Children From Violent Communities

The experience of trauma distorts kids' values. Children's internalization of values in high-risk neighborhoods can reflect a value system that justifies violence and retaliation. Unless their communities reach them with healing experiences and offer them a positive social, moral, and political framework within which to process their experiences, traumatized kids are likely to be drawn to groups and ideologies that legitimize and reward their rage, their fear, and their hateful cynicism.

Focus on Building Trust Among Children, Youth, Families, and Communities

At the heart of the downward spiral in war zone communities is declining trust on the part of children and youth that adults can maintain their safety. Mobilizing the capacity of adults and communities to reduce violence is central to children's perceptions of their security. Because the disintegration of communities is often reflected in the disorganization and ineffectiveness of formal service agencies, support for family resources in violent communities must be linked to reforms throughout the institutions in these communities (e.g., schools, health services, housing; Garbarino & Kostelny, 1996).

POLICY RESPONSES

Developing effective public policy responses that will reduce the potentially devastating impact of chronic urban violence on children presents a complex challenge. There is an urgent need to strengthen the knowledge base concerning the negative consequences of community violence for children and the types of interventions that can ameliorate them. The range of strategies that must be addressed includes not only treating the psychological trauma of individual victims, but also confronting the broader social contexts in which community violence flourishes (see chap. 11, this volume; Tolan, Guerra, & Kendall, 1995). There are also policy options at multiple levels that may serve to buffer youngsters against the adverse effects of being exposed to violence, provide children with skills and environments that protect them from violence, and increase safety by improving conditions associated with violent crime in impoverished neighborhoods. The strategies that follow represent potential public policy responses to children's exposure to violence in urban war zones that could guide a badly needed research agenda to test the likely effectiveness of policy approaches to alleviating the distress of these children and their families.

Individual-Level Policies

Identify and Support Traumatized Children

Community mental health centers remain the predominant location where children receive mental health services (Marans & Schaefer, 1998; Waxman, Weist, & Benson, 1999). However, they may not be the best site for timely identification and service provision to children exposed to violence. Children traumatized by witnessing violence may not be brought to mental health clinics until months or even years after witnessing a violent incident, when posttraumatic symptoms bring them to the attention of parents, school personnel, or court officials (Marans & Schaefer, 1998). With appropriate training and a collaborative relationship with mental health clinic professionals, police officers may be especially well positioned to provide earlier identification of traumatized children and to facilitate more immediate access of these children to a mental health professional. The New Haven Model of Child Development and Community Policing is an example of coordinated police and mental health services to children and families involved in a violent incident, in some cases providing counseling within minutes of the police response to a murder or assault (Marans & Schaefer, 1998).

Provide School-Based Mental Health Services

There is a growing move toward the provision of comprehensive school-based mental health services for children and youth (Waxman et al., 1999).

Children are underserved in the traditional public mental health system; estimates suggest that less than one third of youths in need of mental health services actually receive them in community clinics because of barriers such as stigma, transportation, and cost (Zahner, Pawelkiewicz, DiFrancesco, & Adnopoz, 1992). Schools have special potential as locations for accessible and effective mental health services to help children overcome the effects of exposure to violence (Weist, Paskewitz, Warner, & Flaherty, 1996). School personnel may be among the first to notice symptoms of violence exposure, and, with the availability of on-site services, they can make quick referrals for assessment and treatment of the traumatized child (Lorion, 1998; Waxman et al., 1999).

Provide Universal and Targeted Social Development Programs in Schools and Other Community-Based Settings

Universal social–cognitive interventions equip children with skills to manage anger, exercise prosocial behaviors, and develop or strengthen beliefs supporting nonviolence (Samples & Abner, 1998; Thornton, Craft, Dahlberg, Lynch, & Baer, 2000). Frequently offered in school because of convenient access to the child and youth population, these interventions may also be provided in recreational centers, churches, and other community settings. A mounting body of research evidence suggests the effectiveness of many such programs, and there are helpful guides highlighting model or best practices programs (e.g., Thornton et al., 2000; U.S. Department of Health and Human Services, 2001). Training youngsters to enhance their social relationships and resolve problems peacefully is especially crucial for children exposed to chronic violence because of the significant links between exposure to violence and increased aggression (Lorion, 1998). For traumatized children exhibiting higher levels of aggressive behavior, targeted and more intense preventive efforts may be needed (Thornton et al., 2000). Approaches directed at higher risk youngsters may need to include multiple components such as prosocial and anger management skill development, academic enhancement, peer leadership training, and parent training, among other components (e.g., Conduct Problems Prevention Research Group, 1999). There are also examples of effective treatment programs developed specifically for children who witness domestic violence that merit further testing and replication (Chalk & King, 1998).

Prevent Childhood Exposure to Violence

Children often witness violence or experience victimization in afternoon or early evening hours (Chaiken, 1998). After-school programs offering safe and positive activities can reduce the extent and harm of this exposure, including innovative communitywide collaborative efforts to prevent neighborhood crime and its harmful effects on children in disadvantaged communities. These programs typically bring together the resources of youth organizations, police, churches, schools, businesses, government, juvenile justice agencies, and other local stakeholders to provide a variety of positive skill development activities for children and youths such as academic enrichment, mentoring, sports, crafts, community service, and neighborhood safety programs. Such programs have documented success in protecting youngsters from participating in or witnessing violent crime in their neighborhoods (Chaiken, 1998).

Family-Level Policies

Build Parental Capacity to Protect Children and Facilitate Positive Childhood Development

Parent training programs can serve a vital role in helping parents develop the capacity to mitigate adverse effects that may result from their children's exposure to chronic violence. Because such exposure frequently leads to future aggressive behavior in the child witness (Lorion, 1998), it is especially important to provide interventions that help parents support their children's acquisition and maintenance of prosocial behavior and provide positive models of conflict resolution (Thornton et al., 2000). Parents living in distressed communities may also have need for education and training programs that provide them broad assistance in managing everyday life stresses, including issues related to social isolation, depression, marital conflict, and housing and financial concerns (see chap. 9, this volume).

Provide Home Visitation Programs to Facilitate Positive Child Development

Home visitation programs have had well-documented long-range benefits for parent and child. Successful programs have used home visitors such as nurses to work with low-income mothers during pregnancy and early childhood to provide in-home training, support, mentoring, education on child care, and personal development (Olds, Hill, Mihalic, & O'Brien, 1998; U.S. Department of Health and Human Services, 2001). At 15-year follow-up, adolescent children of parents participating in a home visitation program had fewer incidents of running away, fewer arrests, fewer convictions and violations of probation, fewer sex partners, and less use of alcohol and other drugs (Olds, Henderson, et al., 1998). Positive outcomes for mothers included fewer verified reports of child abuse and neglect, fewer subsequent births, greater intervals between the births of first and second children, less dependence on public welfare, fewer alcohol and drug problems, and fewer arrests (Olds, Hill, et al., 1998). Home visitation approaches have particular promise as a strategy for reducing children's exposure to community violence, because the reported benefits should increase the family's capacity for nurturing and monitoring their children and their general prospects for economic progress.

Provide Exposure to Alternative Positive Role Models

Supportive relationships with caring adults can serve to protect children from the adverse effects of a variety of risk factors, including exposure to negative role models who demonstrate inappropriate responses to conflict. Mentoring programs for high-risk children have been effective in reducing some of the behaviors associated with exposure to violent role models, including aggression, in addition to general benefits such as improved school attendance and academic achievement, social relationships, and self-concept (Thornton et al., 2000; Tierney, Grossman, & Resch, 1996). For children demonstrating severe aftereffects from their exposure to violence, special cautions should be exercised in promoting their participation in a traditional mentorship program (Rhodes, in press). Children whose trust in adults has been damaged may suffer additional harm if they engage in a relationship that fails, and the potential for failure may be higher if the child has difficulties in developing attachments or presents challenging behavior (Rhodes, in press; Thornton et al., 2000). For this population, alternative approaches such as matching them with highly trained, paid mentors for socializing and therapeutic experiences should be considered.

Community-Level Policies

Perhaps the greatest challenge for policymakers is developing community-level policies that reduce violence exposure and harm for children. Invariably, exposure to chronic community violence is linked with residence in areas of concentrated poverty (Laub & Lauritsen, 1998). The interaction of structural and social–psychological factors that often characterize economically disadvantaged communities can catalyze community violence. For example, neighborhood instability (i.e., high resident turnover) contributes to greater levels of community violence because transitory residents are less likely to engage in "guardianship" behavior such as watching out for neighbor children and reporting local drug and gang activity (Laub & Lauritsen, 1998). Inner-city joblessness creates isolation, depriving the community of supportive social resources, conventional role models, and cultural learning that facilitates bonds with schools, churches, jobs, and other traditional institutions that exert informal controls on behavior (Wilson, 1991). Two community-level policy responses are recommended: deconcentrate poverty and provide safe havens for children living in dangerous neighborhoods.

Residential mobility programs can potentially free families from negative, dangerous community influences. Voucher programs that allow low-income families to move from the city to outlying suburbs have had positive effects in helping families leave public assistance (Rosenbaum & DeLuca, 2000) and in decreasing the participation and exposure of children to violent crime (Ludwig, Duncan, & Hirshfield, 2001; Centers for Disease Control and Prevention, 2002). Moving into economically heterogeneous communities improves both the family's immediate safety and its overall future prospects.

Because many children witness violence before and after school, it is important to provide them with safe harbors to go to if they feel unsafe as they go to and from school. Among other reasons for adopting such a strategy, decreasing children's perceived level of danger may deter their feelings of need to carry a weapon for self-defense (Mercy & Rosenberg, 1998). New York City schools have established collaborative safe haven projects with police departments and local businesses that have improved the safety of children and their exposure to violence along school routes (Marans & Schaefer, 1998; Mercy & Rosenberg, 1998).

CONCLUSION

Although it is no easy charge, schools, parents, youth-serving professionals, community leaders, and police can work together effectively to create environments where the extent and effects of urban war zone violence affecting children are reduced. Multilevel prevention and intervention policy strategies can provide parents and children with the skills needed to negotiate their way through difficult environments, provide accessible services to help children recover from trauma, and offer hope for relief from adverse community conditions that foster violence. Future research is needed not only to identify the effects of violence on children, but also, more importantly, to encourage effective prevention strategies.

REFERENCES

Ainsworth, M. D., & Bowlby, J. (1991). An ethological approach to personality development. *American Psychologist, 46,* 333–341.

Apfel, R., & Simon, B. (Eds.). (1996). *Minefields in their hearts: The mental health of children in war and communal violence.* New Haven, CT: Yale University Press.

Bell, C., & Jenkins, E. J. (1991). Traumatic stress and children in danger. *Journal of Health Care for the Poor and Underserved, 2,* 175–188.

Centers for Disease Control and Prevention. (2002). Community interventions to promote healthy social environments: Early childhood development and family housing. *Morbidity and Mortality Weekly Report, 51*(No. RR-1), 1–7.

Chaiken, M. (1998). Tailoring established after-school programs to meet urban realities. In D. Elliott, B. Hamburg, & K. Williams (Eds.), *Violence in American schools* (pp. 348–375). New York: Cambridge University Press.

Chalk, R., & King, P. (Eds.). (1998). *Violence in families: Assessing prevention and treatment programs.* Washington, DC: National Academy Press.

Conduct Problems Prevention Research Group. (1999). Initial impact of the FAST Track prevention trial for conduct problems: II. Classroom effects. *Journal of Consulting and Clinical Psychology, 67*, 648–657.

Conroy, J. (1987). *Belfast diary.* Boston: Beacon Press.

Davidson, J., & Smith, R. (1990). Traumatic experiences in psychiatric outpatients. *Journal of Traumatic Stress Studies, 3*, 459–475.

Dunst, C., & Trivette, C. (1992, October). *Risk and opportunity factors influence parent and child functioning.* Paper presented at the Ninth Annual Smoky Mountain Winter Institute, Ashville, NC.

Garbarino, J. (1995). *Raising children in a socially toxic environment.* San Francisco: Jossey-Bass.

Garbarino, J. (1999a). *Lost boys: Why our sons turn violent and how we can save them.* New York: Free Press.

Garbarino, J. (1999b). What children can tell us about living with violence. In M. Sugar (Ed.), *Trauma and adolescence* (pp. 165–181). Madison, CT: International Universities Press.

Garbarino, J. (2001). An ecological perspective on the effects of violence on children. *Journal of Community Psychology, 29*, 361–378.

Garbarino, J., & Bedard, C. (1996). Spiritual challenges to children facing violent trauma. *Childhood: A Global Journal of Child Research, 3*, 467–478.

Garbarino, J., & Bedard, C. (1997). *Making sense of senseless youth violence: Preliminary report.* Ithaca, NY: Cornell University.

Garbarino, J., & Bedard, C. (1997). Is it self-defense? A model for forensic evaluation of juvenile violence. *Loyola Human Rights Review, 18*(3), 2–12.

Garbarino, J., & Bedard, C. (2001). *Parents under siege: Why you are the solution, not the problem in your child's life.* New York: Free Press.

Garbarino, J., Dubrow, N., Kostelny, K., & Pardo, C. (1992). *Children in danger: Coping with the consequences.* San Francisco: Jossey-Bass.

Garbarino, J., & Kostelny, K. (1996). The impact of political violence on the behavioral problems of Palestinian children. *Child Development, 67*, 33–45.

Garbarino, J., Kostelny, K., & Dubrow, N. (1991). *No place to be a child: Growing up in a war zone.* Lexington, MA: Lexington Books.

Garbarino, J., & Manley, J. (1996). Free and captured play: Releasing the healing power. *International Play Journal, 4*, 123–132.

Garmezy, N., & Masten, A. (1986). Stress, competence, and resilience: Common frontiers for therapist and psychotherapist. *Behavior Therapy, 17*, 500–607.

Growing Up Fast and Frightened. (1992, March 9). *Newsweek,* p. 29.

Harris Poll. (1994). *Metropolitan Life survey of the American teacher: Violence in America's schools, part II.* New York: Metropolitan Life Insurance.

Herman, J. (1992). *Trauma and recovery.* New York: Basic Books.

Kinzie, J., Sack, W., Angell, R., Manson, S., & Rath, B. (1986). The psychiatric effects of massive trauma on Cambodian children. *Journal of the American Academy of Child Psychiatry, 25*, 370–376.

Laub, J., & Lauritsen, J. (1998). The interdependence of school violence with neighborhood and family conditions. In D. Elliott, B. Hamburg, & K. Williams (Eds.), *Violence in American schools* (pp. 127–155). New York: Cambridge University Press.

Lorion, R. (1998). Exposure to urban violence: Contamination of the school environment. In D. Elliott, B. Hamburg, & K. Williams (Eds.), *Violence in American schools* (pp. 293–311). New York: Cambridge University Press.

Losel, F., & Bliesener, T. (1990). Resilience in adolescence: A study on the generalizability of protective factors. In K. Hurrelmann & F. Losel (Eds.), *Health hazards in adolescence* (pp. 15–25). New York: Walter de Gruyter.

Ludwig, J., Duncan, G., & Hirshfield, P. (2001). Urban poverty and juvenile crime: Evidence from a randomized housing-mobility experiment. *Quarterly Journal of Economics*, in press. Retrieved June 15, 2001, from http://www.wws.princeton.edu/~kling/mto/baltimore.htm

Marans, S., & Cohen, D. (1993). Children and inner-city violence: Strategies for intervention. In L. Leavitt & N. Fox (Eds.), *Psychological effects of war and violence on children* (pp. 281–302). Hillsdale, NJ: Erlbaum.

Marans, S., & Schaefer, M. (1998). Community policing, schools, and mental health: The challenge of collaboration. In D. Elliott, B. Hamburg, & K. Williams (Eds.), *Violence in American schools* (pp. 312–347). New York: Cambridge University Press.

Marin, C. (1988, June 21). *Grief's children* [Television broadcast]. Chicago: WMAQ.

Mercy, J., & Rosenberg, M. (1998). Preventing firearm violence in and around school. In D. Elliott, B. Hamburg, & K. Williams (Eds.), *Violence in American schools* (pp. 159–187). New York: Cambridge University Press.

Olds, D., Henderson, C., Coie, R., Eckenrode, J., Kitzman, H., Luckey, D., et al. (1998). Long-term effects of nurse home visitation on children's criminal and antisocial behavior: 15-year follow-up of a randomized controlled trial. *Journal of the American Medical Association, 280*, 1238–1244.

Olds, D., Hill, P., Mihalic, S., & O'Brien, R. (1998). *Blueprints for violence prevention, book 7: Prenatal and infancy home visitation*. Boulder, CO: Center for the Study and Prevention of Violence.

Osofsky, J. (1995). The effects of exposure to violence on young children. *American Psychologist, 50*, 782–788.

Perry, B., Pollard, R., Blakley, T., Baker, W., & Vigilante, D. (1995). Childhood trauma, the neurobiology of adaptation, and "use-dependent" development of the brain: How "states" become "traits." *Infant Mental Health Journal, 16*, 271–291.

Rhodes, J. E. (in press). *Stand by me: The risks and rewards of mentoring today's youth*. Cambridge, MA: Harvard University Press.

Richters, J., & Martinez, P. (1993). The NIMH community violence project: Volume 1. Children as victims of and as witnesses to violence. *Psychiatry, 56*, 7–21.

Rosenbaum, J., & DeLuca, S. (2000). *Is housing mobility the key to welfare reform? Lessons from Chicago's Gautreaux Program*. Washington, DC: Brookings Institution, Center on Urban and Metropolitan Policy.

Rutter, M. (1989). Pathways from childhood to adult life. *Journal of Child Psychology and Psychiatry, 30,* 23–51.

Sameroff, A., Seifer, R., Barocas, R., Zax, M., & Greenspan, S. (1987). Intelligence quotient scores of 4-year-old children: Socio-environmental risk factors. *Pediatrics, 79,* 343–350.

Samples, F., & Abner, L. (1998). Evaluations of school-based violence prevention programs. In D. Elliott, B. Hamburg, & K. Williams (Eds.), *Violence in American schools* (pp. 217–252). New York: Cambridge University Press.

Thornton, T., Craft, C., Dahlberg, L., Lynch, B., & Baer, K. (2000). *Best practices of youth violence prevention: A sourcebook for community action.* Atlanta, GA: Centers for Disease Control and Prevention, National Center for Injury Prevention and Control.

Tierney, J., Grossman, J., & Resch, N. (1996). *Making a difference: An impact study of Big Brothers/Big Sisters.* Philadelphia: Public/Private Ventures.

Tolan, P. (1996). How resilient is the concept of resilience? *Community Psychologist, 4,* 12–15.

Tolan, P., Guerra, N. G., & Kendall, P. G. (1995). A developmental-ecological perspective on antisocial behavior in children and adolescents: Toward a unified risk and intervention framework. *Journal of Clinical and Consulting Psychology, 63,* 579–584.

U.S. Department of Health and Human Services. (2001). *Youth violence: A report of the Surgeon General.* Rockville, MD: U.S. Department of Health and Human Services, Centers for Disease Control and Prevention, National Center for Injury Prevention and Control; Substance Abuse and Mental Health Services Administration, Center for Mental Health Services; and National Institutes of Health, National Institute of Mental Health.

Waxman, R., Weist, M., & Benson, D. (1999). Toward collaboration in the growing education-mental health interface. *Clinical Psychology Review, 19,* 239–253.

Weist, M., Paskewitz, D., Warner, B., & Flaherty, L. (1996). Treatment outcome of school-based mental health services for urban teenagers. *Community Mental Health Journal, 32,* 149–157.

Wilson, W. (1991). Public policy and The Truly Disadvantaged. In C. Jencks & P. Peterson (Eds.), *The urban underclass* (pp. 460–481). Washington, DC: Brookings Institute.

Zahner, G., Pawelkiewicz, W., DiFrancesco, J., & Adnopoz, J. (1992). Children's mental health service needs and utilization patterns in an urban community: An epidemiological assessment. *Journal of the American Academy of Child and Adolescent Psychiatry, 31,* 951–960.

18

COMMUNITY DEVELOPMENT AS A RESPONSE TO COMMUNITY-LEVEL ADVERSITY: ECOLOGICAL THEORY AND RESEARCH AND STRENGTHS-BASED POLICY

DOUGLAS D. PERKINS, BILL CRIM, PAMELA SILBERMAN, AND BARBARA B. BROWN

In this chapter, the authors propose strengths-based community development as a community-level antidote to the economic, political, social, and physical environmental challenges facing communities. Community development initiatives that encompass multiple community domains, build and sustain local community capacity, and bring together the public and private sectors are central to this approach. Special importance is placed on meaningful grassroots (citizen) participation in such community development efforts. An array of strengths-based public policies at the local (e.g., community land trusts), state (e.g., "smart growth"), and federal (e.g., community development block grants) levels are presented. This chapter illustrates the value of recognizing and building on existing community strengths, building new

The first and fourth authors were partially supported during work on this chapter by grant no. 98IJCX0022 from the National Institute of Justice. Points of view are those of the authors and do not necessarily represent the position of the U.S. Department of Justice. We thank Michael Krownapple, Bonnie Leadbeater, Kenneth Maton, Linda McCarter, Kenneth Reardon, Susan Saegert, and Mariano Santo Domingo for their comments.

321

community strengths, strengthening larger social environments, and engaging in a collaborative, participatory community change process.

* * *

Much of the variation in social, economic, environmental, and political adversities and strengths occurs not at the individual or family level, but at the community level. Individual problems are often rooted outside the individual, family, or group and ultimately become community problems (Caughy, O'Campo, & Brodsky, 1999; Wandersman & Nation, 1998). Thus, individual change is not the key to solving community problems. Indeed, unless community adversities are understood to be rooted more in the environment than in individuals or families, we risk blaming the victim. This is antithetical to a strengths orientation. Therefore, we believe that both strengths and adversities must be examined from an ecological perspective, which places individuals, families, and communities in context. That context includes multiple systems, institutions, and environments that, interdependently, both affect people and are affected by them.

This chapter takes such a view of community-level adversities and argues that to address them adequately, our theories, research, and policies must be comprehensive and systemic. We first describe four interconnected forms of community-level adversity—economic, political, social, and physical environmental. We then describe how these adversities can be countered with five strengths-oriented community development (CD) theories: sustainability, empowerment, social capital, capacity building, and asset-based CD. These strengths-based theories have guided many promising and successful local and international CD programs, but their influence on state- and national-level CD policy making has been more rhetorical than substantive. We present an ecological model of community economic, political, social, and physical environmental development with parallel, complementary, and interdependent roles for policymakers and local communities. The chapter concludes with a review of strengths-oriented and ecological CD policies.

FORMS OF COMMUNITY-LEVEL ADVERSITY

Economic Adversity: Neighborhood Decline

With low-wage service jobs replacing unionized manufacturing jobs and welfare time limits expiring, economic problems may be the most pressing adversity to consider. Poverty is also a primary cause of poor health and poor health care, educational deficiencies, and most of the other social, environmental, and political problems discussed in this chapter and throughout this volume. One need only travel from one side of any city to the other to observe the clustered neighborhood-level effects of poverty. Factors triggering neighborhood decline include Skogan's (1990) "four Ds": (a) disinvestment, or even systematic "redlining" (the illegal refusal to make loans in poor communities); (b) deindustrialization (factory closings) and the resulting decline of wages that can support a family, tax base, schools, and services; (c) demagogues (e.g., in media or real estate) whose negative portrayal of a neighborhood creates a self-fulfilling prophecy as the resulting residential instability and fear decrease community confidence, collective efficacy, and safety; and (d) demolition and construction (e.g., of highways, redevelopment projects). Ironically, large-scale building projects are seen by many politicians as the cure for neighborhood decline. But they often lead to what we would call the fifth and sixth Ds: displacement of those who can afford to leave and those who cannot afford to stay and discouragement of those who do stay in communities destroyed by cycles of decline and urban renewal.

Political Adversity: Disempowerment

Communities that are oppressed, that lack political connections and influence, or that have significant segments of disempowered members face political adversity. Government agencies often use community advisory boards and public hearings to pay only lip service to grassroots participation in decision making. This sets agencies up for failure as community knowledge is ignored, and the community is more likely to be suspicious of, and resist, the decisions made (Perkins, 1995).

Disempowerment contributes to all other forms of adversity. For example, the housing crisis is as political at root as it is economic or physical. Since 1980, housing costs have risen, sharply in many areas, while real federal spending on low-income housing has fallen. Shelter is a basic need, yet public housing for the neediest has been all but abandoned politically. The federal HOPE-VI program is an attempt to empower moderate-income residents by rebuilding public housing projects as mixed-income developments, including owner-occupied homes. Because it often displaces low-income residents without providing adequate units of replacement housing, however, this may not be the best example of a strengths-based policy. Housing adversities are political because renters—especially low-income ones—are difficult to organize. By contrast, homeowners participate more in their communities and are more empowered than renters, even among lower-income residents (Perkins, Brown, & Taylor, 1996; Saegert & Winkel, 1996, 1998). The political clout of homeowners may explain why they, not those in public housing or other renters, receive 77% of all federal housing subsidies in the form of tax deductions. Developing and maintaining an adequate supply of safe, decent, and affordable housing is a political as well as economic challenge.

Social Adversity: Crime, Disorder, and Cultural Diversity

Crime is just one manifestation of social adversity, but it is of great and consistent concern to the public. As with poverty, criminal victimization and justice are not distributed equally. Both victim and offender rates are significantly worse for poor, minority communities. More young African American men are serving criminal sentences than in college, and the rate is rising (Palen, 1997, p. 191). There is also geographic variation in police practices, even within the same city.

Much more prevalent than serious crimes are social and physical symbols of disorder. Social disorder includes "victimless" crimes (drugs, prostitution) and such noncriminals as "menacing" youths and homeless persons. There is mounting evidence that disorder begets crime and more disorder (Perkins, Wandersman, Rich, & Taylor, 1993; Skogan, 1990). Residents become fearful and withdraw from outdoor spaces, which reduces community cohesion, informal social control, and organizational and commercial life. Group conflict and actual crime may increase as the downward spiral continues.

Group conflict may also be exacerbated by cultural diversity, which is not in itself an adversity. However, prejudice and discrimination based on race, nationality, religion, income, age, sex, sexual orientation, or length of residence are community problems because of the conflict they engender and the difficulties diverse groups encounter in sharing concerns and goals and working effectively together.

Physical Environmental Adversity: Deterioration, Disasters, and Contamination

The physical deterioration of neighborhoods affects housing conditions and satisfaction (Brown & Perkins, 2001), crime (Perkins et al., 1993), fear (Perkins & Taylor, 1996), and the outmigration of residents, business, and jobs (Skogan, 1990). Urban blight and decayed infrastructure (roads, bridges, water and sewer systems) are fiscal time bombs for older cities and towns and the nation (Palen, 1997). Instead of investing in established urban areas, housing and road subsidies have favored development at the suburban fringe (Calthorpe & Fulton, 2001).

Two other forms of community-level environmental adversity are natural disasters and ground, water, and air contamination. There are an estimated 425,000 toxic waste sites in the United States (Rich, Edelstein, Hallman, & Wandersman, 1995). The distribution of the problem is highly concentrated—geographically, economically, and racially—which has led to charges of "environmental racism" (Bullard, 1994). Consequences of toxic exposure include serious health, psychological, family, and community cohesion problems (Edelstein, 2001). Communities that are decimated by a disaster or merely threatened by contamination or a large construction project may be disempowered by the government response to it. Emergency or recovery policies and agencies often take a top-down, rather than bottom-up, approach and concentrate on rebuilding without necessarily restoring the community fabric.

COMMUNITY DEVELOPMENT: COMMUNITY-LEVEL STRENGTHS BUILDING

What Is Community Development?

All four types of adversity underscore the need for widespread community development efforts. We define CD broadly as a process whereby government, nonprofit organizations, voluntary associations, or public–private partnerships ameliorate or prevent adversities and develop strengths in a community's economic, political, social, or physical environment. Economic CD encourages business and job opportunities. Political CD implies effective community improvement associations with broad and active participation. Social CD encourages safer streets and more neighborliness. Environmental CD improves housing conditions, city services, and recreational facilities and helps clean up or prevent toxic or littered sites and instill residents' pride in their home and community.

We advocate a broad-based, bottom-up, public–private approach to CD rather than top-down public or private efforts that focus on one issue. Government funding, regulation, and support at all levels (federal, state, and local), community support and participation, and an encompassing (ecological) perspective are all necessary for CD to be effective.

Strengths-Based Principles of Community Development

Community development policies have often been paternalistic, imposed from above and from afar, and based on the assumption that poor communities have little to offer besides cheap land and labor and social problems. But CD theory and practice worldwide have become more consistent with the strengths orientation of the present volume. A 1995 United Nations Development Program report cited four essential components of strengths-oriented human development: productivity, equity, sustainability, and empowerment. The last two, along with the equally strengths-oriented concepts of social capital, capacity building, and community asset identification and development, have become guiding principles for CD.

The concept of *sustainability*, popular in international development (Ginther, Denters, & de Waart, 1995; Rao, 2000), is also relevant to CD policies and practices in the United States (see 1999 President's Council on

Sustainable Development). Economic sustainability, developing a local economy that can be maintained without reliance on regular infusions of outside capital or credit, was the original goal. Since the U.N.-sponsored Earth Summit conferences, however, environmental sustainability, or developing means of production that do not contaminate the ecosystem or exhaust natural resources, has also become important. Analyses of sustainable development rarely transcend the economic or bioecological. Yet the principle of sustainability can be usefully expanded to include the political and social domains of CD as well. Political sustainability at the local level can be thought of as developing and maintaining active and meaningful participation in grassroots community organizations. The issues they choose to address can make a big difference (Perkins et al., 1996; Perkins, Florin, Rich, Wandersman, & Chavis, 1990). Development decisions must also be politically sustainable, in legal and governance terms, on a societal level (Ginther et al., 1995). Social sustainability may be considered the degree to which communities develop and maintain social capital. Sustainability is strengths based in its emphasis on ecologically healthy development over time based on renewable community resources.

Grassroots *empowerment* involves residents organizing collectively to influence the institutions and problems affecting their community. Decisions are made, democratically or consensually, from the bottom up by local organizations. Empowerment operates at many levels, from psychological to organizational to community. Block and neighborhood associations and tenant groups aim to empower their members while improving community conditions (Perkins et al., 1990, 1996; Saegert & Winkel, 1996; Speer & Hughey, 1995). Internationally, empowerment has become a guiding principle for many CD organizations (Friedmann, 1992; Perkins, 1995). Empowerment is strengths based in focusing on people's and communities' rights, abilities, assets, and resources more than on their needs or problems.

Social capital, a popular concept among CD professionals and policymakers, is the level of residents' integration into the community in terms of informal networks and mutual trust, participation in civic and service organizations, and links among those organizations (Coleman, 1988). Faith-based CD is a form of social capital with a long and effective history, especially in Latin America and the African American community. Recently, CD researchers have emphasized the role of group learning processes in building social capital in communities and organizations (Falk & Harrison, 1998). Social capital fits well with our ecological focus because, in contrast with the older term "human capital," it focuses on the strengths related to interdependent social networks (not simply on individual strengths, such as education levels). As with empowerment, however, it is important for researchers and policymakers to be specific about defining social capital, its formal and informal sources, the dynamic processes to achieve it, and how to measure these along with its material effects (Saegert & Winkel, 1998). It is also important not to focus so much on social capital that we ignore communities' political, economic, and physical capital (Bourdieu, 1985; DeFilippis, 2001; Perkins, Hughey, & Speer, 2002).

Capacity building refers to the development of skills, information, or other organizational resources or the development of organizations and coalitions within an entire community. Whereas social capital describes the small-scale community social and political conditions for grassroots CD to occur, capacity building is a resource development process applied to extant CD organizations. Both concepts are based on the notion that communities have indigenous human resources that can be developed and used to address community problems.

Asset-based community development (Kretzmann & McKnight, 1993) is an approach to mobilizing people and local organizations for the social, economic, and physical revitalization of a community. It is based on the identification, mapping, and development of community assets or strengths, as opposed to needs or problems. Assets are broadly defined and overlap well with our ecological model: they may be physical (e.g., land, community gathering places), social (cohesion, volunteers), economic (consumers, entrepreneurs and workers, funding agencies), and political (voters, advocates, local officials, community leaders).

An example is Building a Healthier Mesa (Arizona) Neighborhood Development Initiative (http://www.mc.maricopa.edu/academic/compact/carter.html). When residents identified the need for a youth program and community center, they created one in a backyard. When they outgrew that space, the city donated a new property and hired a neighborhood liaison. The Initiative has grown into a coalition headed by block and neighborhood leaders, with representation from United Way, the Chamber of Commerce, public schools, and the local community college.

All five CD principles (sustainability, empowerment, social capital, capacity building, and assets-based CD), as well as the terms *strengths* and *resilience*, are so overused and co-opted for different ends that they have become buzzwords. Despite their popularity, strengths-oriented CD concepts have not received the systematic research and programmatic support they deserve. Although there has been a plethora of government policies based, at least nominally, on empowerment (e.g., Empowerment Zones, discussed later in this chapter), most have failed to apply the concept of empowerment clearly or consistently (Perkins, 1995).

By their very nature, strengths-based CD principles do not generally require large public expenditures. Social capital and asset-based approaches, by definition, rely primarily on local private resources, not public funding. Sustainability implies that beyond any initial investment, the need for new outside resources is limited. Yet many local CD programs would be greatly enhanced with more government funding, technical assistance for capacity building, sponsored research, and dissemination (Schorr, 1997). How to support grassroots CD efforts without compromising their autonomy or making them dependent on that support is both a tremendous opportunity and a challenge for policymakers.

AN ECOLOGICAL FRAMEWORK FOR COMMUNITY DEVELOPMENT: ECONOMIC, POLITICAL, SOCIAL, AND PHYSICAL ENVIRONMENTAL COMPONENTS

Most of the CD literature addresses just one or two domains of adversity. In contrast, our conceptual framework is ecological in placing CD simultaneously in the economic, political, social, and physical environmental contexts in which adversities, and the policies and community action addressing those adversities, reside (see Figure 18.1). It is also ecological in viewing CD as a dynamic and interdependent system operating at multiple levels (individual, small group, organization, community), in which change in one area and level affects the other areas and levels.[1] The following sections give examples of public and private CD strategies. The interdependence of these spheres of development becomes readily apparent in these examples.

Economic Development

Urban redevelopment policies in the United States have focused on large, downtown projects and freeways at the expense of revitalizing older neighborhoods. Cities have experienced fiscal crises, declining federal support, crumbling infrastructure, and myriad social problems (Palen, 1997). But can waterfronts, ballparks, convention centers, and hotels undo the "malling of America" (the flight of economic activity to the suburbs)? If they could, how much good would it do the vast majority who live not in downtowns, but in residential neighborhoods? Following are some promising public and private strategies for community economic development.

Community development block grants represent a large federal expenditure that could address many community-level adversities. But during the 1980s, much block grant funding went to less needy neighborhoods to fund public infrastructure instead of to housing, physical improvements, or economic development in poor areas (Catlin, 1981; Watson, 1992). How should these funds be targeted? Neighborhood revitalization's track record is mixed (Ginsberg, 1983), but four generally successful strategies are (a) involving a

---

[1]For more on the variables and relationships in the framework, see Perkins et al., 1996. For other ecological principles applied to community organizing and development, see Speer and Hughey, 1995. For links to community organizing and development-related Web sites, including many of the policies and programs discussed in this chapter, see http://www.people.vanderbilt.edu/~douglas.d.perkins/cdwebsites.htm.

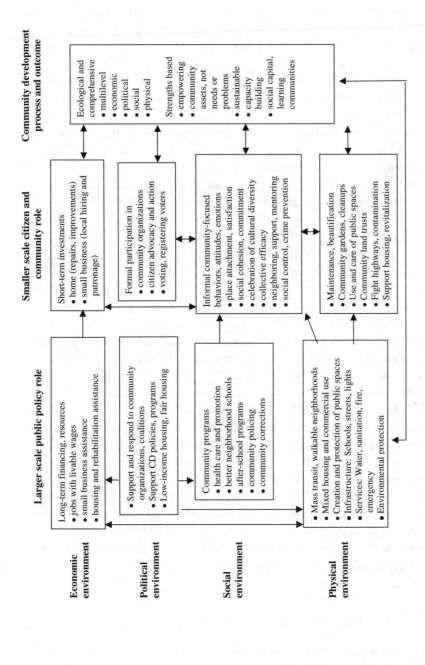

Figure 18.1. An ecological framework for community development. CD = community development. Arrows indicate directions of theoretical causal links. Two-headed arrows imply mutually reinforcing set of variables.

broad base of residents; (b) building on existing community strengths; (c) promoting cooperation among local public and private agencies, along with funding and technical support from higher levels; and (d) targeting common urban problems, such as inadequate sense of community, safety, housing, schools, youth programs, and economic opportunity (Schorr, 1997).

The Empowerment Zones/Enterprise Communities federal policy of the 1990s was based on the 1980s' "urban enterprise zones" of targeted capital investment and training and employment tax incentives. Reviews of the policy have been mixed, with critics arguing that the incentives were either too small (to offset entrenched poverty and related individual and community disadvantages) or too large (essentially a business subsidy that does little for local residents; Palen, 1997). But it incorporated several strengths approaches, including a bottom-up orientation requiring local planning; partnerships between business, government, and community organizations; and local hiring requirements. Some Empowerment Zones enhanced resident opportunities and skills through job training, day care programs, and microcredit.

Community development financial institutions and local exchange trading systems are two of the newest and most innovative economic development strategies. The former include CD-focused corporations, banks, venture capital funds, and microenterprise (microcredit) funds. They are specifically dedicated to serving low-income individuals and communities by developing investments, entrepreneurs, and jobs. Microcredit extends small business loans to those who cannot qualify for a traditional loan because they are poor or have no credit history. Loans are usually small (e.g., for a sewing machine) and come with technical assistance and peer supports. The most famous example of microcredit is Grameen Bank in Bangladesh, which organizes village loan pools, whose collective responsibility for debts gives borrowers more incentive to repay on time. In the United States, South Shore Bank in Chicago has made hundreds of millions of dollars of loans in poor, inner-city neighborhoods. Working Capital in Cambridge, Massachusetts, organizes low-income, small business owners into peer-lending groups.

Local exchange trading systems are bartering co-ops, including local currency programs and "time dollar" exchanges. Ithaca Hours is an alternative economy that pays $10 an hour in a local currency that can be traded for goods and services. Time dollars also equalize the value of work but have no monetary value. In rural Utah, the Emery County CD Initiative developed a Computers for Kids program, which matched junior high tutors with elementary school readers. The tutors earned time dollars, which they used to "purchase" donated computers.

Political Development and Housing Policy

Grassroots organizing, or political CD, is a key, though often ignored, activating ingredient for any CD program's chances of stopping and reversing the process of neighborhood decline. It empowers residents, is a long-term solution, costs little (other than time and energy), and helps maintain neighborhood stability (Perkins et al., 1996; Speer & Hughey, 1995). Political CD means both pressuring every level of government through community organizations and larger coalitions and creating private, nonprofit community self-help programs.

Local, nonprofit CD housing programs address the political and economic gaps in the housing market. They turn homeless people into renters and renters into homeowners. Homeowners are less likely to move and more likely to have a material stake not only in their own home, but in their entire neighborhood, on which property values depend. Many such programs are based on the limited-equity home ownership model ("urban homesteading" or "sweat equity") for providing privately owned housing to low- and moderate-income families. These "third sector" housing programs differ from for-profit housing in both their initial and their permanent affordability (Davis, 1994). A limit is typically placed on the future price at which units may be rented or resold. New York City has seized hundreds of tax-defaulted apartment buildings and turned them over to the existing low-income residents as limited-equity co-ops. Empowering those residents to take control over the revitalization and maintenance of their buildings has resulted in significant improvements in housing quality (Saegert & Winkel, 1996, 1998).

Community land trusts can be used for any particular land use (housing, commercial, or open space) or purpose (historic preservation, local control, neighborhood revitalization; Peterson, 1996). Similar to conservation trusts, which are used to protect open space or agricultural land, community land trusts also acquire land but usually for affordable housing or other CD ends. In general, democratically run groups, such as Share the Future in Heber, Utah, own the land collectively but lease parcels of it to individuals for long-term use. Buildings on the land are sold to the individual lessee. This, along with resale price restrictions, helps keep ownership affordable for the duration of the trust. Community land trusts have preserved family farms, helped stem the cost inflation associated with speculation and gentrification, educated first-time home buyers, and developed special-needs housing and commercial space for lower income entrepreneurs (Peterson, 1996). They protect or improve the physical environment, are a political and economic innovation, and can result in social benefits and so illustrate well the interdependence of all four domains of CD in our framework.

Direct government roles in improving low-income housing rest largely on returning public and subsidized housing budgets to an adequate level. Other housing-focused CD policies include encouraging incumbent upgrading (housing improvements by long-term residents, not gentrifiers and speculators) through CD block grants and subsidized loans, increasing management accountability in public housing through tenant organizations[2] and improved quality assurance and grievance procedures, and mixing housing cost levels to avoid concentrated ghetto effects.

Social Development

Cultural diversity, sometimes described as a potential adversity (if prejudice, discrimination, and conflict are left unchallenged), is better viewed as a community asset. Diverse neighborhoods can be interesting and vibrant places to live. Different groups bring different perspectives, knowledge, connections, and strengths to the community and its organizations. CD efforts must include public events that celebrate diversity and help residents learn about and appreciate their differences. Organizations must actively recruit members of different groups and accommodate differences in language, religious and cultural holidays, and other customs.

Social cohesion consists of a variety of behaviors, attitudes, and emotions that signify the social and psychological creation of community (Perkins et al., 1996). Areas with more neighborliness, greater use of outdoor space, and informal social control of behavior exhibit better quality of life and a greater commitment of members to the community. This commitment both is motivated by and leads to a stronger sense of community and collective efficacy, as well as satisfaction with, pride in, and attachment to the people and place and confidence in its future (Perkins et al., 1990). Social cohesion is the strongest and most consistent predictor of citizen participation in CD (Perkins et al., 1990, 1996). CD organizations, in turn, encourage greater community cohesion by helping residents to discuss and work to address shared concerns and by sponsoring cultural events. Public officials, community leaders, and organizers cannot afford to ignore social cohesion. Communities without it will be hard to mobilize, and communities with it will be better able to change policies with which they disagree.

Community crime prevention programs may be organized by civilians or police or may focus on the physical environment. Civilian crime prevention encompasses both various victimization prevention strategies (e.g., publicizing crimes, increasing home security, organizing resident surveillance; Rosenbaum, 1986) and broader, more strengths-based approaches addressing the root causes of crime (via youth development, employment, or other CD programs). Community-oriented policing consists of a variety of methods (foot patrol, neighborhood miniprecincts, school programs, community crime information meetings and newsletters, home security checks) for officers to interact more with the community, gain their trust, and address local crime and delinquency problems. Related to community environmental develop-

---

[2]It is important that tenant organizations be legitimate, empowered, and active. Just as housing authorities that are unresponsive or disregard agreements erode tenants' sense of collective efficacy, mandated or token participation can undermine community strengths.

ment, Crime Prevention Through Environmental Design, or "defensible space," is a set of architectural and planning principles that encourage natural surveillance and a sense of ownership and limit access in ways that deter crime (Taylor & Harrell, 1996).

Crime rates in the United States have generally gone down over the past 20 years, although there is little empirical evidence for any law enforcement or crime prevention strategy being responsible for that drop. Furthermore, crime and fear tend not to elicit broad or lasting citizen participation (Perkins et al., 1990, 1996). A more promising study of neighborhoods and crime found that, controlling for demographics, communities with more social cohesion and informal social control suffered less violence (Sampson, Raudenbush, & Earls, 1997). Taken together, these findings suggest that community anticrime policy must take a more comprehensive, empowerment approach that addresses the root causes of crime and motivates active community participation through a combination of CD and prevention programs for youth.

Physical Environmental Development

The condition of the local physical environment is closely linked to resident fears, confidence in the community's future, and participation in community organizations (Perkins et al., 1990, 1996; Skogan, 1990). People's attachments to their neighborhood as a place are linked to less crime, fear, and disorder and better housing and home satisfaction (Brown & Perkins, 2001). Organized activities to clean up parks, streets, and yards and to replace vacant lots with urban gardens are excellent ways to get and keep people involved in their community.

New development should promote the quality and vitality of community life and preserve open space. City and regional planning, design, and transportation must be geared toward people and transit (not cars), density (not sprawl), and mixed-use zoning (not suburbia, with its isolated subdivisions, shopping malls, freeways, and office parks; Calthorpe & Fulton, 2001).

Some communities must pay even more serious heed to environmental conditions. Contamination and other environmental disasters and threats require government support for cleanup and protection. But they also require community organization and development to keep local residents united (Edelstein, 2001). Community Development focused on protecting the environment can have an empowering effect at both the individual and community level (Rich et al., 1995).

Although community developers have become more environmentally conscious, they have not benefited from as much collaboration or coalition building with environmental groups as they could. Yet environmental development is perhaps the ideal context for sustainability theory. For new construction (e.g., highway, housing, natural resource development, manufacturing plant) to be sustainable, it must neither pollute or deplete resources nor poison the social and economic climate. It must also be politically acceptable: The decision process must be open and truly participatory from beginning (gathering and evaluating information) to end (ideally, using a partnership rather than an adversarial approach to making and implementing decisions).

The Sawmill neighborhood in Albuquerque, New Mexico, is an example of a community that started out by rallying around an environmental issue and kept residents involved over the long term by thinking ecologically about the economic, social, and political, as well as physical, health of the community. The community initially organized against a particleboard factory that had been polluting the neighborhood for years. After a successful cleanup campaign, the residents formed a CD corporation to help the city develop the abandoned property. As the neighborhood began to gentrify, they formed a community land trust to keep housing affordable to successive generations. The Sawmill Community Land Trust continues to thrive and recently broke ground on a 27-acre commercial, residential, and open space development.

POLICY RECOMMENDATIONS TO ADDRESS COMMUNITY-LEVEL ADVERSITY THROUGH STRENGTHS-BASED COMMUNITY DEVELOPMENT

The strengths-based approaches to community level adversity outlined in this chapter point to specific policy recommendations at the local, state, and federal levels. In most cases, these policy recommendations are not new—they are being implemented in individual communities or states and are included here as examples of policies that can be replicated or adapted in other localities. Some of the federal policies discussed in this chapter can be made more effective by strengthening community control and implementing programs in more coordinated and integrated ways that address all four forms of community adversity.

Although government entities can and should be partners in facilitating, financing, and coordinating CD programs, the process for planning and implementing programs should be community driven. This is a critical point. The call for "maximum feasible participation" of the community has been around for decades. Yet in practice government often makes only minimum efforts to elicit meaningful participation (Perkins, 1995). Both research and practice in participation and empowerment may be helpful in changing this (Friedmann, 1992; Kretzmann & McKnight, 1993; Perkins et al., 1996; Saegert & Winkel, 1996; Speer & Hughey, 1995).

The common thread, and some would say the root cause, running through each form of community adversity is the economic marginalization of certain individuals and communities. Thus, it is in this area that we offer the broadest range of recommendations, all of which attempt to focus economic resources and control at the local level. We have not categorized the recommendations by area of adversity (economic, political, social, and physical environmental), because we believe approaches should be designed to address multiple areas in an integrated manner.

Our recommendations are in the following categories: facilitating the ability of individuals and neighborhoods to address adversity on their own; directing state and local resources to community and economic development, controlled by neighborhoods and communities; and strengthening existing federal policies to support a strengths-based approach. The first category most clearly represents the CD principles of sustainability, empowerment, social capital, capacity building, and asset-based CD. But those working at the grassroots level know best how critical government resources are at every level to address the most entrenched adversities and support communities' own efforts.

Facilitate Grassroots Initiatives

Local governments can support the development of organized mutual supports such as block and neighborhood associations and local exchange trading systems. City staff and resources can be applied to a broad range of indigenous CD approaches by providing training and technical assistance as well as community outreach.

State, Local, and Regional Community Development Policies

State and local governments are well positioned to direct resources to the communities most in need, but they often fail to do so or to connect related policies to each other. Strengths-based local and state CD policies would invest in programs that provide opportunities for economic development at both the individual and community levels, such as microcredit programs, CD financial institutions, community land trusts, and individual development accounts that match the savings of low-income individuals with public or private funds for purposes of education, business start-up, or housing acquisition.

There are numerous examples of communities that use local or state economic development subsidies or financing mechanisms to overcome adversities. These include tax increment financing or industrial revenue bonds for job creation and affordable housing development (e.g., housing trust funds) and tax credits and other incentives to increase wages and benefits or establish "first source" agreements (in which employers commit to offer jobs first to local workers or other target populations, such as welfare recipients, or to promote greater permanence in the jobs created). Other communities use these subsidies to develop industrial retention and expansion programs aimed at keeping higher wage manufacturing jobs in a community. Some communities have successfully addressed economic and environmental adversity by improving transit for low-income citizens, and others have developed elaborate sectoral job creation strategies that target unique local skills, assets, or resources to strengthen the local economy. For example, a rural community in Utah that suffered the closure of a sawmill formed a partnership between local unemployed workers and environmentalists to practice sustainable harvesting of wood products and to develop a market for the value-added products created by a cooperative of local woodworkers.

Local planning and zoning authority can be used in more strengths-oriented ways to promote low-cost housing, improve the social and environmental characteristics of neighborhoods, and assist small business (e.g., mixed-use zoning). Inclusionary zoning ordinances require that a certain percentage of new housing be affordable. Local governments are seizing abandoned, unsafe, and tax-defaulted properties for low-income rehabilitation.

One proposal for keeping the most concerned and resourced residents involved in their own communities is to improve neighborhood public schools (as opposed to magnet or charter schools or vouchers for private schools) so that children stay in the neighborhood. Schools are one of the most important institutional anchors for any community and the second most common place for community participation (after religious organizations). Parents and even local businesses are playing a more direct role in education. Federal leadership and resources are also needed. But the biggest responsibility still rests with state and local government.

Community development policies tend to concentrate on central business districts, residential neighborhoods, or rural areas, but rarely all three at once. This is a serious problem because it tends to preclude mixed-use development, metropolitan region transportation planning, open-space preservation, and other aspects of ecologically "smart growth" and "new urbanism" (Calthorpe & Fulton, 2001).

Strengthening Federal Policies

Fannie Mae, the U.S. Rural Development Agency, and other agencies are beginning to support such strengths-based CD initiatives as community land trusts, self-help housing, individual development accounts, and microlending institutions. The Council for Urban Economic Development recently issued a detailed federal policy agenda, including a focus on skills training for the knowledge economy, encouragement of private investment in CD, and other strengths approaches (Garmise, 2001). We would add that many existing federal programs, although consistent with a strengths orientation to community development, are underfunded (e.g., low-income housing, Empowerment Zones, CD block grants, earned income tax credits). Others have inadequate provisions for private investment, including the Community Reinvestment Act (which is currently under serious political threat), the Home Mortgage Disclosure Act, and minimum wage laws (Center for Community Change, 2003; Federal Financial Institutions Examination Council, 2003; U.S. Department of Labor, 2003). Some federal programs should be expanded to other agencies (e.g., Housing and Urban Development's Community Outreach Partnership Program and its HOME Program's incentives for subcontracts to local CD organizations) or to younger target populations (e.g., Americorps service or CD job opportunities for high school and college students). Student loan forgiveness programs could be expanded to include college graduates who do community development work in poor urban and rural areas (similar to incentives for teachers and doctors to select underserved areas in which to work).

There is also a need for more federal funding of ecological research (i.e., systemic, interdisciplinary, multimethod, longitudinal research analyzed at multiple, ecologically valid levels) and for strengths-based CD research (i.e., participatory, driven by locally defined needs, and leading to the identification and development of individual and community assets). The Ford Foundation is not the major supporter of CD research it once was. The Fannie Mae Foundation has filled some of that gap but tends to emphasize housing rather than the broad range of CD issues. The Department of Housing and Urban Development continues to fund a broad range of CD projects, including some major university-based ones; however, it has always funded more interventions than research. Another important federal role in CD research is to ensure that national data gathering better reflects the ecological and strengths orientation toward community-level adversities and development (and not just individual or household indicators).

Although funding is important, federal leadership is also critical for regulatory changes. For example, often CD block grant and other resources are captured and redirected by political interests outside the control of marginalized communities. State and local applications of federal strategies could have greater impact if their regulations specifically required broader and more meaningful participation, not only by the general public but also by the low-income communities facing the greatest adversities. A more specific example of a regulatory problem is that limited-equity, low-income housing cooperatives do not have access to tax credit financing. Federal underwriting practices often prohibit mortgages for extended families or co-ops and restrict the construction of common spaces that would make group life more productive. A recent exception is the loosening of restrictions on common space in housing for elderly people, which may open the door to better accommodations for collective ownership models.

CONCLUSION

Dividing CD policies by level of government helps to target advocacy, but it runs counter to the ecological and systemic perspective we advocate.

Some of the most compelling examples of CD are the growing number of comprehensive community revitalization initiatives (e.g., Dudley Street Neighborhood Initiative in Boston, Massachusetts, and Sandtown-Winchester in Baltimore, Maryland) and comprehensive community health and substance abuse prevention initiatives, which are encouraged by multiple public and private funding agencies. Thus, CD policies at all levels must include both programs to address as many of the social problems discussed in this volume as possible (not just infrastructure and economic development, as important as those are) and meaningful participation at the grassroots level. By the same token, interventions that deal only with the social and psychological symptoms of poverty and injustice and do not address the economic and political root causes of those problems or make real and tangible gains in people's lives (e.g., decent affordable housing, livable-wage jobs, crime reduction, cleaned up neighborhoods and toxic sites) may be doomed to fail.

Implicit in this chapter are at least three different, but equally valid, strengths-based orientations. These include CD policies and organizations that strengthen individuals and communities by building on existing strengths (e.g., community assets and citizens as social capital vs. communities and citizens viewed only as problems); developing new strengths (i.e., empowering and capacity building vs. top-down, bureaucratic decision making, blaming victims and trying to fix them), and making the goal the development of economically, politically, socially, and physically sustainable and healthy environments (vs. the mere absence of adversities).

CD is relevant to each of the other chapters in this volume because CD programs and policies reduce, at the community level, many of the adversities discussed in the other chapters. Furthermore, CD directly contributes to the capacity of individuals, organizations, and communities to cope with any remaining psychosocial adversities, thereby strengthening children, youth, and families in the process.

REFERENCES

Bourdieu, P. (1985). The forms of capital. In J. Richardson (Ed.), *Handbook of theory and research for the sociology of education* (pp. 241–258). New York: Greenwood.

Brown, B. B., & Perkins, D. D. (2001). *Neighborhood revitalization and disorder: An intervention evaluation* (Report to National Institute of Justice). Salt Lake City, UT: University of Utah.

Bullard, R. D. (Ed.). (1994). *Unequal protection: Environmental justice and communities of color*. San Francisco: Sierra Club Books.

Calthorpe, P., & Fulton, W. (2001). *The regional city: Planning for the end of sprawl*. Washington, DC: Island Press.

Catlin, R. A. (1981). An analysis of the Community Development Block Grant Program in nine Florida cities. *Urban and Social Change Review, 14*, 3–11.

Caughy, M. O., O'Campo, P., & Brodsky, A. E. (1999). Neighborhoods, families, and children: Implications for policy and practice. *Journal of Community Psychology, 27*, 615–633.

Center for Community Change (2003). *Financial modernization moving in the house: Community Reinvestment Act.* Retrieved June 11, 2003, from http://www.communitychange.org/cralinks.htm

Coleman, J. S. (1988). Social capital and the creation of human capital. *American Journal of Sociology, 94*, 95–120.

Davis, J. E. (Ed.). (1994). *The affordable city: Toward a third sector housing policy.* Philadelphia: Temple University Press.

DeFilippis, J. (2001). The myth of social capital in community development. *Housing Policy Debate, 12*, 781–806.

Edelstein, M. R. (2001). *Contaminated communities: Psychosocial impacts from the contamination of home and place* (2nd ed.). Boulder, CO: Westview Press.

Falk, I., & Harrison, L. (1998). Community learning and social capital: "Just having a little chat." *Journal of Vocational Education and Training, 50*, 609–627.

Federal Financial Institutions Examination Council (2003). *Home Mortgage Disclosure Act.* Retrieved June, 11, 2003, from http://www.ffiec.gov/hmda/

Friedmann, J. (1992). *Empowerment: The politics of alternative development.* Cambridge, MA: Blackwell.

Garmise, S. O. (2001). *Ensuring the knowledge economy means prosperity for all: A federal policy agenda.* Washington, DC: Council for Urban Economic Development.

Ginsberg, R. (1983). *Community development strategies evaluation: Offsite effects.* Philadelphia: University of Pennsylvania.

Ginther, K., Denters, E., & de Waart, P. J. I. M. (1995). *Sustainable development and good governance.* Dordrecht, The Netherlands: Martinus Nijhoff.

Kretzmann, J. P., & McKnight, J. L. (1993). *Building communities from the inside out: A path toward finding and mobilizing a community's assets.* Chicago: ACTA.

Palen, J. J. (1997). *The urban world* (5th ed.). New York: McGraw-Hill.

Perkins, D. D. (1995). Speaking truth to power: Empowerment ideology as social intervention and policy. *American Journal of Community Psychology, 23*, 765–794.

Perkins, D. D., Brown, B. B., & Taylor, R. B. (1996). The ecology of empowerment: Predicting participation in community organizations. *Journal of Social Issues, 52*, 85–110.

Perkins, D. D., Florin, P., Rich, R. C., Wandersman, A., & Chavis, D. M. (1990). Participation and the social and physical environment of residential blocks: Crime and community context. *American Journal of Community Psychology, 18*, 83–115.

Perkins, D. D., Hughey, J., & Speer, P. W. (2002). Community psychology perspectives on social capital theory and community development practice. *Journal of the Community Development Society, 33*, 33–52.

Perkins, D. D., & Taylor, R. B. (1996). Ecological assessments of community disorder: Their relationship to fear of crime and theoretical implications. *American Journal of Community Psychology, 24*, 63–107.

Perkins, D. D., Wandersman, A., Rich, R. C., & Taylor, R. B. (1993). The physical environment of street crime: Defensible space, territoriality and incivilities. *Journal of Environmental Psychology, 13*, 29–49.

Peterson, T. (1996). Community land trusts: An introduction. *Planning Commissioners Journal, 23*, 10.

President's Council on Sustainable Development (1999). *Toward a sustainable America: Advancing prosperity, opportunity, and a healthy environment for the 21st century.* USGPO. Retrieved June 30, 2003, from http://clinton2.nara.gov/PCSD/

Rao, P. K. (2000). *Sustainable development: Economics and policy.* Malden, MA: Blackwell.

Rich, R. C., Edelstein, M., Hallman, W. K., & Wandersman, A. H. (1995). Citizen participation and empowerment: The case of local environmental hazards. *American Journal of Community Psychology, 23*, 657–676.

Rosenbaum, D. P. (Ed.). (1986). *Community crime prevention: Does it work?* Beverly Hills, CA: Sage.

Saegert, S., & Winkel, G. (1996). Paths to community empowerment: Organizing at home. *American Journal of Community Psychology, 24*, 517–550.

Saegert, S., & Winkel, G. (1998). Social capital and the revitalization of New York City's distressed inner city housing. *Housing Policy Debate, 9*, 17–60.

Sampson, R. J., Raudenbush, S. W., & Earls, F. (1997). Neighborhoods and violent crime: A multilevel study of collective efficacy. *Science, 277*, 918–926.

Schorr, L. B. (1997). *Common purpose: Strengthening families and neighborhoods to rebuild America.* New York: Anchor.

Skogan, W. (1990). *Disorder and decline.* New York: Free Press.

Speer, P. W., & Hughey, J. (1995). Community organizing: An ecological route to empowerment and power. *American Journal of Community Psychology, 23*, 729–748.

Taylor, R. B., & Harrell, A. V. (1996). *Physical environment and crime: NIJ research report.* Washington, DC: U.S. Department of Justice.

United Nations Development Program. (1995). *Human development report 1995: The revolution for gender equality.* New York: Oxford University Press.

U.S. Department of Labor. (2003). *Minimum wage.* Retrieved June 11, 2003, from http://www.dol.gov/dol/topic/wages/minimum wage.htm

Wandersman, A., & Nation, M. (1998). Urban neighborhoods and mental health: Psychological contributions to understanding toxicity, resilience, and interventions. *American Psychologist, 53*, 647–656.

Watson, S. S. (1992). Decentralizing community development decisions: A study of Oklahoma's Small Cities Program. *Publius, 22*, 109–122.

IV

CONCLUSIONS AND FUTURE DIRECTIONS

19

A BLUEPRINT FOR THE FUTURE

ANDREA L. SOLARZ, BONNIE J. LEADBEATER, IRWIN N. SANDLER,
KENNETH I. MATON, CYNTHIA J. SCHELLENBACH,
AND DANIEL W. DODGEN

In this last chapter, we summarize the key conclusions that can be drawn about the importance and effectiveness of strengths-based approaches. In addition, we present several crosscutting policy recommendations—including directions for future research—and identify key criteria for developing or evaluating strengths-based policies or programs. The conclusions and recommendations presented here are based on a synthesis of the information presented in the preceding chapters, as well as on discussions that took place at a 2-day meeting of the chapter authors, policy experts, and book coeditors.

* * *

Historically, U.S. society has focused on fixing or preventing social problems. This volume argues for a new focus on promoting strengths to sustain healthy individuals, families, and communities and to increase capacities to overcome adversities. It articulates the differences between strengths-based

We are grateful to the Center for Mental Health Services for their support (Order 99M00594801D). At this meeting, chapter coauthors, the book coeditors, and Washington, DC-based policy experts gathered to identify the key policy and substantive points about strengths-based approaches that are important to get across to policymakers and the public. The meeting, which was held in Washington, DC, May 5–7, 2000, was supported with funding from the Center for Mental Health Services and the American Psychological Association.

and deficits-based approaches, presenting clear arguments for the advantages of strengths-based approaches to programming and policies.

Deficits-based approaches—which are currently dominant—focus on "fixing" what are perceived to be problems with individuals, families, and communities. The focus is on identifying problems, identifying risks and weaknesses, and treating disorders or problems to reduce pathology. Strengths-based approaches, however, focus on tapping or building strengths or competencies; promoting healthy development and wellness; strengthening social environments; and engaging individuals, families, and communities in the development and implementation of solutions.

Strengths-based approaches work. They are effective strategies for promoting healthy individuals, families, and communities and reducing major social problems. Although gaps remain in the research base, when considered across the many topical areas presented in this volume, there is substantial empirical evidence for their effectiveness. Moreover, it is evident that promising strengths-based alternatives can be implemented to address a very wide array of adverse conditions.

In this chapter, we present a series of major conclusions, crosscutting recommendations, and research priorities based on the material presented in the preceding chapters and on discussions that took place at a 2-day meeting of chapter authors, policy experts, and book coeditors. First, however, we articulate how to reframe thinking to encompass the key concepts involved in the strengths-based approach.

REFRAMING OUR PERSPECTIVE

The challenge for policymakers, program developers, service providers, and researchers is to reframe their thinking to encompass a strengths-based perspective that focuses on promoting strengths for children, youth, families, and communities. For many, however, this requires a new and unfamiliar way of thinking. Policymakers typically respond once problems have been identified as needing fixing, program developers and service providers typically focus on addressing the deficits of a particular population experiencing problems (e.g., substance abuse, delinquency), and researchers typically study what are perceived to be dysfunctions and pathology. In this section, we contrast strengths-based and deficits-based models, present a set of criteria for evaluating whether existing or proposed approaches are strengths based, and give an example of how to reframe an issue from a deficits-based to a strengths-based approach.

Figures 19.1 and 19.2 present a graphic comparison of strengths-based and traditional deficits-based models. As Figure 19.1 shows, the focus in the traditional model is typically on specific pathologies or problems, such as substance abuse, teen pregnancy, or divorce. Efforts are then made to under-

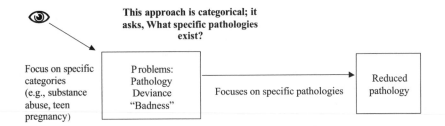

Figure 19.1. Traditional deficits-based approach.

stand and intervene in the etiological processes that led to the development of the problem, with an ultimate goal of reducing pathology (e.g., stopping substance abuse, reducing violent behavior).

The strengths-based model illustrated in Figure 19.2, however, takes a more comprehensive and integrative approach. Rather than focusing on specific, discrete problems, the focus is on healthy development for the individual, family, or community as a whole. Instead of focusing on what is wrong with individuals, families, and communities, the focus is first on what strengths and assets are present. Adversities are seen as developmental challenges that must be understood in a multilevel context of individuals, families, and communities. Strengths and capacities are seen as interactive and crosscutting; for example, healthy and resource-rich communities can help to build or build on the strengths of families and individuals, increasing their capacities to deal with adversities and the likelihood of positive developmental outcomes. The goal of strengths-based approaches is not simply to reduce pathology, but to promote positive behavior and healthy development. These processes are seen as ongoing, interactive, and dynamic.

There are a number of questions that can be asked to determine whether a program or policy approach meets the criteria of being strengths based. In

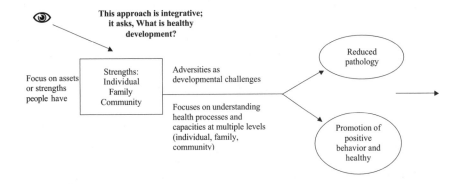

Figure 19.2. Strengths-based approach. The arrow indicates the process is ongoing and dynamic.

reality, of course, programs and policies are likely to incorporate a range of approaches. There are numerous reasons for this, including the philosophical orientation of those developing the approach, the characteristics of programs that already exist in a community, and the political context. The criteria in Exhibit 19.1 can be used by policymakers and program developers both to evaluate the degree to which existing policies and programs reflect a strengths-based perspective and to develop new strengths-based approaches.

It is useful to examine an example of how a problem can be reframed from a deficits-based to a strengths-based approach, taking into consideration the criteria listed in Exhibit 19.1. Table 19.1 illustrates how the issue of low reading scores might be reframed to reflect a strengths-based perspective (there are also numerous examples in the chapters of how problems can be reframed in strengths-based terms). A similar approach can be taken when looking at other challenges or adversities.

MAJOR CONCLUSIONS

There are several major conclusions that can be drawn about strengths-based approaches that cut across the conclusions reached in each chapter about specific adversities and that reflect a convergence of findings across different literatures about the importance of the strengths-based approach.

Conclusion 1: Strengths-based approaches can and do make a real difference in promoting healthy development.

Strengths-based approaches hold a great deal of promise for both reducing the occurrence of a range of negative outcomes and promoting healthy development. Although gaps remain in the research base, in at least some areas there is substantial empirical evidence that supports pursuing these approaches. In other cases, the research points toward "best bets" for practice and programming that can be tested further through pilot or demonstration programs.

There are particular strategies that can be used in the design and development of strengths-based approaches that increase the chances of positive developmental outcomes. For example, programs that include input from the target population in their design, implementation, and evaluation are more likely to be successful. Thus, policies and programs should promote active engagement in decision making and the creation of solutions across levels.

The most effective strengths-based approaches marshal resources across multiple levels (i.e., individuals, families, communities) and systems (e.g., health care, education). Thus, to ameliorate the negative effects of adversity and prevent long-term problems, policies need to build strengths (i.e., competencies, resources, and capacities) at the individual, family, and commu-

EXHIBIT 19.1
Criteria for Evaluating Whether Policies and Programs Are Strengths Based

FOCUS ON STRENGTHS

- Does the policy, program, or approach focus on the key strengths in children, youth, families, or communities known to be related to the target adversity or outcome?
- Does the policy, program, or approach build on existing strengths of children, youth, families, or communities?
- Does the policy, program, or approach build new strengths in children, youth, families, or communities?

PROGRAM DEVELOPMENT AND SUSTAINABILITY

- Is there an empirical or theoretical basis for the policy, program, or approach (e.g., is it based on empirically evaluated interventions)?
- Is active engagement of the affected population promoted in decision making and in creating solutions?
- Are developmental and contextual factors considered (e.g., cultural, social, political, and economic factors)?
- Does the policy, program, or approach facilitate or develop linkages among and within relevant systems (e.g., housing, public safety, health, education, social services)?
- Are essential or basic resources for developing strengths in children, youth, families, and communities present? If these resources are inadequate or absent, does the policy, program, or approach provide them or otherwise work to ensure their availability?

OUTCOMES

- Are the desired outcomes strengths based?
- Is there a focus on developing positive outcomes, and not just on alleviating existing problems?
- Does the policy, program, or approach work to prevent future negative effects?

EVALUATION

- Are mechanisms included to evaluate the presence and development of strengths in children, youth, families, and communities?
- Is an appropriate range of costs and benefits considered, including nonmonetary costs and benefits (e.g., quality of life factors, lost potential)?
- Are both short- and long-term outcomes considered when assessing effectiveness?

---

nity levels instead of simply focusing on ameliorating deficits. In doing so, it is important to facilitate linkages both across systems and within systems.

> **Conclusion 2:** Children, youth, families, and communities facing adversity are far more capable of meeting challenges than has been previously recognized, *if* they have the necessary basic resources (e.g., housing, health care, social support, safety). However, absent these essential resources, children, youth, families, and communities do not do well.

TABLE 19.1
The Reframing Process: Moving From Deficits-Based to
Strengths-Based Approaches

Problem: Low reading scores	Traditional deficits-based approach	Approach as reframed from a strengths-based perspective
The issue	Reading scores on standardized tests are too low.	Being able to read is a critical asset, affecting both individuals and society at large.
The question	How do we increase reading scores?	What factors lead to positive educational development?
The approach	What's wrong with our schools, teachers, curricula, kids, parents?	What existing strengths at the individual, family, and community levels promote reading and positive educational development? How can these strengths be tapped or built on to promote or sustain healthy educational development over the long term?
The strategy	Teach "to the test" Punish schools and teachers if reading scores do not improve or reach certain standards	Promote initiatives that enhance school readiness Ensure that schools have adequate resources for teaching and that teachers have adequate training Promote family involvement in reading
The outcome evaluation	Changes in reading scores	Improvement in reading readiness and ability Changes in reading participation and enjoyment Improvements in overall academic achievement Increased family involvement in learning

Most young people—even those dealing with serious adversities—do okay; they graduate from high school, become gainfully employed, and do not get in trouble with the legal system. In fact, having to deal with adversity is not a unique situation; some adversities are very common (e.g., divorce), and most people must face adverse circumstances at different points in their lives. However, children, youth, families, and communities need certain resources—at multiple levels—to successfully meet the challenges of these adversities. For those who do not have these basic resources—supportive family relationships, access to appropriate services and safe environments, and the like—negotiating these periods of adversity can be particularly risky.

Conclusion 3: There are unique patterns of strengths that children, youth, families, and communities have that contribute to positive outcomes under adverse conditions.

All people can be viewed as having strengths. Existing strengths in individuals, families, and communities can be valued, tapped, and enhanced; new strengths can be acquired and developed. However, people can vary considerably in their strengths and access to resources, so the same, universal approach may not work for everyone. It is important to consider the diversity and heterogeneity of the population of focus, viewing its members within the context of their own particular community, history, and culture. For example, a behavior that might be viewed as undesirable in one setting could be viewed as adaptive in another (e.g., not allowing one's children to play outside if one lives in a dangerous neighborhood). For at least some adversities, a relatively small list of key strengths—such as school engagement, warm parenting, or neighborhood resources—can be identified and developed to increase the probability of positive outcomes for those facing these adverse circumstances.

Conclusion 4: To be effective, approaches must be both developmentally and contextually appropriate.

Building strengths earlier in life may be the most productive approach for reducing the likelihood of a wide range of future problems, disorders, and dysfunctions. Effective programs take into consideration the developmental pathways and trajectories of children, youth, families, and communities, understanding that there are key developmental or transitional points (e.g., the school transition from elementary to middle school) that affect responses when facing adverse circumstances. Strengthening healthy development can help to prevent a wide range of problem outcomes by helping young people successfully negotiate current developmental tasks and by facilitating successful completion of future developmental tasks. But young children do not grow up in isolation from families, schools, and communities. Effective programs must also consider contextual factors, including cultural factors (e.g., capitalizing on unique strengths of particular cultures or ethnic groups), as well as economic, social, physical, and political contexts.

Conclusion 5: There are general, integrated approaches to building strengths that apply across groups and across adverse circumstances.

Interventions are traditionally designed to have a targeted impact on one or a few outcomes. However, many adverse circumstances and negative outcomes are linked, and integrated approaches that work to build or build on strengths at multiple levels and in multiple domains may have the greatest chance for producing positive outcomes. A key adverse condition that clearly relates to numerous negative outcomes is poverty, and approaches that serve to ameliorate poverty or enhance economic resources will have an impact on numerous adverse outcomes. Similarly, exposure to violence—at the individual, family, or community level—is a particularly powerful adverse circumstance, greatly increasing risk for a range of negative outcomes. Other factors cited throughout the volume as being critical for positive outcomes include the importance of engagement in prosocial normative activities (including in the school setting) and of parental involvement and involvement in the community. Home visitation programs are an approach that has led to positive outcomes in numerous settings dealing with various adverse circumstances and working with diverse populations.

CROSSCUTTING RECOMMENDATIONS

Specific recommendations focused on particular adverse conditions are included in the individual topical chapters in this book. In this section, several crosscutting recommendations are presented.

> **Recommendation 1:** Policymakers, researchers, program developers, and service providers should assess whether they are meeting the criteria for a strengths-based approach when developing, delivering, or evaluating programs and policies.

Strengths-based approaches vary; there is no cookie-cutter template that can be used to create a strengths-based program. However, there are some basic features that are characteristic of strengths-based approaches. As has been noted throughout this volume, for example, strengths-based approaches focus primarily on strengths and competencies rather than deficits, cut across and integrate multiple social systems, and target and involve multiple levels (i.e., individuals, families, and communities). A number of criteria can be used to evaluate whether a policy or program can be considered a strengths-based approach (see Exhibit 19.1). Although very few programs manage to incorporate all of these features, these questions can help policymakers, program developers, researchers, and service providers both to craft new strengths-based approaches and to evaluate existing programs through a strengths-based lens.

> **Recommendation 2:** Representatives of the groups that are targeted by programs or research should be involved in meaningful ways throughout the process of program development, implementation, and evaluation.

Strengths-based approaches recognize the importance of involving those who receive services in important roles. The active engagement of representatives of the targeted populations in making decisions and creating solutions is critical for success. Consumers should be included throughout the research and program development process. This involvement is particularly important to ensure that the perspective of a culturally diverse population is represented in both the study of strengths and in the development of strengths-based programs. Public participation is needed to ensure that the interventions developed are ones that meet a public need, that they are acceptable to the groups they will affect, and that they can be readily implemented in communities.

Recommendation 3: Public and private funding to support research on strengths-based approaches should be significantly increased to enhance our basic understanding about how strengths-based approaches work to promote positive outcomes for individuals, families, and communities; to increase knowledge about effective programs; and to improve methodologies for gathering information about strengths-based approaches.

Research on strengths-based approaches, as well as the development of more sophisticated methodologies for conducting such research, will advance scientific knowledge in this area and fill important knowledge gaps. Building the knowledge base will help to ensure the development of effective, evidence-based policies for children, youth, families, and communities. The following are several priorities for research:

- developing more sophisticated research models that can incorporate multiple levels, multiple systems, and multiple points in time;
- developing reliable and valid qualitative and quantitative measures of the strengths of individuals, families, and communities;
- testing the effectiveness of various strengths-based approaches or interventions, including those targeted at the community level, following their effectiveness over time;
- assessing the cost-effectiveness of strengths-based approaches, including long-term studies of development from childhood to young adulthood; and
- developing effective strategies for bringing successful programs to scale in diverse contexts (e.g., in different settings and with various populations).

Specific topics for study include the following:

- normative levels of strengths across individuals, families, and communities (including multiple cultural groups);
- the ways that strengths are developed, maintained, and challenged across individuals, families, and communities and over time and the processes that promote or impede their development; and
- the processes by which individuals, family, and community strengths influence outcomes (both positive and negative) in areas of high national interest, including health, mental health, substance use, work, school, and quality of life in our communities.

Variables that measure strengths-based processes and outcomes, including those at the community level, should be included in relevant national databases. National surveys often do not collect sufficient data to assess strengths-based processes and outcomes. Including more of these variables in relevant national studies (e.g., National Survey on Family Growth, Youth Risk Behavior Survey, National Household Survey on Drug Abuse) will increase our understanding of strengths at multiple levels and their impact on outcomes. Because these data are particularly lacking for ethnic and racial minority groups, qualitative and quantitative studies are needed to identify ethnically and culturally sensitive assessments of individual, family, and community strengths that may be unique to these populations. In addition, secondary data analyses should be conducted of existing national data sets to examine the contribution of strengths to outcomes of high national priority, such as those described in *Healthy People 2010* (see http://www.healthypeople.gov).

> **Recommendation 4:** Public and private resources at the federal, state, and local levels should be allocated to build and support an infrastructure for strengths-based approaches.

Presently, there is no well-developed infrastructure in place that is designed to support the development, implementation, evaluation, and sustainability of strengths-based approaches. Although there are, of course, numerous mechanisms that can be used for these approaches (e.g., information clearinghouses, technical assistance centers), this is typically not their primary focus.

A number of steps can be taken to help build this infrastructure. Funding streams should be developed for research, evaluation, and programs to promote strengths-based perspectives. Strategies should be developed for training researchers in how to conduct strengths-based intervention research, including making training funds available (e.g., through the National Institutes of Health). Resources are also needed to train service providers in how to deliver strengths-based programs and to provide those wishing to develop strengths-based approaches with technical assistance. In addition, mechanisms are needed for disseminating strengths-based knowledge and programs including increasing public awareness about the effectiveness of these approaches.

One strategy for facilitating the development of infrastructure would be to establish a federal interagency task force to assess how strengths-based approaches can contribute to the mission of each agency, to assess how much and what types of resources are currently being allocated for strengths-based approaches, and to develop and implement recommendations for future cross-agency collaborations for strengths-based initiatives.

> **Recommendation 5:** Demonstration projects should be funded to test promising strengths-based approaches.

Pilot or demonstration projects with strengths-based approaches are needed to test the efficacy of promising interventions and policies at the local level. Demonstration projects with long-term follow-up are especially needed to examine the economic usefulness of various approaches and their effectiveness in sustaining positive developmental outcomes. Efforts should be made to identify and evaluate existing promising programs at the local community level.

CONCLUSION

There is a growing interest in the development and application of strengths-based approaches to address the social issues affecting the United States. Researchers, policymakers, and the general public recognize that the solutions to many of our problems can be found in the strengths of our citizens, their families, and their communities. Yet our science has generally not focused on understanding these strengths, and our nation's policies have not focused sufficiently on marshaling them to address adversities.

The chapters in this volume demonstrate the potential of strengths-based approaches for dealing with serious social issues. They present the nascent scientific evidence concerning the contribution of strengths and the policy directions that are needed to marshal these strengths. Collectively, they make an impressive case for the potential of strengths-based approaches and call for concerted efforts to focus on strengths both in science and in practice.

INDEX

Abstinence programs, teenage pregnancy and, 130
Abuse. *See* Child abuse and neglect
    definition of, 77
    physical and psychological, 98
    psychological, 98
Academic achievement
    academic attainment in United States and, 216
    of adolescent mothers, 119
    child outcomes and, 216
    of children of alcoholic parents, 138
    as protective factor, 216
Academic performance
    of abused and neglected children, 77
    decline in
        transition into senior high school, 239
        transition to middle school or junior high, 237, 239
Academic problems
    in children of divorce, 54
Acculturation
    definition of, 287
    educational policies for language of instruction, 292–294
        assimilationist, 292–293
    help seeking in domestic violence and, 104–105
    interaction with enculturation
        in risk and protective processes, 288
    psychosocial effects of
        research limitations and, 288
    research and policy and, 287–288
        resilience agenda for, 287–294
    role of schools in, 289
    stress of
        protective aspects of ethnic culture and, 291
Acculturation and enculturation
    ethnic culture and, 291
    incompatibilities of
        intergenerational differences in values and expectations and, 290
        internal conflict and, 289
        linkages in primary social contexts and, 290

    parental involvement in school and, 290–291
    parent–child relationships and, 290
    internal conflict of
        negative mental health and academic outcomes and, 289
        self-concept and identity formation and, 289
    research and theory on, 289–291
Accumulation of risk model, impact of war and community violence on children and, 306–307
Adaptability and cohesion, familial in adjustment to chronic illness of child, 178
Adaptation
    to adversity, 32
    in children with chronic illness
        child factors in, 175–177
        community factors in, 179–180
        family factors in, 177–179
        physical and social development and, 177
    developmental
        adaptive pathways to, 174–175, 176
    for Latino youths
        biculturalism and, 291–292
    programs for adaptive thinking and, 62
Adaptive functioning
    community, 23–24
    family, 20–21, 22
Adaptive pathways
    enhancement, 175
    hardiness, 175
    resilience, 175
Adjustment
    to chronic illness. *See also* Children with chronic illness
    diversity of pathways to, 183–184
Administration on Children, Youth and Families in, 87
Administrators
    changes in middle- and junior high schools and, 247
Adolescence
    depression in, 160
    early, developmental change in, 236–237

gang violence and, 253, 254
interaction of cognition with environmental risks and protective factors
in, 17
marriage or cohabitation in
maternal education and, 125
Adolescent mothers. *See also* Teenage pregnancy
adjustment problems of
stress *versus* individual deficits and,
122
developmental outcomes of
diversity of, 119–120
housing, marriage, residential arrangements and, 131
individual differences among subgroups
of, 119
interventions for
employment and, 126–127
outcomes of, 126–128
physical health and, 127–128
school engagement and, 126–127
subsequent pregnancy, 127–128
male partner support of, 124–125
policy directions for
family and community resources and,
131
housing, marriage, residential arrangements, 131
individualized, developmentally appropriate approach in, 131
schooling and dropout prevention,
131
research needs and, 128–129
Adolescent mothers and children
research needs
evaluation of community-based interventions, 129
role of fathers, 129
state approaches to, assessment, 129
Adolescent parenting
conflict with normative roles, 122
developmental competence model of,
120–126
biological fathers and stepfathers in,
124–125
community support, 125–126
family resources in, 123
grandparent support in, 123–124
individual resources in, 120, 122
knowledge of child development in,
123

psychological resources and social
adjustment in, 122
relationships with mentors in, 124
school engagement and positive aspirations in, 122–123
strength-based personality attributes
and, 122
Adoption and Safe Families Act of 1997, 88,
88n, 105
family preservation *versus* child endangerment, 105–106
Adoption Assistance and Child Welfare
Amendments of 1980, 87–88
matching grants to states for support
services, 88
protection, safety, removal and support
for care *versus* child and family development, 87
Adversity
behavior problems and
National Longitudinal Study of
Youth data, 36–40
National Survey of America's Families data, 33–36
of children and youths
research on, 32–33
chronic and acute
reciprocal relationship of, 43
community level, 23, 322–325
economic marginalization and, 334–
335
environmental, 324–325
policy recommendations for
strengths-based community development and, 334–338
political, 323
social, 324
conceptual framework for, 40–44
ecological properties of
dynamic relations between, 43
place, 41
time span, 41–42
at individual, family, community level
positive outcomes and, 348–349
resources for countering, 347–348
prevention of, 44–45
protective factors and, 32
quality of, 40–41
Advisory Board of Child Abuse and Neglect,
U.S., 1990, 86
Advocacy
for battered women, 104

in community development policies,
337–338
African Americans. *See also* People of Color
adolescent
social networks of, 276–277
child care and, 276–277
churches of
attitudes and beliefs systems and,
275, 278
vehicle for health care information
and opportunity, 277–278
economic disadvantage of *versus* White
Americans, 271–272
exclusion from asset-building policies,
271
poverty rate in, 270
racial disparity and
net financial assets of, 270–271
net worth of, 271
sources of strength and buffers and
extended families, 276
religiosity, 274–275
social support networks, 276–277
stereotype as intellectually inferior, 272
stressors of
sources of strength and buffers and,
274–277
Aftercare programs
for youthful offenders, 258–259
After-school programs
for children of alcoholic parents, 145
public policy and, 225–226
reduction of exposure to violence and,
314–315
Aggression
and early pregnancy, 119
legitimization of
alteration of, 312
Aggressive behavior
in traumatized children
school- and community-based
prosocial programs for, 314
Aggressive children
construction of positive peer culture for,
260–261
Aggressive friendships, 251–252
Aggressive youths
prevention of exposure to negative peer
influence, 257–259
prosocial and adult-structured activities
for, 257
Alateen, 143–144

Alcoholism
parental recovery, as protective factor
for children, 141, 142
Alexithymia, in children of alcoholic parents,
145
AmeriCorps, youth development and, 89n,
89–90
Antisocial behavior, peer influence in, 252
Antisocial youths. *See also* Peer influences,
negative
construction of positive peer culture for,
260–262
group interventions for
conventional–aggressive mix in, 261
interventions for
iatrogenic effects of homogeneous
grouping, 255
isolation procedures, 256
need for social skills training and
self-regulation, 255
prevention of exposure to negative peer
influence, 257–259
re-entry or aftercare programs for
incarcerated youths, 258–259
social skills training in, 258
volunteer mentors in, 258
treatment in least restrictive setting,
261–262
Anxiety prevention programs, for children
of alcoholic parents, 145
Arrest policies
association with police behaviors and
attitudes, 107
gateway for help seeking, 107
referrals at point of police intervention
and, 107–108
Assimilationist policies
in education
English-only instruction and, 292
reactive identification and, 292

Basic needs of individuals, 41
Battered Immigrant Women's Act of 1994, 105
Behavioral control programs, for children of
alcoholic parents, 144
Behavior problems
of abused and neglected children, 77
prediction of
National Longitudinal Study of
Youth data, 36–40
National Survey of America's Fami-
lies data, 33–36

Belief system, African American, 275
Bernal, M. E., 287
Biculturalism
    positive adaptation for Latino youths
        and, 291–292
    promotion in schools, 298
Bilingual education
    dissatisfaction with, 294
    funding and scope of, 295
    history of, 293
    renaissance of, 293
Bilingual Education Act of 1968, 293
Bootstrapping, personal, 14, 15
Bowen, G. L., 217
Building a Healthier Mesa (Arizona) Neigh-
        borhood Development Initiative,
        327
Bullying, schoolwide programming for, 220

California Proposition 227, bilingual educa-
        tion and, 294
Cambridge and Somerville Program for Al-
        coholism Rehabilitation,
    programs for children of alcoholic par-
        ents, 144
Capacity building, community development
        and, 327
Carnegie Corporation report, *Turning Points*
    communities for learning in middle or
        junior high school, 243, 244
Carnegie Council of Adolescent Develop-
        ment, 236
Child abuse and neglect
    awareness of physical abuse, 74
    building bridges among reseach, prac-
        tice, policy, 85–91
    Child Abuse Prevention and Treatment
        Act of 1974, 74
    developmental impact of, 75, 77, 78
    extant research on, 75–78
        cross-section design, 75–76
        definition of abuse or neglect in, 77
        design limitations in, 75–76
        developmental effects of, 75, 78
        retrospective design, 76
        variability of impact on child, 77–
            78
    federal policy of protective intervention,
        86
    federal programs and
        attention to youth development, 89–
            91

child protection and child welfare
    services, 87–89
child welfare services to adolescents
    and young adults, 89
intervention for results *versus* pre-
    vention of harm, 86
harm *versus* endangerment standard for,
    74
incidence and prevalence of, 74
maltreatment
    age span for, 74
    incidence of, 74–75
National Center on Child Abuse and
    Neglect, 74
as national emergency, 86
parental, 98
policy and
    assessment of programs for building
        on strengths, 92
policy and program services and, 86, 91–
    92
research, programs, and policy
    bridge-building between, 91–92
research on
    maltreated children/adolescents in,
        79, 80, 82
    policy implications of, 91
    protective factors in, 78, 81, 82, 83,
        84
    resilience in, 78, 79, 80, 81
    resilience of child and, 78–85
    sexually abused individual in, 79, 80,
        81, 82
    topics linked to policy and program
        development, 91–92
resilience of child and, 78–85
sexual abuse, 74
social class and, 75
Child Abuse Prevention and Treatment Act
    (CAPTA) of 1974, 74, 87
    Keeping Children and Families Safe
        amendment to, 87
Child care
    African American family and, 276
    school facilities for, 222
Child care centers
    for people of color, 279
Child care programs
    schoolage years, 222, 225
Child characteristics
    in adaptation to chronic illness, 175–
        177

in children of divorce, 61–62
Child development
    adolescent parent knowledge of, 123
    ecological perspective
        community in, 215–216
        family in, 214–215
        reciprocal developmental relation-
            ships in, 214–215
        school in, 215
Child protection
    domestic violence policies and, 105–
        106
    federal services for, 87–89
Child psychoeducation programs, children of
    divorce, 67
Children
    of abused mothers, 99
    of adolescent mothers. See also Adoles-
        cent mothers
        developmental outcomes of, 119–
            120
    exposure to community violence
        prevalence of, 305
    exposure to family violence
        adverse effects of, 99
    involvement in wars, 304
    problems of, research on, 32–33
    ratio of civilian:military casualties, 304
    safety of
        Adoption Assistance and Child
            Welfare Amendments of 1980,
            87
        safety of mother and, 98–99
Children of alcoholic parents (COAs)
    academic achievement of, 138
    action research and, 150
    alcohol and drug use and abuse among,
        139
    cognitive functioning of, 138
    conduct problems of, 138
    diversity of outcomes among, 138–139
    educational interventions, screening,
        and referral, 146
    extrafamilial influences on, 142
    family-focused programs for, 143
    gatekeepers for, 146
    incidence of, 137–138
    mental health problems of, 138
    non-COA-specific programs for
        for behavioral control and social
            competence, 144
        for cognitive resilience, 145–146

for emotional resilience, happiness,
    self-esteem, humor, 144–145
outcomes among, 138–139
parent alcoholism as adverse circum-
    stance, 140–141
policy recommendations, 147–150
    funding for research-based services,
        148
    interagency collaboration, 150
    privacy and confidentiality in treat-
        ment, 149
    promotion of mental health *versus*
        diagnosis and treatment, 147
    resilience-based language in legisla-
        tion, 149
    resilience data in surveys, 148–149
    resilience focus in national drug con-
        trol strategy, 150
    shift to public health model perspec-
        tive, 147
prevention programs for
    nonspecific, 144–146
    specific, 143–144
protective factors for, 141–142
public media and education interven-
    tions for, 146
research needs, 142
resilience development in, 141–142
screening and referral of, 146
sons of male alcoholics
    cognitive deficits of, 138–139
Children of divorce
    adaptive thinking of
        programs for, 62
    "child's best interest" and, 56
    custody and adjustment, 58
    deficit-model findings, 54
    follow-up, case management, monitor-
        ing post-divorce, 67
    internal resources of, 62
    mediating factors in, 65–68
        divorce transition guide, 66
        policy impact on, 63–65
        proactive intervention, 66
        universal interventions, 66–67
    outcomes of, 57
        child characteristics and, 61–62
        child support and, 57, 58
        custodial parent function and rela-
            tionship to child, 60–61
        economic decline and, 62–63
        environmental stability and, 62

interparental relationship and, 59–60

legal context of divorce and, 55–58

linkage of policies to, 58–63

maladjustment risk in young adulthood and, 54

mediating factors in, 59

mediation and, 59

noncustodial fathers and, 61

psychological intervention programs and, 59

parent contact issues and, 56, 57

policy areas of, 57

dispute resolution procedures, 56, 57

substantive domains in, 56, 57

policy impact on mediating factors and

child financial support, 64

custody, 63–64

divorce and dispute resolution, 65

relocation, 64

visitation and access, 64

prevalence of, 53–54

problems of, 54

psychological interventions and, 58

strengths-based approach to findings in, 54–55

strengths-based public health model for, 65–68

Children's Advocacy Centers program, 88n, 88–89

Children with chronic illness

burden on children, families, community, 174

developmental outcomes assessment in, 184

functioning over time in, 175, 176

incidence of, 173

insurance companies and deficits-based model, 174

parental care of, 182

pathways to adaptive and maladaptive development in, 174–175, 176

policy recommendations

collaboration among researchers, clinicians, advocates, policy makers, 180, 182–183

examining consequences of employment practices, 182

examining consequences of health care delivery systems, 180–181

promoting health care systems for family and children, 179, 180

summary of, 180

prevention program studies, 185–186

psychosocial difficulties in, 174

research recommendations

conducting research that will inform policy, 185–186

implementing appropriate study designs, 184–185

recognizing diversity of pathways in adjustment, 183–184

summary of, 180

risk factors in, 175

strengths-based intervention trials in cost-effectiveness of, 185

strengths-building in

child factors in, 175–177

community factors in, 179–180

family factors in, 177–179

Child's best interest, definition of, operational *versus* legal, 55–56

Child support

children of divorce and

outcomes of, 57, 58

policy and, 64

Child welfare services

for adolescents and young adults, 89

federal, 87–89

Child Welfare Services program, 88n, 88–89

Cichetti, D., *166*

Class

exposure to community violence and, 305

Classroom environment

behavioral, role in academic and psychosocial outcomes, 218, 220

middle school or junior high school constraints on adolescent development in, 236

Classroom management

public policy for training and support of teachers in, 225

in shaping prosocial behavior, 261

Classroom size

prevention of formation of deviant peer groups and, 259

Coatsworth, J. D., *16, 120*

Coercion, in families, 98

Cognition

children of alcoholic parents and, 138, 145–146, 146

in trauma, 310

Collaboration
    children of alcoholics and, 150
    of research and policy, 27–28
    women and domestic violence and, 111
Comer School Development Program
    model of home–school–community
        partnership results of, 221
    professional development for cultural
        sensitivity, 219
Committee on Community-Level Programs
        for Youth
    key ingredients of strengths-based pro-
        grams for family support, 201
Community
    adaptation to chronic illness of child
        and, 179–180
    adaptive functioning of, 24
    in design, implementation, evaluation
        of interventions, 8–9
    environments of, 140–141, 329, 333–
        334
    programs for children of alcoholic par-
        ents and, 143–144
    promotion of basic needs and develop-
        ment of competency and, 41
    prosocial adult and youth members of
        against community violence, 312
    in strength-based approach, 8–9
    in strengths-building, 21, 23–24
    strengths in, 5
    support for families of children with
        chronic illness, 179–180
    support of adolescent mothers and their
        children, 125–126
    support of constituents and, 23
    violence in. See also Urban war zones
        effects on experience of childhood,
            305–306
        exposure of children to, 305
Community development
    asset-based versus needs or problems
        approach, 327
    block grants for, 328, 330
    community participation program plan-
        ning and implementation, 334
    comprehensive, 3328
    definition of, 325
    dynamic and interdependent, 328
    ecological framework for, 328–334
        federal funding of research in, 328–
            334
    economic

    public and private strategies for,
        329–330
    faith-based, 326
    physical environmental, 329, 333–334
    policy recommendations for strengths
        based
        facilitation of grass roots initiatives,
            335
        federal funding of ecological re-
            search, 336
        participation in schools, 336
        state and local government policies
            and economic subsidies, 335–336
        strengthening of federal policies,
            336–337
    political and housing policy, 329, 330–
        332
    social, 329, 332–333
    strengths-based principles of
        asset-based, 327
        capacity building, 327
        empowerment, 326
        funding of, 327–328
        social capital, 326–327
        sustainability, 325–326
    theories of, strengths-oriented, 322
Community environment
    of children of alcoholic parents, 140–
        141
Community institutions
    enhancement of personal skills and
        knowledge through, 278–279
    for people of color, 278–279
Community land trusts, 331
Community-level adversity
    economic, 322–323
    physical environmental, 324–325
    political, 323
    social, 324
Community-level policies
    for reduction of violence exposure for
        children, 316–317
        residential mobility programs, 316–
            317
        safe havens, 316, 317
Community organizations
    protective factors in, 21, 23–24
Community Reinvestment Act
    private investment and, 336–337
Competence
    adversity and, 41
    definitions of, 16, 120

developmental indicators of, 120

in middle childhood and adolescence,
42

middle childhood and adolescence and,
42

as protective factor, 41–42

of youths

federal programs and, 91

Competence, individual

characteristics in development of, 20

context and, 16

dynamic, interactive character of, 17

expression of

in adversity, 17

developmental stage and, 17

interaction of protective and stress processes in, 18–19

as process, 17

as protective factor for resilient outcome, 120

Conduct problems, of children of alcoholic
parents, 138

Confidentiality, in services to children of
alcoholic parents, 149

Contraception, teenage pregnancy and, 130,
131

Contracts, relapse prevention of incarcerated
youths, 259

Control. See Locus of control; Need for control

Coparenting

child outcome in divorce and, 60

of grandmother and adolescent mother,
124

Coping

outcome and

children of alcoholic parents, 146

children of divorce, 62

skills training for

for children of alcoholic parents, 145

for children of divorce, 67

Council for Urban Economic Development

federal policy agenda, 336

Crime

as manifestation of social adversity, 324

prevention programs in community development, 332

Crime Prevention Through Environmental
Design, 332–333

Cultural diversity

as adversity, 329, 332

as asset, 332

group conflict and, 324

Curriculum, cultural relevance of, in outcomes, 218–219

Custodial parents

functioning and relationship to child,
60–61

psychoeducation programs for mothers,
67

Custody

adjustment of child and, 58

policy and, 63–64

Custody evaluators (Special Masters)

in divorce, 56, 57, 58

Daily hassles, effect inner city children and
youth, 196

Deficits-based approaches, 344–345

individuals, families, communities as
objects vs. participants, 5

reframing to strengths-based approaches, example of, 346, 348

strengths-based alternatives to, 3

Department of Health and Human Services,
U.S.

Administration on Children, Youth and
Families in, 87

Depression

in adolescence, 160

after transition to middle school or junior high, 238

comparison of women in refugee camps
and public housing projects, 309

cyclicity of, 159

epidemiology and classification of, 158–
159

medication for, 159

of parent. See Depression, parental

prevention of, 158

risk factors for, 158

talking therapy for, 159

Depression, parental

access to care, 165

day-care, 163

effect on adolescents, 160

effect on children, 159–160

family-focused programs

for adults, 164

best practices in, 164–165

early childhood mental health interventions and, 164

integrated prevention, principles of,
165–166

parenting strategies, 164
family programs for resilience enhancement, 160–162
  clinician-facilitated sessions in, 161–162
  intervention framework, 161
  lecture presentation of information for ages 8 to 15 in, 161, 162
family support programs, 160–162, 166–168
mothers in inner city, 163
nurse home visitation, 163
parent–child interactions and, 160
policy recommendations for
  comprehensive mental health system and, 166–168
  foundation for policy making and, 166
  integrative family-centered programs, 166, 167–168
  life-span, developmental perspective in, 166, 167
  programs for specific risk factors, 168
proactive intervention in, 163
programs for children and adolescents, 164–165
programs for infants and toddlers, 162–163
strengthening family as unit, 166
support for parenting and, 162
Toddler-Parent Psychotherapy, 162
treatment of parent and support for parenting, 166, 167
Depression of parent. See Depression, parental
Depressive symptoms
  adolescent mothers
    effect on children of, 119
    negative outcomes for, 119–120
  and early pregnancy, 119
Deviance
  peer support of, 252–253
  social reinforcement and group acceptance and, 253
Deviancy training
  in aggressive friendships, 252–253
Disempowerment
  community-level, 323
Disengagement from educational enterprise.
    See also School engagement
  human and social costs of, 234
  with transition into middle school and junior high, 237

with transition into senior high school, 240
  types of, 234
Dispute resolution, in divorce, 56, 57, 65
Divorce resolution procedures, 56, 57, 58
Divorce transition guide (DTG), 66, 67
Domestic violence. See Women and domestic violence
  economic losses from, 98
  incidence of, 98
  interventions in, 110–111
  public policy and, 99
Drug and alcohol use and abuse surveys, inclusion of resilience data in, 148–149

Eckenrode, J., 15
Ecological framework for community development
  federal funding of research in, 328–334
Ecological perspective
  adversities and, 41–42
  child development and, 214–216
  inner city children and youths, 194
  strengths and adversities in, 322
Economic adversity
  neighborhood decline and, 322–323
Economic decline, children of divorce and, 62–63
Economic inequality, effect on inner city children and youth, 195
Economic resources, African Americans and, 270–272
Economic sustainability, community development and, 326
Emotional management programs, for children of alcoholic parents, 144–145
Employment
  adolescent mothers and, 126–127
  parents of chronically ill children, 182
Empowerment, grassroots, and community development, 326, 330–331
Empowerment Zones/Enterprise Communities, 330
Enculturation
  definition of, 287–288
  interaction with acculturation
    in risk and protective processes, 288
Endangerment standard, rates of child abuse and, 75
Enhanced functioning
  in children with chronic illness, 175

and child's adaptation to chronic illness,
177–178

Environment
classroom, 218, 220, 236
community, 140–141, 329, 333–334
adversity in, 324–325
family, 140–141
neighborhood, deterioration of, 323–
324
physical, deterioration of, 323–324
school, 219–220
sustainability of, community development and, 326

Epstein, J. L., 216
Ethnic culture, in schools, 298
Ethnicity, as risk factor, 270
Ethnic minorities, role strain of, 197
Ethnic minority youths
acculturation stress and
generational trends in, 286–287
psychological and social problems
and, 286–287
enculturation and acculturation and
adaptive resources of, 287
value conflict in, 285–287

Faith-based community development, 326
Familism, protective function of, 291
Family
in adaptation to chronic illness of child,
177–179
of adolescent mothers, 131
African American
as problem-solving stress-coping systems, 276
refuge from harm, 198
as buffer and refuge from inner city
stress, 198
child's adaptation to chronic illness and,
177–178
in design, implementation, evaluation
of interventions, 8–9
enhancement of coping of innercity
children, 199
inner city, 197
involvement in school, 223
life cycle stage and response to stress,
21
normative transitions in, 20–21
promotion of basic needs and development of competency and, 41
in strength-based approach, 8–9

strengths in, 5
support of inner city, 199
lack of program evaluation in, 202
strengths-based programs for, 201
violence in
incidence of, 98
nature and scope of, 98–99

Family environment
of children of alcoholic parents, 140
cohesive and supportive
protective factor for children of alcoholic parents, 141

Family Medical Leave Act of 1993
parental care and
of children with chronic illness, 182

Family Opportunity Act of 2003
financial demands of childhood chronic
illness and, 181

Family Partners Project, 185

Family Preservation and Support Services
Program
for families and children in at-risk situations, 88

Family systems
protective factors in, 20–21, 22
response to stress and protective processes over life span, 21, 22
in strengths-building, 20–21, 22
supportive of people of color, 279

Family violence. *See also* Women and domestic violence
nature and scope of, 98–99
policy, historical view of, 100–101
research on
shift from deficits in women to deficits in justice system, 101

Fast Track Project
promotion of friendships of aggressive
children with conventional youth,
258

Fathers
biological
of children of adolescent mothers,
124–125
of children with chronic illness, 177
involvement of
effect on children of adolescent
mothers, 125
positive, 122–123
noncustodial
parenting and, 61
psychoeducational programs for, 67

role of, research in, 129

Federal Housing Authority (FHA), exclusion of African Americans and, 271

Feelings identification training, 145

Financial institutions, in community development, 330

Financial issues, in divorce, 56, 57

Fine, M., *242–243*

Focus on Families, 143

Foster care, 87

Foster Care Independence Act of 1999, 89

Free African Society, founding and purpose of, 275

Fromer, J. E., *21*

Funding
    of bilingual education, 295
    in community development
        government, 327–328
        private, 327
    of ecological research in community development, 328–334, 336
    of help seeking reseach, 111
    of inner city programs, 204, 206
    for kindergarten access, 225
    of school-based community centers, 202–203
    of services for children of alcoholics, 148
    state, for child protection and prevention, 89
    for strength-based approaches, 351

Gangs. *See also* Peer influences, negative
    adolescent violence and, 253, 254
    increase in, 253
    reduction of
        prevention curricula for, 263
        programs with community-based organizations, 262–263
        social skills programs in, 262
    risk for membership in, 253–254
    in urban war zones
        for sense of affiliation and security, 309

Garbarino, J., *305, 306*

Garmezy, N., *14*

Gender, exposure to community violence and, 305

Genetics, children of alcoholic parents and, 139, 140

Goals, individuals, 41

Good Behavior Game, 260–261

Gore, S., *15*

Grandfather, adolescent mothers' parenting and, 124

Grandparent support, outcomes for adolescent mother and child and, 123–124

Grass roots initiatives, in community development, 335

Gun ownership, children and youth, 305–306

4-H, urban youth focus for positive development, 203

Haggerty, R. J., *14*

Hardiness, 175
    in children with chronic illness, 175
    of family
        child's adaptation to chronic illness and, 177

Harm standard, rates of child abuse and, 75, 76

Head Start programs, 279

Health care delivery system, chronic illness and, 180–181

Health information centers, family-to-family of children with chronic illness, 181–182

Healthy Start programs, 279

Helplessness, in domestic violence, 101

Help seeking in domestic violence
    acculturation or immigration history and, 104–105
    advocacy sources and, 104
    barriers to, 104
        for immigrant and ethnic minority women, 110
    consequences from systems, 105
    coordination of child protection and domestic violence policies and, 105–106
    definition of, 101–102
    demographic factors in, 103
    dimensions of, 102–103
    ensuring success of, 103–106
    entry points in, 102
    identification and prohibition of negative consequences of, 110
    by married *versus* cohabiting women, 103–104
    number and diversity of contacts in, 103
    as process, 103
    reasons for, 103
    resources and, 103
    timing of interventions and, 104

women seeking, 102

High school transition

    decline in academic performance, 239–240

    disengagement from educational enterprise, 240

    interventions and policy responses, 242–243

    negative outcomes, 242

    restructuring in

        impact on life trajectories, 245

    school restructuring for, 242–243

    schools within schools and, 242–243, 247–248

    teacher designed restructuring for, 243

Hinshaw, S. P., 166

Home Mortgage Disclosure Act, community development and, 337

Homestead Act of 1862, exclusion of African Americans and, 271

Home visitation programs. *See also* Nurse home visitation programs

    benefits for parent and child, 315

    in reduction of children's exposure to violence, 315

    in strength-building, 350

Housing

    adolescent mothers and, 131

    African Americans and, 271

    Community Reinvestment Act and, 336–337

    Federal Housing Authority and, 271

    Home Mortgage Disclosure Act and, 337

    local nonprofit programs, 331

    low-income, government roles in, 331–332

    political development and policy and, 330–332

ICPS (Interpersonal Cognitive Problem-Solving), 223

Identity formation, cultural incompatibilities and, 289

Illinois Middle Grades Network (IMGN), 244

    academic, emotional, behavioral performance and

        outcomes in, 244–245

    basis in STEP model, 244

    implementation of, 244–245

Immigrant women

domestic violence and

    barriers to help seeking in, 110

    Battered Immigrant Women's Act of 1994 and, 105

    help seeking in, 104–105

Individual

    promotion of basic needs and development of competency and, 41

    strengths in, 5

    view of in African American religion, 275

Individuals with Disabilities Act (IDEA)

    school participation for children with chronic illness, 179

Inner city children and youths

    developmental-ecological perspective on, 194

    developmental threats as stress for

        chronic environmental stress, 195–196

        life events, 196

        reintegration of inner city into larger political economy, 197

        responses to, 197

        role strain, 196–197

    environmental stress and, 194

    interventions for, 197

        deficits-based for individual and family, 198

        family as buffer, 198

        family coping, 199

        promoting positive youth development, 199–204

    policy solutions for, 204–207

        areas of review and initiative in, 206–207

        empirical demonstrations of effects of community-based interventions, 206

        equal protection, opportunities, and supports, 206, 207

        focus on mentoring and civic engagement, 205

        funding basis of programs, 206

        funding strengths-based *versus* deficit-based programs, 204

        integrated service provision, 204–205

        integration of inner city with broader society, 205

        optimizing local fit, 206, 207

        program evaluation and, 206

promotion of sense of role, 205
research-based, 206–207
supporting skills *versus* remedying
deficits, 206, 207
social problems and risk to, 194–195
strengths-based programs for, 201
Inoculation programs
advantages of, 241
preparation for school transition, 241
in transition to middle and junior high
schools, 247
Inservice training, for teachers, 224–225
Instruction
approaches in
professional development and
inservice training for, 225
cultural relevance of, academic and psychosocial outcomes and, 218–219
Internalizing, in children of divorce, 54
International Youth Foundation, 200
Interparental relationship, child outcome in
divorce and, 59–60
Intraindividual characteristics, and developmental outcomes in abused and neglected children, 85
Isolation procedures, deficiencies of, 256

Junior high school. *See also under* School
transitions
avoidance of, 246
changes in
support of teachers and administrators in, 247
inoculation programs in, 247
restructuring of, 246–247
Justice system
arrest policies and, 107–108
help in domestic violence and, 102
protection orders and, 108
women and domestic violence and,
106–108

Kamehameha Elementary Education Program (KEEP) in Hawaii
culturally relevant pedagogy, 219
Kauai, Hawaii, resilient children of, 14
Key to Caregiving program for new mothers,
164
Kindergarten, access to quality, 225

Language of instruction
assimilationist policies and, 292

bilingual education, 293
Latino youth
acculturation and, 287–294
biculturalism and, 291–292
education policy for
assimilationist, 292, 294–295
compatibility with ecology of school
and community, 295
enhancement of ethnic culture and
biculturalism in, 295
increasing parents' access to schools,
296–297
mental health implications of, 294
recommendations for promoting resilience, 294–298
respecting ethnic culture and promoting biculturalism, 298
supporting teachers in working with
cultural minorities, 297–298
language of instruction and, 292–296
parents and schools and, 290–291, 296–
297
resilience agenda for, 287–294
Leadership development, 90
Leave No Child Behind Act of 2003, 90–91
Legal issues
children of divorce and, 67
in treatment of children of alcoholic
parents, 149
Legislation, children of alcoholic parents and,
resilience-based language in, 149
Life events
of children of alcoholic parents, 140
effect on inner city children and youth,
196
Lifeskills '95 aftercare program for youthful
offenders, 259
Limited English proficiency (LEP) children
English as a second language programs,
294
isolation in separate programs, 293–294
Local exchange trading systems, in community development, 330
Losses, depression and, 158

Magical thinking, as resource for problem-
solving, 310
Maladjustment
in children with chronic illness, 176
indicators of, 55–56
Maltreated children
resilience and outcomes in, 79, 80, 82

Maltreatment, definition of, 77
Managed care systems, consequences for children with chronic illness, 181
Marital separation, as adversity for children, 53
Masten, A. S., *16, 120*
McCubbin, H. I., *21*
Meaning of life, trauma and, 310
Mediating factors, child outcome in divorce and, 57, 59
Medicaid buy-in legislation, financial demands of childhood chronic illness and, 181
Mental health
    of children of alcoholic parents, 138
    of children of divorce, 54
    family systems approach to. *See* Depression; Depression, parental
Mental health services
    for children and parents in urban war zones, 312
    school-based
        for children exposed to violence, 313–314
    for traumatized children
        police officers in identification and referral to, 313
Mentoring
    for children exposed to violence, 316
    for children of alcoholic parents, 145
Mentors
    for aggressive and antisocial youth, 258
    foradolescent mothers
        natural *versus* assigned, 124
Middle Grade School State Policy Initiative, 244
Middle or junior high school transition
    Carnegie Corporation national initiative for, 244–245
    constraints on adolescent development in, 236
    decline in academic performance and, 237, 238
    disengagement from educational enterprise and, 235
    interventions and policy responses, 243–245
    teacher in, 236
    Turning Points and, *244*
Middle school
    avoidance of, 246

changes in
    support of teachers and administrators in, 247
    deviant youth influence in, 260
    inoculation programs in, 247
    peer culture of
        promotion of prosocial goals and behaviors, 261
    restructuring of, 246–247
Middle Start Initiative, Michigan, 244
Minorities
    family response to discrimination, *21*
Moral development, of children from violent communities, 312
Mothers
    abused
        issues in, 98–99
    alcoholic, fetal alcohol exposure and, 139, 140
    of children with chronic illness, 177
    custodial
        psychoeducation programs for, 67
    depression in
        programs for, 162–163
    inner city
        building strengths of, 200–201
    maladapation to chronic illness of child, 178
    parenting skills programs for, 60–61
    substance-abusing, interventions for, 164
Murphy, J., *245*

National Center on Child Abuse and Neglect (NCCAN)
    abolition of abuse, 87
    incidence and prevalence studies of, 74
National Drug Control Strategy
    increase in resilience focus in, 150
National Educational Longitudinal Study, 237
National Family Violence Survey (NFVS), 98
National Institute of Justice Spouse Assault Replication project, 102
National Longitudinal Study of Youth (NLSY)
    adversities assessed in, 36–37
    prediction of behavioral problems
        adversity and strength combinations in, 38–39
    effects of adversity in, 37

effects of strengths in, 40
strengths assessed in, 37
National Research Council, *Understanding Violence Against Women*, 100–101
National Survey of America's Families (NSAF), 33–36
prediction of behavior problems
adversities assessed in, 33–34
effect of combinations of risk factors and strengths in, 34–36
effect of cumulative adversities in, 34
effect of strengths in, 36
strengths assessed in, 34
National Survey of Income and Program Participation (SIPP)
racial disparities in net assets, 271
National Task Force on the Violence Against Women Act, advocacy efforts of, 100
Native American youths, ethnic identification and self-esteem in, 291
Need for control, 41
Neighborhoods
deterioration of, 324
factors triggering, 323
negative environment of
problems associated with, 272
Net assets, racial disparities in, 271
New Chance, the Learning, Earning, Parenting (LEAP) Program
outcomes of for adolescent mothers, 126, 127
New York City Beacons
school-based community centers
funding of, 202–203
for positive development of inner city youth, 202
Normative school transitions. *See* School transitions
Nurse home visitation programs. *See also* Home visitation programs
for adolescent mothers, 130–131
decrease in subsequent pregnancy, 127
outcomes for children, 127
outcomes of, 126
for people of color, 279

Office of Child Abuse and Neglect, 1996, 87
Oliver, M., *271–272*

Parent–child contact
in divorce, 56, 57

Parent–child relationships
acculturation and enculturation and incompatibilities of, 290
development of quality, 257
Parent education programs
for adolescent mothers, 128
for custodial mothers, 60–61
for development of capacity to protect children from violence, 315
in divorce, 56, 57, 66–67
for positive childhood development, 315
in prevention of exposure to negative peer influences, 256–257
Parenting. *See also* Adolescent parenting; Fathers; Mothers
African American
social support network and, 277
of children of alcoholic parents, 140
consistent discipline and monitoring
protective factor for children of alcoholic parents, 142
fathers in, 61
impact of stress on youths and, 198
importance of high-quality, 60
in inner city, 195
parental depression and, 166, 167
programs for custodial mothers, 60–61
protective styles of
as buffer from inner city stress, 198
Strengthening Families Program and, 145
Parents
ethnic minority
access to schools, 296–297
involvement in school, 290–291
involvement in strength-building, 350
welfare-to-work policies
care of chronically ill child and, 182
Partnerships
parents, teachers, community, 221
programs for inner city youth and, 203–204
Partners Project, parent-child interactions, 164
PATHS (Promoting Alternative Thinking Strategies), 223
Peer groups, deviant
prevention of formation of, 259–260
Peer influences, negative. *See also* Antisocial youth

affiliation of agressive and antisocial children and, 251–252
deviancy training and, 252–253
gang reduction and
    prevention curricula for, 263
    programs with community-based organizations, 262–263
    social skills programs for gang members, 262
intervention in, 254–256
    barriers to cross-behavior friendships with conventional adolescents, 254
    for friendship-making deficiencies of aggressive and antisocial youths, 254–255
    before gang membership, 254
    iatrogenic effect of homogeneous interventions and, 255
    parent training, 255
    self-regulation techniques, 255
    social skills training, 255–256
on middle school peer group, 260
prevention of exposure for antisocial youths, 257–259
prevention of exposure to
    parent education programs for, 256–257
    prosocial and adult-structured activities for aggressive youths, 257
strengths-based approach to resilience building, summary of, 264
Peer support
    protective factor for children of alcoholic parents, 142
People of color. *See also* African Americans
    design of strengths-based policies for
        "color consciousness" in allocation of resources, 278
        family supports enhancement, 279
        personal skills and knowledge enhancement, through community institutions, 278–279
        reduction of economic disparities and disadvantage and, 277
        social capital enhancement, 279–280
        strength and resilience enhancement of, 277
    social policy based on inherent inferiority, past, 277
Person

in design, implementation, evaluation of interventions, 8–9
hierarchy of goals/needs of, 40–41
reciprocal, interdependent, transactional relations with social systems, 23
in strength-based approach, 8–9
strengths in, 5
Personal Responsibility and Work Opportunity Reconciliation Act of 1996
    teenage childbearing and, 129–130
Philadelphia School Collaborative, *242–243*
Physical assault, in families, 98
Physical environment, community development and, 329, 333–334
Pianta, R. C., *17*
Pinklining, for help seeking in domestic violence, 105
Police officers, in identification of traumatized children, 313
Policing, community-oriented, 332
Policy, problem-focused *versus* strengths-focused, 25
Political sustainability, community development and, 326
Positive outcomes, factors important for, 349–350
Poverty
    effect at family level, 272
    rate for African Americans, 270–271
Privacy, in services to children of alcoholic parents, 149
Professional development
    for cultural sensitivity, 219
    for teachers, 224–225
Project Before, for substance-abusing mothers, 164
Prosocial normative activities, in strength-building, 257, 261, 312, 314, 350
Protection orders
    extension of full faith and credit to, 108
    implementation of, inconsistent, 108
Protective factors
    child abuse and neglect and, 78, 81, 82, 83, 84
    individual level, 32
    as process *versus* trait, 32
Protective processes, description of, 17–18
Psychological abuse, in families, 98
Psychological distress, after transition to middle school or junior high, 237, 238

Psychological functioning, racism and, 272–273

Psychological problems
    of abused and neglected children, 77
    of ethnic minority youths, 286–287

Public health model, for children of divorce, 55, 65

Quality of life, adjustment to chronic illness and, 184

Race
    exposure to community violence and, 305
    as risk factor, 270

Racism
    biopsychosocial effects of, 273
    definitions of, 272
    effect on inner city children and youth, 195
    impact on psychological and physiological functioning, 272–273
    sociopolitical understanding of, 199

Redlining, neighborhood decline and, 323

Re-entrance programs, for youthful offenders, 258–259

Relational Psychotherapy Mother's Group, for substance-abusing mothers, 164

Religiosity
    as adaptive coping mechanism, 274
    as buffer against race- and ethnic-related stressors, 274–275

Religious organizations
    African American
        benefits of, 274–275
        self-esteem and, 275
        view of individual in, 275

Relocation, children of divorce and, 64

Research, problem-focused versus strengths-focused, 25

Resilience
    accumulation of risk and, 307
    in adolescents with chronic illness, 176
    child abuse and neglect and, 78, 79, 80, 81
    in child abuse and neglect studies
        definitions of, 78, 79, 80, 81
        factors associated with, 84–85
    in children of alcoholic parents
        pathways to, 141–142
    in children of divorce
        enhancement of, 55

in children with chronic illness, 175
definitions of, 16, 17, 32, 120, 137, 175, 214
    need for operational definition, 147
developmental tasks and competencies in, 42
early research, 15
emotional
    children of alcoholic parents and, 144–145
    indicators of, 199–200
parental
    children with chronic illness and, 177

Resilience Framework, 141

Resilient children, definition of, 214

Resources. See also Internal resources
    in competence model of adolescent parenting, 120

Role strain
    ethnic minorities and, 197
    inner city children and youth and, 196–197

Rutter, M., 217

SAFE Children program, 200–201

Safe harbors, for children in urban war zones, 317

Safe havens, for children in urban war zones, 316, 317

Safety
    of children
        Adoption Assistance and Child Welfare Amendments of 1980, 87
        child's sense of, 308
        of mother for safety of children, 98–99

Sawmill neighborhood, physical environmental development and, 334

School
    acculturation role of, 289
    before- and after-school programs
        public policy and, 225–226
    biculturalism in
        promotion of, 298
    as center of community, 223
    comprehensive and integrated approaches of, 221–224
        child care facilities, quality of care and, 222
        in support of family under stress, 221–222

disengagement from. *See* Disengagement from educational enterprise

early care and family support services of, 222

gang violence in and near, 254

in identification of children and families in need of services, 226

increasing parents' access to, 296

parental involvement in
Latino youths and, 290–291

policy implications of, 224–226

prevention programs for children of alcoholic parents, 143

preventive programs for behavior enhancement, 223

programs for nonviolent responses, 312

reform of
holistic, 224

multicomponent and integrated, 226

as risk or protective influence, 216–217

role in academic and psychosocial outcomes, 216–217
classroom behavioral environments, 218

cultural relevance of curriculum and instruction, 218–219

home–school–community partnerships, 221

interactive instructional approaches, 218

school environment and climate, 219–220

teacher attitudes and relationships with students, 217

success of, public policy promotion of, 46

School engagement. *See also* Disengagement from educational enterprise
adolescent mothers and, 126–127
positive adjustment after birth, 122

School environment
role in academic and psychosocial outcomes, 219
bullying and victimization in, 220

exposure to, involvement in, victimization by violence, 220

physical facilities and, 220

School Intervention Program (SIP)
for children with chronic illness, 178–179

School leaving, drop in grades with transition to middle school or junior high

school, 237

School of the 21st Century (21C) program
evaluations of, 223

full service approach of, 222–223

implementation of, 223

partnership of parents, teachers, community, 221

School principal training programs
for prevention of deviant peer groups, 260

School restructuring
transition into high school
schools within schools, 242–243

teacher designed, 243

Schools within schools, 241
in high schools, 247–248

implementation in high schools, 247–248

quantitative evaluations of, 243

research support of, 242–243

in transition into high school, 242

School Transitional Environment Project (STEP), 243

School transitions
developmental needs of adolescents and, 234

intervention and policy responses to, 240–245
high school and, 242–243

inoculation methods, 241

middle or junior high school and, 243–245

restructuring of physical and social organization of schools, 231

schools within schools, 241–242

secondary prevention programs for problems, 240–241

into senior high school decrements in academic performance, 239–240

for whole group or population, 241

junior high schools, organization of, 235

into middle or junior high school, 236, 236–239
constraints on adolescent development in, 236

disengagement from educational enterprise and, 235

middle school and needs of early adolescent
theory and application, 235–236

normative

disengagement from educational enterprise and, 234
lack of academic and social integration and, 234
problems created by, 233–234
after high school entrance, 234
recommendations for policy and intervention
availability of inoculation or pedagogical programs, 247
avoidance of middle or junior high schools, 246
federal role in restructuring, 245–246
restructuring of middle or junior high schools, 246–247
schools-within-schools, 246–247
support for implementation, 247
into senior high school
disengagement from educational enterprise and, 240
Search Institute, 200
Second Chance Homes, 130
Security needs of children
parents and, 308
Self-concept, cultural incompatibilities and, 289
Self-esteem
adversity and, 41
African Americans and
religiosity and, 275
benefit of ethnic identification and, 291
coping and
in children of divorce, 55
decline with transition to middle school or junior high, 237–238
fluctuations in, 238
Self-evaluation, African American *versus* mainstream criteria in, 275
Self-worth, belief in, 41
Services, Training, Officers and Prosecutors (STOP), 100
Sexually abused children
resilience and outcomes in, 79, 80, 81, 82, 83
Shapiro, T., *271–272*
Sherrod, L. R., *14*
Siblings, of children with chronic illness, 178
Single mothers, extended African American family and, 276
Skills training. *See also* Social skills training
for children of alcoholic parents, 145
for children of divorce, 67

federal programs and, 91
Social capital
community development and, 326–327
definition of, 280
enhancement of
for people of color, 279–280
Social competence, programs for children of alcoholic parents, 144
Social-Competence Promotion PRogram, 223
Social context
linkages for Latino youth
cultural incompatibilities and, 290
Social development
adaptation to chronic illness and, 177
in community development, 329, 332–333
school- and community-based programs for children in urban war zones, 314
Social disorder, community-level, effects of, 324
Social maps
children's, 308–309
chronic trauma and, 310
Social networks, as protective factor, 41–42
Social problems, of ethnic minority youth, 286–287
Social resources, of youths, federal programs and, 91
Social Services Block Grant (SSBG)
state funding for child protection, prevention, early intervention, 89
Social skills training. *See also* Skills training
for aggressive and antisocial youths, 258
for gang members, 262
as intervention in negative peer influence, 255–256
Social support
African American networks for, 276
post-divorce, child outcome and, 61
Social sustainability, community development and, 326
Social withdrawal, of abused and neglected children, 77
Special Masters
for conflict resolution in divorce, 67
family of divorce and, 56, 57, 58
Spiritual development, of children from violent communities, 312
Stability or instability, in relationships of poor of young couples, 125
STAR program, for children of alcoholic parents, 143

Strength-based approaches
  ecological perspectives in, 10
  implications of, 9
  linkage of research and policy implications and, 9
  variations in, 5–6
Strength-based research
  early
    bootstrapping in, 14, 15
    environmental risk and protective factors in, 15
    extension of early to family and community, 15–16
    historical perspective, 14–15
    new directions in, 16–18
Strength-building
  in children with chronic illness, 177
  criteria for
    meeting of by policymakers, researchers, program developers, and service providers, 350
    demonstration projects for testing, 352–353
    inclusion of measurement variables in databases for, 351–352
    infrastructure for
    public and private resources at all governmental levels and, 352
    involvement of target groups in program development, implementation, and evaluation, 350
    pathways of public policies in
      counteraction of effects of adversities, 45–46
      positive development, 44
      prevention of adversity, 44–45
      protection from effects of adversities, 45
    positive school engagement in, 46
    public and private funding of research on
      increase in, 351
    research–policy collaboration in, 27–28
    research priorities for, 351
    resources and public policy for, 44–47
    school engagement and activity, positive, 46
    volunteering and, 46–47
Strengthening Families Program
  children of alcoholic parents and, 143, 145
Strengths

versus absence of failure, 33
behavior problems and
  National Longitudinal Study of Youth data, 36–40
  National Survey of America's Families data, 33–36
building new, 7–8
of children and youths
  research on, 32–33
conceptual framework for, 40–44
definition of, 32–33
ecology of, 43–44
  effect on adversities, 43–44
  effect on dynamic relations between acute and chronic adversity, 44
problem behavior and, 33
promotion of basic needs and development of competency and, 41
recognizing existing, 6–7
Strengths-based approaches
  to children of divorce (public health model)
    additional features of, 68
  criteria for policy and program evaluation, 346–347
  from deficits to strengths-based alternatives, 3–4
  effectiveness of, 344, 345
    developmental and contextual appropriateness for, 349
  emerging, 5–6
  existing strengths in
    recognizing and building on, 6–7
  general, integrated across groups and adverse circumstances, 349–350
  individuals, families, communities in design, implementation, evaluation of interventions, 8–9
  goals of, 6–9
  as movement, 3–4
  variations in, 5–6
new strengths in, building of, 7–8
overview of, 3
positive outcomes under adverse conditions and, 348–349
promotion of health development and, 346
reduction of negative outcomes and, 346
social environments
  strengthening of, 8
utilization of resources from multiple levels, 346–347

Strengths-based research and policy
    diversity of response to adversity in, 25–26
    within group differences in, 26
    life-span trajectory in, 25, 26–27
    principles for, 25–27
    strengths and competencies in, 25–26
Strengths-building
    community organizations in, 21, 23–24
    family systems in, 20–21, 22
    processes of, 18–20
    protective factors in, 20–23
    protective processes in, 20–24
Stress
    chronic environmental
        definition of, 195
        effect on inner city children and youth, 195–196
    symptoms of
        perceived racism and, 273
    violence and, 194–195
Stressors
    race- and ethnicity-related
        social adjustment problems and, 274
        source of strengths and buffers against, 274–275
Student loan forgiveness programs, community development and, 337
Sustainability, community development and, 325–326

Teachers
    middle school and junior high school
        challenge of early adolescent in, 237
        changes in, 247
        constraints on adolescent development in, 236
        policy and, 224–225
        prevention of deviant peer groups and cooperative learning methods in, 259
        role in academic and psychosocial outcomes
            attitudes and relationships with students, 217
            interactive instructional approaches of, 218
        training programs for prevention of deviant peer groups, 260
Teenage pregnancy. *See also* Adolescent mothers; Adolescent parenting
    developmental impact of, 118

negative correlates of, 119
Personal Responsibility and Work Opportunity Reconciliation Act of 1996 and, 129–130
protective factors for, 118, 120
risk factors for, 118, 119
subsequent, 127–128
teen birth rate in 2000, 117–118
    comparison of U.S. and other industrialized nations, 118
    racial and ethnic differences in, 118
Teen Outreach Program, 46
Teen Parent Demonstration, outcomes of, 126
Thompson, A. I., *21*
Thompson, E. A., *21*
Toddler-Parent Psychotherapy (TPP), 162
Trauma
    childhood
        adults and, 310–311
        loss of future orientation, 310
        magical thinking and, 310
        terminal thinking and revenge-oriented morality, 311
    in commission of assault, 310
    components of, 310
    early childhood
        effect on brain development, 307
        response to, 311–312
    overwhelming negative cognition in, 310
    physiological responses to, handling of, 310
    as psychological wound, 310–311
Trust
    building, in urban war zones, 312–313
    loss of, trained mentors for, 316

Understanding Violence Against Women (National Research Council), 100–101
Urban war zones
    accumulation of risk factors in
        effects of, 306–307
    children in
        adults as mediators in psychological responses of, 310–311
        policy responses to, 313–317
        research-based principles for increased strengths for, 311–312
    children's beliefs about the world and, 308–309
    effect on brain development, 305–306

experiences of parallel to experiences in refugee camps, 309

gangs in, 309

gun ownership by children and youth in, 305–306

homicide rate, U.S. *versus* all other modern industrialized nations, 305

impact on children

accumulation of risk model and, 306–307

from position of strength, 307

policy responses to

community-level, 316–317

family-level, 315–316

individual-level, 313–315

residential mobility programs for families in, 316–317

social maps of children in, 308–309

violence in

ratio of assaults:homicide and, 305

socioeconomics and demographics of, 305–306

zones of peace for children and, 311

Valued Youth Partnership Program, for inner city youth, 203

Veterans Administration mortgage system, exclusion of African Americans and, 271–272

Victimization

in bullying, schoolwide programming for, 220

in crime

prevention strategies for, 332

of women, violent, 98

Violence

in families, nature and scope of, 98–99

gangs and, 253

in inner city

effect on children and youth, 196

prevention of childhood exposure to, 314–315

as stress factor, 194–195

Violence Against Women Act (VAWA) of 1994

Services, Training, Officers and Prosecutors of, 100

Virginia Commission on Family Violence Prevention

protection orders in

centralized registry of, 108

Visitation and access policy, children of divorce and, 64

Volunteering, needs satisfaction through, 46–47

Walsh, D.J., *17*

Wealth accumulation, Whites *versus* African Americans, 271–272

Werner, E. E., *14*

White Americans

economic advantage of *versus* African Americans, 271–272

racial and ethnic stereotypes of, 273

Willie M. Program, 261–262

Women, violent victimization of, 98

Women and domestic violence. *See also* Family violence

dilemmas of, 108–109

ending the violence *versus* ending the relationship, 109

from helplessness to help seeking, 101–106. *See also* Help seeking

justice system and, 106–108, 109

arrest policies, 107–108

protection orders, 108

use of, 106

losses of, 108–109

policy implementation, interventions for consistent and effective, 106–108

policy recommendations, 108–111

collaboration among systems, 111

effective and consistent implementation, 111

evaluation of of, 111

federal funding for research on help seeking, 111

increase in intervention points, 110

interdisciplinary and interagency or interorganizational training, 111

studies of technology transfer and, 111

system-level interventions, 110–111

safety of mother for safety of children, 98–99

Younger Americans Act of 2001, 90. *See also* Leave No Child Behind Act of 2003

Youth

external and internal assets of

correlation with environmental and individual resilience, 200

federal programs for, 89–91

inner city programs for positive development
   opment
   4-H, 203
   key ingredients of, 201
   National Youth Development Information Center and, 204
   New York City Beacons, 202–203
   Valued Youth Partnership Program, 203–204
   Youth Build, 202
promoting positive development *versus* fixing problems of, 199–204

Youth Build program
   for out-of-school youths, 202
   strengths-based work, 90
Youthful offenders
   aftercare programs for, 258–259
   contracts with, for relapse prevention, 259
   re-entrance programs for, 258–259
Youth Policy Forum, 200
Youths, problems of, research on, 32–33

ABOUT THE EDITORS

Kenneth Maton, PhD, is professor of psychology and director of the Human Services Psychology PhD Program at the University of Maryland Baltimore County. His research focuses on minority youth achievement, empowering community settings, and the community psychology of religion. Recent books (coauthored) include *Overcoming the Odds: Raising Academically Successful African American Young Women* and *Beating the Odds: Raising Academically Successful African American Males.* He is past president of the Society for Community Research and Action (SCRA), represents SCRA on the Council of Representatives for the American Psychological Association, and serves on the editorial boards of the *American Journal of Community Psychology, Analysis of Social Issues and Public Policy,* and *Journal of Community Psychology.* He received his PhD in community–clinical psychology in 1985 from the University of Illinois, Urbana–Champaign.

Cynthia J. Schellenbach, PhD, is an associate professor of sociology at Oakland University in Rochester, Michigan. Her research interests focus on adolescent parenting, child abuse, and the impact of community-based child abuse prevention initiatives. She is a past president of Division 37 (Child, Youth, and Family Services), and has served as liaison to the APA Committee on Children, Youth, and Families. She is an active member of the Healthy Families America Research Network to Prevent Child Abuse in Chicago. She coauthored *Violence Against Children in the Family and the Community* (APA, 1998). She received her PhD in human development from Pennsylvania State University.

Bonnie J. Leadbeater, PhD, is a professor in developmental psychology who joined the University of Victoria in British Columbia, Canada, in 1997 after nine years as faculty at Yale University. She is also the current director of the

University of Victoria Centre for Youth and Society, which focuses on promoting youth well-being through interdisciplinary community research partnerships (www.youth.society.uvic). She holds degrees in nursing and educational psychology from the University of Ottawa in Ontario, Canada, and in developmental psychology from Columbia University, New York. Her recent book *Urban Girls: Resisting Stereotypes, Creating Identities* won the 2001 Social Policy Best Authored Book Award from the Society for Research on Adolescence.

Andrea L. Solarz, PhD, has worked since 1998 as a consultant for behavioral health policy, research, and action, working on such topics as adolescent health, public health advocacy, and the promotion of strengths-based policies. Previously, she was with the National Academy of Sciences Institute of Medicine (IOM), where she directed the studies "Lesbian Health: Current Assessment and Directions for the Future" and "Genetics, Health, and Behavior: Science in Perspective." She has served as assistant director for science policy in the American Psychological Association (APA) Public Policy Office, as a policy analyst in the U.S. Congress Office of Technology Assessment Health Program, and as an APA Congressional Science Fellow in the U.S. Senate Subcommittee on the Handicapped. She is an APA fellow and a past president of the Society for Community Research and Action, Division 27 (Community Psychology) of APA. She received her PhD in ecological–community psychology in 1986 from Michigan State University.

post-traumatic
growth ??!!...
Globe and
mail article
about cancer.
June 6, 2014